Conquer the Planet

A Modern-Day Global Enslavement Handbook

Sir Lawrence McAlister

INGSOC PUBLISHING

Ingsoc Publishing books may be ordered through booksellers or by contacting:
Ingsoc Publishing
PO Box 53
Jim Thorpe, PA 18229

Library of Congress Number: 2024917863
ISBN: 979-8-218-48504-7 (paperback)
ISBN: 979-8-218-62493-4 (hardcover)

Contents

Endorsement

Conquer the Planet by Sir Lawrence McAlister is a serious work written in a unique and entertaining manner to hold the reader's attention to what is, in reality, an encyclopedia of strategies and techniques used by the elitist enemies of liberty to enslave the rest of us by psychological warfare instead of traditional military warfare. It's hard to imagine any serious tactic that is not included. Reading this book as though it is a training manual for conquest puts an unusual twist to information that, otherwise, might seem dull or technical. *Conquer the Planet* is a must read to understand the reality of modern warfare.

G. Edward Griffin,
Author of *The Creature From Jekyll Island* and
World Without Cancer

Dedication

In loving memory of Cecile Lejosne Swolensky (b. 13 February 1929 d. 28 November 2024). Although you never got to see this book finalised, I will always cherish your belief in me, along with your unconditional love and support. Hearing the stories of how you, as a young girl, survived the Nazi invasion of France and afterward lived a long, fruitful life filled with elegance and compassion, taught me something very special. The world needs more love, and if you want to rule the world, it's there for you to do so. But it's only temporary. How we treat each other is forever, and what truly matters. Fly high, angel.

Author's Note

This handbook is a parody of the various conspiracies brought forth by private researchers, published activists and, at times, the conspirators themselves. The concepts are from numerous sources, with credit to the creators where possible. In some instances, the knowledge has been passed along many times and in a variety of formats, making it difficult to credit the original source. In addition, I draw conclusions of my own that may or may not coincide with the source's intent. Please note, because of the dynamic nature of the Internet, links may have been deleted or changed. I created the book for educational and entertainment purposes. It should not be used to commit harmful, criminal or oppressive acts. Doing so can result in criminal prosecution, punishable to the fullest extent of the law. Reproducing and distributing portions or entire copies of this handbook is strictly forbidden.

My own belief is that the ruling oligarchy will find less arduous and wasteful ways of governing and of satisfying its lust for power, and those ways will resemble those which I described in Brave New World.

~ Aldous Huxley

Introduction

So, let me guess. By opening this handbook to peruse the sometimes scandalous yet time-tested principles presented, you feel you have what it takes to reign over a world empire. Or, at the very least, you're curious enough to learn how it's accomplished. Kudos! I applaud your devilish efforts, as the majority of people are much too comfortable in their mundane lives to attempt such an ambitious endeavour.

Furthermore, of great benefit and perhaps relief to you, the same subjects you seek to control will simply brush off such meticulous actions because of the thorough indoctrination processes they've already undergone (techniques to be presented in this manual). Quite humorously, if many such victims were to accidentally stumble across this handbook, they would immediately slam it shut and dismiss the tactics described herein. But, for the privileged few who are courageous and tenacious enough to press on, I'll introduce the best and most up-to-date ruling methods available. Several techniques have undergone thousands of years of refinement and have been passed down through families and secret societies for centuries.

This handbook makes no guarantees for your success. You may find, at some point in your pursuit of world domination, that enslaving humanity is not your cup of tea. There's no shame in that, as many factors, including bloodlines and genetic traits, play a key role in isolating the small number of unique individuals equipped to rule over their inferiors.

For those who are ruthless and cunning enough, not to mention in possession of an insatiable work ethic, this handbook will lay the groundwork necessary to oversee a global empire. In your studies and through practical experience, you'll discover that peasants who believe they are free are easier to control and more useful to you than peasants who are aware of their invisible shackles and chains. Contemporary conveniences such as high-tech devices, the mainstream media, publicly funded schools, commercial entertainment, creature comforts, legal and illegal drugs, corporate foods and well-orchestrated, mass trauma events have greatly assisted current lords in mentally enslaving their subjects whilst hardly raising an ounce of suspicion. As a result, these same complacent subjects vehemently defend their overseers and even make the ultimate sacrifice to maintain the level of convenience they are accustomed to in today's modern world.

You should not underestimate the intricacies involved in deceiving mankind to achieve your own personal aspirations. It's a finely mastered art. Reading this handbook is just the beginning, and much of your learning will come through trials and tribulations should you decide to embark on the often dark, yet exciting journey that is human conquest. All peasants are hereby ordered to put down this manual as we pull back the curtain and discuss the techniques necessary to become a successful, modern-day lord. For the small number of you who are fit to rule, please proceed to the first chapter.

Chapter 1

A WORLD VIEW

The ideas of the ruling class are in every epoch the ruling ideas, i.e. the class which is the ruling material force of society, is at the same time its ruling intellectual force.
— Karl Marx

To conquer the planet, a well-thought-out world view is crucial. What else is going to keep you motivated through those boring board meetings or acts of aggression toward your peers? What will lift you up when it appears the walls are closing in after committing barbaric acts to establish your dominance over your fellow sentient beings, if you don't have a driving force that springs you out of bed in the morning? Many who have aspired to rule the world, like Adolf Hitler and Genghis Khan, had deeply engrained world views and so should you.

Besides keeping you motivated, a specific blueprint for the future of humanity will help you decide how to arrange your peasant farm(s) so your subjects are employed in industries that will bring your deepest and darkest fantasies to life.

Please excuse me for a second whilst I sip on some adrenochrome. Mmmm. Delicious! It's an acquired taste, as you shall soon discover.

To excel as a megalomaniac, your convictions need to be as self-serving as possible. If you are to enslave your fellow man, you cannot have a world view in which everyone can thrive. You must stymie the competition as much as possible. You should provide insider knowledge and privileges, only to those willing to help you fulfil your most twisted and delicious goals.

An ideal world view must keep your worker bees weak, uninformed, unhealthy, spiritually repressed and at odds with each other. We'll discuss techniques to achieve these objectives in later chapters, but the beauty of having a bold and unshakeable world view is that your global empire will naturally present and assemble itself for you whilst you enjoy the spoils of your labourers' blood, sweat and tears.

The mantras that today's peasant farms pump into peasants train them to think that illnesses can be treated but not cured, there isn't enough for everybody and peace can only be achieved through war. It's been quite invigorating to watch large industries arise and develop around this type of world view. Industries like the medical and military-industrial complexes and multinational food corporations have achieved dominance and are now paving the way toward a complete corporate dictatorship over the human race. These industries not only allow you to control the numbers within your peasant populations, but these industries help dominate their minds, bodies and spirits as well.

> NOTE: It'll be very important to keep all known and developed cures, along with any breakthroughs in technology that can make your peasants independent of your corporatocracy, for yourself. Mind control programming will also play a vital role in running your peasant farm at maximum efficiency. We'll discuss these techniques in later chapters.

One of the most important pieces of advice I can give you is to *crush* any type of thinking that encourages your peasants to *unite! This is incredibly important, and you must adhere to it at all costs!*

That isn't to say a unified vision of one language, one religion and one monetary system, etc. isn't desirable. In fact, it should be your end goal. Otherwise, how are you supposed to manipulate all the uprights on the Earth's surface to do your bidding if they're not under the same uniform type of control? Can you imagine a world where car parts like spark plugs come in any shape and size manufacturers randomly choose with directions written in a language you don't speak and made for an entirely different function? The part would be completely and utterly useless. We can say the same about the non-homogenised peasant.

Don't get me wrong. The various cultures and traditions that have organically sprung up have served an incredible purpose and can still be used to divide peasants within your new order, but it'll be helpful if they all have the same reference point regarding money, language and beliefs.

Your world view will help to bring the various peasant farms of the planet together to share one focused purpose—to serve you.

So please, check your guilt in at the door as you learn how to coerce humanity to do your bidding.

Chapter 2

THE CORPORATE PEASANT FARM

If the hammer and the shuttle could move themselves,
slavery would be unnecessary.
— Aristotle

If you want to rise from the multitude of mentally enslaved people wandering the planet, you need to take a history lesson on the various forms of slavery that rulers have implemented throughout the ages. This will provide insight into the best and worst methods to extract the maximum potential from your human chattel.

Originally, the methods of enslaving one's fellow man were blatantly obvious, not to mention, a challenge to maintain. As the tactics were refined over many centuries, they became perfected to such a degree that most peasants today are completely unaware of their bondage and quite content in their servitude. If Malcolm Gladwell was correct in his bestselling novel *Outliers*: 'It takes ten thousand hours of deliberate practice to become an expert in something', imagine what can be accomplished after a few millennia.[1]

We discovered that the most valuable resource on the planet was not an animal, plant, mineral or other substance—it's a human being. When rulers realised they could exploit their fellow human by using fear to get them to do just about anything, human slaves became quite the commodity.[2]

You can't intimidate an apple tree into producing more apples by screaming at it, no matter how red your face gets. Nor can you coerce a hen into laying more eggs under threat of eviction from its coop.[3] But a human? Oh boy, the fun you can have, not to mention the wealth you can acquire.

1.) Malcolm Gladwell, Outliers: *The Story of Success* (New York, Boston, London: Little, Brown and Company, 2008), 41.
2.) Stefan Molyneux, "The Story of Your Enslavement," BitChute video, 13:09, GlobalistKiller, April 2024, https://www.bitchute.com/video/fA27u7L8wukr
3.) Molyneux, "The Story of Your Enslavement," 1:19-2:02.

Can you picture your castle and a multitude of concubines ready to grant any whim you desire? I know I can. Ancient Egyptians implemented the first form of slavery by binding and coercing slaves to perform physical labour. This type of slave driving limited the productivity of slaves because there was no punishment capable of exploiting the most powerful resource of all...the slave's mind.[4] This was also an inefficient means of control because of the amount of energy and human resources required to keep the slaves in line, not to mention preventing them from escaping.

A much more productive method arose under the Roman system that permitted slaves some freedoms like using some of their owner's property as if it were their own and the choice of an occupation or trade where they could apply their individual talents. Educated slaves could even eventually buy their freedom (usually toward the end of their lives when they were of little use anyway). This type of slave system increased the collective output of Rome turning it into an empire.[5] When the Romans curtailed economic freedoms due to over expansion, the Roman Empire began its rapid decline into obscurity. Well, for the time being anyway.

In the feudal system, human enslavement took a major leap forward as serfs were assigned land and required to show unwavering loyalty to their lords.[6] At that point in human civilization, the expanding population had to provide its own sustenance. Allowing serfs to tend to the nobility's land, whilst remaining under their watchful eye, helped maintain the social structure which might have otherwise collapsed due to the absence of a strong central political authority.[7] Not only were serfs restricted in their movements, but nobles, who had to provide protection for their properties amid a plethora of outside threats, were as well. When advancements in farming created much higher yields with fewer hands, this system was, of course, no longer practical.[8]

The overall increase in food production, however, led to the growth of cities and towns, where the disenfranchised flocked to find opportunity. The result was an increase in goods and services and the genesis of industry. Those with a keen eye for profiteering realised the value of a voluntary, although poorly compensated, workforce.

4.) Molyneux, "The Story of Your Enslavement," 3:47-4:13.
5.) Molyneux, "The Story of Your Enslavement," 4:16-4:42.
6.) Elizabeth A. R. Brown. "feudalism social system." Britannica. July 20, 1998. https://www.britannica.com/topic/feudalism
7.) Brown, "feudalism."
8.) Molyneux, "The Story of Your Enslavement," 5:15-5:25.

These labourers were given a mere pittance for their survival and to keep them from becoming a bother to those providing such glorious opportunities.

The modern-day corporation, the gold standard in human exploitation, soon emerged, propelling human potential to new heights. Although the first corporations date back to ancient Rome and India, one of the earliest templates for these modern-day legal fictions was the British East India Company.

Oh, and what a corporation it was. BEIC was unbound by silly laws and possessed unlimited power to make profits.[9] The BEIC even had its own army and when unable to win conflicts on its own, had the distinct privilege of being able to call on the British military. Former governor of BEIC and personal hero of mine, Robert Clive, held a seat in government despite what some whiners today would call a conflict of interest.

It wasn't long after the inception of the BEIC that the seas fully opened for trade, the American colonies formed and the steam engine ignited the industrial revolution, creating a quantum leap in worldwide commerce. The corporation enjoyed renewed importance. Machinery and steam energy were expediting the manufacturing of goods, and hence profits, in a way energy sources like wind and human muscle never could. In the blink of an all-seeing eye, the world suddenly became a much smaller place.

Since corporate structure was needed to create and manage higher profit margins, whilst removing personal liability from its members, these fictitious entities soon emerged everywhere. The corporate peasant farm's unbridled potential led to unprecedented innovations, and an improved lifestyle that many peasants were, and still are, able to attain. Allowing peasants to explore and maximise their potential increased their productivity. Even today, peasants are permitted to create and innovate, as long as they pay a portion of their earnings to their ruler (hopefully—you).

The most important aspect of the corporate peasant farm is the amount of time and attention peasants invest in the corporate economy. Within the corporate peasant farm, energy and ideas are turned into products and services used to create more free time. Peasants, therefore, invest a larger portion of their day producing these products and

---

9.) Dave Roos. "How the East India Company Became the World's Most Powerful Monopoly." History. October 23, 2020. https://www.history.com/news/east-india-company-england-trade

services and then use their wages to acquire and utilise them, hence dividing their time between production and consumption.[10]

You can look at your own life to see this wonderfully ensnaring yet completely efficient system at work. Rather than waking up at 5.00 a.m. to plow the fields and milk the cows, you can work for a company that manufactures the automated equipment that provides this service at a much faster rate than you could with an old hand plow and bucket. Now that you have more time on your hands, since you don't have to tend to the farm, you have free time to watch television, and you can go to the supermarket and choose from a wish list of food items. Then an advertisement for a holiday in the Isles of Scilly piques your interest.

Instead of riding a horse or walking to Cornwall then rowing a small boat to St Mary's Island, you jump in your car, drive to the airport and find yourself basking on a warm beach within a few hours. But you'll need to work longer shifts to afford your car payment, parking fees and air travel, not to mention the money spent on frozen daiquiris.

And so, the process continues.

Although the corporate peasant farm has created extreme advancements and prosperity, there are some stark downsides to this type of enslavement. As corporate peasants begin to establish a true sense of independence and enjoy the creature comforts once available only to the most affluent of society, they may start to question their need for you.[11] I think you can see how this presents a dire problem, which will be dealt with, but first we'll discuss the methods and strategies for creating your very own incorporated peasant farm .

10.) George Reisman. "Production versus Consumption," Mises Institute. March 17, 2006. https://mises.org/library/production-versus-consumption
11.) Molyneux, "The Story of Your Enslavement," 7:19-7:50.

Chapter 3

NECESSARY EQUIPMENT

Let me issue and control a nation's money and I care not who writes the laws.
— Mayer Amschel Rothschild

In this chapter, we'll discuss some of the key materials needed to flourish as a global lord. A few suggestions to get you started are: a laptop, a nuclear arsenal, a private jet, a helicopter (this is especially useful if you need to get out quickly), a bullet proof limo, a seed bank, an underground city with all the amenities, a cache of weapons, a gated mansion with a state-of-the-art security system, six Doberman Pinschers, a ten-man security team, at least one high rise building, a plethora of poppy and coca fields, a few casinos, a well-guarded vault filled with gold, a yacht, a fleet of naval ships and quite a few tanks. You'll also need the best of the best in personnel to operate and maintain these necessary components.

All these items are completely and utterly useless, not to mention nearly unsustainable, if you don't own the single most important piece of hardware required for your goal of global domination—a sturdy and reliable printing press. The purpose of the machine is twofold.

It will print as much written word as possible to create an alternate reality for your *educated,* or should I say, *well-trained* peasants? This will be done through history books, current events publications like newspapers and magazines, religious materials, and books and journals on topics such as law, medicine and the sciences.

Eventually, you'll want to rid your kingdom of all written materials since they make it hard to fudge or remove information you don't want available to your peasants. Digital devices are much more useful when altering publications and hence, history. With these digital technologies, you may also selectively remove any stimulus that enlightens your peasants to their plight. For example, imagine being able to simply delete a telling novel such as George Orwell's *Nineteen Eighty-Four* from the pages of history.

But most importantly, you'll use the printing press to create the debt notes (i.e. IOUs) you'll provide to your peasants for the privilege of participating in commercial activity. Controlling the money supply will be even more beneficial when it's moved to a completely digital medium. Imagine tracking every monetary transaction your peasants make or turning off rebellious peasants' finances so they can't purchase basic living needs. Talk about teaching them a lesson. They won't be raising any eyebrows when they're starving in the streets! We're approaching this reality as we introduce a solely digital monetary system to younger generations. But, for now, the printing press is still a valuable piece of machinery.

Although a printing press is one of the few things you really need to enslave humanity, don't think by owning one that you don't need to read the rest of this manual. If you own a printing press and distribute your crispy green paper without the proper knowledge, you could land yourself in a heck of a lot of hot water. Unless you've carefully positioned yourself, the owners of the current paper money system may find you to be a bit of a nuisance and thwart your efforts to take over their global monopoly.

It's not until you're in control of the laws, government(s), judges, courts, guns and jails that you may operate your printing press with 100% confidence. This cannot be accomplished alone, and you must find those willing to operate outside of *moral* laws to obtain power over others.

Since there can only be one cartel's worthless paper money used as the currency per nation (and eventually the world), whoever rises from the ashes to take over this great privilege must eliminate any competition.

'Why?' you may ask. I'll get to that, but first, a little history to better understand the importance of your printing press.

The first system of trade and commerce was based on the age-old system of bartering where interested parties exchanged one thing of value for another. Then came along the concept of money, which provided a more efficient way to obtain the things one needed.

For example, if you were a carpenter and needed horseshoes from a blacksmith but the blacksmith didn't need carpentry work, you were in a bit of a pickle. But let's say the blacksmith needed milk. Instead of going to a farmer to see if the farmer needed the services of a carpenter so you could, in turn, obtain some milk for the blacksmith, a neutral system of exchange in the form of money arose.

The best money turned out to be something of limited supply with intrinsic value, which was malleable, and could be carried around in one's pocket for easy exchange. Gold and silver made the perfect medium. But people (and hopefully you, after reading this handbook) found ways to exploit others during these transactions.

Shaving a portion of the valuable metal from each piece was one way. Putting the coins in a bag and shaking them vehemently to collect the dust that broke loose was another.

For someone like a king, clipping the coins was easier to pull off than for commoners because merchants would sometimes put the coins on a scale to ensure they were of the proper weight. A typical scenario might transpire like this.

—Blacksmith: 'Ah, excuse me, Your Excellency, but this coin seems to be a few grams short of an ounce.'
—King: 'No, that's impossible, you fool. I just weighed that coin before I left the castle; it was exactly one ounce. Perhaps your scale is broken, you pathetic imbecile.'
—Blacksmith: 'I'm sorry your highness but I can assure you my scale is working quite perfectly and is extremely accurate. All the local merchants use it as a standard of measurement. I apologise for asking your Majesty, but may I request a full ounce of gold in order to give you these fine custom horseshoes that I spent two weeks bending and shaping.'
—King: 'Fine. Have it your way. Cut off his head.'
—The king's security detail would then decapitate the blacksmith and the king would proudly walk away with the coin and the horseshoes (plus the extra gold he shaved off the coin still at the castle) and the blacksmith was out of a job, not to mention his head.
—As the subjects used the currency the king was shaving, the real value of the coins depreciated whilst the king became richer and richer.

NOTE: This can also be achieved with your paper money using a technique called inflation. To cause inflation, simply print more money and, most importantly, use it first. By the time the new money reaches your subjects, it will have less value because there is now more of it in circulation. You'll have real world assets to show for it whilst your unknowing peasants have a depreciating piece of paper.

Quite splendid, isn't it?

Later in history, when people grew tired of hauling around their precious metals, a more user-friendly system of paper money was developed by something now known as a bank. The first banks were run by goldsmiths who issued paper notes redeemable for the gold and silver they stored in a safe place whilst charging a small fee.[12] This type of paper money is commonly known as *sound money* because it is backed by something of value. Gold and silver are also known as sound money because they have intrinsic value and at one time could be used in exchange for goods and services. The value of gold and silver comes from their usefulness in industries like electronics and jewellery. But, as any good ruler who owns a printing press knows, sound money *must* be outlawed because valueless paper (*fiat* money) simply cannot compete with it.

Eventually, the early banks pulled the same trick as the king by gradually taking the gold and silver for themselves with the foresight of knowing that not everyone would come for their metal at the same time. When credit was over extended, and people started sensing their wealth was being stolen, they showed up in droves to reclaim their gold and silver deposits. That's when pesky citizens wanted a head for their trophy case.

> NOTE: This is why it's also important to control an army.

Now that you have a basic understanding of sound money versus fake or fiat money, I believe it should be fairly obvious why you need to eliminate the competition. But, if not, I'll spell it out for you. If someone offers a currency based on real value whether that value is directly in your peasants' pockets or stored somewhere where it can be redeemed, your worthless paper is just that…worthless.

Therefore, you must make laws and be prepared to enforce them rigorously against anyone who threatens your monopoly on the money supply. I mean, are you in charge or aren't you? It's your bogus bills or nothing. As you'll see in the following chapters, you must also create the illusion of perceived value for your paper by pulling a sleight of hand.

'But how?' you whimper. Continue reading and you shall find out.

12.) "The History of Banks. Worldbank.org.ro. https://www.worldbank.org.ro/about-banks-history

Chapter 4

ASSEMBLING YOUR PEASANT FARM

Jobs, as such, are a relatively new concept. People may have always worked, but until the advent of the corporation in the early Renaissance, most people just worked for themselves. They made shoes, plucked chickens or created value in some way for other people, who then traded or paid for those goods and services.
— Douglas Rushkoff

In this chapter, we'll discuss building your peasant farm from scratch. Should a unique opportunity arise, like a global reset, you'll have a huge advantage over other potential peasant farm developers after reading this manual. If no such event occurs, this trusty guide will teach you what you need to know to build your **FARM**, but you'll be faced with the insurmountable task of breaking into the upper echelon of today's corporate structured society. I say this not to discourage your appetite for world domination, but to simply present the reality of entering a tightly monitored and rigged environment designed to keep outsiders like you at a stark disadvantage. If you look around, you may see many of the techniques discussed in this handbook surrounding you in your day-to-day affairs.

Just like adopting a pet or bringing a child into the world, the first order of business is to give your peasant farm a name. This name can come from just about anywhere, but I suggest naming it after yourself or someone you hold in high regard, using a native word that describes the landscape or even taking a word from a religious book that gives your kingdom-in-the-making special meaning. Whatever you choose, if your up-and-coming empire has staying power, it may become the official name of an actual geographical location one day. So, be sure to give it an indelible name with a nice ring to it so people can remember it.

There will be four components to your dominion that you must understand and master in order to operate a successful enterprise. You'll need to select, develop, nurture and control the culture, politics, war and business of your personal nation state to achieve your desired end results. I would love to say that all these four components will be immediately in your grasp, but in reality, this may not be the case.

These building blocks overlap and influence each other, but the most dominant overall force present in your realm will be the culture of your inhabitants. Culture includes things like race, religion, language and customs that deeply influence your peasants' participation in the political, military and commercial undertakings of your **FARM**. For instance, if America were not a Christian nation, leaders would have a hard time convincing their peasants to buy gifts for others on a recognised day each year to stimulate the business sector. Here, culture directly affects business. Likewise, if you need to invade a **FARM** with a foreign religion, your political structure can use fire and brimstone to scare your herd into attacking the outsiders that will drive the business sector. In this scenario, all four components (i.e. culture, politics, war and business) are working together cohesively.

In the day-to-day operations on your **FARM**, business probably has the least immediate impact on your peasants. For example, the exhilaration experienced when offering a new product line will fail in comparison to sending your young men and women off to die in a war. But, over an extended period of time, business can alter the dynamics of your territory until its initial form is unrecognisable. Look at the effect technology has had on the battlefield. Instead of soldiers marching at five mph and loading their muskets to fire upon the enemy, jets travelling at supersonic speeds can bomb villages with pinpoint accuracy with the push of a button.

However, building your **FARM** to this type of efficiency does not happen overnight. In days past, to assemble more workers, you had to conquer a region with your army or trade something of value to obtain additional labourers in your established territory. You could then appoint a religion and language or simply work within the framework of the deep-rooted culture they already possessed. But today, **FARMS** are much more sophisticated, not to mention interconnected, and infiltration takes a vast amount of resources and well-thought-out strategy.

If you're to compete in today's corporate lord climate, it's important, especially when first starting out, to seek talent within your populace and nurture their ability to produce. Whether that entails encouraging them to generate more peasants through the reproductive process or having them manufacture a greater number of widgets that keeps the consumption-driven corporate market moving, your peasants must have the proper incentives to not only be productive, but to remain well-behaved and hence, easier to control.

Religion-based guilt is incredibly useful for this purpose. By creating a mental framework that shapes moral behaviour, your breadwinners will jump up and down for your approval. Self-regulating behaviours such as heterosexual mating, good versus evil and hard work and thrift brought on by mantras like the *Protestant work ethic*, keep your peasants focused on your end goals, leaving little room for any distracting mischief.

Religion can also help instil fear, reminding your peasants that severe consequences may occur if they step out of line. This same fear can be used to manipulate them into doing things they normally might not do, like murder others in the name of their god. As long as you can convince your chattel they're doing things for a noble cause, they'll follow you off a cliff when instructed to do so.

Along with instilling fear, creating the ego-feeding illusion of prestige, or offering greed-satisfying monetary rewards will help spike productivity. Just be sure to have a system set up so you're profiting from the framework you had the audacious courage to create.

It's important to know modern-day societies naturally arrange themselves into a hierarchy made up of three tiers. The first tier is comprised of the most envied and rarest individuals, the entrepreneurs. It includes people like you and me who are the big picture people, otherwise, why would you be reading this handbook? We're the drivers of society and the ones willing to take the biggest risks. We offer bold ideas and possess the tenacity to see them through to completion. But we must rely on the second and third tiers to bring our visions to fruition.

The second tier is made up of competent, organised, and marginally intelligent individuals who manage the third tier made up of the technicians/labourers. The second tier is driven enough to want to control others but typically not to the level of tremendous self-sacrifice and hardship. The third tier consists of individuals who have compartmentalised thinking and skill sets.

Third-tier dwellers should receive training to perform repetitive tasks efficiently whilst remaining ignorant and unenlightened. If they cannot execute simple tasks, they'll most likely depend on you for their provisions. The plight of these third-tier peasants can then serve as a harsh reminder to all tiers what their fate will be if they fail in their endeavours.

In a *free* society, there's more fluidity to move upward and downward from one tier to another. For example, one can serve in their capacity until they've accumulated enough resources and/or knowledge to move into the next tier. In a less *free* society, these positions are locked in place and the top tier is made up of a small, exclusive club that prevents the other two tiers from ever reaching their level.

> NOTE: You must implement systems of control to prevent the lower tiers from uniting. This will be your biggest challenge as a modern-day lord and is essential to thrive as a leader of the top tier.

Getting back to the building blocks of your realm, politics (made up of mostly second tier types with some first-tier plants thrown in to keep them honest) is indeed influenced by the culture of your peasants but, conversely, politics also influences the opinions and day-to-day undertakings of your dwellers. You can cleverly use *government* policy to draw passionate reactions from your peasants or create divisions amongst them, making them easier to control. Second only to culture in terms of impact, a political structure is used to establish a military and hence wage war and can be used to shape business policy.

This handbook makes no assumptions as to the best system of *government* for your realm. You may live in a war torn or impoverished area where a dictatorship is the best method of keeping your *citizens* in line. Or maybe your land mass possesses a valuable resource, like oil, that you and your family want entirely for yourselves. Another possibility is that your territory has many abundant resources, and to fully exploit these *national* treasures, giving others the freedom to profit from them whilst cutting you in on the action is the best way to go. After all, many hands make light work, not to mention huge profits.

In the end, only you can decide the best political system for your **FARM**, but there are a few hidden truths that you must know before you decide how to rule your dominion. Remember, keep this privileged information away from the general knowledge of your peasants. This is especially important if you're providing the illusion of a *free* society. Otherwise, your useless eaters will start insisting that you weren't born with any superior rights or privileges. Who needs that aggravation?

First, it's common knowledge that there are two extremes in government. *Educated* simpletons from universities or mainstream media outlets will argue these extremes are communism/socialism on the far left versus fascism/Nazism on the far right with moderates in between. The truth is the two opposites in government are no government (anarchy) at one extreme and total government (communism/fascism/socialism/Nazism/Zionism) on the other. If one is to balance these two extremes somewhere in the middle, it's necessary to create a system of laws (People's law) that protects citizens from one another (anarchy) at one extreme and keeps the government from infringing on them (tyranny) at the other.[13]

The five basic forms of government that have occurred throughout human history are anarchy (self-rule), monarchy (one person rules everybody), oligarchy (a small group rules everybody), democracy (majority rules), and republics (a system of laws that rules everybody, a.k.a. People's law).[14] As described above, anarchy is zero government and is your opportunity to step in and gain control whenever it occurs.

Anarchy is, by far, the easiest scenario for exerting your will. In this situation, a system has usually collapsed or there has been an uprising against it, and a brief period of chaos ensues. As an aspiring world ruler, you must act swiftly and decisively. The timid will clamour for your protection, and even the strongest in society will miss the freedom that comes with law and order. Even if the new systems of control are highly oppressive and more severe (as they most certainly should be), there will be an overall acceptance of these new parameters just to have the feeling of stability and security return.

A monarchy, unfortunately, doesn't really exist in today's world, even though a spokesperson is usually visible upon whom the peasants can place blame for any ruling group's transgressions against them. As an up-and-coming modern-day lord, you should have a team of people behind the scenes advising you as to the best actions to take against your populous as well as offering general support.

This team should also be helpful in providing any strategic manoeuvres you need to make in foreign lands to expand your dominance and control. This is called an oligarchy. Trust me, exploiting the many is not a job you want to do on your own, at least not in today's fast-paced world. Almost the entire planet is currently running under

---

13.) W. Cleon Skousen, *The Making of America: The Substance and Meaning of the Constitution*. 3rd Edition. (United States of America: the National Center for Constitutional Studies, 2009), 42

14.) The John Birch Society, "Overview of America," You Tube Video, 29:22, TheJohnBirchSociety, April 18, 2012, https://youtu.be/-MzxC8Mqupw

this system. Your main competitors, the banking oligarch, have time-tested many of the principles illustrated in this book. Hopefully, you can give them a run for their money, quite literally.

A democracy is mob rules, and whatever the majority wants, the majority gets, even if it tramples on the rights and interests of the minority. This is not a scenario you want to find yourself in as a citizen or lord, although giving the illusion of a democracy is a great way to pit your peasants against each other.

With a republic (People's law), people assume they can live freely as long as they don't violate the fundamental liberties of their fellow citizens. A republic also allegedly provides each individual protection (laws set up for this purpose) from anyone acting against their fundamental rights, including those in positions of *authority*. This form of government rarely happens (only three times in human history) and is easy to usurp from the cowardly masses since they love to be coddled, not to mention, told what to do.

Also, the concept of a republic was conjured up for a *moral* society, and as you will discover in this book and, hopefully through your own experiences, human beings are susceptible to corruption. Be advised, if this form of self-rule is in place, it's nearly impossible to run your operation as you see fit unless you're able to infiltrate the government and then place it in the caring hands of those you trust. In its purest form, this type of governance is of little use to the modern-day lord and should be subverted, unless it's needed to serve a temporary purpose (see Chapter 5).

The best approach to undermine a free society is to gradually dismantle it over a long period of time. You don't want to raise suspicion from the citizens you're conquering, especially if they can defend themselves. This will allow you to take over the productivity of such a system by leaving its framework in place whilst still reaping its rewards. We will discuss techniques throughout this manual.

Because a gradual takeover of any system takes time, it'll be important to pass your methods and goals to your descendants and people who share your plans for humanity in case you don't live long enough to see your agenda to completion. Unless you're ready to get into a bloody conflict and win outright, gradual usurpation is a much more effective technique, and more stable approach, to gain control over a population and eventually the entire world.

It'll be important to divide your **FARM** into opposing camps. Although there should be both right and left wings in any type of political system you implement, both wings must obviously belong to the same bird…you. It's the framework you create for each *party* that will keep your *citizens* at odds. I hope the purpose is clear…to keep your chattel arguing over trivial matters whilst your agents secretly collude on the issues of major importance. The *political system* is put in place to give your peasants the illusion they have a say in things which, obviously, they should not.

The more conflict you can create, the more allegiance voters will commit to their party. Only conflict within the system will keep your peasants engaged. Otherwise, why would they bother?

Remember, it's important that you *do not let your peasants unite!* So, please pay special attention to the techniques presented throughout this pragmatic guide in order to control your peasants. This is a life and death matter of the highest degree, and the life you save could be your own.

Chapter 14 is devoted to war, but there are a few general points I'd like to discuss here. War is an essential ingredient used to expand the business aspect of your **FARM**. No one territory contains all the resources necessary to maintain a modern lifestyle. Also, differences in one of the four components on another **FARM** may impede your ability to run your incorporated realm to its utmost efficiency. For instance, a *nation's* religious practices (culture) may prevent you from running an oil pipeline through its holy lands. This is a wonderful reason to invade a **FARM** and bomb it back to the Stone Age. Another wonderful side effect of a brutal conflict is cheap labour via displaced *foreigners* seeking refuge on your **FARM**; as long as you're winning, of course.

For your non-thinking foot soldiers to do your bidding, you must always keep your true intentions to yourself, or at most, in complete secrecy amongst your trusted gatekeepers. These confidants will include citizens you blackmail or keep in line via the fear of death. It's not easy, but you must be willing to make an example out of anyone who reveals your actions or true motives.

Moreover, your uninformed sheeple may not be willing to risk their lives, or their children's lives, to take over a banana plantation in Ecuador, but they can be triggered to take down an *evil* dictator if enough fear is instilled in them, even if you put that very same dictator in power. Business is business, and you must find the strongest human emotions possible to motivate your peasants to jump at your command.

Last, war is a great way to focus the energy of your populace and bring your minions together for a common good. Just be sure to undermine your enemies by giving them some sort of label that identifies them as subhuman or, better yet, *evil*. It might be difficult for some to take a life by squeezing the trigger or pushing a button if they see the enemy as another flesh and blood being whose family is awaiting their return.

But, if they can see the enemy as a character in a video game or as a despicable life form like a worm or a maggot, they'll gleefully carry out any task you assign. Past examples include the Nazis calling the Jews *untermensch* or subhuman and the Hutus calling the Tutsi *inyenzi* or cockroaches.

Just the thought of a cockroach scurrying across the floor has my foot in the elevated stomping position. How about you?

Finally, it's important to share a few special ingenious techniques you can use to gain and maintain control of the businesses on your **FARM**. Like in politics, business is conducted under two extremes. One is a competitive free market and the other a monopolistic, state-controlled system.[15] But, in order to confuse your chattel and have them give up control of their hard work and creativity, you must mislead them with key buzz words they don't fully understand. The word capitalism is a perfect example.

If we break down the word *capitalism*, we find the word *capital* which is defined as having the means of production.[16] So, in truth, all systems are capitalistic, even those in Russia or communist China because they have the means to produce, i.e. finances, raw materials and machinery.[17]

But we don't want our toadies to know that.

You see, in a competitive, self-regulating free market system all parties are completely free to transact with one another. The key component is full private ownership, i.e. title, control, use and the ability to dispose of property.[18]

Can you see how this creates a huge problem? Your peasants own the means of production and the products being produced outright, meaning they can buy and sell them without your say in the matter.

In a republic, which is the only political system capable of supporting this type of business activity, the government would simply have the role of providing neutral currency, standards for weights and measures, and neutral courts to resolve disputes.

15.) Birch, "Overview," 20:50-21:02.
16.) Birch, "Overview," 19:00-19:15.
17.) Birch, "Overview," 19:00-20:45.
18.) Birch, "Overview," 21:05-22:11.

But, with this type of system in place, how are you supposed to rig the system so you can control the industries brought about by private ownership? As you can also see, it's pretty hard to give a trusted friend an unfair advantage if you can't regulate other companies out of existence or use your political structure to subsidise those who do your bidding.

Assuming you won't tolerate a competitive free market, you need to decide how much control of the capital you want your peasants to have under the other economic extreme, which is a monopolistic, state-controlled system. In Chapter 7, you'll learn some advanced techniques to trick your peasants into signing their property over to you. But for now, it's important to understand the things your underlings create belong to you and only you. You can, at most, let them *own* the businesses they create, so they take care of the facilities and have some pride in the products they produce, but you must dictate the rules they operate under.

Put a system of penalties in place to shut down their operation should they defy you. Then, you can collect their property via the court system or allow a friend or trusted peasant to take it over. When you're in position for a total takeover, you can demonise the word *capitalism* and trick your peasants into shaming business *owners* into graciously handing over ownership and control of their businesses to the ruling authority.

You can achieve this by convincing your peasants that without your regulations, others would poison the Earth and even drive species out of existence (which a consumption-based society will do anyway). You can remind the working stiffs of the unfair working conditions they may face without your oversight. The hilarity is the regulations will give your apple polishers a false sense of security, letting them think you're attending to a problem when the truth is they would be better off if they regulated themselves. Even the most foolish of business owners know they can't completely destroy the very thing they are trading, as they would be out of business in no time. This would, in turn, encourage responsible business practices, but who needs that poppycock when you have pain and suffering to dole out?

So, in short, to destroy a free market capitalistic system, you'll want to blame the problems on *capitalism,* a.k.a. the means of production, even though it was your regulations that allowed you to show favouritism, oppress non-desirable competitors and create a system of profits for your political structure. You must learn that if you're to thrive as a modern-day lord, you must master the art of creating a problem and then offering a solution that benefits you whilst making conditions worse for your peasants. There's no other way to maintain power and control over a society if you can't accomplish this simple task.

Next, we'll look at applying these strategies to overtake and run a multitude of peasant farms across the globe.

Buckle your seat belt as we focus on eventually running the entire world as one single corporate peasant farm.

Chapter 5

APPROACHES AND TECHNIQUES TO BUILD A GLOBAL EMPIRE

Some even believe we (the Rockefeller family) are part of a secret cabal working against the best interests of the United States, characterizing my family and me as "internationalists" and of conspiring with others around the world to build a more integrated global political and economic structure – one world, if you will. If that's the charge, I stand guilty, and I am proud of it.
— David Rockefeller

To move toward a global system of control, a look at our past is necessary. In a steady march toward a one world homogenised system, much work has been done, either overtly or covertly, to seize control of most of the current peasant populations. At times in the past, exploiting some of these individual **FARMS** fed a necessary purpose that helped bring us where we are today.

As a *crème de le crème* lord, the gory details involved in putting your plans into action should be left to your trusted team of advisors who specialise in battle and covert operations. As the kingpin of a world enterprise, you're simply the idea person. You do, however, need to understand the basic concepts and techniques used to conquer other territories so you can offer the right plan of action to your oligarchy team. It's the bold moves of days gone by that will give us the insight and courage to move forward.

The earliest forms of conquering a territory involved assembling soldiers and leading them into battle to conquer a section of land and its resources, including human beings. Sometimes, an unexpected invasion occurred, and tribes, kingdoms, empires and nations had to defend themselves against these incursions. Other times, the power struggles came from within when two or more opposing factions competed for supremacy over their **FARM**.

All the bloodshed that occurred since humanity's earliest days originated from our lust for power and control. The crowning achievement for any mortal man, I'm sure you would agree, is for complete domination over the entire human race. As you acquire a taste for power, your appetite for it grows, kind of like a yearning for a Whopper or Big Mac.

I happen to own the majority of shares in a few fast-food restaurants. I won't say which ones, but if you find yourself needing a little snack whilst reading these pages, McDonald's and Burger King offer some tasty meals at low prices. I also own the majority of stocks in a few pharmaceutical companies. We'll see later how one hand washes the other.

Even if you haven't gained a sizable advantage over your fellow man by running a huge, multi-national conglomerate, it should be easy to see that the combination of war and business provides the ultimate aphrodisiac. Wars always benefit someone. That's why wars are fought. The goal then, is to make sure that if you enter a conflict, it's beneficial to both you and your businesses, which is why you should be highly invested in wartime industries.

In today's modern society, there are more hands in the pot than ever before. Even simpletons can profit by owning just a few shares in a company that provides a minor component for the war machine. As a push for global control ensues, pockets will be stuffed whilst the poor saps in the line of fire suffer the consequences. If you can't be honest with yourself and admit that this excites you, it's time to tend to your bleeding heart and put down this book.

That's what I thought. Let's continue then, shall we?

The art of deception has consistently served as a powerful weapon in acquiring other farms and their resources. Consider the mythological tale of the Trojan Horse. To finally win the ten-year Trojan War, the Greeks constructed the Trojan Horse to gain access to the City of Troy. When the Trojans found the horse abandoned outside the wall of their city, they wheeled it inside to serve as a victory trophy. But they didn't know that Greek soldiers hid inside. Whilst the Trojans slept, the concealed soldiers sprang from the horse, opened the gates to the city and the Greek army burned Troy to the ground.

Although there is little practical use for a large wooden horse in today's advanced modern warfare, the art of deception is just as vital. Puppet *states* were and are used as an extension of a more powerful *nation state* that has a vested interest in a territory. The lesser *nation state* is permitted the illusion of sovereignty because it's allowed to retain its name, flag, national anthem, laws and constitution. The lesser FARM acts as a puppet by carrying out the will of the greater FARM, hence the name.

Reasons to set up a puppet government are numerous and varied. Here are a few examples to help you decide when a puppet government may be right for you.

For one, you may want to set up a missile system in a territory that neighbours an enemy's border and the current political powers in the potential host country don't want it there. You then consult with your team to decide if bribery (foreign aid), assassination or subterfuge is your best option. You set your plan into action and after a few years, *voila*, you have installed your missile system.

You don't want your enemy to know it was your meddling that allowed this system to be strategically placed, so you leave the façade of the previous nation intact to prevent your nemesis from realising your involvement. Because you are unnoticed, you continue to provide financing and support to your puppet government, so they continue to honour their commitment, leaving your enemy scratching their head wondering how and why this incursion occurred.

Another example: Maybe one of your companies wants to hire cheap labour from a third world *country* to manufacture athletic shoes you plan to sell at enormous profit margins. Rather than spend the money to hire a song writer to churn out a more contemporary anthem and an artist to design a new flag, let alone pay for a long lasting and bloody conflict, you simply spend the money to place a ruthless dictator in power who supports your oppression. You then tax your peasants' productivity in order to send *foreign aid* to the dictator who will squash any dissent amongst peasants who grow tired of working long hours for zero to little pay.

You, in the same breath, win the dictator's loyalty since he could never afford the extravagant lifestyle that you now provide by hocking his wife's luxury shoe and handbag collection.[19] In the meantime, your peasants are too busy staring at the blinking lights on their new trainers to realise they're being exploited. They translate their *happiness* and *comfort* as freedom. It's a win-win for just about everybody, except maybe the young children working in deplorable conditions in the

19.) Taylor Heyman. "Who is Imelda Marcos and why are her shoes famous?" The National.com. May 10, 2022. https://www.thenationalnews.com/world/asia/2022/05/11/who-is-imelda-marcos-and-why-are-her-shoes-famous/

sweatshops. But that's simply their cross to bear for being born onto such an inferior **FARM**. Thankfully, there may be hope for these less fortunate souls which we'll discuss in Chapter 13.

As a last example, it may be in your best interest to implement a clashing political ideology in the midst of a region where the culture doesn't support it. An example may be to insert a Christian or Judeo based system into a Muslim populated area. Remember, religion has a huge impact on a political system and its policies. So, rather than defeat a country in an oil-rich region and re-name it something like *America in the Middle East*, which offers everything from a Macy's to a McDonald's and even hosts an NFL preseason game, you simply infiltrate from within as suggested by Sun Tzu in *The Art of War* as the most effective way to take over a *nation*.[20]

Then, you simply operate from behind the scenes whilst leaving the previous culture and political structure intact. This way you avoid spending time and money on unnecessary clean-ups brought on by car bombs and exploding human beings that would be sent in to resist a more transparent occupation. Just make sure you provide enough military and financial support to prevent this terrain from becoming a slaughterhouse if a neighbouring **FARM** recognises and objects to your silent takeover. Once you get a foothold in such a region, you can also begin your expansion into other nearby realms.

Equally as pervasive as a puppet government is the fictitious entity known as a multinational corporation. This modern-day product and service driven enterprise can be used to bait other **FARMS** into wheeling your *Trojan Horse* onto their territory, providing full access to their natural and human resources. This construct offers the perfect vehicle for subversion and can enhance your wealth, power and influence. You can hide behind an impersonal brand name that few people, if any, will ever associate with you. Well, unless you enjoy that kind of attention. Another perk is that you don't need to be anchored at a specific geographical location to funnel a **FARM'S** riches directly into your bank account. You can start up and govern from behind your protective shield as you eat caviar on your yacht just off the shores of your privately owned Caribbean Island. Your business can take root in one fixed, strategic area or many, including *enemy* **FARMS**.

This corporate guise will also allow you to profit from more than one side of a skirmish that, typically, the political sector of a

---

20.) Sun Tzu, *The Art of War* (New York: Fall River Press, 2011), 9-10.

FARM initiates. Whether you're behind a banking institution, an energy company like Standard Oil in World War I or a technological company like IBM in World War II, you can play all sides of a conflict, guaranteeing that you benefit from the lucrative industry that is war, regardless of the outcome of the battles.

You can also seek talented people from within these profit-driven syndicates who are willing to play outside of the rules to not only further your agenda but to fulfil their own desires. Whilst using your financial influence and top-tier connections, these ambitious diamonds in the rough can then be placed in political positions to work on behalf of your industries and to cater to your personal aspirations as well.

One more benefit of the corporate structure is that you can monopolise an entire industry or diversify in other industries and take over the leading companies in many disciplines, whilst hiding behind various corporate names that seldom point back to you. Just as ruling your political structure from behind the scenes is far more strategic than taking centre stage, the same can be said for your business endeavours. Who's the largest shareholder in the Coca Cola Company? How about the name of the CEO? Even if you know, ask ten people you pass on the street if they know. I'd be surprised if one of them did. But I bet every single one of them is familiar with the Coca-Cola brand.

Do you see my point?

Once your businesses control the **FARM'S** politics, you can use your power to dictate which technologies remain relevant, influence the laws and regulations that hinder competition and ensure that law enforcement protects you from anyone determined to derail your ambitions. After this is accomplished, you can focus on more important things like taking over other **FARMS**.

For example, let's say the chicken feed your pharmaceutical company provides to agricultural companies pollutes a stream with arsenic.[21] Since you completely control the regulatory body that monitors the ingredients and production quality of your product, it's given the green light for distribution even though it poses a risk to human health. Maybe your intent was to gradually make people sick so they come back to your pharmaceutical company for their cancer protocol.

21.) Ecowatch. "Big Pharma Cover Up: Hiding Significant Levels of Arsenic in Your Chicken." Ecowatch.com. November 21, 2014. https://www.ecowatch.com/big-pharma-cover-up-hiding-significant-levels-of-arsenic-in-your-chick-1881975113.html

Even if your plan fails and your company is rigorously criticised, most likely, you can use your connections to downplay the incident. You remove the product from the shelves and have a company spokesperson or CEO vow to never let this happen again.

In the meantime, no one even thinks of singling you out as the majority shareholder or chairman of the board. At most, maybe the public calls for the firing of the CEO, or the company is fined or sued, but you're never personally held financially or criminally responsible. The very purpose of the corporation is to remove personal liability from individuals for any wrongdoing. Can you see how this corporate shield can be used to protect you from other nefarious activities as well?

From the general public's point of view, corporations generate products and services essential for an efficient and modern lifestyle whilst providing employment for peasants. But, just as a pizza parlour in New York City can be used as a front to conceal illicit activity, so can the corporation. An entire government and one or more of its agencies can be used as fronts as well since they are also incorporated (see Chapter 6).

Just be sure to portray your entity of choice as benevolent by offering attractive products and services to your peasants and by honouring the fighting men and women who sacrifice themselves for your entity's endeavours. Also, be sure to inundate your peasants with friendly and official imagery of your corporation(s) through media outlets and marketing campaigns.

Above all else, be sure to have loyal conspirators within the legal and political structure just in case some do-gooders stumble across your shadowy activities.

A few examples of side industries run out of various public and private institutions include drugs, human trafficking, counterfeiting, prostitution, racketeering, theft, arms sales, insider trading, terrorism, wiretapping and murder for hire. As shown throughout history and during such times as prohibition, when authorities deem a product or service illegal, its value increases dramatically. Therefore, doesn't it make sense to outlaw the items you're able to produce without the legal restrictions imposed on the peasants and use your unfair advantages via your political structure to monopolise these markets?

Creating this kind of profit margin will elevate you above the straight schmucks who could never yield the same amount of revenue from their legal businesses. By the way, you'll be taking a percentage. By controlling the laws and law enforcement, you can target any competitor who refuses to include you in the profits or attempts to undermine your dominance. If you're not in control of a political system, is there no better reason to do so?

We cannot have a conversation about world dominance without mentioning the need to take control of your region's (and eventually the world's) land, air and water. If you're going to have total control over humanity, you need to control its most vital resources. This can be done through your political, military and corporate structures and is the key to your prosperity and dominance. Once established, you can micromanage things like food, water, petroleum and even the air your peasants breathe.

Establishing your supremacy over these three jurisdictions will give you greater advantages when it comes to trade and military strategy. The avenues and techniques used to control your fellow man are limitless. Hopefully, this handbook will ignite your creativity and inspire new methods to deprive the unenlightened.

Another tool to use on your road to global conquest is a proxy war. This is another indirect way of weakening a superior **FARM** without getting into a bloody and costly conflict. You can either support a farm that will directly engage in conflict with your rival farm, or you can aid and abet the enemy of your adversary's proxy.

Because technology has dramatically changed the nature of warfare, direct wars with superpower **FARMS** are no longer feasible unless you plan to obliterate the entire planet and its inhabitants. But there are still some outdated **FARMS** susceptible to ideological influence, not to mention invasion. Acquiring such **FARMS** can help put you in a stronger negotiating position when it comes to dealing with other superpower **FARMS** at the world table. Keep in mind, you'll want to collude with and even recruit fellow superpower **FARM** leaders who will be on board with your overall plan, whilst also working behind the scenes to seek advantages over them.

Another way to exert your influence, similar to a proxy war but slightly less involved, is to subvert a **FARM'S** elections or incite a rebellion that will destabilise a **FARM** and place a more sympathetic ally in power. Both types of interference can include psychological and covert operations, propaganda campaigns, financing, arms support and tactical training. Again, this type of infiltration is much easier to achieve on weaker **FARMS**. However, if the centres of power are gradually penetrated, even the strongest of **FARMS** can become vulnerable.

Because both nations and businesses are incorporated, you need to realise that these entities are similar and can be used for similar purposes. They both have a team of people behind the scenes controlling the spokespeople who serve as their leaders, and you can use both to take over other corporations, whether they are entire countries, religious organisations, governments, branches of government or other businesses.

In today's world, both businesses and governments can hire private armies for a variety of reasons, further blurring the line between nations and corporations. Therefore, lords like yourself can hide behind both fronts and use the methods described above to accumulate land, air, water and all the resources (human and otherwise) that are contained within.

Now that we set the tone by discussing proxy wars and corporations, it's time to reveal the ultimate Trojan Horse. What if you could create or take over a nation that is not only capable of generating its own wealth, but is used to fight just about every proxy war on Earth whilst also posing as the beacon of hope for all?

In addition, what if you could create a religious corporation that's a nation itself with its own set of laws and territory and is used to control all other corporations, including the surrogate fighting nation and all properly registered peasants? And beyond that, what if this religious city is controlled by a higher order that hides its occult symbolism in plain sight on religious costumes, accessories, sculptures and paintings?

Finally, what if this is all done through a corporate city state that controls the world's banking and financial system on which the military arm and spiritual centre are dependent? You would have three corporations working in conjunction to rule almost the entire planet.

Looking at the current power structure of the world, it's easy to see this has already been achieved. Of course, this didn't happen overnight. This grand experiment began quite a few centuries ago but took a big step forward when some enlightened businessmen arrived on the shores of a lush territory that possessed many natural resources. There were some minor inconveniences, such as natives who cherished and respected the abundant land. But this would be a minor stumbling block for the oppressed who were escaping a tyrannical system with the hope of achieving the ultimate human experience on this new and wide-open terrain...freedom!

Although the deep-rooted yearning for equality, fairness and achieving one's unlimited potential was and still is the driving force of those who settle or wish to settle in such a place, the reality is this utopian concept of freedom for all is neither achievable nor practical. Even though a gutted version of the original template for a free society still exists today in the United States of America and benefits a good portion of its inhabitants, this system was really intended to benefit only those who penned the social contract.

As even the most rudimentary legal minds can tell you, a contract only applies to those who sign it. *We the People* included only the original peasant farm lords who signed the contract and their prodigy as stated in the agreement. Is this not completely obvious? If it isn't, then why would those who boasted, 'All men are created equal,' also own slaves? Because they were talking about themselves in relation to those who sought to oppress them and not the people they murdered and oppressed.

The American colonies were a robust business venture, and when America's *founding fathers* showed they could do a lot with very little, like win a war against an empire and thrive as a business operation, they created a social contract that protected them against anyone who would threaten their interests, whether that threat came from a fellow citizen, their own government or a foreign creditor/enemy. However, a good portion of the **FARM'S** dwellers benefitted from the many spoils this system generated, ultimately providing a higher quality of life for all who resided within the confines of its geographical borders.

For a short time, a sincere effort was made to operate this new **FARM** as a utopian society, despite its hypocritical beginnings. Many advances, great prosperity and an incredible business model came into being due to the sacred principles of individual ownership and rights. The combination of a free market and its ensuing personal freedoms attracted the best and the brightest from around the world who enjoyed being rewarded for their specialised contributions. Many innovations were achieved in the areas of technology, aviation, energy, transportation and weaponry. These advances made America a powerful force in world affairs.

However, America's greatest source of independence, the ability to coin and regulate the value of its own money, was eventually cajoled by those wanting to harness this grand experiment for their own gain. Inherent rights gradually became privileges that had to be granted via permission. Whilst citizens gave up more and more of their personal liberties, they believed their right to consume meant freedom.

In the marketing of America, peasants on other **FARMS** are led to believe it's the glitz and glamour of the American lifestyle that is desirable and not the moral high road its people once took. What was once, and still is, sold as a land of opportunity and freedom, is now simply a land where one can have modern things and live a comfortable lifestyle. But its citizens must be willing to compromise themselves and pay the ultimate sacrifice to maintain that comfortable lifestyle.

Yes, you heard that right. Americans are expected to blindly enslave themselves, and future generations, to pay for the conquests of other **FARMS** whilst also sacrificing themselves in these battles. They've been used and misled into many wars that served a higher purpose whilst, at the same, further indebting themselves to those clever enough to trick them into these costly endeavours.

'How is this done?' you wonder. I'm glad I asked.

We'll discuss the most successful techniques throughout this handbook, but on a superficial level it's because Americans today have the best of the best in everything, from weaponry to medicine to entertainment, giving them a sense of entitlement that forces their values onto other **FARMS**. Over time, Americans have also been, quite deliberately, made to realise the unpleasant conditions experienced on lesser **FARMS**, making them willing to do just about anything to protect their higher standard of living. Because peasants on other **FARMS** yearn for the hope that America offers, they're also willing to risk life and limb to move there or, at the very least, desire similar conditions on their own **FARMS**, further spreading American ideals. In the interim, barely anyone questions their captivity and servitude regardless of the **FARM** they inhabit.

'But, for what ultimate purpose is America used to attack other nations?' you may ask. Well, I'll answer this question with a question. As an up-and-coming lord, what's the most effective way to control a population aside from brute force? If you answered debt, you're catching on quite nicely and just might have what it takes to rule a world empire.

It'll be your debt-based currency, implemented throughout the world, that will give you complete control over humanity. At the very least, your valueless paper, and certainly not gold, must be the dominant currency of all nations. By strictly ensuring that a commodity such as oil can only be purchased using your fiat money (currently called the *petrodollar),* you'll begin the process of bringing all farms into your dominion. Any non-nuclear **FARM** that resists your currency should be invaded and forced to implement it.

But then the question arises, 'How do I motivate a **FARM** such as America to spill their blood for my paper monopoly money?' An excellent question. I'll provide a few time-tested techniques in upcoming chapters.

However, if you're new to the game of global conquest, you might first wonder how to infiltrate the highly established order of today's modern world. I must be clear; I never said it would be easy. Unless you're born into the ruling class, it may be damn near impossible. If you decide to pursue this undertaking full-time, realise you have set your goals to the highest of the high. To have a real chance at social dominance, you may need to marry into an elite bloodline or, at the very least, befriend those already at the top of the social pyramid. But if you're keen on approaching this challenge the old-fashioned way via grit and determination, I'll provide the information you need to proceed. Enter at your own risk.

For starters, to implement your own monetary, political and religious systems, you'll need a **FARM** with some real firepower. Therefore, subversion of a global police **FARM** could be a viable option. For a military giant like America, infiltrating the centres of power and changing the mindset of its occupants is a possibility. Once you have a foothold in the hubs of influence, like the universities and the media, you must trumpet your mantras through the pillars of the infiltrated **FARM**. You'll, of course, also need willing conspirators who understand and fully believe in your worldview. You must be prepared to tighten your grip on the inhabitants of even an allegedly *free* **FARM** to steer them in your direction.

There's a phenomenon known as Stockholm syndrome in which, for survival, victims empathise with their captors and over time take on their point of view. So, almost effortlessly and quite naturally, peasants on your cherished **FARM** begin to unknowingly adopt and work toward your world view. As a current example, look at how communism has been brilliantly woven into the fabric of American thinking.

As you begin to conquer other territories, these fallen **FARMS** will start to take on your worldview. Like Adolf Hitler said: 'The great strength of the totalitarian state is it forces those who fear it to imitate it.'[22] Like the board game Monopoly, the more property you take possession of, the wealthier you become, and the closer you are to distinguishing yourself as a leader in the human chattel market. Similar to running a business, you'll want to gobble up the competition whilst acquiring more capital and maximising your profits. Your peasants will be a means to this end. The more peasants you can accumulate to do your bidding, the more prevalent your world view will be.

There is, however, one last thing to consider when taking over the planet and all its resources. At the current rate of consumption, there

22.) Adolf Hitler. "Nazi Germany Quotations: Power and Totalitarianism." alphahis-tory.com. https://alphahistory.com/nazigermany/nazi-germany-quotations-pow-er-totalitarianism/

may be little left if the masses continue to decimate the Earth's landscape and raw materials. At some point in the near future, decisive action must be taken because the American model will not be sustainable, especially since it's currently being imposed on the rest of the world. I think it'll be helpful to view this time in history as an opportunity to apply some forward thinking. Instead of taking over the military might of America, it may behove you to infiltrate, sway or convince a *nation* like China to act as your surrogate.

With abundant human resources (pawns to be thrown into battle) and a totalitarian system already in place, this **FARM** has all the amenities conducive to meeting your end goals. Whilst America buries itself in debt and China buys up more and more of its properties, you may be able to get a big jump on those looking to rule from behind the war horse that is America.

At some point, it'll be necessary to pull the plug on the current American system. America has already topped out as far as production and consumption are concerned. *Countries* like China and India will soon replace America as leaders of the global economy. Nevertheless, it'll be necessary to reduce the standard of living for all peasants, not to mention, reduce their numbers.

A nice global conflict orchestrated by many willing players, and fought by the oblivious, will be instrumental in achieving this goal. But, for now, we'll look at the methods for legally enslaving your peasants and the imaginary corporate world those enslaved peasants are subject to versus the real world in which slavery has been abolished. Confused? Then, please read on.

Chapter 6

CORPORATE FICTION VS THE REAL WORLD

It's ridiculous to talk about freedom in a society dominated by huge corporations. What kind of freedom is there inside a corporation? They're totalitarian institutions—you take orders from above and maybe give them to people below you. There's about as much freedom as under Stalinism.
— Noam Chomsky

Until this point in human history, there's never been a **FARM** as efficient, productive, wealthy and dare I say it, exploited, as the American **FARM**. This, of course, includes its human assets. Such a **FARM**, however, is absolutely necessary if you're going to satisfy your lust for world power. Throughout this handbook, to illustrate how to dominate and cunningly use a **FARM**, I'll focus on the American **FARM**. That's not to say that **FARMS** of yesteryear haven't helped pave the way toward the submission of humanity to the ruling few, but special attention must be given when building, capturing, infiltrating and upgrading a formidable **FARM** such as America and turning it into the world's only true superpower.

> NOTE: Ruling with an iron fist is much more straightforward than overseeing a **FARM** that affords its peasants many perks and privileges once reserved solely for the upper echelon of society. To win the human race over to your world view, you must create a system that taps into every man, woman and child's innermost wants and desires until you have successfully funnelled a large majority of the Earth's population into your preconceived order. When this has been achieved, you'll have free reign to rule as you wish.

There are an infinite number of ways to accomplish this, but there are some constants you must adhere to. The concepts behind your ruling methods, no matter how far-fetched or abstract, must make sense to you. They can be completely made up or pieced together from prior disciplines such as law, business, politics, religion, the occult and philosophy. If you implement a strategy, you must be able to justify it and having a historical track record will aid you in this endeavour.

Next, your ruling approach must be esoteric in that only you and your trusted associates understand all its complexities. It's acceptable to have incoherent and even outlandish techniques thrown into the mix in order to confuse your peasants and force them to give up due to the overwhelming intricacies needed to understand your system. As long as you and your associates have a way to benefit whilst also possessing the skill and tenacity to restrict the peasants' utilisation of these methods, you'll reign supreme. Whether you wish to create your own ruling system from scratch, use one already in place or create some sort of hybrid, it's my most sincere hope that the remaining illustrations in this handbook inspire you to dominate, conquer and control the meek.

Let's forge ahead if it shall so please you, my lord.

I'm sure you'll agree, most of the civilised world is aware of the history of Black slavery and the bloody American Civil War that was allegedly fought to end it. Did you ever stop to wonder how and why the rest of the world ended slavery without incident?[23]

So, was all the bloodshed really about freeing the downtrodden African American slaves, or was something more grandiose at play? I think you're getting to know me well enough to correctly answer that question.

If you believe that the American Civil War was fought solely to free the Black slaves, I have a bridge I want to sell you. Does this statement make you feel uncomfortable? Lied to? Confused? As you continue to read, you may notice the mind control programming you were subjected to and experience physical discomfort known as cognitive dissonance. Encyclopaedia Britannica[24] describes cognitive dissonance as:

> *The mental conflict that occurs when beliefs or assumptions are contradicted by new information. The unease or tension that the conflict arouses in people is relieved by one of several defensive manoeuvres: they*

23.) Thomas J. DiLorenzo, *The Real Lincoln: A New Look at Abraham Lincoln, His Agenda, and an Unnecessary War* (New York, New York: Three Rivers Press, 2002), 37, 48-49.

24.) The Editors of Encyclopedia Britannica. "cognitive dissonance." Encyclopedia Britannica.com. April 4, 2023. https://www.britannica.com/science/cognitive-dissonance

reject, explain away or avoid the new information;
persuade themselves that no conflict really exists;
reconcile the differences; or resort to any other
defensive means of preserving stability or order in their
conceptions of the world and of themselves.

You can use this natural, physical response and ensuing denial mechanism to your advantage to keep your peasants in a state of oblivion. Unless, of course, you're ready to quit your ambitious goals of global conquest due to the uneasiness you're feeling. Are you bothered to the point of caving in, or are you resilient enough to go forward? If you're to rise to the position of global lord, you must recognise some hard truths and be willing to push past what is uncomfortable to obtain a higher level of understanding. Knowledge is power and an absolute must if you are to gain an advantage over the misled sheeple grazing in the pasture of ignorance. There are endless possibilities available to you, but only if you're willing to do what it takes to seize power.

So, was the American Civil War really about freeing the Black slaves? Arguments have been made on both sides of the issue, but I'm not here to argue over the details provided by establishment-friendly historians. Let's skip ahead a few years beyond the Civil War to find the truth. According to corporate government schools (i.e. peasant training centres) where most, and maybe even you, received an *education*, the 14th Amendment gives Blacks equal protections under the law by recognising everyone born within the United States of America as a United States citizen. This sounds wonderfully inclusive, but is it?

Before the Civil War, Americans were *citizens* of their respective states (a Pennsylvania citizen, a New Jersey citizen, etc.). After the Civil War, through the District of Columbia Organic Act of 1871, THE UNITED STATES OF AMERICA (singular unit) became a corporation, replacing the defunct and bankrupt republic formerly known as the united States of America (plural, many states). This similar name, but new creation, allowed the switch from people's law to a corporate style of government for the now incorporated ten square mile area known as THE DISTRICT OF COLUMBIA. This act appointed Congress as the board of directors to continue the business functions of government whilst under martial law. Thanks to the Lieber Code (orders regarding the code of conduct for Union soldiers during wartime) the jurisdiction of this new entity not only pertained to captured citizens from the south but to all Americans in their respective states now known as United States citizens.

For proof that the United States is a corporation please see Title 28 United States Code 3002 15(A) where (15) United States means— (A) A federal corporation.

More on codes in an upcoming chapter.

Oh, it's such a golden web of deceit, isn't it?

A new document called THE CONSTITUTION **OF** THE UNITED STATES replaced the Constitution **for** the united States of America and became the bylaws for the newly formed business venture. Anyone who declared citizenship of the United States fell under this new corporation's rule through consent. In other words, a citizen of (state name) became a United States citizen located in THE DISTRICT OF COLUMBIA.

But how can you reside in your respective state and also live in the DISTRICT OF COLUMBIA? Well, a legal piece of paper representing you can be in one place like Washington DC whilst you go about your frivolous existence elsewhere.

'But, for what purpose?' you hum and haw.

Before we continue, you may also be wondering, 'Why does he keep using capital letters? Is this for emphasis or is he angry?' In the case of legal documents and definitions, any name in all capital letters refers to something known as an ENS LEGIS, legal speak for a fictitious/ corporate entity that is different from a living, breathing human being.

Do you write your name in all capital letters, or do you capitalise the first letter of your first and last name and then use lower case characters to spell out the rest? Why then, does your name appear entirely in UPPER CASE LETTERS on documents and financial instruments used in commercial activity like your *commercial* driver's licence, gas bill, bank loans, bank accounts, social security card, court documents, etc.? Is it to draw attention to your name or for some other reason? Now that your wheels are turning, I'll present the wonderful world of the corporate fiction created to enrol real world people like you into *voluntary* servitude.[25]

It is, without a doubt, in your best interest to also find a way to contractually trick your peasants into volunteering their time, labour and property over to you. You've seen the backlash forced slavery generates and you don't want to be caught holding the reigns to this highly frowned upon institution.

25.) Dr. Sym. "'Strawman' The Untold Story." Foundation for Truth in Law.org. https:// foundationfortruthinlaw.org/Files/STRAWMAN_THE_UNTOLD_STORY.pdf

But, if your peasants contractually agree to their subservience, you're not responsible, right? Therefore, as outlandish as this may seem, we must create a parallel universe where your fictional characters not only reside but interact with each other. This world must also be connected to the real world where living men, women and their property actually exist. The beautiful thing about this alternate reality is that most peasants will never even suspect or investigate it and will openly dismiss it as crazy when presented with the truth. In fact, the longer it goes on and the longer your peasants are engaged in it, the harder it will be for them to recognise they've been deceived.

So, to start, I'd like you to think about the three, and only three entities, that are spelled out in all capital letters. I'll give you a hint. Corporations, ships and dead people. If you don't believe me, look at a billing statement with a company name on it, look at the markings on any large oceanic vessel or simply walk through a cemetery and inspect the headstones. All three of these unique and separate entities in the magical land of commerce possess or transmit CAPITAL and are written in all CAPITAL letters. All three also have a direct relationship to the LEGAL PERSON/ENS LEGIS that represents you in commerce.

For one, it's no surprise that CORPORATIONS are *legally* considered PERSONS and have been given rights to protect their property. As I mentioned, both CORPORATIONS and PERSONS are fictitious entities known as an ENS LEGIS, defined in Black's Law Dictionary 2nd Ed. L. Lat. as: [26]

> *A creature of the law; an artificial being, as contrasted with a natural person. Applied to corporations, considered as deriving their existence entirely from the law.*

So then, can you take an actual corporation like WAL-MART or MICROSOFT out to lunch or go bowling with it? Can the COMMONWEALTH OF VIRGINIA or the STATE OF TENNESSEE physically appear at your hearing? Can either SIR LAWRENCE MCALISTER or YOUR NAME go parasailing or play lawn darts? Is then, that NAME on your social security card and birth certificate you? If you've blurted out, 'Hell no!' it's important that you not only hold onto this secret, but defend it at all costs if you, indeed, take this approach. These vessels can be used to trick your peasants into relinquishing their rights, labour and property over to you.

26.) "ENS LEGIS Definition and Legal Meaning." The Law Dictionary.org. https://thelawdictionary.org/ens-legis/

PERSONS, like SHIPS, are also subjected to Merchant Law/ Law of the Sea/Admiralty Law as clearly demonstrated by any court that replaced lawful money (required in common law courts) with negotiable instruments and commercial paper called legal tender found in Admiralty proceedings. The difference between the terms legal and lawful is also important. Anything *legal* has the form and appearance of law where something *lawful* is based on the substance and content of law.[27]

The current financiers of the world have brilliantly tricked men and women into a *legal*, make-believe system by creating codes and revised statutes (Merchant/Law of the Sea/Admiralty Law) that exploit the equity function of the courts. This equity function is best explained as rulings reached according to the conscience of the court as opposed to outcomes based on strict interpretations of the law.[28] If the court's conscience is rooted in commerce and profits, the results can be quite lucrative for the key players involved. Furthermore, if a legal system of conscience can saturate a lawful society, interpretations of right and wrong will be left to the ruling party's discretion. Since agreements and contracts are the backbone of Merchant Law, many clever ploys have been developed to entice the peasants into these Star Chamber proceedings. In short, by offering peasants a semblance of justice whilst duping them into hidden, one-sided contracts, they'll feel compelled to participate.

'But what contracts?' you mutter. We'll look at these *adhesion* contracts in greater detail in the next chapter.

For now, it's useful to know a peasant can grant a court equitable jurisdiction (authority) through implied or expressed consent. It's no fault of yours if unknowing peasants forfeit their basic human rights by agreeing to terms and conditions they're unaware of. As long as your rules make sense to you and your team, and peasants agree to them, then by all means proceed.

PERSONS, like SHIPS, are birthed/berthed when they pass from a body of water (embryonic fluid/sea) through a canal (birth/ narrow waterway) to a delivery (room/dock) on dry land. A CAPtain (derived, in part, from their association with capital) must provide a berth certificate when docking a ship and a DOCkTOR signs a birth certificate after the mother goes through *labour*. The person attains citizenSHIP (citizen of a ship) after presenting the birth certificate and

27.) West's Encyclopedia of American Law, edition 2.S.v. "lawful." April 11, 2023. https://legal-dictionary.thefreedictionary.com/lawful
28.) David Williams. "Courts of Equity – A Brief History." Presto Servers.com. August 7, 2014. https://prestoservers.com/blog/courts-of-equity-a-brief-history/

eventually has ownerSHIP (owner of a ship) of things like real estate which can be put up for sale/sail using the PERSON/VESSEL in the commercial world that operates under Admiralty Law.

Common law or *Law of the Land* is based on natural laws but dependent on geographical location as to which laws are recorded and how they are enforced. That's determined by the culture and politics of a society. Regardless of one's country of origin, at sea everyone is subject to a set of international rules made up of codes and revised statutes that are designed to regulate commerce. *Authority* comes from the *author* of the codes or statutes, an agent of the *corporation*.[29] No explaining is required to see why this system, or a similar one, must be implemented, if your end goal is to rule humanity under one prevailing authoritative order.

Finally, there's also a correlation between a DEAD PERSON and the ENS LEGIS spelled exactly like YOUR NAME. Besides being written out in ALL CAPITAL LETTERS, both require a living man or woman to initiate any kind of commercial activity on behalf of the entity. Since both are lifeless, they need living people to provide the life force necessary to transmit something from the land of the living into the land of paper and titles, a.k.a. the dead.

In a lawful/de jure court, you would need to show there has been a real-world loss or injury, and a man or woman would have to make the claim for a judge to provide a remedy for the harm done. But, in a legal/make believe/de facto court, corporate fictions are in conflict, and all administrative decisions are based on hidden agreements and contracts where any fictitious entity can seize the property of another whether or not a real-world loss or injury actually occurred.[30]

Just to tickle your funny bone, when a judge says, 'Do you understand?' did you know he's really saying, 'Do you agree to the terms and conditions of the contract?'[31] Because he's dressed in a Zorro cape and armed with a wooden gavel capable of bashing in a human skull, most bond servants obediently nod their heads yes and agree to the contract. This is especially true if peasants have been properly trained to fear *authority* or, at the very least, the prison they'll be taken to if they step out of line.

29.) Charles Weisman. "Authority of Law, 2nd Ed." Internet Archive.org. August 9, 2020. https://archive.org/details/authority-of-law/page/71/mode/2up , 6-10, 28.

30.) Robert Kelly, *Redemption Manual* 4th Edition (4.4): How to Become a Secured Party Creditor (Central Point, Oregon: ABS Publishers, 2006), 445-446.

31.) "The Secret to Winning at Court – Court Remedy." Educated in Law.org. March 10, 2017. https://www.educatedinlaw.org/2017/03/the-secret-to-winning-in-court-court-remedy/

How and when did all this happen in a *free* society? To see clearly, we must take a step back in time to the early days of the American colonies and work our way to present day. For starters, the business venture known as America has always had financial trouble, even since the days of its early inception. A simple analogy can clearly show why.

Let's say I fund the mass movement of peasants and their handlers to Ecuador so they can establish and operate a banana plantation on my behalf. Then, once they're up and running, my Ecuadorian ambassadors decide they no longer want me to have a say in things and refuse to give me a return on my investment. In any reasonable court of law, they would, at the very least, be lawfully required to return the startup money plus any additional funding that I provided for an ensuing rebellion. Such is the story of the American colonies and their obligation to their financiers in England.[32]

Furthermore, the French, who aided the American side of the revolution, also accumulated a nice little bill in the process. These liabilities owed to both England and France were negotiated into the social contract penned after the revolution, a.k.a. the Constitution for the united States of America. The evidence is in the provision shown in Article VI to repay any pre-constitution debts.[33] By creating this agreement, the managers of the peasant farm known as America were now able to run the **FARM** as a more profitable business without interference from the Crown as long as they paid their debts.[34]

As a budding lord, it's also important to understand that in order to gain control you must sometimes be willing to give up control. As you'll see a little further into our current example, a little bump in the road was not about to deter the cunning creditors of the colonies from giving up on their quest for global dominance and the promising new land known as America. You'll soon see their patience, determination and use of trusted agents (used to gain access to critical information) beautifully utilised to implement their agenda.

32.) Brian Shilhavy. "The American Revolution: When the Bankers Destroyed the Economy – History Repeating Itself?" Created4Health.org. July 12, 2020. https://created4health.org/the-american-revolution-when-the-bankers-destroyed-the-economy-history-repeating-itself/ and Holly Greig. "The United States Remains a British Colony." Bibliotecapleyades.net. July 29, 2010. https://www.bibliotecapleyades.net/sociopolitica/sociopol_globalbanking92.htm and William Guy Carr. "*Pawns in the Game*: Chapter Five – The American Revolution." Lovethetruth.com. https://www.lovethetruth.com/books/pawns/05.htm
33.) Skousen, *The Making of America*, 654-657.
34.) Greig, "The United States Remains a British Colony."

On the flip side of things, leaders of the colonies had already learned the importance of coining their own money. Before the revolution, they used Colonial Scrip. Having their own scrip allowed the colonists to 'control its purchasing power whilst owing interest to no one', as expressed by Benjamin Franklin to the Bank of England that wanted to know the reason for the plantation's newfound prosperity.[35]

'But why was Ben Franklin reporting to the Bank of England?' you ponder. I'll let you read between the lines on that one.

If you see no connection, you still have a peasant's mentality and have not yet reached the level of a leader who needs to have ears to the ground to obtain an advantage over others. Remember, knowledge is power and so is coercing others to act on your behalf.

Because of the Bank of England's influence over the British government in conjunction with Ben's helpful tip, Parliament passed the Currency Act of 1764 which prevented the colonies from printing and coining their own money. Franklin later retorted: 'In one year, the conditions were so reversed that the era of prosperity ended, and a depression set in, to such an extent that the streets of the Colonies were filled with unemployed.'[36] Franklin would later say this was the prime reason for the Revolutionary War.

Thanks again for your wonderful on-the-ground reporting, Ben!

The production of money was so important to America's Founding Fathers that a provision was placed in the constitution that gave the government for the United States the sole authority to coin money and regulate its value. Do you see the obstacle presented for an outsider trying to muscle in? Well, so did the pioneers of today's planetary takeover.

By provoking and financing the War of 1812, along with the American Civil War, and by buying proponents and eliminating opponents of their policies, these aspiring global lords were able to

---

35.) Mike Kirchubel. "How Benjamin Franklin Caused the Revolutionary War." OpEdNews.com. July 14, 2011. https://www.opednews.com/articles/How-Ben-jamin-Franklin-Caus-by-Mike-Kirchubel-110711-773.html and Dan and Jax Bubis. "Benjamin Franklin trips to England." Revolutionary War and Beyond. com. https://www.revolutionary-war-and-beyond.com/benjamin-frank-lin-trips-to-england.html and George Goodwin. "Benjamin Franklin in London." Mount Vernon.org. https://www.mountvernon.org/library/digitalhistory/digital-encyclopedia/article/benjamin-franklin-in-london/ and William Guy Carr, *Pawns In The Game* (USA: Dauphin Publications, 2013), 57.

36.) Congressman Charles G. Binderup. "America Created Its Own Money In 1750: How Benjamin Franklin Made New England Prosperous." Rense.com. 1941. https://rense.com/general66/nobeyb.htm and Carr, *Pawns In The Game*, 57.

drive America into massive debt and bypass their biggest hurdle to date: the Constitution for the united States of America.[37]

They did this when monies owed from the War of 1812 and the Civil War caused America to default on its loans. Instead of seizing the collateral, i.e. the land that comprised the United States, banking and corporate interests developed a better idea; they decided to suspend the government and form a corporation created for the sole purpose of exploiting this budding new **FARM** and its people.[38] The corporation, owned by these backroom players, would eventually trick the people holding allodial land titles to transfer their property over to them.[39]

This didn't happen overnight. There were still some stodgy members in *government* and private industry who wanted The United States of America, Inc. to coin their own money thereby maintaining control of the country's affairs. Creating an alternate United States was a big first step, but there were still a few obstacles preventing a complete takeover. If these ingenious, behind the scenes opportunists could find a way to cleverly convince their opponents to entrust them with a monopolistic central banking authority with complete autonomy to lend money to the government and the nation's commercial banks, it would pave the way for profitable wars and big business policies that would follow shortly thereafter.

I get a little teary-eyed every time I talk about it but, tragically, a couple of early United States corporate presidents who opposed a central bank met their untimely demise when they happened to be in the direct path of a bullet.[40]

And who could forget those unfortunate, successful businessmen who happened to be on the maiden voyage of an extremely large luxury liner during its regrettable mishap?[41] One must be extremely careful when

37.) Michael Rivero. "All Wars Are Bankers' Wars!" whatreallyhappened.com. https://www.whatreallyhappened.com/WRHARTICLES/allwarsarebankerwars.php and Alain Pilote. "Chapter 49 – The History of Banking Control in the United States." Famguardian.org. First published in the Sept-Oct 1985 issue of the Vers Demain Journal. https://famguardian.org/Publications/InThisAgeOfPlenty/plenty49.htm

38.) David William. "The United States Became A Foreign Corporation in 1871." The Liberty Beacon.com. June 24, 2016. https://www.thelibertybeacon.com/when-the-united-states-became-a-corporation/

39.) Augustus Blackstone. "Allodial Title Via Land Patent." Internet Archive.org. February 24, 2021. https://archive.org/details/blackstone-augustus-allodial-title-via-land-patent/mode/2up , 8-11.

40.) Rivero, "All Wars Are Bankers' Wars!"

41.) Andre Nolan. "Titanic Conspiracy." Titanic Universe.com. September 20, 2022. https://www.titanicuniverse.com/the-titanic-conspiracy#:~:text=Supporters%20

navigating around icebergs at full steam ahead. Presently, even unsinkable ships now provide enough lifeboats due to this huge oversight which could have saved so many, including three self-righteous businessmen whose money and connections stood in the way of progress.

Since there were no remaining objections and many in government were starting to see the benefits of allowing a private group of enlightened bankers and businessmen to control the money supply (wink wink), a secret meeting was held on Jekyll Island, Georgia under the guise of a duck hunt to devise a blueprint for the replacement of the corporation's money supply.[42]

At that time, the money, called a US Note, was still backed by gold and there was no interest charged for the citizens to use it. Oh, what a wonderful asset gold turned out to be for this new corporation and its shareholders. But there were even more assets to be gained through this sleek veil behind which the most powerful global cartel ever formed would soon be operating.

Should you be fortunate enough to join forces with such an eclectic group of power brokers, your way of doing things, your objectives, your connections and even your sparkly personality may not gel with other members. But, since it's a moral imperative to team up with the cleverest and most ruthless of the Earth's lords to enrich and protect each other's stake in the game, you must learn to play well with others and that means even the ones you're not particularly fond of. This was also the case with the diverse, international architects of the creature known as the Federal Reserve.

The name, Federal Reserve, was brilliantly chosen to lead any sceptics into believing the organisation was part of the federal government and that it had reserves backing the new legal tender.[43] The Federal Reserve Act was passed into law in 1913 and for the next twenty years, these newly created Federal Reserve Notes could be redeemed for gold.[44] But there was a lofty little secret looming behind this new note. As opposed to the interest free US Notes issued into circulation by the Treasury, there

of%20the%20idea%20that%20the%20Titanic%20shipwreck,the%20order%20 and%20God's%20will%3B%20Captain%20Edward%20Smith.

42.) Edward Griffin, *The Creature from Jekyll Island: A Second Look at the Federal Reserve.* Fourth Edition. (Westlake Village, California: American Media, 18 June 1994)

43.) Griffin, *The Creature from Jekyll Island,* 1, 16-17.

44.) Dr. Gene Schroder. "War Powers Act." Scanned Retina.com. March 17, 2014. https://scannedretina.wordpress.com/2014/03/17/dr-schroders-work-war-pow-ers-act-2/

was now interest charged to borrow the Federal Reserve Notes, entered into circulation by the twelve Federal Reserve banks. That interest was only payable in gold.[45]

Sorry, I just burst into uncontrollable laughter. Did you?

Coincidently, also in 1913, (ahem) the same year interest to borrow the new paper currency was instated, the 16th amendment, *the power to tax income*, was added to The Constitution of the United States. Of course, there was no need to properly ratify the 16th amendment using the preposterous notion of state's rights since we were now dealing with a corporate charter and not a constitution for a functioning government. As a result, the Bureau of Internal Revenue Service formed in 1913 and this agency would be assigned the task of collecting the interest from US citizens for the privilege of using these new bank notes.

For your own knowledge, should you want to take over a **FARM** that doesn't allow a direct tax on its inhabitants and their earnings, like that of early America, it's important to understand the gradual transition necessary to compel peasants to give into this drastic curtailing of their freedom.

Again, travelling back in time through American history, the only direct tax that was allowed in the original constitution was an apportioned direct tax. First, a direct tax is one that is placed directly on an individual. *Apportioned* means that everyone pays an *equal portion*. This apportioned direct tax was only intended to be applied during times of emergency, for instance, to finance an armed insurrection against a well-established monarchy.

Fools!

A provision was also included in the original Constitution for the united States of America to administer a census that was to serve only two distinct purposes. One was to determine the number of representatives each independent state would seat in the House of Representatives, based on their population, and the other was to calculate how much each citizen of a respective state would owe, should the direct tax be necessary.

For example, if you knew that New York had one million citizens and you determined the state owed ten million US$ to protect the lives

45.) Michael T. Snyder, Esq. "United States Note vs. Federal Reserve Note." NoSue.org. December 19, 2011. https//www.nosue.org/banking/united-states-note-vs-feder-al-reserve-note/ and Earl Frederick. "The "U.S. Government" Went Bankrupt In 1933 And Is No Longer A Republic." Family Guardian.org. https://famguardian.org/Subjects/LawAndGovt/LegalEthics/Corruption/USGovtBankrupt.htm and "Federal Reserve Act." Govinfo.gov. December 23, 1913. https://www.govinfo.gov/content/pkg/COMPS-270/pdf/COMPS-270.pdf and Schroder, "War Powers."

and freedoms of their citizens during a national emergency, each citizen in New York would owe ten US$ in tax regardless of how much each individual made in their occupation.[46] But, how can you control your peasants' finances and hence them, if you can't tax them based on how much money they earn? This is important to recognise as a burgeoning lord. If your peasants can attain unlimited wealth by keeping all the proceeds they earn in exchange for their time, labour and skills, they can also build their family fortunes and maybe even replace you.

You *must not* let this happen!

NOTE: Since this silly people's law republic actually protected the rights of the majority of its members for a brief span of time, when an early day census was required, one was only required to list the total number of household members. At that time, the census couldn't be used for any other type of information gathering. But today, peasants are so well-conditioned to submit to authority that they gladly provide just about any personal detail they're asked to give. As we'll discover later, this is to your advantage. Their willingness to obey will be a testament to your ability to conceal the history of their oppression and will demonstrate your competency in creating obedient responses to you and your associates' instructions.

Back to our story.

If you remember from history class, those poor darling minutemen had to fight barefoot in the dead of winter whilst raiding farmhouses for their next meal due to the populace's unwillingness to contribute anything to their efforts. This clearly illustrates that even back then, citizens enjoyed being subjugated. The cost of attaining freedom was not worth the effort and dare I say, not even appreciated by the majority.

Because the Articles of Confederation gave sole taxing authority to the states that, in turn, failed to properly contribute funds for the *common treasury* of the Confederation, America nearly lost the Revolutionary War.[47] This inability of the national government to raise funds to achieve independence is exactly why the apportioned direct tax was included in the ensuing social pact known as the Constitution for the united States of America.[48] Due to their recent battle cry of *No taxation without representation,* the early do-gooder and idealistic slave owners of that time felt the need to justify the taxes imposed on others (not to mention themselves). This is in stark contrast to the stern and

---

46.) Skousen, *The Making of America,* 378, 477-481.
47.) Skousen, *The Making of America,* 378.
48.) Skousen, *The Making of America,* 378.

highly disciplined lords and barons in control today who scoff at the idea of being taxed themselves but do not hesitate to rip money out of their peasants' pockets.

In the social contract known as the constitution, the only other tax that was permitted beyond an apportioned direct tax was an indirect tax, applied to something a subject may need but was under no direct obligation to buy.

For instance, you can choose whether or not to buy petrol for your car travelling on the motorways where the revenue generated from the petrol tax is supposed to be spent. However, you can also choose to walk, ride a bicycle or even produce your own fuel to avoid the tax. But the direct tax in the US Constitution is paid directly to the federal government and, since it's to be apportioned, can only be applied under certain restricted conditions for which everyone in their respective state is required to pay an equal amount.

But for those adept at exploiting others, this restrictive form of direct tax became the prime target from which to base their takeover. These cunning creditors realised if they could create a large enough debt, the limited revenue stream of an indirect tax would be insufficient to meet the repayment demands. Thus, the government would have to find additional ways to honour its promise to pay.

Once again Abraham Lincoln and the Civil War enter the picture. Money was needed to fund this internal conflict. To make matters worse, the shrewd banks of that time would only loan Lincoln money at 30% interest. *The Great Emancipator* (and I say that very mockingly as you shall soon see why) knew his hands were tied when it came to directly approaching the private sector for money. He knew he could tax any *profit* made on property (which is the original definition of *income*) but he had no authority to tax money paid to Americans in private sector trades and occupations.

That's because providing one's time and skills for a common medium of exchange (money), then used to acquire someone else's time and skills, is an even exchange with no profit gained by either party. If one paid a dollar for a lottery ticket and won a million, that one dollar created a million and could be seen as profit on property, a.k.a. income.

But, under the Revenue Act of 1862, Lincoln was able to justify going directly after monies paid to those who worked *inside* the government (hence the name *Internal Revenue*).[49] He did this by

49.) Peter Eric Hendrickson, *Cracking the Code: The Fascinating Truth About Taxation in America* (United States of America: Peter E. Hendrickson, 2003), 12-13.

pointing out that citizens could freely pursue any profession of their choosing, but only a limited number of people could work *inside* the government. Therefore, holding a position *inside* the government was considered a position of privilege and taxable. As a result, the Revenue Act of 1862 was passed and applied only to those who made a profit on property and those who worked for the United States.[50] There were other revenue streams generated through licence fees and excise taxes, but those are not relevant to this discussion.

'So, why babble on about these trivial distinctions?' you mutter. Oh, I'm bustling with so much excitement I can barely stand it. The foundation for the grand scheme is nearly complete. But first, we must look at the Trading with the Enemies Act of 1917 (TWEA).

The Federal Reserve had been four years into its twenty-year charter in 1917 when the president who signed the Federal Reserve Act into law, Woodrow Wilson, committed the United States to World War One.

> NOTE: Please pay special attention as to how wars are used to enslave nations through debt. The Trading with the Enemies Act (TWEA) was enacted in 1917 for the purpose of giving the United States complete authority over any foreigner living within the United States deemed to be hostile toward the United States. These hostile actions included conducting business with or providing financial support for the enemy whilst being located within the continental borders of the United States of America. If a foreign person/corporation supported an enemy, the US government could seize their/its assets. If a foreign person did not intend on assisting the enemy, they could apply for a licence and be subjected to the full scrutiny of the United States and its agencies. This only applied to foreigners and not US citizens in accordance with the TWEA of 6 October 1917.[51]

Let's fast forward to 1933, when the Federal Reserve's twenty-year charter was set to expire. THE UNITED STATES OF AMERICA, INC. went bankrupt in 1933 because it ran out of gold reserves used as interest payments on the Federal Reserve Notes.[52] *Attention*: when governments fight wars, they need money to pay for them. A central bank can gladly provide this necessary service, with interest of course. With more debt comes more interest, meaning more profits for the bank!

50.) Hendrickson, *Cracking the Code*, 12-32.
51.) Schroder, "War Powers."
52.) Schroder, "War Powers."

Tip tap tip. Tip tap tip. I'm dancing on a cloud.

Where were we? Oh yes, *a national emergency* was declared by banker-friendly Franklin Delano Roosevelt just two days after he was sworn into office. A *switcharoo* had already been planned. In lieu of the now confiscated gold, which was formerly used as collateral for the corporation's debt, a *New Deal* would be formed that made US citizens and all their labour and property collateral for the US debt, i.e. US citizens became enslaved to THE UNITED STATES OF AMERICA, INC.[53]

'But that's absurd', you say. Blasphemy! Do you doubt the brilliant minds who pulled off such a heist?

As I'm sure you'd expect, not everyone fell for this *New Deal*. Many Americans were desperately struggling as a result of the Great Depression and began lining up at the banks to reclaim their gold in order to protect their wealth. But FDR, who's trumpeted as a working man's hero in the public fool system, had ordered a banking holiday due to this *national emergency*, i.e. people wanting their gold, stated in Proclamation 2039 on 6 March 1933:[54] 'Whereas there have been heavy and unwarranted withdrawals of gold and currency from our banking institutions for the purpose of hoarding.'

Ha!

The banks were closed until 13 March 1933, whilst the new Federal Reserve Bank Note, which had already been printed in preparation of this event, replaced the Federal Reserve Note.[55] Can you see the purpose of misdirecting peasants during their formative years in public education? If they knew the truth about President Roosevelt, they would surely become aware of their servitude. But, if the same man responsible for their captivity is painted as a hero, they'll remain ignorantly blissful.

> NOTE: It's not only important to mislead future peasants, but also important to paint their captors as heroes. Heroes to be idolised and worshipped.

As you can imagine, this change in banking policy didn't sit well with most Americans who had an implied contract with the banks

---

53.) Schroder, "War Powers."

54.) Franklin D. Roosevelt. "Proclamation 2039—Bank Holiday, March 6-9, 1933, Inclusive." The American Presidency Project.ucsb.edu. March 6, 1933. https://www.presidency.ucsb.edu./documents/proclamation-2039-bank-holiday-march-6-9-1933-inclusive and Schroder, "War Powers."

55.) Schroder, "War Powers."

to withdraw their gold on deposit at their discretion. Because of this upheaval, it became necessary to deem all United States citizens enemies of the state under the War Powers Act shown in Title 12 USC Section 95(b).

> NOTE: Until the War Powers Act, only foreigners during times of war, under the Trading with the Enemies Act, were considered potential enemies of the state and subject to the full authority of the United States. But now this sweeping authority also applied to US citizens during any declared national emergency, such as, but not limited to, war, as per Public Law 73-1 48 Stat. 1. Not only did the national emergency in 1933 further promote the suspension of constitutional guarantees to US citizens but, as enemies of the state, all previous contracts with US citizens were terminated and their property became legitimate prize.[56]

Whether just for laughs or to add insult to injury, the hoarding of gold then became a crime punishable by no more than $10,000 or ten-years imprisonment or both. You know the real reason for this law and in whose pockets the retrieved gold ended up. Gold was no longer needed to back the new legal tender since the labour and property of US citizens now took its place and Federal Reserve Bank Notes were printed against the labour and property of US citizens each time *money* was needed for borrowing. The notes then entered circulation and became further evidence of the mounting debt since there was no way to actually pay debts now that lawful money (gold and/or the notes that were backed by it) were outlawed.

So, to reiterate, if you're in possession of a US dollar, you're holding someone's promise to pay a debt when indeed lawful money returns. As illustrated on the debt note: 'This note is legal tender for (*for* meaning used to discharge, not pay) all debts both public and private.'

Now you have the historical background necessary to fully understand the two worlds, public versus private. Like in the movie *The Matrix,* there are two separate realities at play. The public is the superficial reality (inside the matrix) where all the funny money and fictional characters reside. It's the illusionary world that has been meticulously created to engage peasants and secure their voluntary compliance. The private world, on the other hand, is where the flesh and blood men and women really exist (outside the matrix) with their real-world assets. They use lawful money (gold/silver) as a means of settling their debts whilst resolving their disputes in common law (*de jure*) courts.

56.) Schroder, "War Powers."

The public, however, tricks people into signing away lawful title to their property over to the public trust for the privilege of operating inside the matrix and using its debt-based currency. It should be noted that those who operate in the public are also agreeing to all terms and conditions of the adhesion contracts presented and to act as surety (those willing to pay) for the company's debt should the corporation be unable to pay.

In short, those who are convinced to trade in their rights in exchange for the perks and privileges the corporation grants them, also pledge their property and labour as collateral for the company's debt. In exchange for this transfer of ownership of property via their signature, men and women are allowed to retain equitable title (possession and use of the property) as long as they don't violate any of a plethora of restrictions placed on them. Perfect title (and hence total ownership) involves possessing both legal and equitable title.

It's all about the terms of the contracts, silly!

As you can easily see, if left to them, peasants would eventually choose to operate outside the matrix and retain their property and what little dignity they still have left. It's for this reason enforcement agents (*The Matrix's* Agent Smith), must be trained to use force, or the threat of force, to keep the real-world men and women inside the matrix— after they *freely* sign the adhesion contracts, of course. The constant threat of force will also help keep them oblivious to the private world in which their rights and property actually exist. Enforcement techniques will be discussed in upcoming chapters.

NOTE: We'll also see how proper training (see Chapter 11) will condition your peasants to prevent others from escaping the corporate plantation. To use The Matrix analogy, this is the equivalent of anyone operating inside the matrix suddenly turning into Agent Smith to defend the illusionary system from those out to disrupt or break away from it. I can't help but think of crabs in a bucket where the others claw and tug at the one trying to escape to freedom! You must bombard your peasants with fear and discourage them from uniting!

So how do US citizens and their property become surety (the responsible party) for THE UNITED STATES OF AMERICA, INC.'s debt? They apply and hence are registered to do so.

I know, quite comical, isn't it?

By filling out the application known as the certificate of live birth, a *cestui que vie* trust is created by the United States for each US citizen who then automatically becomes an employee of THE UNITED STATES OF AMERICA, INC. By applying for and then attaching a social security number (a vessel number) to the trust in return for the corporations' benefits (social security, welfare, etc.), the trust becomes active, and the trustee/beneficiary can begin to hold private property in the trust whilst using public money to do so. This trust is charged interest in return for the use of public money and the ensuing benefits received. All your property and earnings from your *employment* as a United States citizen are run through this trust.[57]

> NOTE: The *cestui que vie trust* stems from England's Cestui Que Vie Act of 1666 that declared one legally dead and lost at sea (maritime jurisdiction) if not heard from for seven years, resulting in a forfeiture of their estate (property) through the creation of a trust.

Like renting a car from Hertz, there's a rental fee to use this trust in the form of a tax. This tax is something the Internal Revenue Service defines as *reversionary interest*. You have a choice in the matter when it comes to registering with the corporation to become a US citizen via a birth certificate and social security number. But to survive in today's fast-paced commercial world, trying to operate in the sea of commerce without a birth certificate and SSN is quite inconvenient, if not impossible. Use of this trust is for the lifetime of the owner, then it reverts back to the corporation that created it.

Again, using the rental car example, you can choose from a variety of insurance packages, elect to include multiple drivers on the agreement or even choose a minivan or convertible, but you must pay the rental fee and incur any costs associated with using the vehicle whilst it's in your possession, i.e. filling the gas tank, adding oil, paying tolls, etc. When finished with the rental agreement, you return the car to its rightful owner, also a corporation.

If damage occurs to the car or others whilst it's in your possession, you're the responsible party, not Hertz. If Hertz is having financial trouble after starting a bloody conflict with Avis and you rent from

57.) Pao L. Chang. "Proof the United States' is a Criminal Corporation." wake up world.com. December 2, 2015. https://wakeup-world.com/2015/12/02/proof-that-the-usa-is-controlled-by-foreign-corporations/ and "Step 1A. Understanding Cestui Que Vie Act 1666 – Existence of Life." New Human New Earth Communties.com. June 30, 2018. https://www.newhumannewearthcommunities.com/solutions-actions-remedy/understanding-cestui-que-vie-act-1666-existence-of-life

Hertz, it'll be reflected in your rental fee. If you kill someone with the rental car, you'll also be *charged* for murder.

Keep in mind, this system has taken a good half of century to be fully developed and about as much time to get the majority of living collateral to go along with it. Early on, a lot of arm twisting, bribery (Example: the Social Security Act of 1935 Title 5 Section 501) and propaganda had to be implemented to garner participation.

But now that the modern-day peasant clamours for privileges in exchange for compliance with the corporation and its policies, you can demand that even the cheap card stock that the **STATE**-created social security number is printed on be returned on demand just to let them know who the true creator is. If you don't believe me, just look on the back of any modern social security card. It reads: 'This card belongs to the Social Security Administration, and you must return it if we ask for it.' Trust me, peasants won't want to let go of it; you'll have to rip it from their cold, dead fingers. But it's their current lords' property and not theirs!

Chapter 7

THE POWER OF THE PEN

Evil requires the sanction of the victim.
— Ayn Rand

In Chapter 6, *Corporate Fiction vs The Real World*, I emphasised the importance of having your peasants contractually agree to their servitude whilst transferring their real-world labour, rights and property over to you via a corporate structure. So, the question arises, what's the most effective tool used to coerce your flocks' servitude?

If you answered whips or chains, you were born centuries too late. In today's commercial world, the most valuable instrument of oppression at your disposal is a pen. Have you ever heard the expression: 'The pen is mightier than the sword'? As evidenced in literature, the pen has been shown to be more influential than violence.

Is there a law saying we can't use the quill in place of violence to achieve our goals?

Of course, we can.

'But how?' you stammer.

Through the most modern and effective means of human compulsion…the contract. But to enforce a contract by law, a signature is required. So then, we must understand the most important aspect of scribbling on the dotted line. Although it can, at times, be used to identify the parties involved, the main purpose of wilfully marking an agreement is—drum roll please—to express *consent*.

'But consent to what?' you howl.

That depends on what you're trying to achieve. However, there's nothing more important than obtaining your peasants' compliance during the entire process.

Not only will their consent obligate them to perform all the terms and conditions you impose on them, but it can also be used to remove all accountability from you since their signature committed them to the obligation. But keep in mind; it doesn't hurt to have the threat of force present in case some encouragement is needed to ensure your peasants' cooperation.

If you look at your own pitiful life, how many loans, permits, licences and other obligations have you signed without reading them, just to avoid the headache of understanding all the legal jargon in fine print? There is an old joke, 'If you read something and you can't understand it, it was probably written by a lawyer'.

Is this by accident or something more devious?

Hold your breath as we dive deep below the glistening veneer.

The etymology of the word *attorney* is quite interesting. *Attorney* stems from the word attornment, which in English property law during the Feudal system, was an acknowledgement from peasants that the land they lived on was being transferred to a new lord. So, doesn't it make sense that the person transferring a peasant's property to a new lord (as per the peasant's *consent*) is called an attorney?

'What?' you exclaim.

Wait, it gets even better. Aren't you curious to know who the new lord is?

Well, if you follow the instructions presented in this handbook, that new lord could indirectly be you (that is, via your corporate fictional entity, of course). That's what makes the transfer of property so simple. Because we're operating in the magical kingdom of the non-living where undisclosed contracts and every other form of legal trickery is not only accepted but welcomed, seizing the peasants' labour, rights and property has never been easier. These undisclosed agreements range from contracts peasants sign directly, to contracts that are implied via the peasants' participation in certain corporate benefits and privileges, like voting, for example.

These optimal agreements, called adhesion contracts, are imposed on your peasants for your benefit. These agreements are notoriously defined by a party in a position of power whilst giving the weaker party no choice but to agree to the unfavourable conditions.[58]

Would you expect anything less?

These contracts are ideal because you have all the bargaining power and your peasants are under strict obligation to endorse them as well as comply to maintain privileges such as licences, permits and registrations, etc. On your **FARM** or any **FARM** you take over, your

---

58.) Cornell Law School. "adhesion contract (contract of adhesion)." Legal Information Institute. December 2021. https://www.law.cornell.edu/wex/adhesion_contract_%28contract_of_adhesion%29

responsibility is to ensure your peasants understand the importance of giving their signed consent on behalf of their fictional selves (ENS LEGIS) that will then permit them to operate in the sea of commerce.

Now, in the real world where people have inherent, and if you believe in such, God-given rights, two or more living people who enter into a contract must disclose and agree to all of the terms and conditions for a pact to be valid. The ultimate purpose of this type of contract is for all parties to mutually benefit. But again, how are you supposed to obtain power over others if they benefit equally? I think the answer to that question is obvious and supports my suggestion that you *must* create a system where hidden and implied contracts are enforced to keep your vassals at a stark disadvantage.

Does this make sense?

You didn't say anything, so your silence is considered your consent.

Did you know that?

> NOTE: When your peasants remain silent for any or all of your undertakings, just know their silence is evidence of their approval. This is an established maxim of law *qui tacet consentire videtur*[59] meaning silence gives consent.

Gratias ago tibi, domine ex inferis. (Thank you dear lord of the underworld).

Don't worry, they're usually too caught up in their mundane affairs to notice your transgressions.

Oh, it's too easy!

Now, without getting into the entire Uniform Commercial Code, the current bible of international, maritime/law of the sea/commercial laws that everyone operating in business is compelled to follow, it should be noted that recipients of presentments[60] are usually given ten days to accept or refute the presentment, or they accept all the terms and conditions of that instrument. The same can be said when the President of the United States receives a bill to be signed into law. If the president does not veto or sign the bill within ten days (excluding Sundays), the bill automatically becomes law. Remember, *qui tacet consentire videtur*.

Finally, if pulled over in the US by a law enforcement agent and

---

59.) Vishwa Patel. Qui tacet consentire videtur Law Times Journal.in. January 6, 2020. https://lawtimesjournal.in/qui-tacet-consentire-videtur/

60.) The People's Law Dictionary. S. v. "presentment." Retrieved April 21, 2023, from https://legal-dictionary.thefreedictionary.com/presentment

issued a ticket/citation, would you care to guess the standard number of days you have to accept and pay the ticket or refute it before more aggressive action is taken against you? If you answered ten days, you owe yourself a biscuit and a pat on the head.

'So, what's this all about?' you bellow from the depths of your soul.

My point is, whether you receive a ticket from a law enforcement officer (of the corporation), or a bill goes before the president of the corporation, it's all about commerce, love, and less about teaching your peasants a valuable lesson. A few lashings would be a much more effective technique if you're trying to get through to them.

I'm sure someone like Martin Luther would've agreed. If you were excluded from this history lesson because you were taught in a *public* training centre that gave you just enough information to function in the public system but not enough knowledge to fully understand it, Martin Luther demanded reform from the Catholic Church when he discovered the church was selling indulgences to fill their coffers. This was achieved by offering worshippers the opportunity to buy their way out of their sins (much like buying one's way out of a traffic citation by paying a fine). Luther was outraged by the Catholic Church's conduct but was deemed a heretic by the Emperor of Rome. Ole Mr. Luther kind of reminds us of that crazy guy who stands up for his *rights* in traffic court.

Burn him at the stake! Better yet, let his fellow peasants ridicule him for the rest of his living days.

> NOTE: If you feel it's necessary on your farm, you can enhance your police state to weaken your peasants financially whilst escalating the level of force used against them just to remind them who is in charge—erm—I mean to show them the error in their ways.

I would like to digress for a second to look inside the animal kingdom to explain the difference between your freedom and the restrictive freedom you'll place on your human herd. Nature operates under the law of necessity. When carnivores are hungry, they hunt and kill animals to survive. If a bird can't make it through the winter in one location, the bird migrates to a more hospitable climate. In these examples, the animal didn't need permission from a group of its peers, nor did it face legal repercussions for its actions. The animal was acting out of the law of necessity. You, therefore, must always act out of the law of necessity.

As applied to the rest of the Earth's snivelling uprights, in theory, if humans need to hunt or fish to survive, no man-made law can prevent them. To do so would be to deprive them of their right to life.[61] The law of necessity trumps all man-made laws. Similarly, if other humans, including those you dress up in government uniforms with shiny badges, try to rob people of their right to life, they are well within their rights to defend themselves against those with shiny badges in order to remain alive. But that is under the law of necessity.

To function as a civilised society, a more restrictive system, known as *laws of the land,* was created to establish a human hierarchy and to explicitly define permissible behaviour for the majority of a **FARM'S** inhabitants and the consequences they face for acting outside these restrictions. There have been rare instances throughout history, however, when laws of the land protected an individual from *any* violation of their fundamental rights by any other individual, even from those wearing flashy government costumes. (Example: the original Constitution for the united States of America). But take note, in these cases, your dominance cannot be fully implemented and, unless being used for a very specific reason, laws protecting your peasants should be subverted and expunged at all costs.

At sea, all **FARMS** currently abide by a set of international business laws derived from long established merchant laws. These laws were implemented to ensure the stability of global trade. Vessels carrying merchandise from all over the world dock at various international ports to deliver and receive goods. Regardless of where a ship docks or what ship you board, the laws governing all maritime transactions are the same. Like on land, there are those at sea who refuse to play by the rules. These expatriates are called pirates and due to their threat to established order they become enemies of nations. Taking what we learned from the last chapter and the War Powers Act, these enemies of your *nation* could be your own peasants if they undermine **STATE** authority and show contempt for **STATE** property whilst operating their *vessels* in the *sea* of commerce.

In both the Constitution **for** the united States of America and The Constitution **Of** The United States, there's something known as the *letters of marquee and reprisal.* The letters of marquee and reprisal have been used historically in other *countries* as well. When applied, these letters gave/give governments like the United States/UNITED STATES

61.) Ken Schoolland, "The Philosophy of Liberty," YouTube video, 8:15, Sidewinder77, December 3, 2006, https://youtu.be/muHg86Mys71

the authority to contract with pirates (who under this agreement operate with total impunity) for the purpose of capturing enemy pirate ships and retrieving the stolen merchandise. Once an enemy vessel is captured, the contracted pirates turn over the apprehended goods to an admiralty court that, in turn, gives a portion of the auctioned off proceeds back to the contracted pirates as payment for their services.

Does any of this seem vaguely familiar? You wouldn't dare assume that today's admiralty court operates in a similar fashion, would you? If so, you're catching on splendidly.

Now, I'll attempt to explain the purposefully distorted logic of a licence. If you think about it, a licence gives a man or woman permission to do something that would otherwise be illegal, i.e. to aid or assist someone with their health, to freely travel from place to place, to marry someone and to engage in business dealings for self-sustenance, etc.

Then why would someone need a licence for activities that common sense tells us all humans already have the free will to do? The answer, my attentive pupil, is that these adhesion contracts (licences, titles, permits, registrations, etc.) allow lords to tightly control and monitor their peasants' activities whilst also obtaining the peasants' consent to do so.

Pure bliss, isn't it? Trust me, peasants delight in kowtowing to established order.

There's no end to the restrictions you can contractually place on your peasants. For comic relief, here's a short list of US permits and licences:

- free speech permits
- moving permits
- dog licences
- private investigator's licences for computer repair technicians
- business privilege licences for bloggers
- snow shovelling licences
- lemonade stand licences
- funeral director licences for monks
- DC tour guide licences
- raw milk licences
- pumpkin and Christmas tree vendor licences
- interior design licences
- licences to close a business

Furthermore, all vending machine operators and chain restaurants must provide a calorie count visible to customers. It's punishable by fine to untangle a whale from a net, and all children in Massachusetts Day Cares are mandated by law to brush their teeth after lunch (preferably with fluoridated toothpaste).

Keep in mind, these permits, licences and regulations not only come with fees to obtain them but can carry severe punishment when stipulations of the agreement are violated, generating even more revenue for the **STATE**.

Oh, to breathe the air. What a rush!

I'll provide just one detailed explanation of a licence agreement so you can gain a full understanding of the effectiveness of adhesion contracts. Now, for our glaring example of word trickery hidden in plain sight: taking a man's or woman's right and replacing it with a privilege provided by you (through your corporate disguise, of course).

Pay attention, boys and girls, because today we'll be discussing the wonderful world of the US driver's licence.

> NOTE: It should be mentioned that only men and women stand up for themselves whereas children do as they are told. In addition, those who are mentally incompetent depend on others to interpret the law for them and to speak on their behalf. Furthermore, it should also be recognised that, as stated in court decisions such as United States v Johnson, only belligerent claimants have rights. 'The privilege against self-incrimination is neither accorded to the passive resistant, nor the person who is ignorant of their rights, nor to one indifferent thereto. It is a fighting clause. Its benefits can be retained only by sustained combat. It cannot be claimed by attorney or solicitor. It is valid only when insisted upon by a belligerent claimant in person.'[62]

Therefore, individuals can only have rights if they recognise and fully understand their rights and are willing to do whatever is necessary to uphold them. Can you help it if people become comfortable with food, distractions and entitlements that pacify them into blindly accepting whatever bunk you feed them? I doubt you'll hear any complaints from your pawns if you also conveniently provide plenty of attention-diverting guilty pleasures that subtly occupy their thoughts.

62.) James Alger Fee. "United States v. Johnson, 76 F. Supp. 538 (M.D. Pa. 1947)." Justia.com. February 26, 1947. https://law.justia.com/cases/federal/district-courts/FSupp/76/538/2304365/

So, back to the matter at hand; am I saying that driving a motor vehicle is a government protected *right* and not a *privilege* contrary to what you've been told your entire life? Not so fast. This is just one example of how you can use wordplay and trickery to undermine your peasants in order to have them willingly forfeit and submit their unalienable rights to you. But first, let's return to the animal kingdom to clearly understand the concept of freely travelling.

As illustrated in our earlier example, if a bird chooses to travel for its own survival or whether a deer chooses to travel across international borders, run down a motorway or simply trot through the wilderness, the animal is free to do so. It doesn't need permission from an agency or department. Since we're all born on this planet for a limited amount of time, doesn't it make sense that the same concept should apply to human beings as well? Well, at least the ones who live in an alleged free society.

If you're justifying the need for a licence by thinking about the damage an automobile can cause, you're demonstrating the peasant programming you've succumbed to. A huge part of controlling your peasants' minds is controlling the information they receive, including the true history of their oppression. If the improperly nourished, sidetracked and conditioned peasants are given the illusion they're being taken care of in exchange for their servitude/cooperation, very few will seek information that may empower them and hence free them from their captivity.

The truth is, the history of the driver's licence and other such usurpations are right in front of their pathetic faces, but many are too busy complying with the myriad of rules and regulations to notice. A quick trip back in time to the *free country* of America will clearly show how and why the citizens on that **FARM** were reined in.

In the early days of travel, whether it was by horse and buggy, statistically much more dangerous than travelling in today's automobile, or up to and including early model Ts, Americans were never under any obligation to ask for permission to travel on roads and highways or, in other words, to obtain a driver's licence.[63] But, as larger vehicles carrying heavier loads entered the roadways for personal financial gain, there were government officials who felt the need to make laws and regulations to protect freely travelling citizens from the dangers of commercial traffic.

63.) Roger Roots, "America's Lost Right to Travel by Automobile," Republic Magazine, Number 6: 21

This led to *commercial* drivers needing a licence (permission from the government) to use the public roads and highways for personal gain. In Willis v Buck: 'While a citizen has the right to travel upon the public highways and to transport his property thereon, that right does not extend to the use of the highways, either in whole or in part, as a place of business for private gain. For the latter purpose, no person has a vested right in the use of the highways of the state, but such use is by privilege or licence...' [64]

Of course, legislators also realised that a generous revenue stream could be created by registering these commercial drivers whilst charging them a fee to subsidise the damage caused by their heavier and more frequently used vehicles.

This additional revenue was so successful that the option was given to everyone to register as a commercial driver despite the fact that many court decisions supported (and still support...shhh) the right to freely travel on the roads and highways. A little nudging in the form of ticket writing was needed to steer the herd away from their cherished right to freely travel and yet another mantra was piped through the **FARM**: 'Driving is not a right, it's a privilege' to further convince them. Boy, was Adolf Hitler right when he said: 'Make the lie big, make it simple, keep saying it, and eventually they will believe it.' It's a good thing his art career never took off because he was much more inspiring as a mass manipulator. Please note that this is an imperative skill you *must* seek in the spokesperson who will be facilitating your burgeoning world agenda.

For many years after it was initially instated, qualifying for a licence (at that time a legalised permit to drive) had nothing to do with passing tests geared toward safe driving or knowledge of the traffic laws. This was a nice little touch to show peasants how much they're cared for and what little interest anyone has in further enslaving them.

Oh jolly, if you believe that one, perhaps you'd like to buy a watch.

If you still can't shake your belief in the mantra that driving/travelling is not a right but a privilege, I ask you, who has more authority over you than you do? Are you not the ultimate source of authority for your own affairs? If you're so fragmented and broken that you believe someone else must give you permission to partake in an inherent right such as travelling, I command you to put down this book now. It's clear you're not cut out to rule over others, as you cannot even empower yourself. You can promptly begin to condemn these teachings

---

64.) "Willis v. Buck." casetext.com. February 4, 1928. https://casetext.com/case/willis-v-buck-et-al

for your media outlet or go to Amazon.com and leave a negative review of this handbook because of your inability to stretch your thinking beyond your peasant mentality. It's quite amusing to watch you flounder when shown the door to your own freedom. As the saying goes: 'You can lead a horse to water, but you cannot make it drink.' This remains accurate, even if the truth is waived right under your nose.

For those still on the fence, I'll make one last attempt to reach you by providing a few definitions right out of such sources as the United States Code and the ultimate dictionary of legalese for the US jurisdiction, *Black's Law Dictionary*. If this still doesn't shake you from your current belief system, do not overly concern yourself. There are those select few fit to preside over others whilst the rest of humanity was born to be subjugated.

For those destined to rule, rest assured that those meant to be ruled will not only justify their subservience but will also fight to maintain it. You can spot them easily, and you *must* be sure to use them wisely. Joseph Stalin referred to his obedient pawns as *useful idiots*, i.e. propagandists for a cause, the goals of which they are not fully aware, and who are used cynically by leaders of the cause.

Oh, how I love to hate them!

First, as noted in a New Hampshire Supreme Court decision American Mutual Liability Ins. Co. vs Chaput: '*Automobile* connotes a pleasure vehicle designed for the transportation of persons on highways.' Conversely, the definition of *motor vehicle* under Title 18 Section 31 (6) of the United States Code states: 'The term *motor vehicle* means every description of carriage or other contrivance propelled or drawn by mechanical power and *used for commercial purposes* on the highways in the transportation of passengers, passengers and property, or property or cargo.'

A few definitions below motor vehicle still in 18 USC Section 31 in subsection (10) we find the definition of *used for commercial purposes*. The term *used for commercial purposes* means: 'the carriage of persons or property for any fare, fee, rate, charge or other consideration, or directly or indirectly in connection with any business, or other undertaking intended for profit.'

Also, according to *Black's Law Dictionary*, a traveller is 'one who travels in any way', whereas a driver is 'one *employed* in conducting a coach, carriage, wagon, or other vehicle.' Aren't these legal definitions, in turn, stating that a motor vehicle is used only for *commercial purposes* by *drivers* who receive payment for their services whereas a traveller uses an automobile to move from one place to another?

So then, when you pick up little Johnny from baseball practice or go to the supermarket to pick up some caviar, are you getting paid to do so? You only wish it were that simple. I think you see my point. Or do you? Regardless, if you're a *driver* of a *motor vehicle*, you're operating in the sea of commerce and an enforcement officer of the corporation can now approach your vessel and further attempt to do business with you since you have agreed to the terms and conditions of the contract (your driver's licence and registration) and have agreed to follow all the rules and regulations those agreements entail. Violating the terms of the contract draws attention to your enemy status and attracts the contracted pirates serving as hired guns for the **STATE**.

With the gradual addition of more codes and regulations, the reasons for routinely pulling over peasants in their *motor vehicles* proportionately increase as well. With enough incentive, enforcement officers can then search cars for just about any reason, providing further opportunity to seize possessions from the peasants' trusts in the form of money, property, and even the peasants themselves.

So then, to fully answer our initial question, being the driver of a motor vehicle *is a privilege* since it is a commercial activity for private gain whereas travelling in an automobile on the public roads *is a right* used to get from one place to another.

But regardless, that's unimportant. Even on an alleged free **FARM** like America, over time and after total *voluntary* compliance is reached, you can gradually bend the wording of laws away from their original intent to bring them up to date. This will prevent your flock from ever realising the rights that were taken away from them whilst you also continue to chip away at more of their freedoms.

Using today's new technologies will greatly enhance the control you have over your peasant farm(s). For instance, what started as a permit on a piece of paper, is now an identification card (Real ID Act 2005)[65] that can provide invaluable information including biometric data, identifying and tracking peasants anytime they pass compatible technology. A mountain of private information can be accessed by simply entering one or two identifying features of the peasants in question. This intrusion on peasants' privacy will be an incredible tool to not only administer your swift brand of justice, but to monitor those you identify as a threat to your world domination plans.

Since a certificate of title and vehicle registration usually work in

---

65.) Jim Harper. "The New National ID Systems." CATO Institute.org. January 30, 2018. https://www.cato.org/policy-analysis/new-national-id-systems

conjunction with a driver's licence, a brief overview is in order. Both of these adhesion contracts further add to the depth of entanglement with the fictitious entity known as the **STATE** (or in some jurisdictions the COMMONWEALTH).

'How?' you bemoan.

This simply occurs with the transfer of the legal title of the automobile over to the **STATE**.

'But I have the *Certificate of Title!*' you cry out.

Sorry to be the bearer of bad news, but the *Certificate of Title* **certifies** that there is a title. The catch is you don't possess it. The imaginary construct known as the **STATE** that the bank or dealership turned it over to does.

The legal title of an automobile is known as the Manufacturer's Statement of Origin (MSO). If a loan is used to pay for the new car, the lender sends the MSO to the **STATE** when the loan is repaid. If the customer buys the car outright, the dealership turns in the MSO. Either way, the **STATE** receives the MSO for all new cars purchased.

Remember to have total ownership of property, called *perfect title*, you must have both legal and equitable title. The **STATE** very graciously provides you with equitable title (the ability to use the motor vehicle) as long as you abide by the terms and conditions of the contracts you unwittingly sign when you register the vehicle and obtain a licence to operate it. The **STATE** in the meantime, maintains legal title. (Remember, peasants and their properties are collateralised by the **STATE** to back the paper money it borrows).

If you think you own the motor vehicle outright, try not following one of the stipulated conditions of the contract and you'll see how fast it takes an enforcement agent assigned by the **STATE** to remind you that you shouldn't be doing what you're doing with *its* property. Beyond that, since driving is such an integral part of today's commercial world, revoking a licence can be a wonderful tool to encourage your peasants to adhere to other rules and regulations that many of them may dismiss as unimportant. These harder to enforce rules don't even have to be related to driving and can include such frivolous infractions as unpaid fines on overdue library books or failing to shovel the snow on their pavements as ordered.[66]

The goal with every type of adhesion contract, besides getting your grunts to voluntarily submit their property, labour and consent, is to also train your chattel to ask for permission for everything they do. This is the same social programming used on prisoners whilst incarcerated. Those

---

66.) Jason Stark, "History of the Driver's License," Republic Magazine, Number 6, 22.

who can't follow simple instructions on the outside must be trained under more intense conditions on the inside.

The last topic I'd like to cover regarding adhesion contracts is the peasants' unwritten forms of consent. In these scenarios, peasants don't sign explicit contracts, but by partaking in certain actions and privileges, they indirectly express their consent. These activities can range from making purchases with public debt notes (commercial paper), to claiming a certain citizen status, to voting. Yes, that's right, voting. When peasants register to vote, they basically give their consent to have those who are elected to offices (corporations have offices) make decisions on their behalf. Therefore, when an *official* is elected as a governor, councilman or even president and then signs something into law, taxpayers have indirectly given their consent to accept the terms and conditions of the public contract brought on by the elected person's signature.

Who better than you to decide what measures are best for your peasants' own good? There's always a *cost* for freedom and *bills* are the perfect way to en-*act* these *costs*. The *bills* signed into law must always appear to be in the best interest of your **FARM** (i.e. providing comfort and security) when in fact they're actually further indebting your servants. Whether you need war to have peace, need a new expansive regulatory commission to monitor (licence) your peasants' activities or need to start an entitlement programme peasants must pay into, these *acts* always come with a price tag. New money will be printed to pay for the initial costs of a war, department or programme and *taxes* will be placed on the peasants to generate revenue streams to *fund* them. To further entrench your worker bees, you *must* also add fines and penalties for those who refuse to pay their *fair share*.

Remember, by submitting the application called the *Certificate of Live Birth* in America, as well as its equivalent on other **FARMS**, one has applied to become an *employee* of the corporation and by claiming a citizen status one is also accepting responsibility for the debt that the corporation accrues. If it's not clear to see, the more programmes, wars and restrictions placed on your peasants to keep them *safe*, the more indebted they are to you—as they should be.

It's good to be the king!

Chapter 8

TAXATION

The power to tax is the power to destroy.
— Chief Justice John Marshall

To illustrate the most effective technique used to enslave a modern-day society, you must first understand the basic operating costs of a **FARM** and the most practical and accepted means of covering these expenditures. Once your corporate grid is set up for commercial efficiency, you can explore more creative ways to gain leverage over your subjects. This will allow you to determine the depths of your herd's enslavement by using the most important tool at your disposal for controlling their wealth and, hence, financial freedom…taxation.

There are nearly infinite ways to *tax* your peasants, and these generous contributions for the common good will also help finance your personal endeavours. In addition, you can use this strictly enforced revenue stream against your underlings. But first, we must look at the history of taxation and the basic needs taxes have provided.

Taxes can be traced as far back as 6000 BC to the ancient city of Lagash, located in today's modern-day Iraq, where early tax records were found etched on clay tablets.[67] Ancient Egypt employed scribes to collect taxes on such things as cooking oil during one period since everyone was required to use it.[68] The scribes entered households to audit the amounts of cooking oil used and to ensure citizens were not using substitutes to avoid paying the tax.[69] Since there was no monetary system, taxes were levied on property and harvests. It was the surplus of goods received as taxes that the Pharaoh relied upon during times of

67.) Jacob Dayan. "Ancient Taxes from Around the World." Community Tax. July 10, 2017. https://www.communitytax.com/ancient-taxes-around-world/
68.) Vern Krishna. "Worldwide: The Ancient Art of Taxation." Mondaq. October 19, 2021. https://mondaq.com/canada/income-tax/1122034/the-ancient-art-of-taxation and Dayan, "Ancient Taxes."
69.) Krishna, "Art of Taxation."

drought, famine and war to secure the safety and health of his people.[70]

In Greece, to fund wartime expenditures, the Athenians were charged a tax (eisphora) everyone was required to pay.[71] Ancient Greece, however, was maybe the only society (and hopefully the last) to refund the tax collected. The Greeks repaid the eisphora with spoils seized in military conquests.[72]

As civilizations expanded, taxes funded central governments. China, in 600 BC, enacted one of the earliest forms of government imposed property tax by requiring ten percent of cultivated land to be donated to the central government as a tax payment.[73] Citizens also worked off taxes owed to central governments by volunteering their labour or by fighting in military conflicts.[74] Those with the means paid for a substitute or sent a slave in their place.[75] These examples are provided to show you that there should be no guilt involved with owning the time and labour of your minions. It's been a common practice throughout history.

Caesar Augustus imposed one of the first inheritance taxes. Interestingly enough, it was the overexpansion of the Roman Empire and the tax burden placed on its citizenry that led to its demise.[76] This should be duly noted for reasons of both caution and strategy. It should also be noted that a sales tax of four percent was placed on slaves as opposed to one percent on everything else.[77] This extra tax slaveholders were willing to pay indicates how valuable an enslaved labour force is when building an empire.

During the mediaeval period, England imposed an early version of the income tax on wealthy office holders and the clergy as well as a tax aimed at merchants on movable property. This tax didn't sit well with nobles who made up the lion's share of poll taxes calculated on a sliding scale according to one's ability to pay. When sales taxes became

70.) Dayan, "Ancient Taxes."
71.) Krishna, "Art of Taxation."
72.) Krishna, "Art of Taxation."
73.) Dr. Richard Willis. "A Brief History of Taxation." Accountancy Age. January 26, 2021. https://www.accountancyage.com/2021/01/26/a-brief-history-of-taxation/
74.) Dr. Tonia Sharlach and Dr. David Silverman. "Taxes in the Ancient World." University of Pennsylvania Almanac. April 2, 2002. https://almanac.upenn.edu/archive/v48/n28/AncientTaxes.html
75.) Sharlach and Silverman, "Taxes in the Ancient World."
76.) Sven Gunther. "Politics of Taxation in the Roman Empire." TTPI. February 28, 2019. https://www.austaxpolicy.com/politics-taxation-roman-empire/
77.) Pulliam, Roscoe. "Taxation in the Roman State." The Classical Journal 19, no.9 (1924): pg. 551. http://www.jstor.org/stable/3289068

so oppressive that the poor were unable to purchase products like grains and meat, taxes led to a revolt.

Speaking of revolt, when the tariffs placed on the American colonies through the Sugar Act failed to produce the revenue stream desired, an additional source of revenue was attempted by way of the Stamp Act. This act required a fee (tax) on all printed materials, like newspapers and documents, with the king's stamp as proof of purchase. The Stamp Act was deemed one of the Intolerable Acts which led to the battle cry 'no taxation without representation' and the subsequent rebellion.

By now, I'm sure you're sick of hearing about grovelling ingrates who refused to do what they were told. However, it does show you why our indoctrination methods must improve, and our broadening control grids must be strengthened through modern means. Regardless, the purpose of bringing this history to your attention is to provide you with an overview of the various taxes still in use today, their history and their initial purpose.

As much as it pains me, early America can be used to illustrate efficient taxation used purely for the benefit of its people and infrastructure. As discussed in Chapter 6, only indirect taxes (sales and import taxes, a.k.a. tariffs) and apportioned direct taxes during times of emergency were permitted in early America.

As a lord, however, it's difficult to live a life of luxury on an indirect tax alone because there's a prohibitive amount of tax you can add before the taxed products are rejected by consumers in the market. Finding a happy medium ensures that revenue keeps coming in but, in the same breath, government keeps itself within the limits set by this restrictive form of taxation. With barely enough cash flow to fund even the most basic operations, there's little money left over for any modern-day excesses.

Another huge advantage early America possessed over other developed societies was that it didn't have a full-time military. As per its constitution, the army was to disband every two years, which just so happened to be the term for members of the House of Representatives, the branch of government controlling the purse strings. The justification for this stipulation was that if a war were unpopular and the house member didn't vote to stop funding the conflict, the people could vote that member out and indirectly end the unpopular war.

Early America was also, in part, defended by a well-regulated militia made up of batches of armed citizens. By breaking the army up every two years, it also served as a check and balance against a standing army which had the potential to be used against its own citizens. This was another safeguard built into this, although I hate to admit it, well-conceived document. Are you beginning to see why it took so long to gain ownership over this **FARM**? During World War II, legend has it that Isoroku Yamamoto of the Japanese Navy stated: 'You cannot invade the mainland United States. There would be a rifle behind every blade of grass.' Regardless of the debate as to the legitimacy of this quote, its meaning should not go unnoticed.

In mediaeval England, peasants and serfs from the age of fifteen to sixty were mandated to practice archery at picnics and festivals to provide for a strong national defence. In short, the more capable members of the population were at defending themselves, the more the **FARM** was able to protect itself from both internal and external threats. Again, depending on the function of your **FARM**, you'll want to strengthen or weaken this ability to maximise your interests.

During America's humble beginnings, to help maintain a check and balance between the people, the states and the federal government, each state legislature would elect two sitting members to serve in the United States Senate for six-year terms. Senate members held a six-year term as opposed to a house member's two-year term because the senators were responsible for developing and enacting things like international treaties. The longer terms, obviously, provided ample time for the completion of these tasks. The framers (America's original lords) also believed that those actively serving in their respective state legislatures were better candidates for federal senate positions since they were most familiar with their state's needs that they were duty bound to represent. Those elected to state governments were also deemed better equipped to decide who in state government possessed the necessary talents for the federal senate positions since these peer-selected federal senators were required to have better insight into international affairs. Who would know better than a group of enlightened men working side by side with a couple of illuminated men?

During this long-forgotten time, senators had a duty to keep the federal government within its constitutional limits. These restraints came in the form of twenty specific enumerated powers that the federal government was confined to in order to protect the states and their sovereignty from federal control. Remember, the states initially came together to oversee a central government not the other way around. In the future, there'll be no need for this type of individual autonomy.

If you recognise it starting to happen on a community or state level, squash it immediately.

The founders of America believed that if the people voted for all branches of government, including senators, they'd start clamouring for all the things they wanted, and the politicians would have no choice but to placate them to get elected. As a result, a senator would potentially bypass their constitutional oath designed to limit the authority of the federal government simply to take office.

Does this ring a bell? Of course it does. That's why it has been skilfully arranged for peasants in America to now elect their senators.

It's a well-known fact that commoners love to be coddled and provided for so much that they simply fail to recognise their own further enslavement by way of debt, not to mention the transfer of their say in things to a more remote location (Washington DC instead of their own local government). At the same time, they're added to a larger group of constituents from which to be heard. With so many voices clamouring for attention, it's easy to drown out the ones that interfere with a well-orchestrated agenda.

Oh, I'm such a bad, bad man.

These twenty original enumerated powers or federal duties include such basic yet necessary tasks as fixing the standards of weights and measures, coining the money and regulating its value, keeping foreign and interstate commerce regular, enforcing five and only five crimes on the federal level (to be discussed in Chapter 10), promoting the arts and sciences as well as protecting intellectual property and discoveries, providing the general defence, establishing post offices and postal roads, and collecting taxes.

As you can also deduce from common sense, assuming you have what it takes to rule over humanity with an iron fist, one central government holding all the power is much easier to control than fifty independent states acting on their own accord. With the few above-mentioned powers and an army that disbanded every two years and was used sparingly in military conflicts, it's easy to understand how a relatively small tax stream could easily fund this type of limited government.

However, this would allow the citizens of the country to keep their earnings for their own needs whilst still providing necessities such as motorways, courts and military protection so each person could live out the pursuit of happiness. What a utopian concept! But, as we've already learned in previous chapters, there'll always be people like you and me who need to rule over others as well as those who need to be blindly led astray.

Therefore, dystopia should be your aim.

Remember, the government big enough to give them everything they want, is the government big enough to take away everything they have. When the time is right, you must make your move to take total control.

I'll expand upon one of the original enumerated powers of the early united States of America to illustrate how to gradually change a FARM from a Promised Land concept to one that's conducive to your wealth and power.

> NOTE: With an alert and vigilant group of free men and women, this is a much more difficult task to achieve. But with a womb society (one that loves to be taken care of at the expense of its own freedom), a slow transition will lure them right into your clutches.

Although I could write an entire handbook on the topic of subjugating a citizenry through the use of everyday government services such as mail delivery, I'll simply present some key points to illustrate how this can be accomplished. Remember, knowledge is power, and learning these effective and established techniques will better prepare you in your quest for global domination.

To begin, before the Civil War, mail was usually delivered to the post office under general delivery where crowds would gather. Names were called out and letters were handed directly to recipients.

But when did free home delivery of what's known today as First-Class Mail (a monopoly still cleverly held by the government) begin?

Despite the heartwarming stories of the government providing soldiers' this complimentary service so they could communicate with their families during the War Between the States, free home delivery was actually a wonderful way to covertly expand governmental services, and hence federal jurisdiction, directly to the *citizens'* doorsteps. Hence, free home delivery began during the Civil War.[78]

> NOTE: It was this expansion of the national government during the War Between the States that served as a catalyst to its broadening powers over the citizenry and ignited the avalanche of federal agencies we have today.[79]

78.) Smithsonian National Postal Museum. "Joseph Briggs and the Free City Delivery." Smithsonian National Postal Museum. https://postalmuseum.si.edu/exhibition/customers-and-communities-serving-the-cities/city-free-delivery

79.) Lisa Rein. "Civil War gave birth to much of modern federal government." The Washington Post. October 7, 2011. https://www.washingtonpost.com/politics/

To briefly recap the timeline, the not so united States of America went into martial law in July 1861, roughly three months into the conflict. In the event you're unaware of this powerful tactic, martial law suspends the *rights of the citizens* during times of emergency and leaves even the most well-intentioned occupants susceptible to unlawful searches and seizures, not to mention wrongful arrests. To the crafty despot, this is the perfect time to shake down a **FARM** to discover where each *citizen's* true loyalty lies. However, to provide a legal framework for this extension of military power, the Lieber Code: *General Orders No. 100 was* instated on 24 April 1863, and led to the military taking silent control of all local and state governmental functions as well as the post office under Article 15.[80]

Ironically, and not so coincidentally, home mail delivery in the US began in July of 1863, just three months after the Lieber Code was instated.[81] Although it's openly recognised that the State and War departments detained and opened letters in search of treasonable correspondence[82] wouldn't such a subtle takeover of this new communications service also provide the perfect opportunity for Union agents to dress up as mail carriers to spy on possible Northern dissidents who were opposed to the expansion of an all-powerful government?

I thought you might like the idea. Please keep it in mind as you impose similar civic benefits on your **FARM**.

This early form of mail surveillance inspired today's undercover US Postal Service surveillance network like the Internet Covert Operations Program, a.k.a. iCOP (Internet spying on those with dissident thoughts), the Intelligent Mail system (a tracking programme for the entire postal network) and the Address Management System (AMS), a database of all addresses and residents in the United States, all run under the watchful eye of the Committee on Homeland Security and Governmental Affairs.[83]

civil-war-gave-birth-to-much-of-modern-federal-government/2011/09/22/gIQA43EFSL_story.html

80.) Francis Lieber. "General Orders No. 100: The Lieber Code." Yale Law School. The Avalon Project. Documents in Law, History and Diplomacy. https://avalon.law.yale.edu/19th_century/lieber.asp and James G. Randall, Ph.D., *Constitutional Problems Under Lincoln* (New York-London: D. Appleton and Company, 1926), 215-218

81.) USPS. "Free City Delivery." Postal Facts. https://facts.usps.com/free-city-delivery/

82.) Randall, *Constitutional Problems Under Lincoln*, 500.

83.) Natalie O'Neill. "USPS admits to spying on Americans' social media posts: report." New York Post.com. April 28, 2021. https://nypost.com/2021/04/28/usps-admits-to-spying-on-americans-social-media-posts/ and Geoffrey Block. "Why is the Postal Service Critical to National Security?" Lawfaremedia.com. May 1, 2020. https://

It also illustrated two essential world domination techniques.

The first is the appointment of political insiders and proven associates to important **FARM** positions. The character of the entire US postal system was notoriously changed when Andrew Jackson appointed former Kentucky Senator William T. Barry to Postmaster General in 1829 after which the Post Office Department infamously became known as the chief dispenser of political patronage for the party in power.[84] Other notables in the Who's Who of national superstars tapped for the esteemed position of Postmaster General included Ben Franklin, Harry Truman and even the notorious, not so Honest Abe himself, Abraham Lincoln.[85] A cushy job is the least you can provide for someone who does your bidding. Assigning the title of PostMASTER gives them the thrill and experience of being in their majesty's shoes by asserting jurisdiction through the use of paper and services onto unknowing beneficiaries. As shown by those who emerged from the mailroom into great historical prominence, a post office tenure could catapult someone with proven administrative talent into a top leadership position on the American **FARM**.

The second, and equally important, world domination technique is the use of communication services such as mail delivery to regulate the information your peasants receive. This is especially true if it's from sources undermining your official narratives and policies. Censors in the North and South rummaged through and removed traitorous citizen correspondences travelling through their territories.[86] Publications such as newspapers and journals opposed to the war were also denied delivery services. An obvious example is when Postmaster General Blair, in the latter part of 1861, denied mail service to newspapers condemned as disloyal by the Federal Grand Jury at New York. When raising the

www.lawfaremedia.org/article/why-postal-service-critical-national-security and "JURISDICTION AND RULES." U.S. Senate Committee on Homeland Security & Governmental Affairs.senate.gov. https://www.hsgac.senate.gov/about/jurisdiction-and-rules/

84.) Cathleen Schurr. "The History of the US Postal Service – And That Time Someone Sent Their Kid Through the Mail." HISTORYNET. August 19, 1997. https://historynet.com/history-us-postal-service/

85.) "Postmasters Abraham Lincoln and Harry Truman." USPS. https://about.usps.com/who-we-are/postal-history/abraham-lincoln-harry-truman-postmasters.pdf and Schurr, "History of US Postal Service."

86.) Jesse Walker. "Postal Censorship and Surveillance: A Timeline." reason. September 2021. https://reason.com/2021/07/15/postal-censorship-and-surveillance-a-timeline/ and "Mail Service and the Civil War." USPS. 2012. https://aboutusps.com/news/national-release/2012/pr12_civil-war-mail-history.pdf

question of Mr. Blair's right to do so, the Judiciary Committee of the House of Representatives formed an obvious conclusion…of course he does.[87] A useful lackey like General Blair would not have been placed in such a critical **FARM** position had he not been entrusted with the authority to make controversial decisions on behalf of the ruling power. However, the appearance of concern for his fellow citizens' rights was a wonderful display of political pageantry used to disguise his hidden overseers' more insidious aims.

So, to recap, free home mail delivery began forming the intricate dynamic of *citizens* receiving a government benefit in exchange for their submission to federal jurisdiction. Included in this exquisite sleight of hand were the hidden intrusions required for a **FARM'S** ruling authority to impose and expand itself. The Lieber Code provided the legal smokescreen needed to do so whilst loyalists, placed in key positions, were instrumental in producing the desired results. Not only did this early form of censorship help the central government achieve more power—ahem—I mean, achieve the perfect union, it helped develop the early framework for today's expansive control grid.

A true long-term victory, indeed!

Since the government and its Union Army won the conflict in 1865 with such brutal campaigns as Sherman's March to the Sea, and because a peace treaty was never officially signed, the country remained in Martial Law, as well as under the edicts of the Lieber Code. This can easily be seen during the implementation of the Reconstruction Acts in 1867 and 1868 when military districts replaced acting Southern governments. Commanded by generals, districts were set up in the South to ensure that the Southern states accepted the 14th Amendment in order to rejoin the Union. And what a perfect union it became! To refresh your memory, the 14th Amendment was responsible for the creation of United States citizens, as opposed to being citizens of their respective states, which was a roundabout way of dismantling the state's authority over the federal government. Can you see the importance of gaining the South's cooperation, even if it was through the barrel of a gun?

There was plenty of opposition to this military takeover, including three vetoes of the Reconstruction Acts by President Andrew Johnson. Similar defiance from North Carolina Governor, Jonathan Worth, led to his expulsion under general orders #120 issued by General Canby of the United States Army. These orders were enforced by the arrival of

---

87.) Randall, *Constitutional Problems Under Lincoln*, 499-502.

troops at the North Carolina state capital on 1 July 1868, the day the orders were to go into effect.

In his letter addressed to his replacement, Governor W.W. Holden, Governor Worth wisely vacated his office despite some whimpering and claims of surrender due to military duress rather than fair election.[88] Both President Johnson and Governor Worth understood the illegality of the military's strong-arming tactics to gain state compulsion, not to mention the underlying plan to thrust all citizens into a deepening state of servitude.

Illegality schmegality. Please note the importance of carrying a heavy club to gain compliance. Do you want results or don't you?

As discussed in Chapter 6, a corporation was formed in 1871 under the Organic Act to carry out the business duties of the defunct government of the united States of America which had adjourned *sine die* (indefinitely) ten years prior. This is when the land of fiction, if you will, began to blossom.

As we continue, please pay special attention to how the real world and the world of make-believe closely resemble each other. Great care has been taken so that only insiders can detect it. Remember, your peasants should be so well indoctrinated that even when confronted with this truth, they'll dismiss it to remain in their state of servitude and complacency.

'So, what does all this ballyhoo have to do with mail delivery and hence taxation?' you bark.

It has to do with Zip Codes and their real purpose. Just like the Reconstruction Acts set up military zones during post-Civil War America, zip codes became boundary lines on a paper map that divided up the Washington DC Municipal Corporation into legal (fictional) military districts. This was even further justified when all United States citizens became enemies of the state in 1933.

If you remember, the War Powers Act of 1933 brought United States citizens into the licensing control of the US Corporation. One of the first licensing requirements was the Agricultural Adjustment Act, passed 12 May 1933. This was nothing short of a federal takeover of the agricultural industry, allowing *government* control of everything from prices to production to the very farmland where the crops were and still are grown. Comically, Stalin was also seizing control of the farms

88.) Jonathan Worth. "North-Carolina Surrender Letter." North-Carolina American Republic Resource Library.org. July 1, 1868. www.ncrepublic.org/lib_surrender-letter.php

in the Soviet Union around this same time, leading to the starvation of millions. Fortunately, those living on the land mass known as America were being groomed into a military superpower to be used by the illuminated minds of those orchestrating a unified global peasant farm. Hence, American citizens were spared such harsh consequences.

During comrade Roosevelt's first hundred days, many other seizures by licensing authority took hold over such industries as transportation, communications, public utilities, securities, oil, labour and all natural resources. The justification of such usurpations goes back to the implementation of the Lieber Code in 1863 and the resulting loss of each citizen's property and rights. Now that a new money system based on the property of US citizens had taken effect under the Emergency Banking Relief Act of 1933, Public Law 1, Stat 48. 1, it was made clear in Senate Document 43, who really controlled the property. This manuscript boasts ever so proudly: 'The ultimate ownership of all property is in the State; individual so-called *ownership* is only by virtue of government, i.e. law, amounting to mere user; and use must be in accordance with law, and subordinate to the necessities of the State.'

In other words, it doesn't matter if gold is taken out from under citizens' noses, now citizens have to buy things with worthless paper. Therefore, it's of little importance how they gain use of something, because whatever property of the state they use can just as easily be revoked.

Although a licence was, and still is, a *voluntary* contract, only those who had one would receive government subsidies for counterintuitive practices such as a farmer not growing food. These illogical incentives provided a nice transition into gaining compliance from US citizens when they were previously free to act on their own accord. But despite the broadening powers and revenues achieved through licensing, only 3.9% of the population filed an income tax return in 1936.[89]

But how was THE UNITED STATES OF AMERICA, INC. supposed to gain acquiescence from every American to pay this *income* tax if they were domiciled outside of *federal territories* and not employed inside the federal government as discussed in Chapter 6? By first offering them a biscuit, that's how.

We're in the money! We're in the money!

Both Hitler and FDR had studied Otto Van Bismarck and his social insurance programme, a compulsory insurance against worker's old age, sickness, accident and incapacity. First implemented in Germany

---

89.) Hendrickson, *Cracking the Code*, 47.

in 1881 by Chancellor William the First, at the behest of its creator, Otto Von Bismarck, this social insurance programme was organised by the state yet entirely financed by employers and employees.

As an up-and-coming dictator, it's important to understand why pyramid schemes like Social Security fail in private industry yet succeed for governments.

First, a pyramid scheme works like this. 'Hi Bob, its George. How are you mate? Listen. I've got this great opportunity for you. Give me one thousand quid and I'll return your investment by forty per cent. Yes, I'm serious. Okay lad, if you don't want in, that's your call.'

Bob contemplates for a moment then realises George was the best man at his wedding. He then reluctantly withdraws some money from his son's university savings and gives it to George whilst maintaining a natural dose of scepticism. Then, one week later, George approaches that recent divorcee he met at the gym who looks splendid in a pair of leggings.

'Hi Susie. You're looking great, love. I have this wonderful investment opportunity where you can get in on the ground floor. It'll give you a 40% return.'

Susie is impressed by this opportunity, not to mention George's dazzling charm. Over dinner at an opulent restaurant, she hands him twice what Bob gave him. George waits a few days to rope in a few more stooges...um...I mean investors, and then once again approaches Bob.

'Hi Bob. Here you go chap. I told you this was the real thing. Here's your thousand plus four hundred. It was a pleasure doing business with you mate.'

Bob is so ecstatic; he empties his entire life savings via a wire transfer into George's business account. And so, the process continues.

As you can see, a pyramid scheme rewards those who are first to get in as long as they get out before things go south. For example, the first recipient of a Social Security check, Ida May Fuller, in January 1940. Ms Fuller worked for three years before retiring at age sixty-five, paying a grand total of $24.75. She lived to be one hundred years young and collected a total of...drum roll please...$22,888.92. The early upsides make implementing these programmes fairly easy to do because those at the beginning of the programmes are most handsomely rewarded and therefore, will enthusiastically support them.

The problems start when the chickens come home to roost like during the retirement of a baby boomer generation. Again, we go back to the example with our friend Boob—oh crumbs, I mean Bob—to illustrate the long-term downsides of a Ponzi scheme. We'll pick up where George receives a call in the middle of the night from a panic-stricken Bob.

'Hi Bob. What's up, mate? Bruv, you're starting to freak me out. I know you want to pull your money out; everybody's hurting right now. No one saw this economic downturn coming, including me, but just keep your money in a little longer until the economy turns around. You'll be on the upside of this thing. Fraudulent? Would a government agency allow this type of investment to occur if it were fraudulent? And you think it's because my niece is marrying a higher up?[90] You're really pushing our friendship here, Bob. Okay. We'll talk more about this tomorrow. Cheerio.'

Whilst alone with his thoughts, George starts to think about the repercussions of such a grand heist and admits to himself that it's quite a thrill. But he also hopes and prays that all his investors don't demand their money back, like Bob. If they do, and since he doesn't have an army to back him or the colour of law to use against others to extract the money he already spent on hookers, beachfront property and holidays, he contemplates the possibility of receiving plastic surgery, changing his identity and then faking his own death.

Again, notice the importance of having an army and using the colour of law (to be discussed further in Chapter 9). As applied to today's Social Security programme, many US citizens who obediently pay into the system their whole lives will get back less money than they actually paid in, even though the majority of them probably won't bat an eye at the projected shortfall. Mugs!

This is again why peasants must be conditioned to faithfully and trustfully turn matters over to you. If not obvious, the reason Ponzi schemes work for governments is because they can force people to pay more to keep the programmes afloat even when the programmes go bankrupt. This appropriately leads us back to taxation.

Not only did the Social Security Act, passed in 1935, require active registration for a US citizen to receive the benefit (thereby creating an implied contract with the federal corporation making those doing so liable for the shortfalls), it provided for the creation of the Social Security Board which created ten *Federal Social Security Districts* that combined to form a *Federal Regional Area* that covered the several states like a plastic tarp draped over a dead body.

90.) Brian Ross and Joseph Rhee. "SEC Official Married into Madoff Family." abcnews.com. December 15, 2008. https://abcnews.go.com/Blotter/WallStreet/story?id=6471863&page=1

The Buck Act (4 USC Sect 105-113) then came along in 1939 and authorised any department, agency or establishment of the federal government to create a *Federal Area* for the implementation of the Public Salary Tax Act of 1939. This was a municipal law aimed at taxing the *income* of all federal and state employees and those who live and work inside a *Federal Area*. This new law happened to arrive just before World War II when public financial support was greatly needed. It should also be noted how simple visual tools like cartoons can help muster support and cooperation for hard to swallow policies imposed on your herd. For a prime example, you may want to seek out such masterpieces as Donald Duck and the Spirit of '43 to watch the power of suggestion at its finest.[91] Oh, these simple-minded adults can be manipulated as easily as children.

Also, important to note is how just about every federal agency falls under control of the executive branch. If you set up your **FARM'S** political structure this way, you can control all the agencies through one man or woman, i.e. your corporate government's president.

Just because the Buck Act permitted any agency, department or establishment of the federal government to extend themselves into these imaginary military venues did not mean that real men and women could actually exist in them. Similarly, just because an unsuspecting benefit seeker signed a contract or used an assigned number to receive a benefit or privilege, it still did not physically place him in a federal district/area.

So then, how would you trick inhabitants of your **FARM** into these imaginary districts which, in turn, make the fictional entity representing the peasant directly responsible for the corporation's debt? I'll give you a hint. The initials are Z.I.P. (Zone Improvement Plan) Code. Please also take note that an endearing character named Mr. Zip and a catchy little jingle were created to pacify reluctant peasants whilst turning them into residents of a federal district. Come to think of it, lollipops may have worked just as well.

By claiming a zip code (i.e. an imaginary federal zone) whilst accepting the privilege of home mail delivery from the now private corporation and quasi government agency known as the United States Postal Service, one concedes to be a resident (*res: a thing, ident: identified*) in a federal district of the District of Columbia and hence under the jurisdiction of THE UNITED STATES OF AMERICA, INC.

91.) Walt Disney Productions, "DONALD DUCK: The Spirit of '43," YouTube video, 3:06, 8thManDVD.com, July 9, 2015, https://youtu.be/XNMrMFuk-bo?si=UhV-JTzKOPSjiBZij

located in Washington, DC. Furthermore, the Internal Revenue Service has adopted zip codes as Internal Revenue Districts as published in the Federal Register, Volume 51, Number 53, Wednesday, 19 March 1986, and as stipulated in 26 USC Section 7621. This means when you use a zip code, you're saying you're not a Citizen of Alabama but instead a resident in the Alabama area of the District of Columbia (a federal district). Now, you're within the municipal laws of the United States and within range of agencies working to collect the federal debt on behalf of the federal corporation.

'But how much debt can there be?' you cry out.

Here's where yet another imaginary idea of *interest* comes into play. I suppose this is why some suggest that Einstein purportedly said compound interest is: 'the eighth wonder of the world', 'the most powerful force in the universe' or 'the greatest invention in human history'. I must admit, juxtaposing such a brilliant mind next to such an abstract concept really drives the point home. Whether he actually made any of these statements or not is of little consequence. The hidden punch line is, how can one give back more than was originally created? But it sure is fun to watch them try.

By charging a modest interest fee of say, around six percent on every bill that is printed, then running off more *money* every time a war for *freedom* is fought, or a department needs funding, or a poor college student needs a loan to attend one of your institutions of *higher learning*, more corporate federal debt is created. Your toadies will never be able to pay you back more than you originally *lent* them, thus rendering them perpetually enslaved to you. Are you starting to see the value of a good printing press? They'll be working themselves into oblivion whilst those you hire simply hit the print button and load the machines.

> NOTE: Just be sure to keep this handbook in a very secure place. If it falls into the wrong hands, the possibility of a peasant uprising exists.

As previously discussed, using a social security number, a zip code and claiming US CITIZEN status further binds a peasant to the federal corporation and puts them within the jurisdiction of the agencies used for debt collection. By using street addresses owned by local municipalities, peasants become residents of those subsidiary corporations as well. Notice how brilliantly the use of services, benefits and resident status creates a contractual nexus that identifies the peasant as the fictional entity within this fictional military venue. The most glorious part of this whole ploy is that it's all done by way of the peasant's own unknowing consent.

Although most well-trained peasants will use skewed logic to debunk this rather obvious scheme to suit their own motivations or to avoid cognitive dissonance, when agitators catch on to it you should also make it a point to compel your trusted peasants to harass, badger, arrest, mock and prosecute any peasant seeking to escape your corporate plantation. That's why it's important to control all the information sources your peasants have access to. Obviously, you can then use these platforms to rebuke any truthful claims your peasants make regarding your underlying intent. Controlling the media will also play a crucial role in preventing the undesirable outcome of your peasants *uniting*.

Strict adherence to *income* tax laws should be instilled in your peasants through the use of aggressive enforcement. This will help keep your underlings in fear of repercussions for any acts of rebellion. You can also pipe mantras into your **FARM** such as: 'Pay your fair share' (teaches them shared responsibility for the debt owed to you), 'I'm a taxpayer. I have rights' (makes them think that because they pay taxes, they have a say in things which, obviously, they should not) and 'Nothing is certain but death and taxes' (browbeating them into believing taxes are inescapable). These catchphrases will also help convince your peasants that if they can't get out of paying taxes, neither should anyone else. These obedient peasants are nice to have on juries, in human resource departments and tax agencies, for instance, when thinking peasants try to escape the corporate **FARM**.

You can also encourage your peasants with more positive methods like returning a portion of the money collected from them each year. This will make them grateful to you, earning their loyalty. Giving them the feeling they're being *responsible citizens* will also lead them to police irresponsible citizens who aren't contributing to things they are led to believe the taxes are used for, like education, roads, wars for freedom, etc. Again, there are many ways to extort the time and energy of your peasants. An income tax should be used to pay the interest owed to you for the money you so graciously lend them.

Those who continue to resist *must* be made an example of and humiliated in the public eye. Historically, those who verbally attacked creditors who were loaning money to others at an interest (known in the olden days as *usury*) ended up nailed to a cross.

NOTE: Most of society will idly stand by whilst anyone with the courage to speak out bears punishment for their rebellious actions. Many hopeless peasants will actually cheer at these events or take part in their execution (this can be attributed to Stockholm syndrome: empathising with their captor). This is the equivalent of a herd of wildebeests trotting away from a lion that snatches one of their own. We repeatedly see the same mentality on domesticated human farms throughout history.

Tactics used to degrade dissidents can range from dragging them from their houses naked (or barely clothed), to humiliating them in front of their neighbours, to stripping them of their property, to seizing their actual bodies. A heavy tax can naturally confine your peasants' movements, but when further restrictions brought on by fines and penalties do not earn their compliance, their movements must be further restricted to a jail cell until they fully understand the consequences of their actions. Enforcement must be strictly administered if you're to gain your peasants' full cooperation. Otherwise, why would they pay?

Wealth means a lot of different things to a lot of different people. Perhaps being wealthy is simply owning a lot of land outright via Allodial title (i.e. title for land, buildings and/or fixtures that is independent of any superior landlord, a.k.a. a government, imposing property taxes) or having one's health. But, one must admit, purchasing power is the most important aspect in today's commercial world. If you're able to finagle things so that your trained monkeys and their property and labour are possessions of the **STATE** and collateral for the debt owed to you, we can really begin to have some fun.

If you can get your **FARM** running efficiently, there are an infinite number of ways to exploit your chattel. Please note, besides filling your own pockets, you can also use tax revenue streams to:

1. Subsidise other nations via foreign aid (a.k.a. paying off willing associates in sympathetic *countries by taking it from subjects in affluent countries*).

2. Show favouritism to certain corporations through government contracts, tax breaks, guaranteed loans and monetary grants, allowing you to subtly enrich associates through their businesses. This type of corporate welfare will work best when you can privatise profits, to you and your associates, and socialise losses.

3. Fund quasi-governmental private corporations (federal agencies) by appointing trusted associates from government and private industry to watch over and manage your subjects and all their activities.

NOTE: Politicians should be funded and work for you as should your national and international affiliates mentioned above. Otherwise, how are you going to bring the **FARMS** of the world together into one harmonious, blissful hodgepodge? Even though aspiring and established officeholders will be sponsored by you and your wealthy associates, political rhetoric should express concern for the peasants along with a pledge to make their conditions better. This will help provide the illusion of freedom, (see Chapter 13).

The following is just a partial list of taxes currently used in the *free* country of America, that you can also use to fleece your flock: [92]

accounts receivable tax	automobile registration tax
building permit tax	capital gains tax
CDL licence tax	cigarette tax
corporate income tax	court fines (indirect tax)
dog licence tax	federal income tax
entertainment tax (PA)	fishing licence tax
federal unemployment tax	fuel permit tax
food licence tax	hunting licence tax
petrol (gasoline) tax	inventory tax
inheritance tax	IRS penalties (tax on top of a tax)
IRS interest charges (tax on top of a tax)	local income tax
liquor tax	marriage licence tax
luxury taxes	parking meters
Medicare tax	septic permit tax
real estate tax	social security tax
service charge tax	sales taxes
road usage taxes (truckers)	road toll booth taxes

92.) Aaron Russo, "America: Freedom to Fascism," YouTube video, 1:47:45, Revolution Your Mind, May 10, 2011, https://youtu.be/uNNeVu8wUak?=tNbZf-Gk-Fw1Vffq

recreational vehicle tax	state income tax
school tax	telephone federal excise tax
state unemployment tax	workers compensation tax
telephone federal universal service fee tax	toll bridge taxes
telephone minimum usage surcharge tax	traffic fines
toll tunnel taxes	vehicle sales tax
trailer registration tax	well permit tax
watercraft registration tax	telephone federal, state and local surcharge taxes
death tax (yes, you can tax them to death. It's wonderfully cruel, isn't it?)	

Now for some really amusing and creative ways to bilk your peasants.

Card tax (10 cent tax on a deck of playing cards in AL)	yoga tax (tax on health clubs in Washington, DC)
glow worm tax (6% tax on glow worms, noise makers and sparklers in WV)	occupation tax (tax for working in a particular occupation in PA)
tethered balloon tax (tax on hot air balloons tethered to the ground for use as a ride in KS)	nappy (diaper) tax (only applies to children's nappies and not adults (thank goodness) in CT)
holiday decorations tax in TX	dance tax in WA
soda fountain drink tax (in Chicago IL fountain sodas are taxed at 9% as opposed to canned sodas at 3%)	nudity sales tax (10% tax on any sexually explicit business where someone appears nude or partially nude in UT)
blueberry tax in ME	per capita tax (tax for being alive in PA)
fruit tax (33% tax on fruit bought from vending machines in CA)	tattoo tax (6% tax on tattoos or body piercings in AK)
litigation tax in NY	bagel cutting tax in NY
air tax (tax on any item that comes out of a compressed air vending machine in PA)	rain tax (dependent on surface area of property in MD)

federal dirt tax (per ton)	bingo and raffle tax in NM
jock tax (most states with professional sports teams charge a per game state tax on any paid athlete playing a game in their state)	illegal drug tax (a.k.a. crack tax in which a stamp is received to place on illicit drugs in TN)
belt buckle tax in TX	

This is just a short list of the fun you can have as your peasants frantically busy themselves in their meaningless jobs to pay tribute to you. As you can hopefully see, there's no end to the types of duties you can impose on them, and the possibilities are only limited by your reluctance to assert your will.

I would now like to elaborate on three particular taxes to show how you can minimise your peasants purchasing power whilst also working against their best interest. Reducing your proletariats' wealth will force them to work longer hours on the corporate plantation and you can then use their time and labour to build and enhance the control grid around them.

First, a property tax is one of the best weapons available to keep peasants in check. This tax makes them renters instead of property owners and not paying rent to the government can result in dire consequences. If their possessions can be readily seized, depriving peasants of secure places to sleep, not to mention confiscating the amenities they have toiled countless hours to obtain, they will think twice about bucking the system. We saw how the state should be set up to be the true owner of all property, but providing peasants the illusion of ownership will trick them into thinking they're in control of their lives. Revenue from property tax can then be channelled into things like public training centres, where future peasants will be indoctrinated to fit into your system.

Next is an example of how government regulatory agencies can be used to siphon the financial freedom of your peasants as well as track and penalise every unauthorised move they make. Such agencies can be instrumental in targeting a competing business or industry or your personal or political nemesis. Occasionally, you may want to unleash one of your enforcement squads on a random innocent bystander, just to demonstrate your authority and serve as a fresh reminder that you're in charge. These agencies should have little to do with the functions presented to the peasants. Their existence should give peasants the impression they're being protected when quite the opposite is true.

This is another tool to work toward the peasants' demise if necessary.

I'll use a fictional environmental regulation agency as an example. However, before we discuss how to exploit something as important as a healthy environment, we must first discuss the ideal way to protect it from damage. Obviously, humans must produce things to survive and waste byproducts are, unfortunately, the inevitable result. These unwanted leftovers occur regardless of the type of government and business system you choose for your **FARM**. So then, which system is most effective at minimising the damage from the contaminated surplus?

To answer this, let's look at our two basic choices, communal ownership versus private ownership. With communal ownership, the resources are free for everyone to use for the *common good*. Profits are not allowed by the established government that also defines the *common good*. Since profits aren't involved, there's no incentive to fully utilise a resource to its full capacity or to conserve it for future profits. Common sense clearly shows that less care would be invested. Also, under this type of arrangement, it's easy to see how an *acquire-it-before-someone-else-does* mentality develops since the resources are fair game, and a resource may not be there when one goes to retrieve it. For a real-world illustration, please reference the all too frequent and large-scale environmental tragedies in Russia and China which serve as glaring examples of communal ownership.

On the other hand, with private ownership, a price must be paid to acquire property. A price measured in one's time and energy. Quite naturally, this creates a deeper respect for the assets. Furthermore, if one paid a price to own the property, more care is not only expended on its maintenance but on the conservation of its resources. A profit incentive only adds to the need to protect and take care of the property. Finally, it's only under the system of people's law coupled with private ownership where, if one harms another's property, whether it's land, an asset, or an individual's own body, a valid claim can be filed in a common law court and a remedy for damages sought.

Now enter an environmental regulation agency into the picture. Since we discussed how real-world property has been voluntarily turned over to THE UNITED STATES OF AMERICA, INC. and how the US Citizens have now become mere users of the property, it makes sense that an environmental regulation agency's main function is to protect the **FARMS**' resources so they can be exploited by the **FARMS**' owners. Whether peasants attempt to use property (even the land they think they own) in a way restricted by the overseeing lord...eh hem...I mean agency, or a competitor tries to skirt around the restrictions, these rule-breaking debtors *must* be forced to pay for their transgressions. The regulatory body usually manages these infractions through fees and fines, but if a lesson needs to be reinforced, the peasant is arrested. Your court structure should be set up to compensate your agencies before providing any relief to a peasant injured as a result of a violation.

Whether it's these corporate regulatory agencies' staffing needs, their equipment and operational costs, or funds needed to kick off a new programme, policy or subsidy, peasants should obviously be responsible for their overhead even if money must be borrowed against the collateral for the debt (i.e. your peasants and everything they own). In the event there's some sort of blunder by an agency causing the damage they were set up to prevent (like accidentally releasing a million gallons of contaminants from a mine into a creek)[93] your peasants should bear the cost. Just put it on their bill. They don't mind paying for it.

Oh jolly. By doling out so much suffering I can literally feel the stress releasing from my body.

There's one last tax I'd like to mention before the big reveal. Hopefully, this one inspires you to find even more magnificent ways to further deceive the masses for your own gain. This spell first recognises and then exploits the warming and cooling trends that the Earth has naturally undergone for millions of years. The key to pulling off this type of unbridled, worldwide revenue stream is the time-tested method we've already discussed that demonstrates: 'If you tell a big enough lie and tell it frequently enough, it will be believed.' A healthy dose of fear must be sprinkled in to traumatise subjects into submission along with two heaping cups of *scientific evidence* (which is nothing more than the creation of results to support your narrative). The new religion of science worship has been carefully engrained into the psyches of modern-day peasants and can be used to convince them of just about anything.

Here's how it works. You tax peasants for anything that emits *carbon dioxide*. You know, the stuff plants convert into oxygen and peasants exhale. Should I repeat that? The stuff plants convert into oxygen and peasants exhale!

93.) Jessica Glenza. "Toxic mine water accidentally released by EPA in Colorado river flows south: An estimated 1m gallons of the orange-brown water broke free from a shoddy dam and is flowing down the Animas River towards a lake in a national park." The Guardian.com. August 7, 2015. https://www.theguardian.com/us-news/2015/aug/07/toxic-mine-water-epa-colorado-animas-river

Ha! I wish I could be there when, despite soaring food and fuel costs brought on by their *carbon footprint*, they receive a tax bill in the mail for breathing.

Ha-ha-ha-ha. I'm rolling on the floor right now!

The most side-splitting part of this whole thing is that taxing carbon dioxide or similar greenhouse gases does nothing to reduce the amount of gas spewed into the atmosphere. It just drives the costs of those products through the roof, thereby enriching you. Just be sure your financial institutions create carbon credits and watch your revenues skyrocket. Since you know the whole thing is a racket to further enrich you and your brazen business associates, you can continue funding beach front properties on the coasts, through your financial institutions, since you know that they won't be underwater anytime in the next millennium.

Bwah-hah-hah! I need a five-minute break!

Ah. Okay, I'm back.

I'm finally ready to present the most stealthy and sinister tax known to siphon the labour of your peasants, putting me in a more serious and predatory mood. The carbon tax is hard to beat due to the sheer size, scope and insidious deception involved. But this next tax is so covert, yet so magnificently impactful, it's inspired the founding father of modern-day economics, John Maynard Keynes, to say: 'By continuing a process of inflation, governments can confiscate secretly and unobserved, an important part of the wealth of its citizens. There's no subtler, no surer means of overturning the existing basis of society than to debauch the currency. The process engages all the hidden forces of economic law on the side of destruction and does it in such a manner which not one man in a million is able to diagnose.'

If you missed the clue, this secret weapon is inflation. This hidden duty (as discussed in Chapter 3) comes about by simply printing more paper money that, over time, reduces the value of each bill. Since your government and subsidised businesses are the first to receive the new money, they receive the benefits because of the money's stronger purchasing power. Prices are still based on the previous money supply when each bill carried more value and, hence, prices were lower. This stronger money can be used to acquire capital, bribe foreign diplomats, fight wars or demonstrate the pretence of caring for your peasants (a new programme perhaps).

But by the time this new money trickles down to your subjects, its value diminishes, forcing your peasants to work longer hours whilst at the same time reducing their economic freedom. If done gradually, their loss of purchasing power will appear to be caused by rising prices and not by the devaluation of the currency. The following example will illustrate how drastically you can deprive your peasants of their wealth.

When I was a young man in the 1970s, dashing and debonair of course, I could put a Washington quarter (made from 1932 to 1964, containing 90% silver) into an American vending machine and receive a bottle of Coca Cola. Today, the same can of fizzy drink, on average, costs $1.25. That's five times the price it was in the 1970s. However, the new coins aren't made of silver, they have a copper core encircled by nickel alloy. The melt value of the silver in a 1932-1964 Washington quarter, as I write, is $3.01. That means you can buy at least two cans of fizzy drink today with the actual value of the 1932-1964 Washington quarter because production methods and the true costs of manufacturing and distributing the product have gone down in relation to silver. But the fiat currency (not made from a precious metal) has lost five times its original purchasing power. Thus, peasants must dedicate more hours to their work as well as send their spouses and children to work on the corporate plantation just to have what peasants in the 1970s could achieve on one income.

If you choose, you can have the entire plantation living in complete squalor as they complain about the rising prices, whilst not one of them will know who to blame. As you run off more paper, you'll collect more interest on the paper you lend to the *government* (creating a national debt) whilst also lessening the value of each bill. The more money and more debt you create, the more hopelessly indentured they'll be to you. The inflation tax is a wonderful tool that can be used by the political system to keep taxes taken directly from peasants to a bare minimum whilst the cost of everything around them escalates. Having them pay into things like retirement programmes also gives you access to the newer money they pay in whilst leaving it nearly useless by the time the gullible peasants receive it.

Ah, the utter brilliance! If this doesn't motivate you to aspire to the level of world emperor, nothing will!

Chapter 9

LAWS

When plunder becomes a way of life for a group of men living together in society, they create for themselves in the course of time a legal system that authorises it and a moral code that glorifies it.
— Frederic Bastiat

Let's start with you. Say for a moment that you're the only living human being on the planet. You, by default, are the sovereign ruler of your domain. No other man or woman has authority over you because, quite frankly, there isn't anyone else. A lion may try to eat you out of the laws of necessity, but you have the inherent right to defend yourself and kill the lion. If you need to eat, you can also hunt lions for food, but you better have a well-thought-out plan because lions may not take too kindly to your encroachment on their territory. If you fail, you might become their next meal. To add a little more complexity to the situation, let's add more people to the mix.

In theory, the above principles also hold true with the addition of more human beings. No other human has authority over you. If another human being tries to kill you, out of the laws of necessity, you have every right to defend your life. That doesn't always mean you'll be successful but, obviously, to survive, no other human being, or group of human beings (even ones wearing matching uniforms and shiny badges) has a higher vested interest in your life than you, and you have the inherent right to preserve yourself.[94] Remember this, as it's the foundation of your sovereignty. As the Dutch philosopher Baruch Spinoza once theorised: 'If men were born free, they would, so long as they remained free, form no conception of good and evil.'

94.) Schoolland, "Philosophy of Liberty," 2:35-3:34

NOTE: To be a powerful ruler, you *must* be willing to operate outside manmade laws and not look at your actions through the lens of good and evil but rather from the standpoint of, 'Is every move I make necessary to more effectively rule over others?' In fact, you can create laws that legalise your actions or find creative ways to distort, misinterpret, confuse, hijack or tamper with the common laws and maxims (established principles) already set in stone.

As more and more people enter a geographical area, there's more and more interaction between inhabitants. Being the social creatures we are, alliances and conflicts arise for a variety of reasons. You may want to rip a switch from a tree and beat a nearby dweller like a *piñata* because they have a funny walk, but it turns out they are highly skilled at blowing glass which you find quite useful. The ability to reason separates us from the animals and moves us away from the laws of necessity.

For laws to work properly they must have certain attributes. We're going to visit the unicorn **FARM** of Utopia to describe how laws would work if we all had equal standing in a free and open society.

The laugh never gets old, does it? Please keep in mind these types of laws will liberate your peasants and should not be used on your **FARM**.

First, under the ridiculous presumption that all humans are on equal footing, laws would be an utter blessing to everyone, as they define acceptable and non-acceptable ways of interacting and determine repercussions for transgressions. But, to create laws and give them enforceability, a state must be formed. This is nothing more than a group of selected individuals from a society chosen to act as representatives to those who put them there.

NOTE: Something to keep in mind; if you're the one who puts representatives in place, shouldn't they work for you?

Anyway, these representatives in this fairytale storyline would then, under oath, adhere to a prescribed set of limited powers approved by all members of the society or, at the very least, those who wish to participate in it.[95]

In this whimsical scenario, the laws would be clear and simple to comprehend so that people of average intelligence could fully understand precisely what's expected of them and how others will formally respond if they don't play by the rules. Likewise, the laws

---

95.) Hendrickson, *Cracking the Code*, 35-38.

would only apply to those who both understand and agree with them.[96] This, in turn, would make bad laws quite simple to eradicate, as no one would support them. In early America, jurors sometimes had the audacity to find someone innocent through jury nullification if they believed the law itself was unethical or immoral.

> NOTE: Having agents in place to preside over your courtrooms to make sure just the facts and not the laws are decided upon is imperative to preserving your laws.

In a perfect world, a state would be unable to take on any new powers of its own since what is created cannot be more powerful than its creator, i.e. the people from which it came. A state is granted *authority* by those who agree to support it and actively participate in its existence. Those who represent the state also wouldn't suddenly derive any new superior powers over those they represent, as they're also members of the same society that agrees to engage in the state's existence.[97]

Since our current example is based on the noble attempt to achieve a people's law society in early America, I'll once again use it for reference to make a few additional points. For those to whom a law applies, there must be proper notification of the laws' existence and from where the law gets its derived authority.[98] Because we are referring to the original Constitution for the united States of America, this ambitious framework prescribes certain agreed upon powers, so the state can enact and enforce a specific and limited set of laws, which again, is the main reason to form a state. If any law falls outside the original enumerated powers granted to the state or is in conflict with these limited powers, that law is null and void. This is yet another reason laws were to be written in clear and concise fashion with no ambiguity. It allowed lawmakers, judges, juries and those to whom the law applied to also decide if that law had legitimate authorisation to be created in the first place. As previously mentioned, this type of lawful system would empower your peasants and should be avoided or, if already in place, dismantled.

In the land of milk and honey, proper notice of potential violations of the law is important and is why there must be at least two actors involved in a conflict. The one can serve proper notice on the other before a physical or financial injury is caused. If notice is served and

---

96.) Hendrickson, *Cracking the Code*, 38-41.
97.) Hendrickson, *Cracking the Code*, 35-37.
98.) Hendrickson, *Cracking the Code*, 41-44.

the law is clearly understood by all involved, the injured party then has a legitimate claim because of the harm done by the reckless action of another.[99] The accused can then be brought before their peers where they face their accuser and discuss the details. In this system, the accused does not need anyone to interpret the law for them nor speak on their behalf unless they're mentally incompetent or a child.

There are plenty of the latter breathing our air, aren't there?

Here, the laws are enforced under proper authority and consent and an unbiased remedy is provided based on the facts and the law.

Have you had enough of this bloody nonsense?

In a robust and dynamic society, even though more conflicts are likely to occur, having access to a stable system of justice where all can be heard helps maintain domestic tranquillity. This is exactly why we must seek to subvert it if it occurs.

Dear Lord of the Underworld, I can't take it any longer! Let's smash this system and turn it on its head, what do you say?

But, in order to do this, we must establish the Golden Rule: He who has the gold makes the rules. If you're to operate outside of the formalised legal system, you must first acquire and control that **FARM'S** wealth. You can work hard in a nine-to-five job to build up your financial portfolio, but I think you'll find it quite impossible to achieve the level of prosperity required to dictate a nation's laws by playing within the rules. Actually, unless you can indebt your society to you through a monetary system, your actions will be for naught. Once you're in financial control and can dictate the laws, you can then creatively use them to protect and enhance your interests.

Whether you need to start your own federation, infiltrate an idealistic construct like early America or seize a government whose legal system lies somewhere in between, the same techniques apply. After securing the finances, you'll need agents in the area of law operating on *your* behalf. If your country is made up of citizens freely pursuing their own interests, wielding your influence will be difficult. Therefore, you must have those operating within the system take an oath to you (even if unwittingly) which takes precedence over the one ceremoniously declared before their fellow inhabitants.

Please understand that to become the next big thing in world conquest, you must either take over the current hierarchy as is or create a brand-new world order from scratch. As you'll see, this may be quite

---

99.) Hendrickson, *Cracking the Code*, 41-44.

challenging because of the well-established institutions and behind-the-scenes collusion that has developed over many, many centuries. Also know that modern-day technology and infiltration will be used to prevent you from organising your minions, making the implementation of your system of rule even more difficult. But these are the same tactics you must use to topple your competitors.

Remember, it's a deadly game, but where there's a will, there's a way.

First, I'll give you the theory behind how and why to hijack a legal system and then show you a real-world example of how it's been done previously. To begin, if you want to be a dignified modern-day lord, you must be able to recognise and partake in social Darwinism. This is a belief in the laws of natural selection displayed in the plant and animal kingdom where the weak fall prey to the strong. In human circles, it takes a certain *chutzpah* to play outside the rules and break established spiritual laws, like that of murder and usury, to assert your dominance. For example, if you can create a scheme to fleece your brothers and sisters to enrich yourself, it's the targeted victims' own ignorance and mental weaknesses that will part them from their riches and no fault of yours for outfoxing them. This does not mean, once realised, they will not seek revenge or legal recourse.

So, my budding little flower, what shall you do to protect yourself in such a scenario? If you said, 'Take some of the snatched proceeds and pay off the best people in the "just us" system to escape prosecution', you're well on your way to grasping the concepts in this handbook.

Furthermore, what if, through your new associates, you infiltrate a long-established and reputable institution and not only form an alliance, but also have the *state* grant you and your conspirators titles of nobility to present the illusion you've achieved your success in a legitimate way?

There is nothing like being a wolf in sheep's clothing whilst using the guise of the **STATE** as your wool costume.

Baaaaa, baaaaa. Ahoooo.

But, be advised, this may come with a price, and the state may want something in return for their benevolence, like using you and your ruthless tactics to gain control of other **FARMS**. This should be embraced, as it will further build your network of influence and this symbiotic relationship will allow you to attain more wealth and power than you could ever acquire on your own. Secret oaths punishable by death when broken will, of course, be necessary to ensure that you and your colluders' interests are constantly protected and advanced for centuries to come.

Assuming you make it to this point and have taken over the entire legal enterprise and also own and control the financial system of a **FARM**, you can then begin to colour the law (also known as the colour of law) to suit your whims and fancies. But first, you must set up your legal club so that its first obligation is to the system you recreate and not to those it purports to serve. One way to do this is to establish a *reputable* organisation one *must* be a member of to *practice* law and whose inductees are chosen by other proven associates. This exclusive club membership (not a licence) *must* be revoked from any member who does not tow the proverbial line.

We talked about licensing in Chapter 7, and every meaningful profession, minus law, on today's corporate plantation receives a *licence* from the imaginary legal construct known as the **STATE**, thus giving the political structure leverage over almost all the vital industries and occupations. But with something as important as the rules that control the herd, regulation of the legal system should not fall into the hands of an authoritative entity that could find commoners amongst its ranks. That's why a private, self-governing and self-appointed affiliation that answers to no one (except, of course, a supreme ruler such as yourself) must be formed and maintained. Once in place, in order to neutralise any riff raff that finagles its way into key positions on a **FARM**, at least one private *legal* club member should be present at every important corporate and governmental gathering to shrewdly influence decision-making processes. Your trusted plants can then use the scare tactic of—drum roll please—*potential lawsuits* to frighten bureaucrats, board members, and executives, etc. into submitting to their suggestions.

> NOTE: Some may consider this extortion, but it's a very effective tactic, especially when you're in control of the court system.

Fear of legal backlash will also help push your operatives' input and legal interpretations to the forefront of every agenda. With your middlemen in place, you'll assure your system, and not the desires of your subjects, remains intact. As an added layer of protection, these exclusive club members should infiltrate every relevant institution to guarantee you control every aspect of your **FARM**.

As a reward for their participation, your ambassadors will be welcomed and esteemed card-carrying members of a superior, privileged class created by the imbalance in the justice system. Let's see how current modern-day lords have turned the land of the free into the land of the legal ball and chain, and maybe it'll spark some ideas.

First, I must ask you, where's the best place to hide something? Some think in a shoebox under a bed or in some hard-to-reach place but, oftentimes, the best place to hide something is in plain sight. Cue the BAR association. Although some have referred to the BAR as the British Accreditation Registry, its history is even more significant. If you're unfamiliar, the Temple *Bar* is one of the *gates* leading into the financial centre of the world, The City of London. Whenever the Queen of England enters *The City*, she must go to the Temple Bar and ask the Lord Mayor for permission to enter. She must remain two paces behind the Lord Mayor with her head bowed whilst walking within *The City*.[100]

It's also within THE CITY OF LONDON, INC. (an incorporated area of one to two square miles) where the private, unincorporated associations known as the Inns of Court are headquartered. They've been responsible for calling men and women to the BAR since their inception.[101] The four Inns of Court were used to control all the law in England (the first, named the Inner Temple, was established in 1346)[102] and their libraries house eight hundred years of jury trial decisions.[103]

Sounds like a legitimate law centre to me.

'So, what does all this poo pooey about the Queen and THE CITY OF LONDON, INC. have to do with taking over American law?' I can hear the thoughts racing through your inquisitive mind as I write. Please be patient with me, oh wise one, as the hysterical—my word, I mean historical—layers of the *legal* onion are peeled.

If members of a well-established, private institution receive a British title of nobility like Esquire (one rank above a gentleman but one below a knight),[104] there's no cause for alarm, correct? Well, that depends on your game plan. If you're taking over or colluding in the current system, you can always have BAR members continue to profess, through ignorance or self-preservation, that this title means nothing. Or, to weaken your adversary, you could expose this subtle clue and reveal that this title does have relevance (if indeed you have a better means of implementing and

100.) Glenn Winningham, "BAR Members 1 of 3 – they are all Agents of the Roman Cult," YouTube video, 52:42, sovereignliving, July 11, 2014, https://youtu.be/JnRJ8R7ccy8

101.) Glenn Winningham, "BAR Members 2 of 3 – They are all Foreign Agents of the Roman Cult," YouTube video, 28:23, sovereignliving, January 2, 2015, https://youtu.be/1TDs8VrVAB8

102.) Amanda Ruggeri. "The hidden world of the Knights Templar." May 13, 2016. https://www.bbc.com/travel/article/20160510-the-hidden-world-of-the-knights-templar

103.) Winningham, "BAR Members 1 of 3," 6:26-7:04.

104.) Winningham, "BAR Members 2 of 3," 18:22-18:32.

enforcing your rules), thereby subtly destroying this long-established institution.

But before I press on, 'What relevance?' you badger.

As applied to early America, there was no obligation for you to obtain a lawyer as counsel in court nor did you need to be a lawyer to act as a DA, Attorney General or judge.[105] Remember the courtroom scenes in the old classic movies where the judge is wearing a suit and not a robe? If not, I suggest you view one for a good laugh. Anyway, because bankers in England and other European countries, who were amassing great fortunes through what we now know as social Darwinism but what the meek populace refers to as fraud and theft, were seeking to escape prosecution, they began forming alliances with the best judges and lawyers' money could buy.[106] (A technique you should also apply.) Eventually, this new coalition began working in concert to deprive the easily deceived public out of their prosperity.

Along with their collaborative wealth came respectability, and the members of this growing world conquest enterprise wanted to be recognised as legitimate members of their professions. The Crown, finding some usefulness in this highly successful group of profiteers (especially when aimed at a territory like the newly formed united States of America) began doling out titles of nobility like candy at a Halloween parade. But, at the time, the International Bar Association based in the City of London was the only BAR organisation in existence and therefore was the only BAR affiliation in the world to admit members into its private club. Because the International Bar Association was aligned with the world's most influential banks, the title of Esquire was shared between the two professions.[107] But unlike today's well-trained and docile society, early Americans were quite aware of the ruthless tactics these two professions employed to achieve their wealth and power.

105.) "Formation of an Early American Legal System." US Legal.com. https://attorneys.uslegal.com/licensing-of-attorneys/history/formation-of-an-early-american-legal-system/ and Kristopher A. Nelson. "Early lawyering in colonial America." in propria persona.com. September 2011. https://inpropriapersona.com/articles/early-lawyering-in-colonial-america/ and Winningham, "BAR Members 2 of 3," 0:30-8:35.

106.) "Titles of Nobility." American History: From Revolution to Reconstruction and beyond. https://www.let.rug.nl/usa/essays/general/the-missing-13th-amendment/titles-of-nobility.php

107.) "International Bar Association." American History: From Revolution to Reconstruction and beyond. https://www.let.rug.nl/usa/essays/general/the-missing-13th-amendment/international-bar-association.php

> NOTE: This lethal combination of controlling the nation's credit, money and laws eventually allowed this newly formed syndicate to exploit the efforts of the productive, obtain their riches, taint the fairness of the laws, corrupt the courts, compromise public servants and destroy the morality of a nation.

Perfectly done I say!

This infiltration first became apparent in the United States by the early 1800s with such instances as the Jay Treaty. This back room deal in the Senate authorised a $600,000 payment of sterling silver to King George III as retribution for the American Revolution which allegedly America had won.108 Well, if America had won the conflict, why were they paying remunerations to the king? (Never underestimate the power of a good bribe to trusted agents!) By 1802, when the US government lost all its shares in the US Bank to foreign entities by way of strategically placed agents, the threat became, dare I say, very real. (Sulky Jeffersonians opposed the US Bank from the onset.)

Due to the naivety of some early Americans who hung onto the gleaming illusion of limited government of the people, by the people and for the people, these senseless altruists felt that they needed to act decisively to stop the incursion. Although titles of nobility were forbidden in Article One Section Nine of the Constitution for the united States of America specifically to prevent members from the International BAR Association from holding positions of public trust, there was no punishment included for such a breach of this provision.

In 1810, the Titles of Nobility Amendment (TONA), also known as the missing 13th Amendment, was one of the most powerful obstacles introduced to stop this brilliantly conceived foreign coalition from seizing absolute power.

'Missing? But whatever do you mean?' you ask as you scratch the casing of your befuddled brain.

Well, it's been widely accepted that TONA was never ratified into law. And it would have remained that way if it had not been for some pesky purists and their discovery found buried deep in the archives of a few historical libraries. You see these persistent parasites uncovered state constitutions published between the years of 1822 and 1860.109

108.) David Dodge. "The Missing 13th Amendment: *No Lawyers Allowed In Public Office*." The Millennium Report.com. October 24, 2015. https://themillennium-report.com/2015/10/the-missing-13th-amendment-no-lawyers-allowed-in-public-office/

109.) David Dodge. "The True Back Story of the Missing 13th Amendment." The

Unfortunately, these older state constitutions included both federal and state constitutions in the same booklet for cross referencing to prevent the state from overstepping both federal and state restraints and, in turn, acquiring unauthorised power.

Now, we wouldn't want that to happen, would we?

Regrettably, at that time, every state had a constitution containing the *missing* 13th Amendment. But is this enough proof to show the *missing* 13th Amendment had been ratified? Well…ah…of course not, that's why it's important to direct any doubters to the National Archives building where records of this so-called ratification can be found. Unfortunately, the building burned to the ground during the War of 1812 and all its records were destroyed.

Oh my, what an unfortunate event. I suppose it's a mere coincidence that the same country, England, hosting this noble alliance, which was subverting America with its agents, was the same country that torched this glorified warehouse and converted it into a pile of smouldering ash. For now, they'll just have to take our word for it that the Titles of Nobility Amendment was never ratified, won't they?

> IMPORTANT NOTE: When programming the masses, such a purposeful undertaking as the burning of the National Archives building should be presented as a minor chronological detail whilst the backstory and the real reason the event occurred should be deliberately omitted from the storyline.

The beautiful thing about being on the winning side of history is that you can change the facts to fit your narrative. Things can disappear with barely a trace, as they should if you're to keep the confiscation of your peasants' wealth and freedom from them to present the illusion of freedom (Chapter 13).

'But what is in the *missing* 13th Amendment that incited all of the fuss?' you lament.

Quite simply, it reads as such:

'If any citizen of the United States shall accept, claim, receive or retain any title of nobility or honour (Your honour), or shall without the consent of Congress, accept and retain any present, pension, office or emolument of any kind whatsoever from any emperor, king, prince,

---

Millennium Report. April 11, 2016. https://themillenniumreport.com/2016/04/the-true-back-story-of-the-missing-13th-amendment/ and Alfred Adask interviewed by William Wagener, "Thee MISSING Original 13th Amendment, part 1," YouTube video, 14:26, William WAGENER, March 28, 2011, https://youtu.be/Qpp6sIP19dM?si=7Hon-1Cu9M1DmXLu

or foreign power, *such person shall cease to be a citizen of the United States and shall be incapable of holding any office of trust or profit under them, or either of them.'*

Well, those are fighting words if you're a foreign power looking to covertly hijack a nation.

Also, if you're trying to subvert a **FARM** and a similar measure is put in place, you must do whatever is necessary to infiltrate and take control of the financial and legal systems whilst also keeping its people ignorant of this fact. Fortunately, you can keep a nation of people so uninformed that they actually assist you in your endeavours.

Stockholm Syndrome anyone?

In previous chapters, we saw the dramatic change in America after the Civil War when the District of Columbia was incorporated. With the original united States of America bankrupt and on its knees, this was an opportune time to move in the first American BAR association, which was established in New York in 1878.[110] Once in place, changing the laws for the benefit of the money trust behind THE UNITED STATES OF AMERICA, INC. began its wonderful evolution. Early on, only one branch, the judicial, contained members of the BAR association. But by the 1960s, sixty percent of all elected members of the American government belonged to the BAR, allowing a complete takeover of the *government* by a foreign power.[111] This was done by joining all three branches together with members of one exclusive organisation.

Infiltration, infiltration, infiltration, I tell you!

'So, in what form did the manipulation of the people's law appear?' you excitedly persist.

Well, I'm aching to deliver this crafty colouring of the laws to you. So, let's proceed, if it's fine by you.

To start, BARbarians were people who did not speak the common language and hence could only be understood by those inside their tribe. Similarly, legalese is a language that's only understood by those within the legal profession—BAR members. The wonderful thing about this codified language is that it's used as a deterrent against peasants looking to speak for themselves. If peasants did speak for themselves, their mutterings could be entered as testimonial evidence. To avoid

---

110.) "History of the American Bar Association." Upcounsel.com. https://www.up-counsel.com/lectl-history-of-the-american-bar-association
111.) Brett D. Gilman. "Why Are So Many Politicians Lawyers?" Hill Reporter.com. March 27, 2022. https://hillreporter.com/why-are-so-many-politicians-law-yers-127943

this, peasants are made to feel they aren't qualified to offer their own version of the events because they don't speak the language of the court. Instead, peasants are directed to accept a hearsay substitute to act as an interpreter/translator for them. Attorneys are never under oath and can say just about anything you need them to say. This allows the court to base its decisions on third-party interpretations and translations of the facts rather than direct testimonies.

> NOTE: This surrogate can also be of great service to you when it comes to protecting you and your associates from things like self-incrimination and perjury if the unfortunate scenario arises where you or one of your associates ends up in court.

Today, BAR members condemn witless peasants for not knowing how to fill out proper lawyer forms, criticise them because they aren't trained in law and shame and harass them because they don't know court rules. All these tactics are used to trick peasants into delegating their authority to an officer of the court whose first duty is to the court and to the public not his client as per CJS (*Corpus Jurus Secundum*) *Volume 7 Section 4*. With private members controlling all aspects of the proceedings, peasants have little hope of receiving a fair trial and are subject to whatever outcome you and your associates desire.

But even more pleasing and dastardly is using legalese to muddy the laws so much that only those with *special training* can interpret them. This not only gives BAR members an unfair advantage when it comes to decoding these hard-to-understand decrees for their own use (creating a superior class), but it also leaves room for members of the club to interpret a law to their liking and use it against a peasant regardless of the edict's true intent.

Consequently, with attorneys also filling the legislative branches of the US government, they can further lengthen the laws with so much legalese that peasants will pay any amount of money to avoid the headache of having to decipher the jibber jabber contained on an onslaught of pages. Therefore, they'll simply go along with anything they're told to do for fear of getting caught up in a ball of legal red tape. The ambiguity created by the handsomely paid legislatures to craft hundreds of thousands of incomprehensible words will also allow other BAR members the wiggle room necessary to use the law for political not societal gain, thereby enriching the **STATE**, its corporations and the grandmaster of it all—you. Of course, no one actually reads the gibberish contained in the bills that later become laws anyway, especially the *representatives* elected to serve the peasants. This will leave the courts plenty of latitude to improvise when it comes to interpreting the meaning of a law. As long as a law's content lands somewhere in the ballpark, it can be bent to suit you and your associates' agendas, not the peasants'.

Finally, a confusing law can trick most members on a **FARM**, rich and poor, young or old, into feeling obligated to follow a dictate that excludes them from its application. The thousands of confusing pages found in the Internal Revenue Code serve as a gloating illustration of this technique. *The code* is also an example of *positive law*. This is yet another shade of colour in a scheme that leaves the accused with no human victim or notifying party which, as discussed, is a qualifier for a legitimate law. Instead, a positive law requires a positive action and is very unnatural as compared to a law requiring restraint such as one to prevent murder or theft. The beauty of a positive law is that when violated, its only victim is the hapless peasant. It's as if the peasant has signed some sort of contractual obligation to perform for the imaginary entity known as the **STATE**.

It's quite beautiful how this all ties together, wouldn't you agree?

It should be noted that, in a true people's law society, a man or woman would only have to contend with laws setup to protect themselves and others from harm to their persons and property, or for a breach of contract. In this type of system, there are few laws, and therefore each one carries more weight. But when inserting your agents to defend and prosecute for a make-believe construct known as the **STATE**, there's no limit to the oppressive boundaries you can place on your subjects.

You see, with a godlike, imaginary entity called the **STATE**, it can appear everywhere, at all times, and can be offended and violated even when there's no actual victim or claimant. An example of this is a crime against oneself like the use/possession of drugs or not properly securing one's seatbelt. No one's hurt in such a situation but potentially the peasant, but why ruin all the fun? It's important to make peasants comply with things that you insist are good for them so your **FARM** can operate the way you want it to whilst allowing you to profit from every infraction peasants commit. Remember, peasants signed a contract called a licence to obey all the rules and regulations of the road that are bestowed upon them.

When an alleged victim drops charges, your all-powerful **STATE** can take over the charges. Remember, it's the peasants' consent to the commercial system via their ENS LEGIS that ties them to its corporate laws and therefore binds them to the outcome in the form of jail time.

Oh, how fun it is to watch them squirm without the slightest idea why.

You can also use case law to further empower your judges. This is the art of allowing a judge's decision to become the law instead of following the traditional route through the legislature where a few peasants could become elected members. Instead of a judge's verdict being an example of the application of a specific law used in a court decision—voila—the judge's ruling is now the law of the land. This little shortcut is a much quicker and more expansive way to pin your vassals down under the entangling web of the state.

Now's the perfect time to point out that real crimes involving peasants against other peasants or their property—whoops, I mean your property—as well as breaches of contracts should also be punished by your *legal* system to give it the appearance of serving your inhabitants. The only part of the notification process that should be legitimate is the court's correspondence through the mail and its record keeping duties. This will help create the illusion of authenticity.

In addition, laws against hate crimes and hate speech can further regulate peasants' freedom to express themselves because they may cross the sensitivity threshold of those who belong to a different social group or race. This alone achieves a myriad of objectives. For one, it prevents peasants from being disruptive and ensures a proper respect for authority. Peasants must be trained to be timid especially when facing oppressive policies from your political structure. If limited speech is the norm, outspoken peasants will need to second-guess any decision they make to inform others. Actual hate crime laws will help keep your peasants divided into subgroups and will have them at odds with each other, leaving less work for you. If one of your peasants commits an injurious act against another peasant, in theory, it's a crime regardless of the race or subgroup the victim belongs to but, as you can clearly see, the proclamation of a hate crime allows you to pit group against group, further widening their division.

Hate crimes can also be used as a protective device for your peasant management team. If you can assign a race or religion to your organisation and then victimise the disposable members of that same chosen subgroup, you can create laws to punish anyone who lets even the slightest derogatory term about your chosen cartel front slip off their filthy tongues. As you can probably deduce, especially if you're cut out to run a world empire, you can create sympathy and protection for a chosen subgroup by creating, funding or facilitating a publicly traumatizing event against a subgroup's members, especially one of horrific proportions. This can be real, imaginary or both and can be accomplished through war, psychological operations or false flag events and must be trumpeted through your information outlets.

If you can successfully criminalise words peasants speak (even though their words may or may not incite the actions of others) the exciting possibility exists to punish them for their thoughts even if they don't follow through. Just for fun, imagine a peasant relaxing on their sofa, only to have their door kicked in by armed soldiers who drag them off to an interrogation centre because they formed the thoughts of a dissident? When you own your peasants' thoughts, you'll completely own the peasants, making an Orwellian superstate a real possibility.

Ew, I just got chills! I do hope I get to see it in my lifetime.

Since laws are established to protect you and your associates' interests, once you gain your peasants trust and compliance, the laws should be gradually morphed into a working playbook that justifies your trespasses against them. This was done in Nazi Germany just before Hitler turned his country into a genetic laboratory and is currently taking place in the United States under the guise of the War on Terror. This brilliant scheme, via legislation, has allowed **FARM** owners to legally assassinate their own *citizens* without a proper trial under *laws* like the Authorization to Use Military Force Act (PL 107-40). An enactment like this will come in handy when peasants question the events used to justify a new system. As an additional safeguard, a measure like the 2013 National Defense Authorization Act *legally* allows government propaganda to be presented as factual stories to keep obedient dwellers in a state of denial and, hence, under your control. Even though false reporting has been in practice for quite some time, the responsible parties are now *legally* covered if enough peasants wake up to the totalitarian world being built around them.

Well, it's not like anyone was breaking the law. Nudge, nudge. I don't hear anyone complaining, do you?

> NOTE: If you aren't cut out to run the world (don't despair as many are not) you can still use several of the techniques in this handbook to reach higher levels of society through such avenues as industry, the military and government.

Since being elected to a position in government takes funding, the candidates willing to compromise their *principles* will have much more success in raising the money necessary to gain both public awareness and acceptance. Once in office, if they aren't already an agent, these anointed baby-kissers can be approached by agents ready to grease their palms in order to put your rules and regulations in place. This backdoor influence is especially important if the illusion of freedom must be maintained. The term *lobbyist* refers to an earlier time when interested parties waited in the hallways of parliament for a recess hoping to influence decision makers. Legend also has it that those seeking political favours would similarly wait in the lobby of the Willard Hotel in Washington DC to access President Ulysses S. Grant who would frequent the bar to enjoy brandy and a cigar.

Oh, the promises that can be obtained when one has such a magnificent vice.

To keep the illusion of freedom going, crafty orators are assets well worth nurturing. They'll work on your behalf yet skilfully tell the ignorant public what it wants to hear. That's why the following stratagems should be applied to provide cover for their allegiance to your agenda. A few quick examples will illustrate these useful techniques in action.

The NDAA (National Defense Authorization Act) is renewed by vote every year on the American **FARM**. Since peasants seek a ruler's protection, only one in a million will object to spending *public* money on their *safety* as insinuated by the National Defense Act. This is especially true if you can jolt them into a good little scare from an outside bogeyman (more on this topic in later chapters). Therefore, such a bill makes the perfect cover for any oppressive legislation that needs to be subtly snuck into law. Furthermore, it gives *representatives* the justification needed to vote for the measure despite any grumblings from those paying close attention to your back door efforts. You must, however, be sure to drown out these agitators through persistent media propaganda and political fear mongering. If you can keep the majority of your peasants busy, ill-informed and scared enough, you can completely rewrite an entire system of laws without the peasants noticing.

To show the stark contrast between working for you and, I can barely say it, working for them, two points should be brought to the forefront. Let's start with the gut-wrenching notion of representing an entire society in a fair and compassionate way. If a law/bill is to be accepted, funded and followed, it should be simple to understand and should only contain one subject matter.

Second, it should be read and understood by those voting on behalf of the benefactors so a determination can be made as to whether the new law meets the proper requirements of constitutional authority. However, if the officeholder is working for you, a modern-day lord, the laws should be confusing, lengthy, contain multiple subjects and avoid serious scrutiny. The orator can then use their talents to justify their vote by using the latitude provided in varying parts of the legislation. Inundating peasants with an onslaught of laws/bills will stymie their efforts to single out and stop laws most detrimental to their interests.

This brings me to the summation of this chapter. To allow your **FARM** to grow and prosper, there should be few laws. They should contain details of the expectations placed on its societal members and the repercussions for violations. To take the reins and regulate every aspect of the peasants' lives, statutes and codes should be abundant and should flow from as many avenues as possible, including federal, state and local governments, as well as from agencies created to monitor peasants and their every move. As you instinctively know, he who has the gold makes the rules. If you're to be the self-professed ruler of your **FARM**, the most important law passed into existence *must* prohibit any competitors from threatening your dominance over the money supply. Once achieved, all further laws can be craftily applied to bleed the wealth of your peasants and further restrict their independence and movements. A law is nothing without enforcement, as you'll discover in the next chapter.

Now the fun really begins!

Chapter 10

ENFORCEMENT

What good is a smooth tongue without sharp teeth?
— Jocelyn Murray

Assuming you have what it takes to carefully select and place your skilled orators in political offices and establish the rules, these efforts are completely for naught if you don't have the threat of a heavy club ready to crash down on your peasants' thick skulls should they step out of line. As discussed in Chapter 2, if you can establish fear in your herd, especially for infractions of your rules, you'll create order on your **FARM**. Remember, humans can fear tomorrow, therefore strong and reliable enforcement actions will keep them aware of the repercussions for daring to cross your boundaries.

> NOTE: It's amusing that American peasants are actually advised through the subtle expression Attorney at law (versus Attorney in law) that those purportedly representing their freedoms and rights are actually hacking away at the just us system by dabbling at law rather than being rooted in law. This isn't just for laughs, although it does provide a hearty chuckle.

This also goes back to the time-tested, well-established legal maxim *qui tacet consentire videtur* (silence gives consent). As long as peasants are told those representing them are tinkering around with law, rather than being based in law, it's no fault of your own if they never figure out this brutal, in-your-face reality. It really is this easy.

The level of enforcement and harshness you use on your human nursery will depend on the type of goals you have for your **FARM**. First, we'll discuss moderate and useful forms of enforcement for more *open* societies until we arrive at the more deeply satisfying jack-boot-in-the-face type methods used on more restrictive **FARMS**.

A word of warning: too much force can result in a violent backlash from your herd, so use extreme caution when implementing these methods. Typically, force is used to gain immediate compliance during times of civil unrest, but it can also be creatively used to pit peasants against each other on the same **FARM** or on opposing **FARMS**, leading to such profitable outcomes as war. This will be more deeply discussed in Chapter 14.

Before we discuss well-intentioned enforcement approaches naively designed to benefit a *society,* another incredibly useful concept needs to be brought to the forefront. Like the idea of *interest* that'll have your peasants spending much of their precious time and labour to repay you for something that doesn't exist, the illusory idea known as *authority* will not only have your peasants quivering in their boots at the thought of defying you, but they'll turn over their decision-making abilities to you as well. This can be efficiently accomplished through early age training where you begin to teach your peasants to entrust you with all their important decisions whilst allowing them to manage their more frivolous affairs.

Developments into this type of training have been so effective, you can make your subordinates completely dependent on you. Once peasants submit to your system, you'll not only solve their biggest problems (usually problems you create to enrich yourself and your associates), but you'll tell them how to dress, what to eat and what to think. You can even control their relationships to others regarding class, sexual orientation, religion, nationality, race, political affiliation and any other divisive issues. Remember, it's of the utmost importance to create separations in your herd to prevent them from *uniting.*

Also, the powerful phenomenon known as Stockholm Syndrome will have peasants obeying your orders and holding others accountable to your dispiriting policies. This will make enforcement easier. Those who disobey your laws must be taught a valuable lesson. Someone needs to have the courage to manage the herd. Give me one good reason why this shouldn't be you. As I was saying…

Peasants would much rather experience the tranquillity of their familiar lives than take a leap of faith into the unknown and be truly free. Being free makes them responsible for their own protection and sustenance. The ruler providing these comforts will win their loyalty. It's a sliding scale as to how much oppression you can impose before creating a backlash. As long as you keep them fed and entertained, as the old Roman adage of bread and circuses dictates, they'll find little reason to revolt. Over time, they'll simply learn to adapt to their tighter yet more invisible bondage. Remember, strictly enforcing the rules on your **FARM** will bring about a preferred familiarity that'll have them warmly accepting your guidelines even though these *laws* benefit you and not them.

> NOTE: There's no greater way to pass an oppressive new policy than to tell peasants it's for their own good. If they trust you enough, most will gladly open their wallets, not to mention their eager hearts, to put this new tenet in place.

The most important enforcement action you can execute on your **FARM** is both the protection of your monopoly over the money supply and the collection of the interest on the debt your peasants owe you for the privilege of using your paper banknotes. Otherwise, how are you to reign above them, a pitiful nine-to-five job?

Your tax collection policies and agents should be the most stringent and most feared. To stay on top, even the slightest compromise in this area will result in the loss of your ability to thrive off the toil of your inferiors.

Enforcement of fines and other ways of depriving your peasants of their time and personal wealth should also be met with dire consequences should they refuse to cooperate. But all other enforcement actions will fail in comparison if you cannot persuade your peasants to fund the corporate construct via taxation.

> NOTE: The more ruthless and brazen you are in terms of creating a highly productive and obedient **FARM**, the more leverage you'll have in taking over other **FARMS**, and eventually, the world.

This is the perfect segue into another important enforcement action, desertion during times of war. The matter of taking over other **FARMS** is serious business, and one wrong move can result in a great loss for you and your ambitions. Can you imagine what would happen if the grunts fighting your bloody conflicts felt they could just lay down their arms and walk away? The results would be devastating. Therefore, it's critically important that any dereliction of duty be met with swift consequences. The stakes are high, that's why your military must be the most focused and clearest thinking in society. Capital punishment should be a very real consequence, leaving peasants with the choice of death if they walk away from a battle or possible survival if they continue to fight.

> NOTE: On most **FARMS**, you'll find it necessary to make military service mandatory to protect your interests. Remember, other **FARMS** will want to take over your **FARM** since it's a race to the top. The ruler with the strongest world view and the one able to convince the most people to fight for their cause will be the self-proclaimed ruler of the world.

Finish this handbook as soon as possible! There isn't a second to spare.

Before the modern-day control techniques illustrated in this manual were fully developed and available, keeping peasants from becoming unruly was a necessary objective. A large mob forming at the entrance of a castle could be quite a threat. As more advanced systems of *national* defence came into being and production methods improved, keeping those whose talents were being exploited for the advancement of their **FARM** content and on point was of the utmost urgency. Therefore, there are two early forms of *peacekeeping* that led to modern-day policing.

Over a thousand years ago in Anglo-Saxon England, the king appointed a reeve (an agent of the crown) to a shire (county) to tend to the peasants and their trivial disputes. The reeve reported back to his sovereign lordship.

But when those in the *land of the free,* a.k.a. America, got the preposterous idea that each inhabitant was their own sovereign (king), the shire-reeve (sheriff) began working for his new kings, a.k.a. the people of the land, to protect and defend their rights and interests.[112]

Well, of course, you cannot assert your dominance over so many rulers without running into some obstacles, like a well-armed sheriff's department. Over time, this position had to be taken back under the control of a self-appointed ruler. Can you see what must be done if the **FARM** you wish to control has such a distribution of power in place? It's my pleasure to report, in many areas of the American **FARM**, the sheriff has been reduced to a courthouse lackey who doesn't even have the power to make an arrest. That's important if the person they try to arrest, upon demand from their boss (the people), is you.

In some counties in the United States, the sheriff is appointed by those representing the ruling power's interest (such as county commissioners) rather than elected by the whining peasants who clamour for their rights, something a ruler grants them anyway. There are even some subdivisions of the American **FARM** (**STATES**)

112.) Richard Mack, The County Sheriff: America's Last Hope (Pima, AZ: 2009), 23.

where this nuisance of a public servant has been completely eliminated.

The second peacekeeper, known as a Bobbie, was established in 1829 and named after the founder of England's first government created police force, Sir Robert Peel.[113] At first, as I'm sure you can imagine, there was great concern amongst peasants that a monopolised enforcement unit created by the state would be used to crush political opposition and squash privileges that the whimpering populace were so kindly granted. (I've heard of worse ideas.) In England, before the Bobbies, the majority of criminal matters were handled by constables, night watchmen and red coat soldiers. The soldiers, whose loyalty belonged to the ruling class, would not only be called upon to restore order during times of civil unrest, but dabbled in local crime as well. But would a full-time, state-created gang responsible for maintaining law and order abuse their power?

Unfortunately, during the Bobbies' formative years, they did not. Instead, they protected and served their fellow citizens. Hilariously, the success of this early form of state policing was not measured in terms of tickets or arrests but by the absence of crime and disorder. Talk about missed opportunities. This early form of *consent* policing focused on crime prevention and the Bobbies were to offer service, courtesy and friendliness to all members of the public despite their social status. Of course, these bumbling fools carrying only billy clubs and whistles were prevented from expanding their jurisdiction into the financial centre, a.k.a. THE CITY OF LONDON, INC. where a more finely groomed department patrolled.

> NOTE: This primitive form of policing, that encouraged physical force only when absolutely necessary, wasn't used to enforce the moral behaviour of individuals. That was left to the family, the community and the churches (institutions you must break down and corrupt for total control over your **FARM**). The Bobbies were simply instated to protect peasants from each other.

This should raise a few red flags from those advanced enough to recognise the most effective ways to rule over their subjects. First, and foremost, if you don't lead with the threat of force, you cannot whip your peasants into compliance with your dictates, let alone cause an underlying resentment to your rule which will typically appear in

---

113.) Elizabeth Nix. "Why are British police officers called "Bobbies"?" History.com. December 10. 2104, last modified August 22, 2018. https://www.history.com/news/why-are-british-police-officers-called-bobbies

peasant against peasant transgressions. Whether this has the police warring against citizens or has some peasants acting more viciously towards other peasants, the result is the same. As the old saying by Aristotle goes: 'Anybody can become angry–that is easy, but to be angry with the right person and to the right degree and at the right time and for the right purpose, and in the right way–that is not within everybody's power and is not easy.'

In short, the majority of peasants are not smart enough to realise it's your rule causing their hardships, and they'll turn on each other because those within their sphere of society are easier targets to retaliate against. This is why you must divide them in as many ways as possible. Infighting leaves them too distracted to focus on your encroachments, and if you set yourself up correctly, leaves them unable to set their differences aside to unify against you. Of course, any good modern-day lord is completely prepared for the unfortunate scenario of a peasant uprising.

Secondly, to totally regulate the peasants' behaviour, and profit from their weaknesses, it's important to not only criminalise their transgressions toward each other but also against themselves (a.k.a. victimless crimes). Since mankind is riddled with flaws and many of these modern-day Neanderthals are both aimless and careless, there are many ways to prosper from their imperfections.

As discussed previously, the Catholic Church first implemented such a profitable system on human frailty when parishioners could buy forgiveness for their sins. This type of profiteering was maybe a bit too obvious but led to an enforcement system that was devised to keep citizens *safe* from others and most ingeniously of all, from themselves. This scheme not only left peasants screaming for its implementation but as still shown today, also secured their strict adherence.

I hope you're learning that the world isn't one of nations and ideologies but a business operating under the law of contracts (Admiralty Law/Law of the Sea). Enforcement agents are usually the ones who engage the easily fooled peasants into negotiations. A ticket (also known as a presentment) is made by a corporation's enforcement officers for any infraction of a previously signed adhesion contract (such as a commercial driver's licence) a peasant has tacitly agreed to. Peasants will unknowingly sign the new business offer and even thank the agent for not pulling them out of their car and beating them to a bloody pulp, although this threat should always be ominously present. Otherwise, why would peasants agree to such a lopsided arrangement?

Even if peasants resist and refuse to sign, if they don't contest the presentment before a proper *authority* or don't provide a proper remedy for their infraction, they'll be *charged* for it. Remember, silence is consent, and if the peasants do nothing, they passively agree to the terms and conditions of the newly administered contract. They are in dishonour if they don't settle the offer.

It's important to keep cost-free remedies out of the peasants' realm of understanding so you and your associates can apply them to your advantage whilst leaving peasants uninformed. Peasants will then be forced to settle offers with their time, labour and energy.

My aim isn't to teach you the ins and outs of the current system, but to simply advise you how to gain complicity from your herd. However, for a contract to have merit, all terms of the contract *must* be revealed. But, as always, there's some wiggle room if your peasants are neither smart nor inquisitive enough to discover any hidden terms of a contract or seek remedies available to them. This is why a variety of adhesion contracts (if you decide to use them) should be as lengthy and confusing as possible. This alone will exasperate even the most analytic of your chattel, leaving them no choice but to comply. For those who persist, a winding maze of obstacles from within your system should be used to block any awakened peasant's path. The heavy hand of force must be applied if a peasant refuses to concede. This is also why control of the courts and prisons is so important.

Last, allotting any sort of power to families, churches and communities also directly takes power away from their ruler, a.k.a. you.

Families, churches and communities are much more effective at resolving personal demons of the afflicted but, as I hope you're emphatically asking yourself right now, how am I to profit from their vulnerabilities if I allow others to rehabilitate them?

Oh, how I love your magnificent train of thought!

NOTE: If your aim were really to change the peasants' behaviour, perhaps pulling them over and giving them thirty lashes for such violations as speeding would slow them down a bit. This technique can be seen on **FARMS** where, for instance, a hand is removed from those who steal to discourage theft. Remember, there are two ways to conquer a nation and hence its people. One is by sword, the other by debt. Having peasants buy their way out of their wrongdoings forces them to turn their money and property over to you, further indebting them, whilst harsher penalties make them more obedient and more under your control. Perhaps a healthy combination of both is the way to go. Again, this manual simply illustrates the various techniques available whilst leaving it up to you to choose the ones you'd like to impose on your **FARM**.

As societies advanced beyond the days of Machiavelli and his ruler's handbook, *The Prince*, the dangers of having a standing military enforce law and order became more common knowledge amongst peasants. Although some societies such as China, North Korea and Russia still overtly use their military against civilians, **FARMS** that attempted more *humane* forms of domestic civility had to be infiltrated with more care.

As we learned in Chapter 8, there was an overreaching use of military force during the Civil War and its ensuing Reconstruction Era that provoked a bit of whimpering from former Southern slave owners who were demoted to the same menial social standing (14th Amendment Citizens) as the Black slaves they once subjugated. To temporarily appease these howls of inequity and such claims as voter suppression by the Union Army at the polls, the Posse Comitatus Act was passed in 1878, long after military law and order in the south was fully established. This act essentially prevented the Army, and later Air Force, Navy and Marines, from being called upon to enforce the laws of the United States against its own citizens.

NOTE: This act doesn't say anything about prohibiting law enforcement agencies from using military equipment. These specialised munitions, of course, must be carefully maintained and operated by full-time military personnel, rather than hapless, untrained civilians.

You see, it just goes to show, there is always a work-around.

Furthermore, once you control the laws and courts, there's a sliding scale as to what can be considered a rebellion, an insurrection, domestic violence/terrorism, or an unlawful conspiracy that can then be used as reasons to override attempts to block your military dictatorship. If your lawmakers are crafty enough, you can even pin any one or all these egregious civil disturbances on any one of your peasants for simply waking up in the morning.

Finally, as will be discussed later in this chapter, the door has already been flung wide open in regard to information sharing between law enforcement agencies, intelligence communities and militaries worldwide due to a bold and bloody experiment during the Vietnam War.

Like a shark in the ocean, you must thrive on the scent of blood. I know I certainly do.

Since the Posse Comitatus Act was a noble attempt to prevent an incredibly sexy…I mean, a malicious dictator from overstepping their bounds, we'll now discuss the five and only five crimes United States federal law agencies were originally granted jurisdiction over.

At this point it should come as no surprise that the American *freedom* experiment is over. But, as I'm sure you can see, it's sure fun and insightful to learn from its gradual demise.

These initial five federal enforcement duties did not involve drugs, tobacco, firearms or even missing children, as your television might lead you to believe. The original five were:

1. those within the military
2. those against the law of nations (violations of international law)
3. piracy/misconduct committed on the high seas
4. counterfeiting
5. treason

Did a bead of sweat just roll down your forehead, especially at the mention of the last three? Don't be concerned. Well, unless you lack the courage and are completely unable to reverse such federal actions for your benefit. Still confused? Let me further explain.

First, if you didn't recognise that piracy has already been set up in America and much of the world in the form of a *maritime* legal system, you need to study Chapter 7 more carefully. Admiralty law is the law of contracts and since the world is now a giant business, to become its CEO, you'll need to seize the vessels and property of disobedient peasants when necessary. Modern-day pirating on these cleverly established imaginary waterways has allowed lords to covertly accomplish this *legal* form of piracy with barely a whimper.

Brilliant, I say.

These bold and creative moves will be necessary to inconspicuously hijack a FARM, especially a free one. Perhaps you can conjure up a more highly efficient and profitable imaginary system that can be implemented for your benefit. Just remember: this is one of the many reasons you cannot let your peasants *unite,* as they may one day want to take back the property you've ingeniously seized from them.

Secondly, since it's explicitly stated in both the Constitution **for** the united States of America and The Constitution **of** the United States that only gold and silver coin are to be used as a tender in the payment of debts, any digression from these specific instructions is clearly considered counterfeiting.

> NOTE: On any **FARM**, you can at least remove scrutiny of your counterfeiting activities if you can provide a convenient money system that will allow subjects to shed cumbersome remunerations like gold and silver from their pockets in the name of expediency. Just remember, as a ruler, you need to do most of the work. Keeping your peasants comfortable will shut down their critical thinking skills and allow you to unobtrusively operate behind the scenes.

Even if you're able to divert the average peasants' attention away from your financial takeover, you *must* also direct those sworn to protect the issuance of sound money elsewhere. Maintaining the integrity of the currency is one of the key ingredients for a *nation* to achieve wealth and freedom. That's why you must subvert it. Since the primary goal of any good modern-day lord is to set up a counterfeit system of cheaply produced and readily available paper, you must obviously misapply such a highly esteemed federal policing duty. As discussed, this is done by outlawing and strictly enforcing any competition to your clearly marked and identifiable paper bills which hopefully, one day, have your picture on them.

In this scenario, since lords and their associates were (and still are) successfully committing the most serious charges (treason, counterfeiting and pirating) it was of the utmost importance to turn federal agents outward toward peasants rather than at them and their, at one time, punishable-by-death activities.

> NOTE: The aim of enforcement agents should be at peasants and their more mundane or even pithy infractions rather than at you and your more serious crimes. Remember, commit a small crime, go to jail. Commit a monstrous crime, become a king. You must have the chutzpah to break all rules if you want to emerge from the plethora of wannabe lords reading this handbook. This is true even at the risk of death or being incarcerated for the rest of your life.
>> Do you still believe you have what it takes to rule the world? We shall see.

Once *authority* is established and then deeply entrenched on your new **FARM**, you can begin to branch out by placing enforcement agents everywhere to track all peasant activity whilst simultaneously protecting your own interests. As just discussed, this must start at the top of the pyramid, or in the American **FARM** example, the federal level. This is shown by agencies like the Federal Bureau of Investigation (FBI) and Central Intelligence Agency (CIA), repeatedly used to facilitate the lawlessness of the current rulers of the American **FARM** by suppressing incriminating evidence pointing back at them. The examples are too numerous to mention but can be seen in such hustles as the drug trafficking used to fund the Iran-Contra affair, the plane part serial numbers withheld after the 9/11 attacks and the sabotage of evidence found after the Koresh standoff in Waco, Texas.[114]

What? Surprised or even amazed by these statements? If you still don't see the importance of partaking in such illicit activities to accomplish your goals whilst reading this handbook perhaps you can instead bask in the glory of being a cashier at a local knitting shop.

> NOTE: The term national security, meaning cover-up in layman's terms, should also be added to your lexicon. You can more easily disseminate this term once you have placed the fear of God in your peasants and assured them you must keep certain secrets from them to protect them. Isn't it invigorating to know the details of the assassination of the leader of the free world (i.e. John F. Kennedy) have been kept under lock and key for more than fifty years? This type of loyalty is required from your most trusted agents to prevent dissension and the revealing of state secrets on your **FARM**. On other **FARMS**, similar secret services exist such as the Mossad in Israel, the KGB in Russia, the MI6 in the United Kingdom and the crème de la crème of all intelligence agencies, overseeing the Holy See and working for the Superior General of the Society of Jesus, a.k.a. the Black Pope, the Jesuits.

This is the primary organisation you must subdue or eliminate if you're to become the new ruler of the planet. You will, however, need a little more than dumb luck to accomplish this lofty task because *they* probably know you're reading this handbook right now whilst you have no idea who or where *they* are. A healthy dose of paranoia will serve you well. You need to be looking over your shoulder constantly on your way to the pinnacle of society.

114.) Gary Webb, *Dark Alliance: The CIA, the Contras, and the Crack Cocaine Explosion* (New York: Seven Stories Press, 1998), 481-485. Aidan Monaghan, *Declassifying 9/11: A Between the Lines and Behind the Scenes Look at the September 11 Attacks* (Indiana: iUniverse, 2012), 29-35. Jason Van Vleet, "Waco – A New Revelation," YouTube video, 1:49:50, rtxyz1, January 8, 2014, https://youtu.be/Xr9pQ1pIbiU

It's also important to realise that the most horrific atrocities throughout history have been carried out by order takers. You must fill the ranks of your enforcement arms with order takers if you're to carry out your darkest whims and fancies whilst keeping your own hands blood free. If you seek a high level of control over your peasants, a monopolised **STATE**-sanctioned system will serve you and your associates best. On the federal level, enforcement in every area of the peasants' lives, including the food they grow and eat, the land they use, the substances they put in their bodies, their means of travelling, what they hear and see on media distribution outlets, the things they purchase and the way they earn their money, must all be tightly monitored.

The enforcement agents closest to you (secret service, federal agents, etc.), must be the best of the best and generously compensated. This will win their loyalty and give other order takers something to aspire to. A brotherhood should be established, and perks and privileges not afforded to other peasants should be granted to members of this esteemed fraternity. Of course, trumpeting the fact that these *secret* services are provided for the peasants' safety should be repeated often. In some instances, this may be true and will serve as motivation for your chosen few to put themselves in harm's way.

Enforcement agents willing to put the needs of peasants ahead of yours and your associates should be demoted, fired or, at the very least, prevented from advancement. The bullies, people who were bullied in their formative years, those seeking power over others and especially those returning home from combat, are the ideal types to be recruited and promoted. Critical thinkers in the field of law enforcement are detrimental to your objectives. Candidates with low IQs are ideal. Their training should only teach them how to enforce laws not how to interpret them. An enforcement agent must be willing to *legally* extort peasants for the good of the **STATE**.

The best candidates are those who are unable to succeed in the private sector, making them quite useful in collecting revenue for the **STATE** by taking it from those who are productive.

Besides the onslaught of federal enforcement agencies on the American **FARM** that have been set up to arrest peasants for such frivolous infractions as removing a stone from federal lands, subsidiary enforcement services have also been established. Some examples include state police, municipal police, college campus police, regional police, sheriffs, probation departments (tighter enforcement on those proven brazen enough to defy the laws) and just about every other form of herd control you can think of. The primary goal of all peasant regulating departments should be to protect your interests whilst picking the pockets of your peasants. This will be yet another way to transfer their time, energy and skills over to you. Protecting docile peasants from the opportunists also keeps your worker bees loyal to you and your protective services whilst allowing the do-gooder peasants to carry out their mundane tasks on the **FARM**.

Law enforcement agents will be more effective if there is a personal emotional connection to the laws they're enforcing. For example, perhaps as a boy, a police officer lost his father due to a drunk driving accident. Now he has an axe to grind with any peasant travelling with even the slightest amount of alcohol in their system. Or maybe a special agent grew up in an abusive home and is deeply intrigued by the motives of a serial killer. As long as their thinking is compartmentalised (more in Chapter 11), these agents should be allowed to thrive in their enforcement actions. In the interim, their personal crusades will keep them blind to the sometimes-illegal actions they take on behalf of the corporate construct known as the **STATE**.

As explained earlier, just because a select few get dressed up in matching costumes doesn't mean they suddenly derive any new superior powers over others. But that's exactly what's happened throughout history, isn't it? Weren't the inquisitors allowed to carry out criminal acts against suspected heretics as permitted by the supreme authority of its time, the Catholic Church (examples include torture and burning people at the stake)? And all this to hunt for imaginary witches! Wasn't the SS sanctioned by the German government to commit what was seen by the outside world as war crimes to stomp out those branded undesirables in their society and, in turn, the world?

These, of course, are extreme examples, but to assert your dominance, resistors, traitors and dissenters must be beaten down, silenced, imprisoned or murdered by those swept up in the fervour of loyalty to you and your **STATE**. Creating powerful emotional triggers will override the critical thinking skills of the majority and create a dangerous pack mentality you can use to your advantage to incite massive nefarious undertakings against those on your **FARM** and on other **FARMS** that you target.

In the event the leader with the silly moustache you select to actualise your world view gives an impassioned speech to a stadium full of adamant supporters, but his animated diatribe falls on deaf ears, not all is lost. If the **FARM** you're infiltrating, or seizing outright, already has a totalitarian policing system, simply keep these rigid and respected enforcement tentacles in place whilst implementing your new rules. However, if you wish to rapidly expand your grasp on a more liberated **FARM**, you'll need a strong spark that ignites the populace's deepest fears to justify your more invasive obtrusions into their daily routines.

This strong example will help explain. Are you acquainted with the *Burning of the Reichstag*? In 1933, one month after Adolf Hitler took power, the German parliament building was set on fire. The German regime cleverly pinned the arson on a *communist agitator* even though the strong possibility exists that the regime itself lit the fuse. This led to the subversion of the rights and privileges of the citizenry in exchange for their safety. It also eliminated the communist party from parliament and cleared the way for Hitler's pursuit of absolute power. This was, of course, the precursor to the establishment of Nazi Germany.

Baby steps I tell you, baby steps!

> NOTE: You *must* disarm peasants to the best of your ability during any major upheavals on your **FARM**. Peasants are very reluctant to change and may resist, especially if there's a sudden loss of privileges or a threat to their numbers. Again, if you can find the right emotional catalyst, they'll gladly turn over their weapons to you, even if it's against their own best interest. Stripping them of their self-protection will be even more difficult on a well-armed **FARM** able to defend itself from both foreign and domestic enemies. It should be quite obvious that having them voluntarily relinquish their munitions is more practical than a round up. Techniques to achieve this and more will be discussed in upcoming chapters.

The wonderful thing about human beings is that they can love, but even more beneficial to you is their propensity to fear and hate. If you wish to keep others under your control, it's important that you tap into these negative emotions to lead them in your direction. Love will bring them together and allow them to *unite*. As mentioned throughout this handbook, this should be prevented at all costs. Fear and hate also allow you to override their critical thinking skills, an important attribute for those carrying out your enforcement actions. Those most suited for law enforcement should be driven by anger and should lack the emotional intelligence to sort out, analyse and control their visceral responses to antagonistic stimuli. This is why soldiers returning from combat make ideal candidates. Techniques to trigger peasants on an individual and mass scale will be presented throughout the rest of this modern-day ruler's handbook.

In an extremely rare people's law society, such as early America, the power structure was flipped on its head, giving local governments (towns, cities, counties) the utmost authority. States, which were mapped out based on natural boundaries, railways, political controversies over slavery and proportionate latitudinal and longitudinal coordinates,[115] were formed to represent all dwellers within their borders in matters concerning the very bottom of the political hierarchy, i.e. the federal government. As discussed in Chapter 8, the federal government was given twenty and only twenty enumerated tasks designed to promote the general welfare of the participating members.

Ha! Is your blood boiling from the audacity of such nonsensical thinking?

In such a preposterous scenario, can you see the difficulty with asserting your will if *peacekeepers* elected to protect the freedoms of the people, such as sheriffs, who also have the authority to deputise private citizens, have more say in the laws than your federal enforcers? There would be thousands of self-righteous John Wayne wannabes painting up the landscape as if it were the Wild West. If elected by the people rather than appointed by your associates, this county peacekeeping outfit would then, theoretically, have more power than the mayor's police (municipal and city police), the governor's police (state police) and the president's police made up of both your three letter friend enforcers (ATF, FBI, etc.) and the military.

It should be completely obvious why a *civil war* (one of my favourite oxymorons) had to be instigated to seize power and make the execution of laws a top-down monopolised system of enforcers appointed by trusted officials working in accord with the new owners' interests and not that of the meaningless *citizens*. Had this not happened, American citizens would have had way too much say in how they were governed and what laws were created and enforced. In the event you're unfamiliar, the **execut**or of laws at any level on the American **FARM** resides with the chief **execut**ive of their respective corporate office, a.k.a. the **execut**ive branch. In a town or city, it's the mayor. On the county level, it's the sheriff. On the state level, the governor and on the federal level, the president. I think it's easy to see why the executive branch is given protectoral duties. Can you imagine various members of Congress trying to convene to determine the appropriate response to an encroaching squadron of enemy planes and battleships? This same

---

115.) Mark Stein. "How did the States Get Their Shapes?" Wonderopolis. https://www.wonderopolis.org/wonder/how-did-the-states-get-their-shapes

opportunistic group of easily swayed puppets doesn't have the collective intellect to agree on what to order for lunch yet alone make a timely decision about something as important as the defence of their *country*. By giving the executive branch, and in effect one person, the power to control the military and law enforcement officers, decisions can be made in emergency situations where the immediate use of force is necessary.

'Ah, but will I need to use force?' you quiver.

If there's an uprising, or an enemy's hell-bent on taking over your **FARM**, you damn well better be ready to retaliate with a vengeance. If not, immediately put down this handbook and enlist in a game of croquet.

Throughout history, the individual privileges and rights of the *citizenry* had to be retracted under the threat of invasion or rebellion to protect the integrity of the **FARM**. Even on a **FARM** like early America, if one owned a ship but a fleet of enemy ships was approaching, the government could seize the private ship to defend the country. That is, however, as long as the ship was returned, or the owner compensated, once the threat subsided. The thought process behind this practice was that, to protect the rights of its citizens (like the right to life and the right to own property), the government would sometimes have to resort to such necessary tactics.

In today's corporate world and as the future CEO of PEASANT FARM, INC., can you see the absurdity of such a policy? Paying back peasants isn't conducive to making large profits, and that policy assumes the property isn't yours after the peasants contractually agreed to turn ownership of all that is theirs, including themselves, over to you.

Now it's time to put on your thinking cap. Is there a broader scenario *legalising* or, at the very least, justifying the same results gained from the undisclosed adhesion contracts that hand the peasants' rights and properties over to the **STATE**?

If you said a national emergency or state of emergency, I expect to see you hosting a G20 Summit Meeting one day.

Just think of what happens during a catastrophic storm. Travel is restricted, curfews imposed and military units dispatched. There are even times when *residents* must leave *their property* behind and relocate. Although we'll be discussing advanced uses of this technique in upcoming chapters, you need to know that these emergencies can be real, imaginary or an innovative combination of both. Once in place, even the right to a fair and speedy trial can be suspended and enhanced enforcement tactics applied. The beauty is your peasants will be left no choice but to comply.

Oh my, what a rush! My whole body is pumping with adrenaline!

Excuse me whilst I take a brisk five-minute power walk.

Drats! Never mind. I'll finish my little stroll later. I couldn't wait to hurry back to my typewriter to write this.

If you're having difficulty processing such slippery techniques, when at war, isn't it better to assume one is an enemy (guilty until proven innocent), and to dispose of or seize them, rather than have that person turn around and destroy you? In a state of emergency, isn't it better to incarcerate someone rather than have him commercially harm you or others (guilty until proven innocent)? With so many enemy vessels operating in the sea of commerce, as established by such legislation as the War Powers Act, why take that chance?

A telltale sign that such a proclamation has been declared can be felt when a peasant looks into their rearview mirror and spots a police car. If the peasant has an unsettling feeling that they may be harassed for any unjustified reason, you can rest assured a state of emergency has been implemented, and the agents are serving and protecting the ruler's interests, not the peasants.

If you, as the orchestrator of such a plan, get that same uneasy feeling when you see a sheriff's car, you have much work ahead of you.

In order for your *government* to retrieve its property from an enemy ship that violated the rules on international waters in a breach of contract, the letters of marquee and reprisal can be applied and other pirates, in the form of the corporate courts and law enforcement agencies, can seize the vessel and any incriminating property. This booty, also known as civil forfeiture, then gets divided between the **STATE** and its pirates-for-hire. The majority of the pirates' cut comes in the form of salaries, benefits and department funding.[116] Keep in mind, if peasants are found innocent after their possessions are sold, the possessions were never the peasants' to begin with. The operation of your **FARM** takes precedence over bickering peasants upset about their mistreatment.

NOTE: It's human nature to want other people's things, especially if one is a pirate. A few marauders may feel, since there's no personal attachment between their department and the seized items, that they may benefit directly by keeping or re-selling these legally obtained possessions. You can determine what degree of stealing you find acceptable, but if a pirate's

116.) "How Crime Pays: The Unconstitutionality of Modern Civil Asset Forfeiture as a Tool of Criminal Law Enforcement." Harvard Law Review. March 2018. https://www.harvardlawreview.org/2018/06/how-crime-pays-the-unconstitutionality-of-modern-civil-asset-forfeiture-as-a-tool-of-criminal-law-enforcement/

serving you well, it may be in your best interest to allow them
to personally prosper on such confiscations, and in unique
situations, permit them to trump up charges for the sole purpose
of taking desired personal property from another.[117] Always
remember, in a looting and pillaging system, bad behaviour may
become the norm not the exception.

Can you help it if they adore their leader and want to
emulate him? Of course, if one wishes to keep the illusion of a
legitimate system in place, this behaviour must be curtailed or,
at the very least, frowned upon.

As the justification for your intrusions on your peasants' rights and
property increases, so can the enforcement techniques imposed upon
them. As long as subjects are led to believe these national emergencies
are for their protection and well-being, they'll learn to be thankful for
them. The wars on drugs and terror are prime examples.

To illustrate, before both national emergencies, there was less
danger for both the public and enforcement officers, making the use
of aggressive enforcement tactics harder to justify. But, with larger
profits generated by the illegal drug trade, even a simple traffic stop
had the potential to lead to a shoot-out or worse. Failure to respond to a
simple command in such perilous situations could then easily warrant
an electrical shock, a stream of pepper spray to the face or a jackboot
to the groin. Searching a vehicle could also move to the forefront since
the peasant could be harbouring an illicit substance, even if it's a father
returning his family home from Sunday school. But then, maybe Dad
likes to take a toke from the ole peace pipe after dropping the kids off for
a few hours. Upon returning home with his children, Dad's pulled over
and the officer detects a slight hint of marijuana. Now the officer has
the grounds to not only rummage through Dad's minivan in search of
anything at all, but in collusion with lawmakers, has the *legal authority*
to confiscate Dad's property, including his children, for endangering
them whilst driving.

Your chosen lawmakers can further protect your encroachments
by giving the officers the discretion to terminate a peasant if the officer
feels their own life is in danger. There could be a spooky terrorist set on
wiping out an entire city driving through a neighbourhood, or perhaps
a house is suspected of drug activity and BLAM, just like that, you're

---

117.) Larry Light. "Feds: IRS seized millions from innocent people and businesses."
CBSNews.com. April 6, 2017. https://www.cbsnews.com/news/irs-seize-mil-
lions-innocent-people/

more than justified to call in a military swat team. The beauty of such breeches to protect their safety is that it conditions peasants to adapt to this new level of enhanced enforcement until it's accepted as the new normal. Once established, you can redraw the lines on their privacy to take even more from them.

> NOTE: Blaring a loud siren, flashing bright lights and travelling at high speeds whilst pursuing and then pulling over an enemy ship on the side of a busy or dark motorway doesn't necessarily promote a safe travelling environment, but it does remind all peasants who is in charge. Shining a bright light on a suspect and his vehicle is the equivalent of shining a flashlight in a frog's eyes to paralyse them and will give your agents an advantage when approaching a defiant peasant.

The crescendo of this bone crushing chapter will proudly unveil the bloody experiment that arose from the ashes of the Vietnam War to serve as a template for today's modern-day global peasant farm, *The Phoenix Program*. This wonderful yet little known operation provided the genesis for today's super state enforcement system merging intelligence sharing, policing and military functions into one common, *international* network. This constantly evolving nexus indeed has the potential to finally bring the entire world under one giant totalitarian umbrella, surpassing George Orwell's wildest dreams. Perhaps a little background into its origin will help explain its practicality in today's planetary takeover.

First, at an early point in the Vietnam War, the United States realised it couldn't militarily defeat the deeply entrenched Viet Cong. There was a shadow government made up of civilians that were providing political leadership and various administrative functions for the VC insurgency in the South. This network wasn't made up of North Vietnamese soldiers or armed guerrillas but simply citizens who wanted their country to remain autonomous. How dare they! The only way for the United States to get their way in the conflict was to destroy this civilian infrastructure by using interrogation and assassination techniques.[118] Hence, *The Phoenix Program* was born.

This covert programme coordinated members of the intelligence community with police and military personnel for one single purpose,

---

118.) Douglas Valentine interviewed by James Corbett, "Trump Admin Raising Phoenix Program From the Ashes – Douglas Valentine joins Corbett Report, YouTube video, 51:05, Jane Marple, February 4, 2017, https://youtu.be/C0PLKj4bBpg

to destroy the civilian infrastructure aiding and abetting the enemy. US Representative Ogden Reid remarked during a Congressional Investigation: 'If the Union had had a Phoenix Program during the Civil War, its targets would have been civilians like Jefferson Davis or the mayor of Macon, Georgia.'[119] Since Phoenix was aimed at civilians and not military personnel and its activities, the CIA was responsible for its inception, funding and operation.[120] Information was extracted at Provincial Interrogation Centers (PIC's) where extreme methods of torture were often used to collect data.[121] This information was shared and gathered by intelligence agents, police and military personnel and stored in computers at the Intelligence Operations and Coordination Centers (IOCC's) located in districts (counties) and provinces (states) throughout Southern Vietnam.[122]

> NOTE: There were two ways to impose fear on the enemy. One was the direct method of explicit fear which would employ such tactics as beheading VC sympathisers in front of their villages and then placing the dismembered heads on stakes. The other was the indirect method of implicit fear that carried the notion if one didn't accept or support the American backed government being imposed on them, they were a VC sympathiser and could be blacklisted.[123]
>
> Does the phrase 'You're either with us or against us' ring a bell? Oh, such beautiful words!

Once a civilian profile was established, they could be detained, tortured, recruited for counterintelligence or targeted for assassination, depending on their determined level of usefulness or threat. Various techniques to *neutralise* those on a hit list included military bombing strikes of villages where suspected VC supporters were assumed to be located, starving captured suspects in a cage and murder by way of assassination teams called Provincial Reconnaissance Units (PRU's).[124] The PRU's, by the way, initially recruited the most ruthless criminals from Vietnamese prisons to commit what some might consider to be horrific murders.[125] Obviously, this is a technique to keep in mind should you need it to strike fear into the enemy.

119.) Douglas Valentine, *The Phoenix Program* (New York, Avon Books, 1990), 13.
120.) Valentine, "Raising Phoenix Program From the Ashes," 11:45
121.) Valentine, *The Phoenix Program*, 85, 347, 383.
122.) Valentine, "Raising Phoenix Program From the Ashes," 14:57
123.) Valentine, "Raising Phoenix Program From the Ashes," 20:55
124.) Valentine, *The Phoenix Program*, 159-173, 348-349, 381, 399.
125.) Valentine, *The Phoenix Program*, 10, 170.

Such a delightfully brutal operation did not, of course, transpire without a few glitches. There were some Vietnamese citizens who took the opportunity to rid themselves of a political or business rival by reporting them to Phoenix operatives as a VC sympathiser.[126]

Conversely, some unethical district officials accepted bribes from the VC to release certain legitimate suspects being detained.[127] When high quotas of 1800 neutralisations per month were put in place to kick the programme into high gear, I think it's easy to see how some innocent bystanders may have been swept up in the fury to reach those ambitious numbers.[128] Human ears not only served as wonderful trophies but as a confirmation of kills made during the sweeps, even if there may have been a few cases of mistaken identity.[129]

Even though *The Phoenix Program* got a little messy, especially when quotas were instated, can you see the usefulness of such an information gathering and dissension targeting apparatus on your **FARM**? If so, could this also be used on multiple **FARMS**, whether they are *free* or oppressed, to bring them all under your control? If only there was an event to justify a worldwide clampdown.

Hmmm. Now what could that be? If you're thinking along the lines of some sort of multi-national state of emergency, you've soaked up the material in this chapter like an absorbent paper towel.

Before I reveal more wonderful techniques for world domination, I must first set the stage a little further to be sure all preparations for global conquest are in order.

126.) Valentine, *The Phoenix Program*, 359.

127.) digigod. "The Controversy of Phoenix Program." StoptheCrime.net . January 24, 2019. https://stopthecrime.net/wp/2019/01/24/the-controversy-of-phoenix-program/

128.) Valentine, *The Phoenix Program*, 13.

129.) Valentine, *The Phoenix Program*, 170, 384.

Chapter 11

TRAINING YOUR PEASANTS

The schools must fashion the person and fashion him in such a way that he simply cannot will otherwise than what you wish him to will.
— Johann Gottlieb Fichte

In a letter from Aldous Huxley (author of the 1932 dystopian novel *Brave New World*) to George Orwell (author of the 1949 dystopian novel *Nineteen Eighty-Four*), Huxley thanked Orwell for the complimentary book he received from Orwell's publisher but disagreed with the method to which a ruling party could assert its dominance over its subjects. Huxley stated: 'My own belief is that the ruling oligarchy will find less arduous and wasteful ways of governing and of satisfying its lust for power, and those ways will resemble those which I described in *Brave New World*.'[130]

The methods Huxley spelled out in his inspiring futuristic publication involved indoctrinating infants according to their pre-chosen role in society, whilst numbing adults with a pharmaceutical drug called Soma when they felt agitated or uncomfortable. The drug prevented them from analysing the root of their angst. In contrast, Orwell uses surveillance and implicit and explicit fear, including such things as continuous war, the thought police and the threat of a boot-on-the-face to maintain order and loyalty to Big Brother. Since both authors were illuminated men, it would be wise for you to consider both approaches on your **FARM**.

The key to successfully enslaving a subject mentally is to begin the indoctrination process as early as possible. This works best if the biological parents are themselves already domesticated peasants.

130.) Rob King. "In the future, I'm right: Letter from Aldous Huxley to George Orwell over 1984 novel sheds light on their different ideas." Daily Mail.com. March 7, 2012. https://www.dailymail.co.uk/news/article-2111440/Aldous-Huxley-letter-George-Orwell-1984-sheds-light-different-ideas.html

If they are forced to conform, individuals in each subsequent generation will be more easily moulded.

Even though newborns are in the temporary care of their biological parents (until they enter early programmes such as pre-school) you can start shaping their perception of the world as well as sharpen their engrained responses to authority figures. This process begins in the hospital when nurses rip the infants from their parents' arms and place them in a nursery. Just exposing the newly birthed peasants to the giant medical and pharmaceutical industries will leave quite an indelible impression on these producers-in-the-making.

> NOTE: It's important to establish whose property the children are by registering these freshly arrived peasants as subjects via the birth certificate.

Injecting newborns with pharmaceutical drugs will begin their transmutation. As illustrated by Aldous Huxley in *Brave New World*, altering the inherent biological environment of these little sucklings with experimental chemicals will allow you to override their natural biological responses, bypassing millions of years of evolution. This will give you greater control over their immune systems' ability to cope with the various viruses and bacteria they come into contact with and make them more dependent on your pharmaceutical solutions. You should view institutions such as hospitals as profit centres where you can reap the benefits throughout a peasant's lifetime.

> NOTE: One very lucrative and widely accepted practice in creating functioning yet physically compromised peasants is injecting infants with toxins like those found in the Hepatitis B vaccine. In this scenario, the nippers' biological parents are told, if they even bother to ask, that this injection protects their toddler for up to twenty years should the child embark in such risky behaviour as sharing intravenous drugs and fornicating with multiple sex partners. We all know how wild those nurseries can be, especially when the nurses step away to attend to other matters.
> Can you say…PARTY?!

Of course, it's obvious that, for at least the first decade of a young peasants' life, this type of exposure is quite impractical, if not irrational. However, this formality allows you to gauge the effectiveness of your training tactics by observing the number of peasants who willingly follow these orders from medical authorities. Of course, pharmaceuticals are only used to keep the chattel safe from a myriad of dreadful diseases.

Mugs! As you'll learn in subsequent chapters, it's quite the contrary.

As peasants progress from infancy to childhood, it's crucial for the white coats to strongly coerce obedience since these are the primary agents these budding consumers will most often encounter during their formative years.

Doctors and other authority figures such as scientists, CEOs, lawyers, celebrities, professional athletes and politicians should all be generously compensated and presented to all peasants at various ages, as more knowledgeable and superior. This will develop hero worship rather than critical thinking. These prestigious professionals will subconsciously rob your less accomplished peasants of their personal power and autonomy. These heroes will appear more desirable than those in other roles and will attract the best of the herd to your ruling party's cause and not to the empowerment of their fellow man.

Other conditioning tools such as televisions, entertainment *programmes*, technological devices, mass sporting events and state-approved *learning* materials can mould a peasant's reality.

Biological parents will pass on their self-limiting beliefs to their children, steering future generations into similar occupational roles on the corporate **FARM**. Here are a few beneficial ways parents can indoctrinate your budding peasants.

First, however, I need to mention that lords across the globe have had to collude and agree on certain parameters on all **FARMS** to maximise peasants' allegiances and contributions to their territories. Some of these necessary features include borders, taxation, national flags, anthems, national debt, rules on immigration, state-controlled education and the widespread belief that governments are necessary and virtuous. Rulers build the peasants' belief systems with these elements and integrate them into the storylines taught during their indoctrination.

Once a reference point is established, you can use an influential tool like the television to strike fear into the hearts of your **FARM'S** inhabitants to gain their compliance, much like the wizard behind the curtain in *The Wizard of Oz*. Such fear mongering can include paralysing narratives such as warning them of an upcoming plague that could wipe out the entire population. Then the narrative can sell an experimental vaccine. Or perhaps you can manipulate the inhabitants of your **FARM** to participate in a profitable war against an evil enemy who you claim is constructing a secret weapon capable of killing millions. Boo! As long as the information comes from an authoritative source and fits into the peasants' core belief system, very few will dare to question its validity.

Indoctrinated biological parents are perhaps your most useful assets because they'll have the biggest influence over the young peasant's development. If biological parents put doctors on pedestals, their children will quickly learn to obey their godlike instructions. If biological parents believe things provide happiness, they'll shower their children with toys. This will eventually turn the up-and-coming wage earners into adult consumers who equate material possessions with happiness. This will create yet another generation with a debt slave mentality they'll pass on to their own offspring. If biological parents rely on corporate foods with pleasing artificial tastes as a family staple, this will direct their children's palates away from wholesome foods that will benefit their health and instead eventually lead them into the clutches of the lucrative medical industry.

> NOTE: Misguided biological parents should encourage their developing offspring to consume *approved* corporate products that compromise their health instead of improving it. This list can include, but is not limited to, pharmaceutical drugs, vaccines, sugars, trans fats and chemical-laden snacks containing artificial ingredients like aspartame, etc. It also includes items that cloud their thinking, such as fluoridated products, behaviour-altering drugs and anything with mercury (tuna, vaccines, fillings, etc.). This will allow you to profit handsomely, whilst more easily controlling your peasants. Again, a systematic trust in doctors and government health officials will facilitate this endeavour.

Finally, you should create public holidays that stimulate the business sector. The unwitting peasants will emulate their neighbours to avoid bringing disappointment to their children who should be domestically and culturally trained to associate happiness with *approved* corporate products. Various mediums can reinforce this by bombarding the modern-day peasant's subconscious with a barrage of images, ideas and subliminal messages. Have you ever wondered why places like doctors' offices and malls have become saturated with television screens? Many billboards litter the landscape, displaying more obvious subliminal programming. Remember, being free is a state of mind, and enslaving their minds must start at the earliest age possible. To do this, you must dominate their thoughts with the things you want them to believe are important and the things you want them to desire, so you can more easily manipulate their behaviour. They'll spend their time, energy and talents producing and consuming your approved products and strive to succeed in your controlled institutions such as universities, the military or (dare I say) the entertainment industry, thereby creating many ancillary enterprises.

Patriotic biological parents who are loyal to their **FARM** will infuse these invaluable attributes into their children and give all involved the feeling they're contributing to a greater purpose. You see, peasants will die and sacrifice their biological offspring to win their ruler's approval and see that the ruler who provides the greatest illusion of freedom maintains his lavish lifestyle.

It's bloody good to sit upon the throne!

Remember, as much as the world needs peasants, it also needs brash rulers like you. Therefore, I'll make a few comments to assist you in passing the reigns to your privileged descendants who have the good fortune of benefiting from the risk and hard work you put into becoming a global lord. This will come with a price. First, you should be very selective with whom you procreate. As Charles Darwin alluded to in 1871, in his book *The Descent of Man*, based on scientific proof, only a small percentage of humanity is evolving; the rest (around 95%) have reached a developmental dead-end.[131] Heaven forbid advanced bloodlines such as yours and mine intermingle with the undesirables. It would cause an evolutionary backslide too horrific to imagine.

A good state-controlled schooling system not only helps prepare peasants to be competent enough to fill out paperwork and operate machinery,[132] but it also helps determine what function they're to fulfil within society and allows for the arrangement of the most preferred breeding stock. Based on what's available, you may even want to consider keeping your lineage pure by inbreeding or, at the very least, choosing a similar advancing genetic seed with which to reproduce.

NOTE: It should be your aim to become godlike in terms of human perfection. That's why science, and its pursuits, should be worshipped and encouraged over frivolous religions and

---

131.) John Taylor Gatto, "John Taylor Gatto, Three Time New York City Teacher of the Year, Interviewed in Sweden (3/3)," YouTube video, 9:44, ProfanityAlertMedia, December 6, 2011, https://youtu.be/VeQe32wR9yI

132.) George Carlin, "George Carlin – The American Dream," YouTube video, 4:52, snackle, August 4, 2009, https://youtu.be/-54c0ldxZWc

superstitions. You can then become the new god of a world rebuilt according to your design. Imagine an existence where we mix and match the best traits of all living things to create various super species, and then integrate technology to connect and manage it all. It will, however, be essential for you to own and control these technologies for you and your accomplices' benefit only. This will be yet another tool that will put you at a stark breeding advantage over your underlings.

State-controlled schools allow the **STATE** to shape peasants into productive and responsible *citizens*, whilst *private* schools benefit the upper echelon by teaching our sons and daughters the skills and techniques necessary to rule over our genetic inferiors. As a ruler of society, the best existence you can provide for all inhabitants is one of abundance. Therefore, refining the underprivileged into reliable and predictable producers is paramount. Once accomplished, peasants can work to manufacture and then acquire a plethora of creature comforts that will facilitate your rule over them. Creating an industrious **FARM** will provide the best human society possible. Why shouldn't the pioneers of such a system reap great power and profits for arranging such a wonderful utopia? There should be a clear distinction between the two types of education afforded to evolving bloodlines versus dead end stock, private versus state-controlled schooling, respectively.

We'll discuss the primary goals of state-controlled schooling shortly, but since this chapter focuses on training your peasants, I'll only briefly mention the subjects that private institutions should teach for the appropriate growth of future lords. To ensure they possess the social skills necessary for getting what they want from others, up-and-coming lords should develop the art of writing and public speaking and sharpen well-ingrained manners. A reading list that has inspired many of the principles in this handbook and an in-depth critical analysis of complex information is also imperative.

Correctly parenting the rulers of tomorrow plays an important part in their preparation for world dominance. However, parents also pass on essential personality traits and genetic qualities to future generations. One personality trait of great interest to today's rulers is the dissociation characteristic. To make tough decisions, like who lives or dies and for what reasons, one must lack an ability to empathise with others. Tests can determine if your child possesses this desirable attribute, but if required, one can develop it through rather harsh methods. These practices are beyond the scope of this handbook, but leaving a mousetrap in a baby's crib and withholding the mother's comfort until the child stops crying after being snapped by the device is just one such technique. The lesson learned is that the infant will not receive its mother's solace until it separates itself from the physical and emotional pain inflicted.

To be a leader in society, individuals must possess a high tolerance for emotional and physical pain whilst also receiving nurturing that fosters clear and profound critical thinking. Exposing future oligarchs to proper imperial etiquette demonstrated by their parents' actions toward others will also benefit them greatly, as will encouraging their independence and allowing them to develop a strong sense of self.

In some ways, productive peasants require similar attributes as their rulers. They must also be able to withstand high levels of emotional and physical pain to perform their routine jobs consistently and predictably. Authoritative parenting can be useful for this purpose. Physical punishments like a smack on the bottom will help sharpen the young peasants' decision-making skills and will teach them respect for authority. Various sociological tools can trick peasants into wallowing over these so-called *abuses* rather than thriving from such disciplinary measures.

The stark difference in bringing up young peasants, however, will arise from exposure to their biological parents' lifestyles and social networks. Much of what young peasants perceive will shape their reality. If they witness their fathers and mothers going to work every day in the parents' chosen occupations, young peasants will aspire to thrive in the same line of work or, at the very least, one on a similar societal level.

Guilt-based religions can also stymie peasants' natural instincts. Morals will put peasants at a stark disadvantage when it comes to courting mates, crossing spiritual thresholds and doing whatever is necessary to rise to the top. As I will demonstrate shortly, peasants *must* receive an education that gives them only enough knowledge to operate within their compartmentalised roles on the **FARM**. Each **FARM'S** academic standards will be based on a sliding scale, depending on that **FARM'S** level of sophistication.

At the time of this writing, the world's farms are experiencing abundance, and experts have developed many of the technologies required to achieve this level of comfort. Therefore, most modern-day lords agree that the majority of regressing stock is most beneficial in the role accredited to Vladimir Lenin's *useful idiots*. That is, indoctrinated propagandists who blindly promote their ruler's ideology without fully understanding it.

Like their leaders, these *useful idiots* are often morally depleted but don't have the skill sets, knowledge or connected channels to rise above their current status. Quite pitifully, they falsely believe if they take on their ruler's point of view, they too can become rulers. In my opinion, they're the most pleasurable to mould, even though they lead a meaningless existence and often fall into the even more deplorable category of *useless eaters*. That is, members of society who provide no real value, innovation or societal worth and are conditioned to be mindless consumers. Both useful idiots and *useless eaters* will endorse a ruler's methods as long as that ruler enables and continues to fuel their delusions. This is in a ruler's best interest because maintaining a large number of *useless idiots* and *useless eaters* will drown out any opposition against **FARM** policies raised by awakened peasants.

Creating this breed of peasant has never been easier. I'll present many techniques to keep peasants on the illusory and well-established, product-driven corporate **FARM**. Even though we must apply these stimuli throughout the peasants' lifetimes, we can achieve the greatest benefits by conditioning their minds from infancy to adolescence, which will reduce the burden of keeping them within a suitable mental paradigm once they reach adulthood. Peasant training centres, a.k.a. state-controlled schools, have been revamped for this purpose. Most people will not only cling to their originally programmed beliefs but will argue vehemently to defend them to remain in a mental and physical state of equilibrium. This self-induced mental prison will be useful. Once you imprison their minds, they will willingly make their bodies, emotions and health fully available to you, allowing you to achieve your innermost whims and desires through their unconscious compliance.

To remove competition, you can legislate the influence of biological parents to near extinction by prohibiting any autonomous actions they take that oppose those prescribed by the **STATE**. You can also encourage child worship (idolization of children) through various information outlets and should label children not deprived of their childhoods through enrolment in early learning programmes as inept or behind. Teachers can instil in children the belief that no one's a loser, and everyone wins, so when they encounter difficulties as adults, they struggle to cope and seek solace in things that bring them comfort. As in *Brave New World, soma,* a.k.a. pharmaceutical and recreational drugs, can pacify peasants whilst also generating huge revenues. These funds can then be used to develop a new **FARM** or conquer other **FARMS**. If you have a limited knowledge of history, you must gain an understanding of how such illicit means have always provided funding for imperialistic endeavours.

You should view peasant training centres, a.k.a. state-controlled schools, just like hospitals and other communal institutions, as factories for your raw materials. Once you've imprisoned their minds, you can gradually turn these *schools* into physical prisons that will condition your developing *human resources* for the broader plan, which is total subjugation of the human race. By incrementally morphing your peasant training centres into physical detention centres, peasants will acclimate to this new environment.

We should continue embedded practices such as requiring peasants to ask for permission for everything they want to do and following senseless orders/instructions/assignments. Placing peasants in actual prisonlike structures during their formative years will also teach them to live under constant surveillance, to be where the authorities tell them to be when they are told to be there and to stay in confined areas for extended periods of time.

Nineteen Eighty-Four anyone?

Homogenised peasants will feel more at home in these institutions than they will with their own biological families. The law should mandate that all children attend peasant training centres, and authorities should use force if biological parents refuse.

Once biological parents teach your human collateral basic life skills, i.e. how to walk, talk, use the loo, etc. it's time to shape their minds for your benefit. Peasant training centres will be more effective in creating homogenised peasants if they're controlled by a strong central government. Having peasants pay into your central government via taxation, and then having it redistribute the money to complicit institutions, will allow you to control the curriculum in the centres at the peasants' own expense. The **STATE** will become the parents of the budding producers/consumers-in-the-making and will thoroughly prepare the children for life on the corporate **FARM**. Standardised testing is an excellent tool for measuring their adherence to uniform thought. Putting emphasis on the results will further pressure developing peasants into groupthink. This will give you greater control over your herd.

Mantras, pledges and songs are important indoctrination tools. Since, by nature, human beings are social creatures who want to belong, patriotism is the perfect way to tap into this innate quality that gives peasants a higher sense of purpose for your benefit. If instilled early enough, catchy melodies along with often repeated **FARM** slogans will strike an emotional chord with your peasants through all phases of their lives. That's why you should repeat them at all meetings, athletic events and any other public functions, including international sporting events that encourage spirited competition and personal pride in one's farm. Stimulus, like a *national* flag, will serve as a constant visual reminder of their *pledged* loyalty to their **FARM**.

Regardless of which **FARM** a peasant belongs to, someone must teach them why their **FARM** is exceptional, and they must learn as early as possible to worship not only their leaders but also those who fight for the cause of the **FARM**. This will also give the peasants purpose, and will add to their productivity on the **FARM**, whether or not they serve in the military. If you expect one or more of your **FARMS** to take over other **FARMS**, you must teach blossoming peasants that their **FARM'S** leaders and way of life are superior to any other **FARMS**. History has shown that subtly planting the seeds of supremacy is most effective. For instance, training your peasants to appreciate the *freedom* you provide will be more effective than telling them they are part of a superior race that should repopulate the planet. This low-key strategy will also reduce suspicion from other **FARMS**, making them more willing to assist you in your conquest efforts. Freedom is an inherent, deep-seated desire in all living creatures, and creating the illusion of freedom (see Chapter 13) will secure your peasants' loyalty to your **FARM**.

If you own more than one **FARM** and need a **FARM** specifically for attacking other **FARMS**, you can smoothly slip warlike lyrics into that **FARM'S** anthems and pledges. In upcoming chapters, you'll also learn various techniques to inject a warlike mentality into your peasants using covert programming. You should routinely drill fear of foreign invasion or horrific devastation into young peasants' heads, making them thankful for the protective services you provide. This will give them a sense of honour and urgency when taking part in your **FARM'S** defensive/offensive efforts when they mature. Hero worship and teaching all peasants to thank members of law enforcement and the military for their service will give peasants the impression the sacrifices made are for their benefit and not their ruler's. The leaders you select will be more effective if they facilitate and encourage this propaganda. This will disarm non-combative peasants, who'll then turn their sense of self-preservation over to peasants designated with the duty of *protecting* them, whether they be intelligence officers, members of the military or local police officers. Panic-stricken peasants are the easiest to coerce. They should face unfathomable despair when you need their conformity.

> NOTE: Be aware that winners write history. If you wish to control the narrative your peasants receive, you must be victorious in your battles. Winning military conflicts is not synonymous with virtue. Only rulers who break natural and spiritual laws are guaranteed success. Treaties, pacts and rules should not apply. Rulers willing to go to the greatest extremes to subdue humanity are the ones who will rise to the top. The ruler who can best manipulate their subjects' emotions will motivate the largest number of peasants to join their cause and win the peasants' loyalty and compliance. Effective and systematic early life training is essential in achieving this task.

Therefore, doesn't it make sense that establishing a self-policing mechanism within each peasant is an efficient way to keep your peasants in line? Once ingrained, peasants will not only police themselves but will chastise others who try to break free from their social programming.

In the battle of Jena in 1806, Napoleon's ragtag fighting forces defeated Prussia's mighty army because the Prussian soldiers were thinking for themselves rather than following orders. This realisation prompted the development of the concept of free and compulsory schooling, which involved teaching all Prussian citizens skills like reading, writing and arithmetic—skills necessary for the developing industrialised world. And even more importantly, they also received strict instructions on the concepts of duty, discipline, respect for authority and following orders that prepared them for military service and subservience to government.[133] This new type of forced schooling led to the unification of Germany and eventually paved the way for the rise of the Third Reich.

Oh, the beauty of conformity.

Even the founding fathers of America realised that good citizens, i.e. those who put the needs of the **FARM** above their own and their families', had to be made and were not born. Schoolhouses made the perfect domestication centres, and the Prussian model was eventually introduced in America by the father of American education, Horace

---

133.) Brendan Conway-Smith and Eve Zarifa, "The Origins of the American Public Education System: Horace Mann and the Prussian Model of Obedience," You-Tube video, 8:19, Police State USA, July 29, 2013, https://youtu.be/HZp7eVJNJuw

Mann, in Massachusetts in 1846.[134] Since peasants' minds are blank slates when they're born, I think it's quite easy to see that the evolution in schooling has led to the sculpting of the ideals, skill sets and discipline necessary to not only make *citizens* obedient but to also prepare them to be productive in the advanced technological climates of industry and warfare. The perfection of this type of peasant training will lead the world into one homogenised system where peasants will be under such effective thought control that gaining compliance using soldiers or police officers will become obsolete.

The ability to make sense out of available information (critical thinking) must be removed from peasant training centres and replaced with regurgitating the thoughts that a few privileged members of the ruling party deem important. The result will be an efficient policy-making class and a sub-class.

Eliminating critical thinking also ensures that peasants gain a minimal understanding of the words they use. By parroting what they're taught, peasants will regurgitate *deaf Phoenicians* or, as the peasants recognise it, *definitions* of words without further understanding their origin or the duality in their meanings and sounds.[135] This is known as phonics, derived from the word Phoenix, stemming from the word Phoenician. This didn't happen by coincidence. Words (or when the letters are rearranged *sword*) are powerful. That's why peasants should only obtain a basic understanding of language and should remain deficient when speaking or writing.

An in-depth study of words unlocks their power and is useful for aspiring rulers who are looking to subjugate their inferiors. Or should I say, have them languish in the language? For peasants trapped under the power of words, obfuscation can blind them further. For instance, have you ever wondered why feet smell and noses run or why you drive on a parkway and park in a driveway?[136]

Quite comical, isn't it?

If trained correctly, the peasants' illusory prison can sit in plain sight for you and your colleagues to revel in, whilst the peasants are none the wiser. The etymology of words (mostly from Phoenician, Greek and Latin origin) and examples of their hidden meanings will be discussed

---

134.) Conway-Smith and Zarifa, "The Origins of the American Public Education System," 2:37-3:34.

135.) Jim Farley, "The Real Deaf-Phoenician Of The Words We Speak Today And Why We Speak Them," YouTube video, 14:57 , June 15, 2017, https://youtu.be/L277s6IkdOI

136.) Farley, "The Real Deaf-Phoenician Of The Words We Speak," 7:32-7:40.

throughout this manual when applicable. [137] Since modern language has also been brilliantly developed to deceive, I think you can see the importance of implementing one carefully crafted, uniform language for the eventual goal of a unified, one world, peasant farm.

If you're going to create a stable and predictable corporate peasant farm that consumes your worker bees' time between production and consumption (see Chapter 2) and that consistently enriches you and your associates, it's incredibly important that free market principles be destroyed. By indoctrinating your peasants in training centres in *what is* rather than *what could be,* you eliminate future competition whilst encouraging your chattel to thrive in the industries benevolently provided.

You only need to look at the American **FARM** to see a highly successful producer/consumer training programme in action. Alexander James Inglis drafted the blueprint for this technique in 1918. The Harvard Graduate School of Education established the Inglis Lectureship in Secondary Education in his honour. In order to extend adolescence and continue *schooling* not only at the secondary school but university level, Inglis crafted a discreet book called *Principles of Secondary Education.* In it, Inglis spelled out the six primary principles that every high school in America was to implement and adhere to.[138] I think the results speak for themselves in terms of the devouring of goods and services that, until this day, takes precedence on the American **FARM**.

NOTE: True learning only comes from within, an axiom as old as time. If you dared to even consider sending your royal offspring to complete strangers in a state-controlled schooling system outside your supervision for twelve of their most formative years to shape their thinking, I would highly question your sanity and worthiness to rule. Yet, this is the type of crass action you must force upon your herd. You must mould young peasants like products on an assembly line to maximise their worth. Even though there's no link between performing well in an occupation and schooling, your herd should be convinced otherwise. You must also be willing, through the use of force, to encourage their compliance with your schooling requirements. As a final note, state-controlled schooling teaches peasants to function in a public capacity and not a private capacity where people like you, after reading this handbook, must masterfully

137.) Farley, "The Real Deaf-Phoenician Of The Words We Speak," 0:17-0:25.
138.) John Taylor Gatto, "History of American Education – John Taylor Gatto – BEST INTERVIEW!" YouTube video, 5:46:59, Education Options TV, July 11, 2014, https://youtu.be/28uPtl5sWVI

operate (see Chapter 6). You should lead your herd to believe that their illusory commercial public selves are their private selves and make sure they are unaware of the distinction. This will allow for the smoothest transmittal of their time, skills and energy over to you.

Enough chatter, let's get to it, shall we?

Before discussing Ingles' six imperative principles, it's important to mention the three overall aims of secondary education that have become the backbone of modern-day peasant training. One aim is to prepare the individual as a prospective citizen and cooperating member of society: The Social-Civic Aim. The second is preparation of the individual as a prospective worker and producer: The Economic-Vocational Aim. The third, is preparation for The Individualistic–Avocational Aim, primarily involving individual action, the utilization of leisure and the development of personality.[139]

'But how do we achieve this?' you quiver with excitement.

The first of Ingles' six principles, held mostly within the upper echelon of peasant training circles, is what he called *The Adjustive Function*.[140] This is by far the most essential of his six principles, establishing fixed habits of reaction to authority.[141] This is extremely important and should override the peasants' critical thinking skills. You should introduce this early in the peasants' training and continue throughout their lifetimes by requiring obedience to stupid orders and whimsical assignments and by punishing individual thoughts and actions. For example, if a peasant skips school to read a book, they should face discipline for not attending school instead of being rewarded for learning on their own. Giving peasants answers to remember rather than problems to solve will weaken their analytical skills. We'll discuss how to use and manage peasants who have an aptitude for critical thinking.

When peasants follow controversial orders, you know your training methods are working to the utmost capacity.

Hopefully, by the time schooling begins, biological parents and other forms of social programming have shaped peasants' responses to their superiors. For example, following doctors' orders even when treatments and medications are detrimental to their health.

139.) Alexander Ingles, *Principles of Secondary Education* (Cambridge, Massachusetts, The Riverside Press, 1918), 368.
140.) Ingles, *Principles of Secondary Education*, 376-377.
141.) Gatto, "History of American Education," 4:51:45

NOTE: Weakening your peasants' ability to reason by hooking them on habit-forming substances like opiates, cleverly promoted as medicine, is the quickest way to expand your plantation, undermine an enemy **FARM** and fill your coffers.

Oh, it's so dirty, yet so effective!

I expect most people who relied on teachers' presentations of approved information to achieve good grades, advance to the next level, earn diplomas, find a career, etc. in state-controlled institutions have already rejected the material in this invaluable handbook.

For those still pressing on, you most likely had the esteemed privilege of attending a private boarding school like St Paul's or Westminster in the UK or Exeter or Andover in the US. If my assessment is correct, unlike the shabby, state-controlled schools where the teacher's ramblings fill eighty to 90% of the students' class time, elite boarding schools encourage independent learning in the true spirit of education. It's easy to see that your private boarding schoolteacher was simply there to guide and assist you in your endeavours by only lecturing for ten to 20% of your class time. After all, an outstanding teacher will tell you where to look, not what to see.

As adults, graduates of the peasant training centre will carry with them the lasting impression that social worth is found in collective environments and that only experts, title/degree holders or those who rise to positions of authority possess the independent thinking ability to handle important issues like the peasants' very own health.

NOTE: Part of the collective learning of peasants should include glorification of their current authority figures and those who have subjugated them in years gone by. Peasants should be constantly reminded of how awful conditions would be if not for their authority figures, even if a different historical outcome would have benefitted them. Such factual details should remain hidden, and a true depiction of monumental events should be fabricated to deceive peasants and keep them ignorant of their past. This is also a great way to keep problem solvers from getting to the root of their societal woes and working toward solutions. Sharing the success stories of those who overcame adversity to rise to positions of prominence in areas like business will inspire a new generation of peasants to uphold a system of dominance and exploitation, so they too can reach for, and hence support, what will be an unattainable lifestyle for most of them.

Lastly, local and high-profile authority figures can visit or be promoted or involved in state-controlled schools to inspire and congratulate obedient young peasants for their achievements. Local authority figures may also intervene when any of these clock-punchers-in-training become agitated and defy their indoctrination processes. You can reestablish obedience through pharmaceutical drugs, legal/police actions or the removal of unruly subjects for placement in more stringent indoctrination centres.

> NOTE: These unruly students will serve you well in the military if they can be browbeaten into following orders. Either way, since state-controlled education is built on the Prussian model, schooling will prepare citizens for soldierly duty.

The second of Ingles' principles of secondary education is *The Integrating (Conformity) Function*.[142] The desired outcome with this principle is to make children as alike as possible which will serve you in many ways.[143] For one, it'll allow you, through such methods as market research, to predict the things peasants will find attractive and what they'll spend their time, skills and energy to acquire, resulting in your lucrative competitive edge. This will come in handy when selling your corporate products to the populace. Those in groupthink won't want to be left out when other peasants obtain these goods and services. It'll also prevent random, unpredictable behaviour from the herd, making them easier to manage—not to mention more reliable as devout consumers. For example, farm planners have crafted public holidays to create predictable periods of consumerism to stimulate the business sector. This keeps the machines running around the clock and peasants running on the corporate rat wheel year-round.

Peasants trained in groupthink can also be manipulated into wanting something by creating a false demand or myth around a product. For instance, if the *useless eaters* share a common belief that 'breakfast is the most important meal of the day', they'll eat a heavier breakfast, including meat, as originally intended by the inventor of this slogan and father of public relations, Edward Bernays.

Bernays was the nephew of Sigmund Freud and, at the time of the creation of this catchphrase, he was employed by Beech Nut Company which was hoping to expand its operation by selling more of its ham and bacon. Bernays convinced just one doctor to concur that eating a

---

142.) Ingles, *Principles of Secondary Education*, 377-378.
143.) Gatto, "History of American Education," 4:53:40

protein-based meal in the morning was essential to being productive throughout the day and then simply asked five thousand other doctors to support this claim. When newspapers published the signings of his petition as *scientific evidence,* Beech Nut sales blossomed and Bernays proved how easy it is to deceive the masses.[144]

A herd mentality is never more important than when it comes to your peasants' belief in your **FARM'S** political system. Faith in your civil foundation will not only translate into all other pillars of your **FARM**, but it'll excuse the use of force against others to justify its existence. Engraining youngsters with the belief that the authorities are benevolent and have their best interests at heart will instil a high level of scepticism should they be told otherwise as adults, allowing you to get away with, well, quite literally, murder. Peasants who break free from their programming will be ostracised and attacked by those who wish to remain in the comfort of the collective and away from the throes of cognitive dissonance.

After all, it's easier to fool people than it is to convince them they've been fooled. Wouldn't you agree?

Normalising the thought process of developing corporate peasants can also be accomplished in less obvious ways. For instance, if your carefully groomed and chosen pedagogues praise total conformity whilst condemning individual thinking as a threat to the system, peasants will learn to sacrifice their individual thoughts, pursuits and desires for the benefit of the **FARM**. Conditioning *students* to attend school at the same time every day will prepare them for a daily routine when they enter the corporate **FARM**. Ringing the bell as in a monkey training exercise and moving them from class to class, as discovered by Pavlov's experiments, will jar the lessons from students' minds and condition them to move to the next meaningless situation with the herd, where again, little information will be retained. It's that same bell sound that's going to jolt peasants from their peaceful slumbers every workday throughout their lives. Boring subject matters will also condition peasants to find contentment in their mundane jobs and careers.

Conformity also has its place on the **FARM** in terms of efficiency and productivity. Learning to eat, be open for business and move about at the same time every day will allow schedules to align, not to mention develop stable habits, keeping peasants comfortable with the familiar.

144.) Abigail Carroll. "How lobbyists made breakfast 'the most important meal of the day'." The Guardian, November 28, 2016. https://www.theguardian.com/lifeand-style/2016/nov/28/breakfast-health-america-kellog-food-lifestyle

Such subtle actions will ensure a predictable consumption of products whilst also discouraging spontaneity. Requiring peasants to conform to certain standards, like driving on the same side of the road, in the same direction and at posted speeds, will add to their conditioning. You should use enforcement officers to find abnormalities to keep the **FARM** stable and in good working order. As you can see, this creates a more fluid **FARM**.

The third of Ingles' cardinal principles is that of *The Differentiating Function*.[145] In order to compartmentalise non-desirables and keep them from interacting with more esteemed members of society, it's important to categorise peasants early on so they can begin learning only what's necessary to fulfil their assigned role on the **FARM**. Not only will this save valuable time and money when developing your human resources, but it'll make them more proficient in their trades of choice that, of course, should be congruent with your worldview. Remember, peasants shouldn't learn *anything* beyond their given societal role. This will limit their interactions to like minds creating stark divisions in the social strata, allowing you to rule most effortlessly.

As far back as Ancient Rome, leaders knew that to continue a social form you had to appoint custodians who were well-trained to perpetuate and manage it. Ingles fourth principle, *The Propaedeutic Function*, calls for the careful selection of those responsible for adhering to and preserving the core principles and objectives of schooling as laid out in his book.[146] Doing so eliminates the need for wasteful undertakings such as class warfare. If you have the proper guardians in place to make sure that the general peasant population remains intellectually simple and childlike, the political and economic functions of the **FARM** will operate with as few disruptions as possible. There's no need to seek the best and the brightest for these positions, as students are byproducts of their teachers. Tapping into every child's deepest talent and genius is not the aim. To fill these important positions, you should choose disciplinarians over intellectuals, conformists over freethinkers and the lazy over the productive. These types of successors will ensure the greatest stability and continuation of the indoctrination methods.

Ingles' fifth principle, *The Selective Function*, paints a clear picture of the type of compassion you *must* have for those with deficient genetics.[147] Unbeknownst to teachers and most administrators, this is the

---

145.) Ingles, *Principles of Secondary Education*, 378-379.
146.) Ingles, *Principles of Secondary Education*, 379-380.
147.) Ingles, *Principles of Secondary Education*, 380-382

assessment of the breeding potential of developing peasants, where the poorest amongst them should be prevented from reproducing. This can be secretly accomplished systemically by giving them low grades, tagging them unfit by hanging humiliating labels on them and by placing them in separate remedial classes so their peers perceive them as inferior. This will cause below average peasants to withdraw from possible mating opportunities out of despair or will influence those with desirable breeding traits to reject those deemed outcasts based on the institution judging them inadequate.[148]

Remember, as one who has climbed to the top of society, you'll be responsible for the progression or recession of humanity, so don't louse it up!

Last, Ingles' sixth principle, *The Diagnostic and Directive Function,* calls for teachers and administrators to assess each developing peasant's role on the **FARM** and to keep records that lock peasants into their assigned social compartments for the duration of their lives.[149]

Again, by having those with marginal intelligence in the custodial role, *educators* will be ill-equipped, not to mention too busy and overwhelmed, to recognise and nourish unbridled potential within each peasant. Only those who show a propensity for a *field* within the **FARM'S** framework should be actively recruited to further develop their proclivity for the shown skill.

Peasants who play a more significant role on the **FARM** should be courted early and showered with positive reinforcement to keep them compartmentalised in their areas of interest. Those with a knack for the sciences and mathematics are of special interest, as these fields will be used to further enslave humanity by disconnecting them from their spirits whilst turning their focus toward their intellect.

Those in the state-controlled system with problem-solving abilities will, again, be more reliable peasants if they never learn factual history or the theory of human nature. As you probably remember from your private boarding school education, the secrets of how humans were, are, and always will be, can be found in five documented fields of study. They are, in no particular order, philosophy, theology, literature, law and true world history.[150]

By withholding information that would allow peasants to understand the age-old system of oppression, not even the problem solvers will be able to recognise, let alone remedy their subjugation. By keeping these overachieving peasants financially comfortable and

---

148.) Gatto, "History of American Education," 4:55:07
149.) Ingles, *Principles of Secondary Education,* 382-383
150.) Gatto, "14 Principles of Private Schools," 1:04

satisfied by rewarding work, they'll also lack the desire to change things for the betterment of their fellow man. If unaware of their effect on the big picture, these compartmentalised peasants can be skilfully used against their own best interests. This can be seen in military operations where soldiers blindly follow isolated orders, even though they'd probably be opposed to certain missions if they knew a mission's true objective, especially if said mission unnecessarily put them or others in harm's way.

> NOTE: Even on alleged free **FARMS**, peasants should *not* be taught their fundamental human rights or how to stand up for them. Can you imagine the problems this would create? Presenting history as a childlike fairy tale instead of an in-depth exposé can serve you greatly. You'll want to leave out many important details, for instance, who financially benefitted from a major historical event and the sensitive information that led to its occurrence. This is especially true if it exposes a myth propagated from a historical situation that is, in turn, used for control purposes.

As a wonderful example, did you know that the first legal slave owner of a Black man in America was a Black Virginia tobacco farmer named Anthony Johnson?[151] This puts an interesting spin on one's perception of history, wouldn't you agree? Until the court made its breakthrough decision to allow this former servant to legally own a human being, slaves in America were indentured (under contract), usually for a limited period of four to seven years, to work off things like travel costs to the New World, room and board, etc. Mr Johnson had four White indentured servants and a Black one named John Casor.[152] Both Whites and Blacks could serve as indentures throughout their lifetimes.

Is there much difference between an indentured servant back then and a professional athlete or corporate professional signed to a contract today? Sure, they're paid much better and treated more kindly in today's modern world, but that's exactly what enslaves them more securely to the corporate plantation. Besides, it's difficult to sell products to peasants who have no money. In the same vein, it's tough

151.) Bridget Boakye. "The fascinating story of Anthony Johnson, the black man who was the first to own a slave in the US." Face2FaceAfrica. June 05, 2018. https://face2faceafrica.com/article/the-fascinating-story-of-anthony-johnson-the-black-man-who-was-the-first-to-own-a-slave-in-the-u-s

152.) AAREG. "Anthony Johnson, Indentured Servant Owner born." AAREG. April, 2010. https://aaregistry.org/story/anthony-johnson-indentured-servitude-owner-born/

to keep peasants working constantly when there's no demand for goods and services.

Can you see where this is going? For those who can't read between the lines, let me drag you along. Lofty sums of money are required to perpetually stimulate the business sector. The majority comes from non-essential industries.

There. I said it. Moving on.

When John Casor felt his contract was up and he was being held against his will, he contracted with another farmer, Robert Parker, who Mr Johnson sued in civil court to regain his highly skilled and sought-after planter. Upon losing the first case but winning his appeal, Mr Johnson was awarded Mr Casor as his property in perpetuity throughout Mr Casor's lifetime.[153]

> NOTE: I should've had all those who purchased this handbook sign a disclaimer to keep its content confidential, but if one is serious about becoming a global lord, there's no upside to sharing this information. Your network should be made up of people with the ability to rise to the top regardless of their race, religion or creed, as long as they're committed to subduing humanity and are trustworthy associates.
>
> Use things like race and religion to divide the have-nots but not the haves. It'll behove you to enter this limited circle by any means possible if your thirst for conquest is real. Sure, fairer skinned people were historically given advantages, but perhaps it's even more beneficial to flip the script and advance those with darker skin to widen the racial divide that keeps the peasants squabbling with each other. As long as you fully use those who are willing to sell out others of the same race, nationality, etc. you'll do just fine.
>
> Let's return to our main discussion, shall we?

You'll want to keep a watchful eye on peasants who think outside the box. They'll be the pioneers of advancement on your **FARM**. You must keep all their useful discoveries and inventions for yourself whilst allowing improvements to flourish that make your **FARM(S)** more efficient, profitable and under your control. If these entrepreneurial peasants aren't already working in your tightly controlled corporations, their ideas can be bought or even plucked from their grasp if they lack the knowledge to thrive in the commercial world. Remember, you don't always have to be the brightest to rise to the top, but you, with absolute certainty, must be the most ruthless. For peasants who refuse to turn

---

153.) Boakye, "The fascinating story of Anthony Johnson."

their discoveries/inventions/creations over to you, they can be financially destroyed, publicly slandered or eliminated from the planet altogether if necessary. We'll discuss techniques in upcoming chapters.

Your peasants can also develop a false sense of intelligence and superiority when they hold diplomas, degrees and titles, just like the Scarecrow who suddenly becomes all-knowing when the Wizard of Oz grants him a degree. In fact, chasing such achievements will distract and delay them from thinking about solutions to real-world problems.

Psst...Would peasants really be in such a dire predicament (constant war, debt, environmental ruin, racism, classicism, etc.), if secondary schools and universities were producing geniuses? Since peasants have become dependent on authority figures to provide pre-approved information, they'll also refuse to believe any information that contradicts the narrative provided by *official sources*.

Higher education, a.k.a. extended adolescence, will delay peasants from thinking about their future and will prolong their entry into the workforce. Peasants should be led to believe that if they get into a university, they'll be on the road to success. Remember the Catholic Church and their priests (i.e. authority figures) selling parishioners forgiveness for their sins if they paid a modest fee for their salvation? Isn't this the same as educators promising a great career if one earns a university degree? This will be even more effective if you can create a false demand on your **FARM** for such a debt-creating pursuit by requiring a degree for even the most trivial of occupations. Can you see the *¢ents* in having a clear understanding of history?

> NOTE: Since most farms have already achieved a state of abundance today, there's no need to hurry peasants onto the plantation or train them in trades through such archaic methods as apprenticeships. This would make peasants more self-reliant and productive at an earlier age by working in such practical settings as farms and local communities. Peasants can become more independent through this type of learning, particularly when they acquire skills and knowledge from their elders. For example, how to repair things. You'll know your corporate **FARM** is operating at high efficiency when peasants simply throw out items rather than fix them. The more dependent your human resources are on mass produced corporate products, the further entrenched they'll be in the **FARM'S** production and consumption cycle.

Speaking of debt, your corporate **FARM** will operate to the utmost efficiency, and you'll subsequently reap the biggest rewards if you require your peasants to pay for their own indoctrination. After all, why should it come out of your pocket? You simply provide the framework that consumes the majority of their time and energy.

On the American farm, for example, the entire peasant population will foot the bill for mandatory programming (K-12) when you tax such things as the homes peasants believe are theirs. You'll receive interest payments on their *mort-gages* (death-pledges[154]) throughout the peasants' lifetimes via your banking institutions and you can empower your state, city and local corporate municipalities to borrow against your peasants' and *their* properties by guaranteeing repayment of municipal loans through the power of taxation. You'll be indoctrinating students in training centres, and simultaneously browbeating a debt slave mentality into your **FARM'S** communities by having them finance the extravagances of your **FARM'S** infrastructure. This, even though the credit is actually based on your peasants and their ability to produce things of value.

If you want the **STATE** to have more influence over these young, budding peasants, you can increase government funding to your peasant training centres. This will, in turn, force one or both biological parents to spend more time working on the corporate plantation to pay their rising taxes, thus leaving them less time to devote to their children. From this point on, it's a simple matter of gently guiding these parentless little darlings into the caring hands of the **STATE**. Should the biological parents refuse to pay their property taxes (a.k.a. their rent to you through your corporate government entities), they should be swiftly reminded who truly owns their homes.

> NOTE: Quite naturally, school board positions will attract those with a vested interest in the schooling system. Whether it's someone looking to hand a lucrative contract to an associate or a relative looking to grant a job or higher salary to a family member, these public positions should be left autonomous and unbridled. This will allow guardians of the schooling system to flourish whilst enriching you and your associates and further indebting your peasants. Schooling has emerged as one of the most lucrative industries on a **FARM**, not just because of the

---

154.) Libby Kane, CFEI. "The origins of the word 'mortgage' will make you think twice about buying a house." Insider.com. March 16, 2016. https://www.businessinsider.com/mortgage-means-death-pledge-2016-3?op=1

amount of revenue it generates, but because of the obedient workers, consumers and soldiers it produces.

As far as university degrees are concerned, even more debt can be created if a greater number of peasants borrow money for their *continued education* as encouraged and enforced by your political structure. More borrowing equals more debt, which equals more profits.

Great balls of fire, there are mega shekels to be made!

Not only will you profit from the loans you give through your paper money system, but you can also profit immensely if you own the institutions of *higher learning.* Your political structure can ensure that these entities are *tax free,* giving you an advantage over other industries through such untouched revenue streams as state subsidies, endowments, donations, fundraisers, tuition prices and ticket sales to campus events. You can also get your associates in on the action by having your political pawns appoint them to the board of trustees of state universities seeing that their businesses reap the benefits for contracts such as building a new stadium, providing waste management services or operating a new coffee shop on campus.

You may immediately realise that loaning large sums of money to eighteen-year-old peasants in an extended state of adolescence who own no real-world property as collateral seems like a risky business venture. This is especially true when you understand that many of these peasants are unqualified for more prominent positions on the **FARM**. By lowering standards and flooding the market with as many universities and colleges as there are worthless university degrees, you'll not only create a booming market that will further indoctrinate and enslave your human resources but will support many ancillary industries around these learning centres. It's important that your political structure make the repayment of these loans inescapable whilst also subsidising only those institutions and faculties that fall in line with the scientific research and, hence, *results* you wish to achieve.

These centres of higher learning are also prime targets for infiltration should you wish to change a **FARM'S** political, business or social climate. Even though these institutions should be staffed with status quo advocates, both professors and students alike will be barking like sea lions for a fish to obtain their degrees and get promoted in their **FARM'S** ever-evolving configuration. This will make them willing to do or say just about anything to ensure their own advancement. You should discreetly manipulate both students and faculty to achieve your desired results.

Through your institutions of thought control...oops-a-daisy...I mean *schooling*, you can adjust the level of brain power your herd possesses through a variety of methods, depending on your **FARM'S** needs. As previously mentioned, if you live in a state of excess where most of the important discoveries in a myriad of fields have been made, you can serve yourself quite well by dumbing down the populace. This will leave them virtually helpless should you decide to restrict their freedoms, lower their standard of living or reduce their numbers whilst also retaining all their discoveries and advancements.

Your training centres should aid you by leaving peasants susceptible to your control techniques. For instance, making peasants dependent on technological devices to store information or make routine calculations will diminish their aptitude and analytical skills. Creating complicated techniques to solve mathematical problems will leave them frustrated, shutting down their critical thinking skills. Putting more emphasis on sports and entertainment will shift their focus away from learning and their desire to make more constructive contributions to society. Leisurely activities like sex for pleasure and partying will cheapen their self-worth and lower their moral standards, making them more willing to support the unscrupulous actions you and your associates use to acquire more power.

To produce homogenous, productive and compliant peasants, your training methods should focus on habit training as opposed to intellectual development. I'll leave you with an excerpt from former Harvard professor and father of American Psychology, William James, from his book, *The Principles of Psychology.*

> *Habit is thus the enormous flywheel of society, its most precious conservative agent. It alone is what keeps us all within the bounds of ordinance and saves the children of fortune from the envious uprisings of the poor. It alone prevents the hardest and most repulsive walks of life (a.k.a. jobs) from being deserted by those brought up to tread therein. It keeps the fisherman and the deckhand at sea through the winter; it holds the miner in his darkness and nails the countryman to his log cabin and his lonely farm through all the months of snow; it protects us from invasion by the natives of the desert and the frozen zone. It dooms us all to fight out the*

battle of life upon the lines of our nurture or our early choice, and to make the best of a pursuit that disagrees, because there is no other for which we are fitted, and it is too late to begin again. It keeps different social strata from mixing.[155]

My goodness, I couldn't have said it better myself! Let's press on, shall we?

155.) William James, *The Principles of Psychology* (New York: Henry Holt and Company, 1918), 121

Chapter 12

CONTROL TECHNIQUES

The conscious and intelligent manipulation of the organized opinions and habits of the masses is an important element in a democratic society. Those who manipulate this unseen mechanism of society constitute an invisible government which is the true ruling power of our country.
— Edward Bernays

Up to this point, I've presented quite a few control techniques in great detail, for instance, laws (and the bending thereof) and the invaluable uses of a printing press. There are a few more beneficial tactics for a modern-day lord to explore, like the application of religion, technology and false flag operations. This chapter will, in most instances, just list and skim over the many ways to control your minions. Some tactics are long-established and quite self-explanatory, whilst others are still being perfected and implemented and require a deeper discussion.

> NOTE: As always, I encourage you to remain open-minded and creative to discover even more effective ways to subdue humanity whilst reaping the benefits of its productive capacity.

Because this chapter is an overview of the various methods used to maximise your peasants' fears, whims and desires for your ultimate benefit, it's an excellent one to return to for a quick reference. You *must* possess an unquenchable thirst for knowledge and readily absorb pertinent information to obtain the greatest competitive edge. I strategically chose the placement of this chapter to help strengthen your cross-referencing skills, especially if you don't have a legal background or come from a state-controlled education system that discouraged critical thinking and focused on pre-approved facts and a diluted version of history.

Because we have established the fundamental principles of world domination in the first third of this tutorial, this chapter will serve as a brief recap whilst also foreshadowing the more cryptic and ensnaring techniques yet to come. This handbook is like a set of Russian Matryoshka Dolls where each smaller, encapsulated figurine reveals a vital component of the whole. In our scenario, various topics are disclosed in the very intricate, yet nearly invisible, control grid that's carefully woven into the fabric of today's **FARMS**.

Foremost, when effectively controlling any **FARM**, let alone the entire world, if you wish to establish and maintain a powerful ruler's position, it's imperative that you operate in secrecy. Your pawns, a.k.a. *elected leaders,* can come and go, but you must always remain in control of your **FARM(S)**, and it's best to do so from behind the scenes. This will help keep your motives and objectives concealed and ensure your longevity. Peasants will blame your transgressions on those within their periphery and in positions of *authority*. By staging elections, you can lead peasants to believe that *office holders* work for them and not you and can *vote* them out if not performing to their liking. Just be sure all the influential candidates are on your payroll and part of your secret fraternity, leaving you in a perpetual win-win situation.

Always use your information outlets to make yourself appear benevolent and to conceal your role in your **FARM'S** affairs. Although you might be tempted to flaunt your superiority, you must blend into the background even if you climb to the highest of highs…Lord of the entire world. Think of it this way, the more peasants you subjugate, the more there are to rise up against you. Operating in the shadows will redirect their attention to more visible and accessible targets and will allow a longer lasting reign.

Entering the race to the top, you'll discover that you're not alone in your quest. Ruling just one **FARM**, let alone the entire planet, is nearly an impossible task by yourself. Accomplices and foot soldiers will be instrumental in shepherding the flock in your direction. You can convince humans of just about anything. This is especially true if you've trained them properly and robbed them of their personal power and autonomy. Keeping peasants blissfully ignorant just adds to the delight of watching them beg for their rulers' good graces.

Since there are many aspiring lords just like you, it'll be important to network with the best of the best to reach your global conquest goals. The crowning of the King of the World and the responsibility of paving the way for the upper echelon of society will be decided based on talent and execution.

NOTE: Once you have established your fraternity and its networks, it's important to maintain *order*. You must do this by any means necessary. Compromise will leave room for a new, more natural order to develop, resulting in the loss of your clans' superiority. The techniques in this chapter will help you achieve and maintain *order* and aid in preventing peasants from uniting.

Whether you're building a world domination team from scratch, planning to ascend through the system already in place, or aim to usurp it, you'll need to understand and master the art of infiltration. You saw how this was done on a free, people's law **FARM** like early America that, until now, has been the most difficult to wrangle yet the most important in terms of world domination. A weak **FARM** can obviously be taken rather quickly by way of military defeat, debt or both, but a strong, moral, prosperous and independent **FARM** requires a more methodical approach. This is especially true if its framework is to be turned upside down from a utopian concept into an Orwellian super state. As a general rule, the bigger the goal and the stronger the opponent, the more cautious and precise your calculated takeover must be.

NOTE: Like the ruler who remains in the shadows, the inner machinations of your secret society should remain obscured by rumours and by acts of good deeds in the community. You'll further lend credibility to your fraternity by filling its ranks with upstanding members of a **FARM'S** society. You can be certain that most inductees into your private cartel won't argue over such perks as political and judicial favours. Please recognise this is not simply a suggestion, but a directive. You'll find that most humans will jump at the opportunity to gain an advantage over their inferiors. Very few will look out for the best interest of their fellow man unless their self-interest is at stake. In rare cases, those acting on principle or out of concern for others must be decisively targeted, discredited and eliminated.

Once you've aligned yourself with people who share your vision for the fate of those who clutter the highway during rush hour traffic, the **FARM'S** centres of power *must* be created or infiltrated and then controlled. A shortlist of these institutions includes governments, churches, banks, media outlets, opposition movements, universities, charitable organisations, associations, lobby groups, large corporations, the courts, police agencies, military branches, etc. Trusted agents must be in place to prevent peasants from gaining control of associations that they would use for their own gain.

As discussed earlier in this sacred writing, the most important centre of power used to enslave your commoners, an entire **FARM** and eventually the entire world (insert your own blood curdling laugh here) is a private, monopolised banking institution that you own and operate. This will allow you to weigh down peasants with debt and interest. Once you have staffed the government with your agents and burdened it with debt, you can use the various forms of taxation (see Chapter 8) to further entrench peasants in the economic and political system of your farm.

Since controlling the supply of a rigged fiat money system is the single most effective way to enslave a **FARM**, it won't be easily won or achieved. Again, you'll need accomplices who are enticed by the advantages your system provides. If starting a **FARM** from scratch, simply conjure up a banking system and charge others for its services.

Because almost the entire land mass of the Earth already has well-established **FARM** boundaries with accompanying political and economic systems in place, you may need to invade and defeat a **FARM'S** military to seize its centre of power. However, if you have the time, a more effective approach is to infiltrate a **FARM'S** seats of power with your generously compensated agents to begin your gradual take over.

When scattered tribes occupied the land, the *modus operandi* was to form an imperial army and decimate anyone in the way of targeted resources, whilst implementing a more efficient wealth generating system in the conquered territory. Today, militaries can still take over weaker **FARMS**, but with the advancement of both weaponry and social structures, this isn't as straightforward as it once was, especially if a **FARM** contains nuclear warheads or similar technology capable of mass carnage.

> NOTE: If you're ruling a **FARM** that doesn't have a weapon of mass destruction, you should acquire one, allowing you to be taken more seriously by the international community of lords.

If you wish to succeed in global conquest, loyalty to a particular **FARM** and its political or economic system is to your detriment. Your goal should be to profit from as many **FARMS** as possible through both your banking and corporate structures. This is especially true with military conflicts. It's incredibly important that you seek to profit from all **FARMS** engaged in a battle, regardless of their *national* persuasions and ideologies. By financing and supplying all the key players involved in combat, you'll earn their compliance through the terms and conditions of your financial contribution, regardless of the outcome. Building a superior economic **FARM** will allow you to do this more readily. Operating through a variety of corporate structures will also help conceal your support of more than one **FARM** involved in a skirmish. Once you have dominated all the *nations* on the globe, you can continue applying the techniques provided in this handbook to rule the entire human race.

I say! I do hope you keep me posted on your progress.

Once you firmly establish the political, economic and banking systems on a farm, they're yours to take over or to lose. By keeping members of your secret fraternity both content and in positions of power, the engine of commerce will smoothly chug along, as there are few who'll want to disrupt a system that gives them an advantage over others. Even peasants who recognise they're suffering the adverse effects of the situation won't want to disrupt a system that allows them the comfort of a day-to-day routine.

Only by *uniting* can peasants overcome a system implemented for your benefit. It's my great pleasure to present some of the most effective methods used to distract and divert them from accomplishing this task.

This first tactic known as *divide and conquer* goes as far back as war and politics. It was used by Julius Caesar and even accredited to an alleged slave owner, Willie Lynch, who in 1712 purportedly delivered a speech that instructed Southern plantation owners on how to control unruly Black slaves. Instead of *lynching* slaves, which he stated was counterproductive to the plantation owners' interests, he supposedly advised pitting them against one another using fear and envy. The following is an excerpt from his speech.

> *I have outlined a number of differences among the slaves, and I take these differences and make them bigger. I use fear and envy for control purposes. These methods have worked on my modest plantation in the West Indies, and it will work throughout the South. Take this simple little list of differences and think about them. On top of my list is "Age", but it is there only because it starts with an "A"; the second is "Color" or shade, there is intelligence, size, sex, size of plantations, status on plantation, attitude of owners, whether the slaves live in the valley, on the hill,*

East, West, North, South, have fine hair, coarse hair, or are tall or short. Now that you have a list of differences, I shall give you an outline of action—but before that I shall assure you that distrust is stronger than trust, and envy is stronger than adulation, respect or admiration.

The Black slave after receiving this indoctrination shall carry on and will become self re-fueling and self-generating for hundreds of years, maybe thousands. Don't forget you must pit the old Black male vs. the young Black male, and the young Black male against the old Black male. You must use the dark skin slaves vs. the light skin slaves and the light skin slaves vs. the dark skin slaves. You must use the female vs. the male and the male vs. the female. You must also have your white servants and overseers distrust all Blacks, but it is necessary that your slaves trust and depend on us. They must love, respect and trust only us.

Even if the origin of this speech is a little suspicious, there are certainly a few vital and deeply resonating points you can apply in today's modern world. On an international level, you can create fear and/or envy of another **FARM** by highlighting its race, religion, political ideologies, economic systems, customs, laws of the land, wealth disparities, military capabilities, language, affiliations with other **FARMS**, ties to radicalism and just about any other reason you can think of to highlight the stark differences between peasants from opposing **FARMS**. The primary purpose of F.E.A.R. or as I like to say a *False Emotion Appearing Real* is to override your peasants' critical thinking skills, so they act on irrational, emotional impulses brought on by characteristics like those listed above. Just be sure to use your information outlets to inflate these discrepancies to astronomical proportions in order to have your peasants risk life and limb to achieve your objectives.

War is a necessary endeavour. It's human nature to want more. To fulfil this innate desire, you must take from others who actually wish to do the same to you. Since the earliest days of human history, there have been those who tried to conquer and control others through brute force and strength. Why not use this instinct to your advantage? If you don't, someone else will. Again, if this frightens you, not everyone is born to be a ruler. Perhaps you would be more comfortable mastering the craft of whittling. A quick Google search will direct you to the best deals on starter kits that will fill the abundance of time your meaningless life now provides. For those with a little *chutzpah*, let's talk war.

> NOTE: To incite a war, you need not be a war veteran. You should avoid the battlefield at all costs since you not only have a lot to lose in terms of wealth and power, but you're much more valuable as your **FARM'S** decision maker. You're a commodity far too important to be used as cannon fodder. Assuming you've had the proper upbringing, you'll be seeking peasants that require the discipline, focus and structure your military provides. By giving them a purpose, you will earn their loyalty and commitment regardless of how you use them.

Overall, war is a fabulous control technique because it achieves several objectives at one time. Sure, without war, all **FARMS** could acquire a large amount of wealth. As food and other necessary essentials are produced, they'd become more abundant, to where peasants would no longer need to work so hard to meet demand. Even the less fortunate of the world's **FARMS** could be provided for with the surplus in productivity. But, as a ruler-in-the-making, can you see the problem? For one, peasants would have far too much time on their hands once they reach a state of abundance, allowing them relief from their mundane affairs and giving them time to critically analyse the world around them. Peasants could then freely pursue their own purposes whilst becoming wiser, more independent and hence, less controllable. A scenario that is very detrimental to your plans.

War also requires great capital in the form of loans, and it's quite difficult to exploit peasants through the interest on your paper money if **FARMS** have no need to borrow for such an extravagant expense. In addition, a wonderful instrument such as the phallic shaped bomb is an incredible tool that can be used to drive the wheels of industry. Not only does it require peasants' time and labour to assemble, but the devastation it brings once activated keeps them building and rebuilding, allowing no real increase in wealth…well, for them anyway. Whilst peasants are busy blowing things up and putting them back together, it keeps them far too occupied to take a step back and see your methods at work, thus protecting your dominance.

On a darker note, as a **FARM'S** population grows to unsustainable levels, war is a helpful way to keep the peasants' numbers in a manageable range. With humans at the top of the food chain, a large conflict pitting human against human can serve as a helpful way to reduce growth spurts that arise from a void in natural predators. The lower echelon of society will keep replicating itself with reckless abandon if you don't put control measures in place. Reasons range from peasants wanting to escape their economic condition by creating more potential breadwinners, to simply having no greater matters of importance to address. By sending your undesirables to the front lines, you can more discreetly cull the herd whilst you simultaneously use them to achieve your objectives.

Since your goal is global conquest, it'll be necessary for you to construct the most robust economic farm possible from the beginning or, even better, take control of an existing one that can be utilised as your global enforcement arm. In either scenario, you'll need a **FARM** with a strong economy able to withstand the perils of war. It's also imperative that you silence and, if necessary, eliminate any objectors to your overall agenda, especially upon conquest of a newly acquired **FARM**. Many remnants of the old guard will be in the upper ranks of its intelligence, military and political structures, and having your associates ready to step in and replace them will be crucial to your success.

There are many ways to achieve important alliances, some include bribery (foreign aid), threats, infiltration, debt, economic leverage, military conquests, fear, sabotage, regime change, shared business endeavours, cultural and/or military interests or any other inventive way you can think of to draw other **FARMS** to your cause. There's no set method or blueprint for achieving important alliances, but it's incredibly important that your network of associates runs deep into the veins of the **FARMS** you've acquired.

You *must* be in firm control of these captured **FARMS**. As emphatically mentioned throughout this handbook, implementing your debt-based money system is the most important thing you can do to seize and maintain control of these *nations*. Having a strong military presence in an occupied territory to assert your gentle influence when required is a close second.

By slightly revamping conquered farms that already have an oppressive system in place, you can give the citizens the illusion of freedom and win them over to your cause. Shifting and manoeuvring to gain control of all **FARMS** on the planet is a delicate skill and has taken thousands of years to arrive at the point we are today. I say this not to discourage you, but to give you a realistic understanding of the type of commitment required. Your descendants must continue with your bold vision for a world of tomorrow to reach your ambitious aspirations.

The encouraging news is that technology, in combination with the well-established methods presented in this handbook, has made world conquest a real possibility. Even just a century ago, enslaving all of humanity under one system would have been nearly impossible.

If you're fortunate enough to have a warlike, military nation as your world police force, you'll need a bogeyman to keep this **FARM** in a constant state of fear, so your peasants are ready to jump at your command to intrude on other **FARMS**. As we've already discussed, there are many ways to create and propagate the fear of a physical, philosophical or spiritual enemy which can be real, imaginary or a combination thereof.

Fear and envy aren't only great inciting elements for war but can also cleverly drive your **FARM'S** business sector. Not only will you repress your peasants financially, physically and spiritually but you can bring yourself and your associates great prosperity. For example, by delivering a good scare into *patients* of the current medical system, one can more easily guide them into treatments, products and procedures that not only line your pocket but more deeply entrench them into a system of sickness, giving you and your fraternity of world marauders a distinct advantage. If this is unsettling, perhaps you should consider the following advice from Napolean Bonaparte in his will to his son on the topic of ruling: 'To govern is to diffuse morality, education and well-being.'[156]

You should know that generating envy on your farm is straightforward, but it can also be amplified to new heights using today's media outlets. By making a false need sexy, admirable or trendy, you tap into the peasants' yearning for fulfilment. As a result, peasants will feel more desirable if they obtain/consume these products, leaving them feeling as if their self-worth depends on purchasing these commodities. Since we've already explored how human societies always arrange themselves into three tiers, these class distinctions can trick peasants into wanting things their peers have or, better yet, can coax them into acquiring said products so they appear to be part of a higher social order. Trying to outdo their neighbours will keep them spinning indefinitely on the corporate rat wheel.

Another key element is an aspiring ruler's ability to create and use poverty to their advantage. Like war, the use of squalor is multifaceted and is another useful tool in establishing a purpose for the political

---

156.) Frederic Bastiat, *The Law* (Auburn, Alabama: the Ludwig von Mises Institute, 2007), 41.

structure on a **FARM**. If not for war, there really wouldn't be a strong need for people to organise into a society.[157] Once a society is formed, however, poverty helps provide the necessary incentive for its peasants to be productive. This is where you come in. Someone is needed to harness and manage the peasants' output whilst also maintaining order and stability. Are you starting to see why you must be well compensated for your efforts? Not only is your responsibility quite enormous, but if everyone benefitted equally there would be no concentration of power from which to delegate.[158]

Naturally, there'll be peasants who are more motivated, productive and skilled than others. To prevent backlash from the impoverished bottom rung against the upper two tiers, a war system provides the anti-social, disenfranchised and unemployable of the lower echelon one last opportunity to fill a useful purpose on a **FARM** before taking more extreme measures.[159] For those beyond reach, the prison system can be used.

In relation to the war scheme, poverty not only creates the desperation needed to fuel military enlistment, but it helps justify the robbing of resources from other **FARMS**, giving your witless plunderers extra hidden incentive even if they're sometimes unknowingly used for this purpose. An air of superiority is natural on a **FARM** with a more lavish lifestyle, just like it'll be for you as an individual lord. Envy is a powerful force that will inspire others to be more like you. When they take on your worldview, they also strengthen your system of conquest. Poverty on your **FARM**, as well as other **FARMS**, will put peasants in a more vulnerable position when it comes to protecting and utilising natural resources. Once these raw materials are under your well-managed control, you'll have the luxury of creating shortages, real or imaginary, that allow you to raise the prices on necessities peasants require, giving you incredible leverage over them. Poverty is also a key component to poor health that can generate profits on sickness and grant you more control of a **FARM**.

Finally, impoverished subjects will be forced to depend on your political system for their sustenance, making them loyal supporters. All *citizens* can be made to rely on a **FARM'S** government for its good favours that come in the form of subsidies, salaries, programmes

---

157.) Leonard C. Lewin, *Report from Iron Mountain: On the Possibility and Desir-ability of Peace* (London: Bridger House Publishers, Inc, 2008), 38.
158.) Lewin, *Report from Iron Mountain*, 41.
159.) Lewin, *Report from Iron Mountain*, 41.

and undertakings. The result is a transfer of wealth from the hands of the productive into the hands of your associates within the political structure and the swarm of aspiring beneficiaries hovering around it. Once again, as long as you're the one reaping the greatest rewards through the interest charged on your valueless paper, you can drop money from a helicopter if necessary.

Since a **FARM'S** government will be the primary apparatus in achieving your goals, we'll delve into the many crafty techniques that can be embedded into its framework to bring your wildest fantasies to life.

> NOTE: There should always be at least one perceived upside for peasants, however slight, to justify any system, programme or venture that requires their adherence. This will help prevent retaliation and will prod their participation, even if reluctantly so.

First, the political structure itself can be used to divide and conquer peasants on a **FARM**. By splitting alleged *representatives* into at least two parties (two works best) and by giving these parties firm defining guidelines they're *supposed* to adhere to, you can coerce peasants into choosing a team that they feel most aligns with their interests. Usually, their choice of affiliation is passed down through the familial unit.

Giving each team a colour and a mascot turns what should be the peasants concerns and interests into a sporting event, where each side deeply entrenches itself in the political process and applies whatever tactics are necessary to emerge victorious. As long as peasants feel their team is fighting for them, they'll overlook any transgressions their *representatives* commit to win. Creating an overall atmosphere of acceptable, illicit behaviour from those in such frivolous disciplines as sports, entertainment and politics will condition peasants to place results over principles.

> NOTE: When financing candidates to represent your interests in the political *arena*, find or create compromised individuals to maintain the greatest leverage possible. A few quick examples include discovering or entrapping those who partake in such publicly despicable acts as extra-marital affairs, drug usage/dealing or, most egregious of all, paedophilia. As a general rule, the lower you're willing to go, the more control and power you'll have. You can also flip around this same technique to discredit a worthy opponent to your rule. Simply throw out a broadly despised accusation against your adversary, and watch as he tries to refute the allegation, whilst your trusted agents uncover the set up that has been placed around him. If all else fails, simply accuse him of having sex with a pig. Watching him scramble for words is amusing, but a vehement denial will have

you rolling on the floor. If veins start bulging from his forehead as he emphatically defends himself, you just may rupture your spleen.

Oh, great lord of the underworld, I do hope this is all sinking in.

By assigning confusing positions like pro-life but for the death penalty to a party's platform, you can greatly distort your chattels' logic and ability to think clearly. There's a concept known in the world of philosophy as the Hegelian Dialectic. At the principles' core, we see that the human brain must have one extreme to fully comprehend the other. For instance, one could not totally grasp fat if unfamiliar with skinny. In every discussion/conflict, there are always two opposing points of view. When applied to politics, you should control the two sides of the peasants' perceived paradigms which, by the way, you must operate beyond. By controlling the extremes peasants are familiar with, you can mentally entrap them in this more limited level of understanding whilst keeping your trespasses beyond their purview.

Once this has been achieved, they'll argue the positions you create for them. This is why authority over the major media outlets is incredibly important. Keep in mind, what you don't tell peasants is often more important than what you do tell them. Overall, you'll need to emit as much bollocks and create as many distractions as you can to consume the peasants' attention, especially if you're making major moves you wish to keep hidden in plain view.

NOTE: If you manufacture a news story, you must sprinkle in a dash of truth to give it an air of legitimacy. This will help it resonate as authentic in what's hopefully a sea of clouded intuitions. Above all, please remember the wise words of Adolf Hitler: 'If you tell a big enough lie and tell it frequently enough, it will be believed.'

Once you divide peasants into political ideologies, *wedge issues* can trigger peasants to scratch each other's eyes out whilst occupying their thoughts with matters of little importance. A great modern-day example is unisex public toilets, which makes amusing workplace chatter. To add a little obstacle, mix in a dash of political correctness to stymie their voices to just above a whisper. Ultimately, they'll go along with just about anything to feed themselves and their families.

Abortion is one of the most instrumental wedge issues of all time.

The beauty of this practice is that, in reality, it possesses many grey areas. To illustrate, many women who believe they should have the right to choose would never, for any reason, undergo the procedure. However, even the sternest of pro-life advocates would, at least, consider letting the mother choose her fate in a life-or-death situation during childbirth or perhaps out of outrage in a case involving the incestual rape of a young girl. The pro-life/pro-choice debate is also an excellent tool you can use to alienate men from women on a **FARM**. Religions and other cultural constructs, such as the women's liberation movement, aren't only excellent divisive measures but can be used to inflame powerful moral and philosophical dilemmas.

From a structural standpoint, it's important for you to understand that human offerings have been historically necessary to control population sizes, whilst also serving as a useful tool to target certain fringe elements, leading to *social purification* and *state security*. The Spanish Inquisition serves as a shining example.[160] Peasants must fear the repercussions of abandoning groupthink, essential for a unified and cohesive **FARM**.

On a spiritual level, a ruler's metaphysical convictions are a crucial component of their success or failure in the material realm. Since one cannot serve two masters, it's important to make a firm choice between a god that subtracts and divides or one that adds and multiplies. From our discussion thus far, I think it should be obvious which one you must choose. Blood sacrifices are instrumental offerings for power in this principality and puts you in good favour with the deity that historically all successful rulers have turned to in order to assert their dominance, despite the one they publicly profess loyalty to.

Lies and deceit are necessary tools of effective leadership. It'll behove you to pursue a form of worship that explores and embraces these darker characteristics of human nature whilst peasants should be directed toward belief systems that restrict their natural impulses, providing a wonderful form of self-regulation.

I mean, what else is there to prevent these poor saps from seizing you and your well-groomed estate?

Finally, if you can diminish the peasants' respect for human life through a wedge issue such as abortion, you can eliminate other aspects of a peasant's dignified existence such as their privacy, free speech, due process and the like. Even on an alleged free **FARM** such as America, it's

---

160.) Lewin, *Report from Iron Mountain*, 71.

amusing to find that the destruction of an eagle egg carries a harsher penalty (a $1,000 fine and one year in prison), than the abortion of a budding peasant. Lawmakers can loosen regulations on embryonic terminations once they have reached a maximum threshold of useful peasants.

Government is the hub where important **FARM** decisions are made. For example, which *country* to wage war against, the acceptable number of peasants allowed to occupy a **FARM** and the number of laws needed to regulate the peasants' behaviour.

There's no other authoritative measure that takes greater precedence than to outlaw all competing currencies.

If you're still unable to form the words on your lips, you may need to limit yourself to more menial affairs and should instantly put down this handbook.

For those with the courage and talent to rule, this means you *must* create your own legal tender and forbid the use of any other money. Once your fiat money is fully protected through the use of force, making your peasants collateral for the debt should be a top priority. Using a nexus of hidden adhesion contracts, discussed in Chapter 7, is one method that has worked quite splendidly. In fact, many participants in such a **FARM'S** political, legal and economic systems have little to no awareness of this technique. That's why it works. Just be sure to include a perceived benefit for peasants to engage themselves in what should be a very lopsided arrangement in your favour.

Similarly, creating corporate constructs for a **FARM'S** civil and commercial endeavours will allow you and your associates to fade into the background whilst removing all personal liability for wrongdoing. The more false realities you create, the more protection your syndicate has.

Licences force peasants to seek permission for just about everything they do. In the professional world, a licence allows you to intimidate the **FARM'S** industries toward your end goals whilst giving peasants the illusion that you're protecting their interests. In the same breath, burdening your flock with an overabundance of rules and regulations allows you to railroad a targeted peasant for any reason.

The look of confusion on their faces is priceless as is watching them beeline to your trusted gatekeepers (a.k.a. lawyers) to avoid the headache of trying to decipher all the legal mumbo jumbo that pertains to their situation. Most will gladly empty their pockets to appoint such a surrogate to speak on their behalf and to help them navigate through the star chamber proceedings that will contractually obligate them to whatever outcomes their stand-ins can muster.

Other examples of fake worlds used to consume the peasants' attention, wealth and autonomy include Hollywood, the Internet, virtual realities and extravagant material pursuits.

Whether you already sit atop a **FARM'S** pyramid and run your political construct through a descending hierarchy of associates or you plan to rise to prominence the old-fashioned way via such avenues as a *coup d'état* or popular vote, tapping into the herd's fears, frustrations, prejudices and concerns is a *must*. This is true even if your underlying intent is to steamroll over the peasants' needs and wants once you take power. Therefore, you should limit peasants' understanding of a **FARM'S** clandestine affairs. As long as you sell hope and pretend to have their best interests at heart, you'll win their support.

In rare situations, it'll be necessary to put a tyrant in charge of a **FARM** to bring about extreme changes or to sacrifice a portion of a **FARM'S** herd for a larger purpose. It should be noted that only those who possess absolute power should orchestrate this advanced technique. To gain insight into the human psyche, maybe you need to run questionable experiments on a segment of the population. Or maybe you need to drum up sympathy and support for the creation of a new **FARM** operating under the guise of a haven for a targeted race/religion, whilst simultaneously acting as a front and aggressor for your world domination objectives. Either way, you'll need to stir up and capitalise on as much fanatical sentiment as you can to justify your radical measures. Just be sure to criminalise and manipulate public sentiment against any boisterous critics undermining *official* narratives that have the potential to expose your more controversial undertakings.

Political leaders who make outlandish statements (the more the better) help keep peasants occupied as they contemplate and debate such purposeful yet frivolous articulations. This helps humanise the leader, making them appear fallible to which, of course, peasants can relate. This may also lead a **FARM'S** subjects to falsely believe they're more qualified to rule, leaving them less inclined to see a leader's harmful transgressions as deliberate but more as acts of incompetence.

As history has shown, how can you persecute a president like Ronald Reagan who declared, 'Ketchup is a vegetable', or Bill Clinton who dismissed his marijuana usage by claiming, 'I didn't inhale'? If your luminary isn't publicly expressing such outrageous thoughts, they become just like everyone else, the peasants lose interest and disengage from your civic system of control.

You'll have more success advancing a political ideology, agenda or major shift in a **FARM'S** landscape by focusing the peasants' attention on a leader's personality or other defining characteristics as opposed to an in-depth analysis of their policies. This is more appealing to peasants because it's more in their realm of understanding and gives them the illusion they get a choice amongst all your bought-and-paid-for candidates. A great modern-day American example is the cowboy versus the maverick versus the first Black president, all of whom pushed America's imperialistic, pro big business, pro big bank agenda whilst differing wildly in personality, presentation and approach.[161]

You *must* be in charge of all sides of your **FARMS'** conflicts and debates. On more sophisticated **FARMS**, having an actual outlet to reveal dark truths is a nice pressure release that can be further used to divide your **FARM'S** inhabitants. Just be sure to control this opposition, not so ironically known in the global lord lexicon as *controlled opposition*. You'll want your controlled opposition to have some sort of outrageous side to them you can use to destroy their credibility and any momentum they achieve. The dividends from this smearing technique will pay off, as it will also tarnish anyone else who shares a similar position. This exploited blemish can be real or, better yet, manufactured, and is especially useful if a reputable truth teller draws unwanted attention to your motives and tactics. Just be sure to have your media attack dogs ready to rip any legitimate opponent limb from limb. As usual, assassination, character or otherwise, must be a viable option. Like in George Orwell's novel *Nineteen Eight-Four*, a contrived adversary like Emmanuel Goldstein can also be used to draw out and identify any potential resistors to your rule. Since the truth always becomes known anyway, why not use it to your advantage to find out who and where your detractors are? Just be sure to monitor and track anyone with the ability to disrupt the social order you've worked so tirelessly to create.

Since a **FARM'S** governing body will be the apparatus used to oversee and set policies for all aspects of a plantation's day-to-day affairs, you'll need to have a firm grasp on it. This framework will, in turn, be used to ensure the proper operation of your **FARM'S** more

---

161.) David Icke interviewed by Eamonn Holmes, "David Icke discusses theories and politics with Eamonn Holmes," YouTube video, 36:41, TalkTV, April 26, 2019, https://youtu.be/GaUKOQ4rsdQ

direct control mechanisms such as banks, prisons, religious centres, medical institutions, food and drug suppliers, the courts, the military, corporations, literature, the arts, media outlets, communication and transportation networks, intelligence services, law enforcement, natural and human resources, education, etc. To ensure the peasants' confidence and patronage, there must be a real or perceived benefit to justify the existence of these institutions.

For example, a bank can be seen as a safe place to store one's wealth or a jail can keep communities safe from those out to do them harm. If under physical duress from an injury or health crisis, medical professionals in clinics and hospitals provide a necessary community service, as do learning centres that teach the fundamentals of reading, writing and arithmetic. But it's the skill of the crafty lord to bend and twist these basic **FARM** provisions for their own benefit and the benefit of their associates.

On new or expanding **FARMS**, control measures on productive portions of society should be lenient to allow the growth necessary to become profitable. Once you reach economic proficiency, you can use your government structure to regulate these industries for your benefit. If an associate rises to prominence in the business world, they can then further use their influence, via the political structure, to stymie or eliminate competition in their field of achievement. As long as you have a way to cash in on all aspects of a **FARM'S** profitability through both a bureaucratic apparatus and, more importantly, a paper money system, you'll remain Emperor Supreme.

Only individuals who meet the criteria and are advanced into your private fraternity should be allowed to reach upper levels of status on your **FARM**. A legislative body backed by the force of law and a military should protect you and your affiliates' properties, investments and interests and to keep unwanted members from entering into your social strata. On more established **FARMS**, a slew of agencies, staffed by insiders from industries they're supposed to be overseeing, can be used to create and enforce regulations on unwanted intruders whilst providing a false sense of protection for peasants. Keep in mind, it'll be the business ventures deemed *illegal* by your political institutions that you should own and control with maximum efficiency to give you an advantage over those solely producing products/services for legal purchase.

NOTE: If you're a member of the mafia, a criminal enterprise or a street gang, it's in your best interest to move your talents over to a **FARM'S** political structure. Using the force of law against obedient citizens (instead of it being used against you) takes much less effort than an illegal extortion racket and provides much greater yields. For example, using a systemic chain of command the public willingly complies with is much more efficient than sending your goons out to local businesses to collect protection money. Just be sure to afford peasants a possible upside whilst making an example of any peasant who steps outside the rules.

Please be advised; the world's global lord alliance is always looking for associates willing to go much further in terms of violence and oppression to extract wealth and productivity out of others, even if it puts their own **FARM** at risk. As many current lords can attest, why not turn enforcement actions against you into protection services for you? Historically, some of the world's most cherished lords have gotten their start by way of illicit activities. Then, by using one or more of the tactics in this manual, have risen to prominence by exploiting their fellow countrymen.

To establish credibility for your governing body whilst also validating any decisive measures it must take to impose its will, it's imperative that you create, control and/or swiftly react to any crisis, emergency or disaster that arises on a **FARM**. There's no better reason to have a top-down, chain of command organisation ready to respond to a calamity at a moment's notice. It's imperative that you protect *all* your property to the best of your ability.

Political issues too complex, too frightening or too confusing for the commoners to understand will increase their dependence on the **FARM'S** governing bodies. By presenting those in positions of authority as saviours during a crisis, the populous will be more willing to go along with any course of action these *experts* must take. By having a desired outcome pre-planned (legislative or otherwise), you can simply wait for, encourage or ignite a situation on a **FARM** and then execute your strategy. Useful examples range from disarming or displacing a segment of the population to waging a war against another **FARM**. Remember, national emergencies provide the perfect justification to clamp down on your peasants' movements, transactions, behaviours, and overall independence, putting you in complete control of their fate. As American political fixture Rahm Emanuel once proclaimed:

'You never want a serious crisis to go to waste.'[162] In such extreme circumstances, you must be ready to act swiftly and decisively, as there's a small window of opportunity to capitalise on the fears of a **FARM'S** inhabitants.

Ideally, you'll want your most dominant governing body as far away from the peasants as possible. This will give peasants less control and you more. Obviously, the closer in proximity peasants are to their governing authorities, the more pressure they can apply. Placing the top ruling body in its own isolated city away from the commoners will serve as an added layer of protection from their demands and influences. Also, having private club members such as lawyers and secret fraternity members operating within all levels of a **FARM'S** power structure will help keep outsiders from infiltrating through the ranks and diverting your agenda.

When the time comes to conquer the entire planet, you'll want an exclusive world governing body of appointed accomplices to whom peasants have no access, sway or electing powers. This carefully arranged alliance should contain the *crème de le crème* of the world's intellectuals and social elite, including you as their esteemed leader. Once established, this body will simply pass down orders and directives to all humankind. To reach this point, it'll be necessary to draw in conspirators from every single **FARM** who'll bring about your vision and desired fate for the aimless hordes scattered across the globe.

As we're about to discover, by offering your peasants the illusion of freedom, you'll more emphatically gain their allegiance to your rule and will more easily garner their participation when building your world empire. For those who resist or need further incentive to see things your way, I'll show you the most persuasive approaches to gain their compliance. At the very least, you should familiarise yourself with ways to prevent nonconformists from obstructing your agenda. Therefore, please stay focused and pay close attention as I present the remaining hidden secrets required to fulfil your quest for global dominance.

If it may humbly please you, Your Excellency.

162.) Rahm Emanuel, "Rahm Emanuel on the Opportunities of Crisis," YouTube video, 2:47, The Wall Street Journal, November 19, 2008, https://youtu.be/_mzc-bXi1Tkk?si=-wSZ8W6R16EkXTcE

Chapter 13

THE ILLUSION OF FREEDOM

None are more hopelessly enslaved than those who falsely believe they are free.
— Johann Wolfgang von Goethe

Whether you choose to rule your **FARM** with an iron fist or have the vision, confidence and experience necessary to allow your peasants more privileges, it'll behove you to always lead peasants to believe they are free. At the very least, you must convince them they're indebted to you, the ruler, and wouldn't have the quality of life they have if not for your good graces. In many cases this will be true, especially with technology and the conveniences it affords.

However, if you implement a more stringent governing style than those administered on more *liberated* **FARMS**, it's in your best interest to operate within a closed system to prevent your peasants from being influenced by the less restrictive lifestyles experienced elsewhere. If you allow dominated subjects to be exposed to less oppressive herd management styles, you risk insurrection.

Conversely, if you have the good fortune of successfully managing an open system, you'll find that closed systems can inspire your herd to both exploit and wage war against these *inferior* **FARMS** to prevent their systems from reaching your shores. Once you've conquered most **FARMS** on the planet and moulded a good portion of its inhabitants into ideal subjects, you can begin imposing a closed system on the entire world whilst also reducing the Earth's population to more sustainable levels. It'll be important, however, to retain enough useful peasants to not only maintain the technologies and breakthroughs you and your predecessors extracted from the productive portions of society, but to continue to develop them as well.

By entrapping a simple life form such as an ant in a jar, this poor and dear insect will spend its remaining days striving to break free once aware of its confinement. This built-in desire to be free is a powerful, innate force in all living creatures, causing them to act instinctively and without reason. This includes your producers and warriors-in-the-making. Once again, the wise and skilful ruler will harness this natural driving force for their own benefit whilst simultaneously keeping their subjects under control.

The promise of freedom provides power, as illustrated by previous historic occurrences such as the Bolshevik Revolution and the American Civil War, even though the substantial number of commoners who were led into a deepened state of enslavement far outweighed the few who were actually liberated.

> NOTE: The most dominant members of a society always rise to the top and will accomplish this by any means necessary. Otherwise, why would you be reading this handbook? I think you'll be quite delighted when you find yourself in a more advantageous position than those entering the rise to power without the insight of this trusty little guide.

Now, as I was saying…

In Russia, it was the craftiness of Lenin and his fellow Bolsheviks who tapped into the angst of the poor and working class whilst capitalising on their simmering anger toward the oppressive Tsar and sitting aristocracy. By promising freedom and power to the people, the Bolsheviks garnered support of the disgruntled workers, peasants and soldiers who eventually led them to victory.[163] But as any thirsty despot knows, it's impossible to secure your power without taking power from the many and expanding the size and scope of the state. This historic example shows that it matters little what you say to win the support of the *people* as long as you can assert your dominance once you're in charge. Unfortunately, those willing to sacrifice themselves for the promise of freedom were corralled into a den of state slavery where human life became less than worthless.[164]

In the American Civil War, very few were interested in helping solidify *a more perfect union* or in laymen's terms, *an all-encompassing state*. It wasn't until the Emancipation Proclamation, signed by President Lincoln on 1 January 1863, that the war became about—what else? Freedom. This freedom, of course, only applied to slaves in the rebellious

163.) Gregori Maximov. "Bolshevism: Promises and Reality – Gregori Maximov." lib-com.org. June 28, 2017. https://libcom.org/article/bolshevism-promises-and-real-ity-gregori-maximov

164.) Maximov, "Bolshevism: Promises and Reality."

Southern states, not to slaves in the Northern or pro-Union border states. This freedom for slaves in the Southern states was only to be granted upon a Union victory. But who's counting? To win this, eh hum, freedom, the Enrollment Act of 1863 was passed on 3 March of that same year, forcing all Northern males between the ages of twenty and forty-five into mandatory military service.

So, by promising to potentially free one group of people, a larger group was enslaved through conscription, inflation and taxes.[165] It wasn't long until this War Between the States was known as 'a rich man's war and a poor man's fight'. Perfectly done if I do say so myself. Similar examples from modern history are too numerous to mention and therefore beyond the scope of this handbook. But, hopefully, you have the perceptivity of a brilliant ruler-in-the-making and can spot the pattern. From our discussion in Chapter 6, you may remember that the 14th Amendment to the US Constitution actually led to the enslavement of all Americans by turning them into United States Citizens.

Has there ever been a greater misdirect?

This is the perfect segue into my next point, allowing peasants the freedom to choose their own enslavement. Confused? Then please read on.

It was indeed a grand experiment, perhaps conceived to create a modern-day Atlantis; a utopian civilisation filled with enlightened members who could enjoy all the creature comforts life offered. It would still be necessary, nevertheless, to preserve a hierarchal society complete with impassioned worker bees that had the liberty to choose their own occupations whilst being rewarded generously for their contributions to society. However, similar to liberties granted to sailors when their naval ship docks, they're not completely free but can roam the landscape whilst still being obligated to their ship and duty. It's easy to see that regardless of one's standing within an organised society, these commitments are also the key elements of a **FARM'S** preservation and long-term success, even though some may be required to toil and spill their blood more than others.

Those bold enough to forge ahead with this idealistic concept, provided for themselves and their prodigy certain protections via an abstract moniker known as *We the People* which, in the same breath, afforded all inhabitants the starry-eyed belief they were included in this social contract.

Not that those living within such a righteous premise didn't reap its benefits. However, for individuals to have rights, those rights must be granted by someone or, if looking at it from a ruler's standpoint,

165.) Griffin, *The Creature from Jekyll Island*, 379-389.

provided by those willing to make the ultimate sacrifice to protect them. As the dust settled, it was plain to see that these inalienable rights *for all* were gradually turned into restrictive privileges for which less established members of this *free* FARM had to ask permission. Credit for this magnificent turnaround can be attributed to the world's most dominant opportunists who usurped and exploited this short-lived fairytale.

To trick members of this formerly *free* FARM into registering their offspring, the newly established corporate government provided such legally binding instruments as the Birth Certificate. These unknowing mugs turned their offspring into collateral for the debt owed to the financiers of this pioneering system. This has also become quite fashionable (by design) on many other FARMS and sold to peasants as a bag of goods that allows them to prove their age and nationality; to receive healthcare; to go to school; to take exams; to be adopted; to have protection from underage military service or conscription; to marry; to open a bank account; to hold a driver's licence; to obtain a passport; to inherit money or property; and to vote or stand for elected office. Offering such golden carrots as a STATE-managed retirement programme usually kick-starts peasants into official voluntary consent, when at eighteen, they legally tie their peasant numbers (SIN, SSN, NI number etc.) to their public identities (ENS LEGIS) and begin signing as many lopsided adhesion contracts as you can throw at them.

Like Plato's Atlantis folklore, keeping the freedom myth alive allows one to replace the age-old system of forced compliance that's not as effective and long-lasting as the peasants' voluntary commitment. Men are still willing to die for the idea of freedom. Freedom must be at the forefront of every important discussion and civic action. For example, if you insist your peasants have the right to such things as clean water and healthcare, your system should make every attempt to provide these conveniences, particularly if it deepens the peasants' servitude and dependence on the framework you supply. Like caging animals in a zoo, giving the animals the best food and medicine doesn't grant them their freedom, but depletes them spiritually, an important ingredient in their submission.

In later chapters, we'll explore how to convert even the most basic of human needs into weapons of oppression. Eventually, you can convince peasants that such allowances are their freedom, giving them more than enough incentive to do your bidding.

Opposing viewpoints and materials such as books, magazines and films that are critical of a *free* FARM'S policies, inner workings and institutions should be tolerated up to a certain point to give the impression that dissenting voices, as well as all *free speech,* are protected. However, you'll want to have a firm handle on the major distribution outlets and credible review services to restrict or, at the very least, soften the impact of damaging materials against the image of liberty you project. This is the equivalent of a skilled comedian taking full advantage of their most useful tool, the microphone. Just be sure to chart the content and momentum of any dissident's message; to not only see what they know, but to know exactly when to silence them if required.

If laws have been properly established to criminalise large disturbances on your farm, you'll have no problem railroading any rabble-rousers through your court system. Take the persistent pest and disillusioned author G. Edward Griffin, for example. This dolt believes the freedoms listed in the US Constitution were meant for him and weren't exclusively for the visionaries and risk takers who not only formulated and set into motion this ideal business model, but those who continue to make the bold decisions necessary to expand its sphere of influence. Despite the publication of his well-researched book, *The Creature from Jekyll Island,* which exposed the global banking system, there was little impact in challenging this established cartel and its revealed intention to dominate the world. A speech Mr Griffin made post release in a shoddy conference room in front of about fifteen white-haired coffin dodgers would be laughable if it didn't allow me to expand on a few of its points.

As part of his rambling diatribe, labelled on YouTube as, *An idea whose time has come*, Mr Griffin builds the scenario of a cruise ship, *The US Pleasure Ship*, that's hijacked by a group of pirates who kill the captain and replace the crew in order to take the vessel and its passengers to Slave Island. Thus far, I think you'll agree, it has a nice ring to it. Anyway, you and he purportedly stumble upon this grisly takeover during a stroll you and he take to grab a glimmer of fresh air. Upon returning to the ballroom where the food's being served, the band's playing and the slot machines are loose, you try to interrupt the festivities to break the horrifying news. Because the pirates, now dressed as crew members, replace the hired hands and maintain the appearance of normalcy, the people you try to inform find your discovery quite preposterous. Mr Griffin believes there are seven possible reactions to this dire situation.[166]

166.) G. Edward Griffin, "An Idea Whose Time Has Come – G. Edward Griffin – Freedom Force International – Full," YouTube video, 1:23:37, mercen144, Febru-

Before we continue, I need to digress for a second to bring an added awareness to the forefront. There's one important law in the occult/satanism that I'll use to pick apart Mr Griffin's example. Please don't be frightened, as I'm not about to recite a Catholic mass backwards or draw attention to the upside down cross on the Pope's chair. Well, not quite yet anyway. Rather, for now, I'll discuss duality and the importance of seeing things from one perspective whilst the masses are purposefully guided to see them from another. Once again, since Satan is known as the great deceiver, it'll be the art of deception that you *must* fully master to rule most dominantly. Now, back to our illuminative example.

The first response to the hijacking that Mr Griffin unveils is for the passengers to do nothing. This is actually the most common retaliation, especially on a placated **FARM**, and the most ideal for any lord. As covered in other parts of this handbook, this is also consent. By using the techniques revealed in this chapter, along with many others pointed out in this sacred manuscript, peasants can easily be swayed to go along with just about anything.

The second, and most delectable plan of action, is for those heading to Slave Island to join the pirates. This will sometimes be a conscious decision, but if done right, and in line with the incisive teachings in this glorious handbook, will be an unwitting choice on behalf of many, including those within your secret order.

Unfortunately, for these quite useful folks and depending on your plans for humanity, your need for these inadvertent collaborators and their offspring will expire once the entire planet is secured under your full control. You can rest soundly at night knowing these exceedingly useful instruments, once terminated, sacrificed themselves for your worthy cause, assuming you have one. If not, it's still quite a rush to have godlike powers that grant you the final say in who lives and who dies, a prime motivator for any lord-in-the-making.

The third way to deal with the discovery of such a wonderful—dear me—I mean insidious plan plays into the fight or flight response of your subjects.

> NOTE: You must fully educate yourself on *all* such human coping mechanisms.

Here, the orator discusses grabbing the nearest lifeboat and jumping ship to escape the clutches of these dastardly devils. It's what he says next that we need to recognise for our benefit. He doesn't see

---

ary 9, 2011, https://youtu.be/y1-0o0cSw24

this third countermeasure as a viable option because the pirates have hijacked all the other ocean vessels and have seized all the world's ports! What this means to a rising emperor like yourself is that you must carefully build your network so that your insiders staff every point of refuge. You'll most certainly thank the lord of the underworld when their chilling cries for help fall on deaf ears.

Fourth, Mr Griffin theorises that an astute passenger could drop out of sight by taking the room number off their door or by hiding in the boiler room, but this will end up in failure because the pirates will eventually scour the ship and find the stowaways. Here too, we pull an about face and view the scenario from the vantage point of the pirates. If any peasants attempt to drop out of your purview, you must round them up and usher them back into the pen. If you choose to operate your **FARM'S** financial matters on the sea of commerce, you must have your agents constantly seeking and engaging fleeing peasants in as many hidden contractual obligations as possible. As a natural consequence, you'll need to have a firm handle on the courts and jails, which leads us to our next plan of recourse.

You should openly encourage this next remedy. To firmly support the illusion of freedom, you must also simultaneously create an illusion of justice to guide your peasants into this well-lubricated mechanism. By allowing peasants this fifth option, to sue in court, you'll generate a win-win for you and your trusted agents, as well as reinforce the peasants' belief in the *legal* system and the *fairness* it provides. By allotting peasants a civil course of action, you'll give them a false sense of hope whilst simultaneously providing an outlet for their anger. This will also afford you the luxury of buying them off to dispel any rebellious intentions they may have. In the same breath, a major ruling can set a strong precedent for any new policies you'd like to implement on your **FARM**, leaving your peasants, once again, holding an empty bag.

This sixth alternative will also deprive peasants of their valuable time and resources whilst doing little to change their ultimate fate. By pretending to honour petitions for a redress of grievances, you'll delay any drastic actions peasants are considering and provide a nice forewarning for any unsettling feelings they're having regarding your method of rule. The more you can sell the illusion of freedom, the less likely they'll be to partake in Mr Griffin's solution that encourages the unfortunate scenario of peasants *uniting*, organising a counter coup and taking back the ship.

Over time, however, those you subjugate can be conditioned to believe they're free even when they're enslaved. To illustrate, I'll use the example of rats born inside of a box labelled 'Freedom'. If the rats remain inside the box for their entire lifetimes, they know no other existence and will equate their confinement to their freedom because they have nothing to compare to (a tightly controlled play on the Hegelian Dialectic where the rats experience only one of the two extremes).

As applied to world domination, you and your successors will want the entire human race to acclimate to a new form of very isolated and self-contained bondage brought forth during the latest technological revolution by none other than the peasants themselves. Like incrementalism, compartmentalisation in education, occupations, the military and even within your trusted circle of associates will need to be applied if you're to ensnare humanity with its own effort and consent.

During the heyday of the Roman Empire there was a popular term *Civis Romanus sum* meaning *I am a Roman citizen* that wasn't only a source of pride in Rome but inspired others to desire assimilation.[167] As projected by those within the community of lords, by following the techniques in this chapter, you'll not only provide the illusion of freedom that will more easily subjugate your own pawns but will embolden peasants on other **FARMS** to aspire to a similar way of life, leading them right into your trap. These modern techniques are most effective when applied on a **FARM** that has reached a state of excess.

Oh, I love painting such a deceptive picture onto a plethora of fresh, blank slates, and you *must* allow me to share. The anticipation is killing me.

As previously discussed, groupthink's essential for any unified and cohesive **FARM**, and the most important type of groupthink to evangelise is freedom. We don't just offer these comparatively free peasants more advantages than those on oppressive farms, but like the rodent, we condition them from birth to believe that things like perpetual surveillance and the myriad of corporate products they have to choose from are their freedom. This is where incrementalism plays a key role in normalising even the most blatant and heavy-handed control techniques. Gradual scientific advancements lead each generation into a more entangled form of servitude. Although some may resist these changes, the majority will readily follow suit,

---

167.) Zbigniew Brzezinski, *The Grand Chessboard: American Primacy and its Geostrategic Imperatives, Updated with a New Epilogue* (New York: Basic Books, 2016), 11.

especially if these *innovations* afford convenience. Gently guiding those in peasant training centres to build on your worldview within the industries already established will encourage them to continue erecting this cleverly *hidden in plain sight* control grid continually being assembled around them.

Peasant training centres should offer peasants the *freedom* to choose which controlled and established *field* they'd like to enter. It's human nature to want to thrive using one's talents and skills and providing the platforms from which to do so will benefit you greatly. Offering prestige and handsome rewards such as salaries, bonuses and a comfortable lifestyle will also aid in not only incentivising peasants to enter the corporate plantation but will keep them within their compartmentalised set of skills. Even if peasants realise their contributions are working against the greater good of their brethren, very few will sacrifice their own advancement and well-being to benefit others. Enticing peasants with financial security will motivate them to act against their own best interests. Ultimately, this will also draw them into a large web of complicity, making it difficult to establish accountability for any wrongdoings if the majority of a **FARM** is actively participating.

Since freedom is a state of mind, filling peasants' thoughts with your systematic version of independence will form a rigid, preconceived belief system in their malleable brains. This will also help inspire an air of superiority over those on other **FARMS**, thus aligning a fresh batch of conquerors with your worldview, which they, if done right, will provide the ultimate sacrifice to uphold. Once deeply rooted, peasants will prefer to put themselves in harm's way rather than experience the cognitive dissonance that occurs from shedding their deeply rooted convictions. The freedom myth can be propelled in a variety of ways because, as we know, all humans love a good story.

Presenting heartwarming biographies of those who succeeded through the exploitation of others helps propel a system of profiteering that you and your associates *must* master to gain control over your **FARM**. Similar tales of a *country's* forefathers rising up against their oppressors and superior adversaries ignite an allegiance, pride and sense of duty amongst those you're grooming to do your **FARM'S** bidding. Patriotic pledges, chants, anthems and hymns, as well as a fervent commitment to flag worship, will provide the triggers necessary to remind your subjects of their commitment to your **FARM**. Public holidays and boisterous celebrations, including such warlike reminders as song lyrics and fireworks, can help amplify the images of war and the euphoria experienced from victory. To quote the incomparable Sir Winston Churchill: 'There is nothing so pleasing as to be shot at by one's enemy without result.'

Once you've implanted the foundations for the peasants' mental imprisonment, how you sell your illusion of freedom is a matter of artistic flair and personal choice. As you now know, mandatory state-controlled schooling was put in place to teach all peasants to follow orders and respect authority, particularly for imminent military service. Many **FARMS** have no problem standardising their children in peasant training centres by telling them not only how and what to think, but what to wear. Perhaps freedom on your **FARM** means allowing students to dress according to the social group they identify with as opposed to regulated school uniforms. The gain is twofold as it also conditions peasants to be reliable consumers when presented with trends and alternative choices that keep your **FARM'S** economy turning.

> NOTE: A word of caution, outside of military service, too much uniformity can be problematic, especially in a *free* society. When you entrust peasants with weapons and the ability to move about and communicate freely, they have greater potential to unite. According to Seneca of Rome (4 B.C. - 65 A.D.), a proposal that all slaves be made to wear a particular type of clothing was abandoned for fear that slaves would realise both their own overwhelming numbers and the vulnerability of their rulers.[168] Again, the more convenience and the greater illusion of freedom you provide, the less likely you are to encounter such detrimental conclusions from your chattel.

Obviously, the **FARM** living in the greatest state of abundance is the one that has achieved the most economic, political and military success. Once achieved, these spoils can attract the best and brightest minds and talents from other **FARMS**. Peasants will perceive this openness as freedom, as will offering high earning potential and lucrative investment opportunities in a **FARM'S** resources, real estate and businesses. Not only does this openness make this type of **FARM** a stronger opponent to topple (making it ideal as a global enforcer), but it helps provide a built-in layer of protection as well.

Many less fortunate peasants will want to migrate to such a promised

---

168.) Professor Keith Bradley. "Resisting Slavery in Ancient Rome." BBC. February 17, 2011. https://www.bbc.co.uk/history/ancient/romans/slavery_01.shtml#top

land, providing a deep-seated detriment for enemies to attack because their own lineage may reside there or because destroying a safe haven that welcomes the world's tired and poor (like the children from the sweatshops mentioned in Chapter 5) could ruin their chances of achieving a higher standard of living one day. By putting a For Sale sign on such a **FARM**, other peasant farm owners won't want to destroy its infrastructure since it's now a financial investment. Moreover, foreign invaders would also have to contend with a multitude of feeder **FARMS** that have grown dependent on the handouts and services this more dominant *nation* provides. Constructing such a **FARM** is a great momentum builder toward any lord's ultimate goal of ruling the entire planet.

The following techniques will not only sell a land of plenty's inhabitants on the illusion of freedom but will help promote its cultural superiority to other **FARMS** as well.

We'll begin with a **FARM'S** politics and the ritual of voting, which gives peasants the impression they have a say in things. They, obviously, should not. It's important to select your farm's most influential leaders, not elect them. High office candidates like those running for president/ prime minister should be sold to the herd based on their differing personality traits, unique ways of communicating and their enthusiastic promises as opposed to their proven track records and commitment to your agenda. This is all done to cleverly deceive the masses into thinking they have a choice, and by voting they can implement change which again, should be staunchly prohibited. *Change*, by the way, is a powerful buzzword that can rally disenfranchised peasants to invest their valuable time and energy into the already predetermined political process that's tailored to you and your associates' needs, not theirs.

Using the words *freedom* or *liberty* in such things as a **FARM'S** anthems, hymns, declarations, important addresses, songs, architecture, statues, names of schools/universities and policies will only add to the illusion. For example, a policy such as the Freedom of Information Act gives the appearance of transparency and *openness* by giving a **FARM'S** *citizens* access to a government's *sensitive* documents. However, very few peasants will attempt to look at such revealing archives simply because they know the information is available to them. I think the phrase hidden in plain sight once again applies. Making peasants follow a series of steps to retrieve such transcripts will also discourage most from trying. Of course, you'll want a wish list of exemptions to block whole documents or, at the very least, certain portions of them to protect *national security* and its accompanying leverage gaining secrets your peasants have no business knowing.

Obviously, you won't want to leave a paper trail or electronic footprint regarding any of your more sinister plots and practices. For those that you must record for inter/intra departmental approval and cryptic communications between willing players, you can mark the compromising memorandums *classified* or even *redact* certain elements by removing incriminating information that you wish to keep buried before a document's public release.

Granting your peasants *rights* is also another wonderful method of luring them into a state of complacency and passivity. Once citizens become dependent on a government to provide and protect these birthright benefits, the government can eventually trick them into exchanging their rights for privileges that can ultimately be revoked. Since freedom must be earned, you can lead future generations of a *free* society to believe such perks are guaranteed, creating a sense of entitlement. You'll have the advantage if you can convince them they're free whilst not understanding what freedom truly means. Misleading information coupled with enticing catch phrases like 'I have rights, I'm a taxpayer' and 'Proud to be a Roman Citizen' ignite a false sense of empowerment and superiority whilst giving peasants no leverage at all in the big scheme of things.

Speaking of superiority, it's not only beneficial to flex your military muscles toward other FARMS but at your own subjects as well. This will encourage them to empathise with you (their captor) and take on your dominant worldview through the condition known as Stockholm Syndrome. With added brainwashing, you can convince your peasants that peasants on other FARMS are inferior, especially if opposing FARMS don't provide the same standard of living provided by your FARM. Continuous warfare will have your chattel cheering for their own enslavement, as it'll be their own time, labour, energy and sacrifice that pays for your military conquests and global ambitions. Entertainment, such as films glorifying war and sporting events, can divert peasants' attention away from your more nefarious undertakings and will also promote nationalism and its accompanying mirage of freedom.

If you think about it, what purpose does a national anthem have at a sporting event other than to emotionalise the crowd as fighter jets roar overhead? For many, this is two minutes of what they think is patriotism but what is really nationalism. The fundamental difference being patriotism involves questioning one's own government whilst nationalism blindly supports it, even when the nation acts against the best interest of its citizens. Both philosophies can be useful to you depending on your objectives, but for a conquering **FARM**, nationalism is the preferred sentiment. When fever pitch levels of flag waving are required, patriotism can be quickly redefined as terrorism to stymie and, in extreme cases, apprehend any detractors objecting to the methods used to achieve your **FARM'S** overall goals. You can even paint those who refuse to cheer on the aggressive actions of the state as dissenters who don't cherish their **FARM'S** *freedoms*.

> NOTE: Remember, when making bold moves with your **FARM**, you place yourself in a vulnerable position. Therefore, you must garner as much support as possible. If you train your peasants properly, groupthink will assist in this effort.

Contemporary gladiator games like football, boxing and the UFC are perfect venues to ramp up the herd's thirst for blood, enthusiasm for self-sacrifice and pride in its **FARM**. Once a **FARM** establishes a dominant fighting force, there will hardly be a need for such things as military drafts or mandatory service requirements because of the allure associated with battlefield glory that only a winning army can bestow. Voluntary enlistment will also help keep the illusion of freedom burning brightly, as peasants will feel they have a choice (and therefore a responsibility) in protecting the privileges they cherish. This will, simultaneously, further enforce the peasants' belief in their own self-determination. Remember, throughout history, men have been willing to kill and be killed to preserve their *freedom*.

Giving the poor a chance at a more secure modern-day existence covertly squeezes those at the bottom of the food chain into military service. Offering enticements on advanced **FARMS** like hands-on training in a specialised *field*, a career in uniform and university tuition assistance can help drive military enlistment whilst also shifting focus away from the dire risks involved in warfare. As the roles on a **FARM** are more deeply established, children will replace their parents and military service will become generational and therefore promoted from within the walls of the family home. Very few will dare to venture outside their parents' footsteps, especially if the descendants are hard-wired with a sense of duty that's engrained in them by their ancestors.

Making it commonplace for *citizens* to thank the military for protecting their *freedoms* adds a nice touch to the illusion. There aren't too many lords who will find fault with you for sharing globalist Henry Kissinger's position that: 'Military men are dumb, stupid animals to be used as pawns for foreign policy.'[169] This reflection will help you cope with the fact that you must always sacrifice a portion of your herd for the *common good* which can more appropriately be referred to as your agenda. Unlike Kissinger's revelation to Alexander Haig that was regrettably documented in Bob Woodward and Carl Bernstein's *The Final Days,* just be sure to keep such startling introspections to yourself or, at the very least, strictly between trusted blood oath associates. Consistently showering your troops with high praise and routinely paying homage to them will smoothly conceal any lack of care and concern they experience when returning home from battle. The sprinkling of departed soldiers' remains over a landfill in Virginia or providing lacklustre medical provisions for returning troops serves as a shining example of the level of blatant disregard that can be displayed toward service men and women on even a *free* **FARM** whilst experiencing no drop-off in willing combat participants.[170]

Humans are creatures of habit and, as a result, don't want their way of life disrupted. If you can stir up the hive through real threats, imaginary or a combination of both, you can motivate your obedient *citizens* to cooperate with any drastic actions they're convinced must be taken to restore tranquillity. Tying your **FARM'S** *freedom* into these necessary courses of action will win you the most support.

> NOTE: For your own knowledge and certainly not for your peasants', true freedom for a society is only attainable by a moral people. As James Madison wrote in the Federalist No. 51: 'If men were angels, no government would be necessary.' To expand your power and influence whilst limiting the quality of life for your inferiors, it'll be necessary to further corrupt their ethics. This will aid in breaking down their respect for one another and open the door for a variety of encroachments that will keep them at odds with each other and at war with other **FARMS**.

As you spread the idea of freedom from your plantation to other nations, whether that means showcasing your **FARM'S** chosen deity, possessing the most impressive gadgets or living a hedonistic lifestyle without restrictions, peasants on other **FARMS** won't want to lose

---

169.) Waffles. "Did Kissinger Call Military Men "Dumb Stupid Animals"?" wafflesatnoon. August 26, 2016. https://www.wafflesatnoon.com/kissinger-military-men-dumb-stupid-animals/

170.) Mark Memmott. "Report: Hundreds of Troops' Ashes Were Dumped In Landfill." npr.org. December 8, 2011. https://www.npr.org/sections/thetwo-way/2011/12/08/143334376/report-hundreds-of-troops-ashes-were-dumped-in-landfill

their own cultural practices and norms. This means you'll have to force your methods of control on them. Some modern-day examples include things like your paper money system or convenience items such as sports, entertainment, processed foods and consumer technologies.

If your military **FARM** believes these items are their freedom, you can threaten them with the loss of these provisions whilst the actual reasons for your breaches of the peace on other **FARMS** remain secret. It'll be a good idea to give peasants on your enforcement **FARM** the option to freely choose items of their own oppression like implantable microchips, mobile phones and smart appliances even though you should constantly encourage them to use these devices for a more modern lifestyle. You can then use these products to not only enslave your dominant **FARM** but all the other **FARMS** that fall under its influence.

Mainstream media outlets, promoting your blueprint for global enslavement, work best if there's an appearance of differing perspectives. However, these news programmes must be unified when presenting carefully selected stories along with the pre-determined courses of action that must be taken to satisfy your ambitions. Highlighting political nuances and emphasising stark differences in matters of little importance will help sell the phony conflicts needed to achieve your **FARM'S** political divide. You must control the overall **FARM** narrative to get peasants to react in ways that help bring about your worldview whilst your clandestine operations, techniques and underlying plans never reach the point of critical mass awareness.

NOTE: If, for some unfortunate reason, this critical threshold of mass awareness is reached, and the herd feels threatened, peasants may unite to counteract you and your associates' supremacy. Keep in mind that compartmentalising, distracting and depleting peasants intellectually, spiritually and physically will be your best defence. Creating and maintaining as many false realities as possible will keep peasants wrapped up in the illusory worlds you provide whilst they unconsciously participate in the expansion of your global dominance.

The most important aspect of successfully filling peasants' lives with pleasing distractions is that they'll have a hard time believing the drastic and inhumane measures that are a violation of both man-made and spiritual laws that you must take.

Decent and honest people will assume everyone thinks like they do, giving you a huge advantage, since these unwitting targets would never suspect someone would resort to such drastic measures to enslave them. Plato's *Allegory of the Cave* is a must read for any planetary ruler-in-the-making because it highlights the lengths peasants will go to protect their perception of reality once it's firmly established. Once again, it's the wise and crafty ruler who will imprison humanity by using the peasants' own minds against them for the ruler's own benefit.

We spoke earlier of gradual usurpations as the most subtle way to exchange freedoms on a **FARM** for a deepening state of enslavement. Like the US Pleasure Ship hijacked by pirates heading for Slave Island, peasants should be fed and entertained whilst the boat chugs along toward its final destination. Distractions, false realities and conveniences can all be used to sell the semblance of normalcy whilst the peasants' ghastly fate appears on the horizon. If you plan and execute in accordance with this manual, you'll reach a tipping point when it'll be much too late for the passengers to change their fate.

One last thing to keep in mind is that freedom is a driving force that *unites*. Just as you and your associates will team up to subdue humanity to achieve unlimited power and freedom to do as you wish, so will the peasants. It's my hope that you apply the techniques contained in this handbook to satisfy all your indulgences whilst exploiting and restricting theirs.

Chapter 14

WAR

Only the dead have seen the end of war.
— George Santayana

Well, my wonderful protégé, we've come to a critical juncture in this handbook. Since I've laid the foundation for the creation of a global empire, we'll now tackle the most effective and important means of subjecting the world to your will—war. I'll try to sum up a topic that has riddled humanity since its most primitive days. Nothing will bring your deepest and darkest fantasies to life and make a more impressionable footprint on the pages of history than your success in battle.

Various scholars and psychologists have tried to determine whether or not warfare is innate in humans. Beyond perhaps rats and ants, no other living creatures kill their own kind in such large quantities. I'll skip the philosophical debate and get right down to the benefits of war and the best techniques known to round up willing participants. But first, why is war an important part of your quest for global dominance?

This is perhaps the most important question posed in this handbook and possibly one of the biggest secrets I reveal. Startlingly, war is the primary driving force of a society.[171] Without war, governments would have no legitimacy or right to rule. Peasants would grow tired of the restrictions placed on them and the personal wealth taken from them through taxation.[172] War gives value to the political structure and allows for the acceptance of its leaders. Nations need war to exist and to maintain the world's internal political structures.[173] Can you imagine trying to rule even a small tribe without a social hierarchy and organised chain of command? Much of the burden would fall on

---

171.) Lewin, *Report from Iron Mountain*, 29.
172.) Griffin, *The Creature from Jekyll Island*, 517.
173.) Lewin, *Report from Iron Mountain*, 38.

you, leaving you quite like a paperboy trying to collect money from customers who refuse to answer their doors. A three-tier system of rulers, managers and foot soldiers driven unconsciously by the threat of a lurking enemy (real, imaginary or both) simplifies the task of barking out and enforcing orders, leaving lots of free time for more important things like blood rituals, orgies and sacrifices.

Throughout the ages, wars have been fought primarily for conquest and plunder. History also shows that **FARMS** that manufacture the largest amount of munitions whilst rallying the most enthusiastic, obedient and skilled fighting forces are the ones that dominate militarily. A **FARM** that efficiently uses its peasants to develop the machinery and technology necessary to continually advance its killing power will also have a distinct advantage over those who live on berries and prepare for combat by sharpening their stone-tipped spears.

Generating surplus justifies invading other **FARMS** and lures those who enjoy the perks to believe that the conveniences they spill their blood for and toil most of their lives to attain is their freedom. Flaunting an exuberant lifestyle can also provoke leaders with selfish interests to embrace and implement such a system on their **FARMS**.

One clever way to achieve world domination is through a **FARM** that produces the most advanced excesses whilst jointly packaging the best ideology to attract others to your cause. Whether you create this type of **FARM** from scratch, conquer one outright or infiltrate and take over such a **FARM**, once it's in your control, you must cultivate its war-making ability and then aim it at the rest of the world. It's only natural that you must eliminate those who stand in your way. Whilst conventional warfare may be necessary to assert your will on **FARMS** that are philosophically united against integrating your particular system, many times you can use more subtle techniques to win their hearts and minds. Although the techniques we'll discuss should be used to facilitate the implementation of your financial and political objectives whenever possible, never underestimate the value of a brutal and bloody war.

> NOTE: Please keep in mind that the techniques used to cajole the herd into their own enslavement are the same techniques applied on the **FARM** used for military conquests. You should take a more subtle approach however, since a dominant military can overthrow you. Detractors will emerge on the conquering **FARM** when they're unable to reap the benefits of your system, oppose your methods or object to your skilful acquisition of the world's resources. Therefore, you should not give any alliance or sense of loyalty to any particular **FARM**. A healthy form

of contempt is natural toward even those who blindly do your bidding. If you think about it, how else are you going to separate yourself from the pack if your sense of self is not superior to all others?

The threat of force must always be present against other *nations* to ensure the performance of international agreements. You can achieve this only with a ready and willing military that simultaneously provides its citizens with a sense of duty and loyalty. Once you choose your military **FARM**, you can consider marking its landscape with art and architecture that galvanises your mission. Although you may be tempted to erect large statues of yourself and place them everywhere, it's important to exercise some healthy restraint. As we discussed in Chapters 5 and 12, it's best if you remain incognito.

Today's network of lords has garnered inspiration from their families' deep-seated, ancient heritages where polytheistic religions ruled the day. Sun worship was common in many ancient religions since they viewed the sun as the giver of life. In both yesterday's and today's male-dominated world, the erect penis is also seen as the giver of life. This has been common practice in Baal worship and the occult for centuries, with the symbol being that of a giant obelisk pointing toward the sun. In the current military capital of the world, Washington DC, one of these huge phallic symbols, the Washington Monument, faces another fertile landmark, the dome of the Capital Building (representing the female womb) which not so ironically contains the Oval Office (denoting the female reproductive organs).

> NOTE: I'm sure you've heard the expression 'make love not war'. Being that war, with penis shaped missiles and bullets flying everywhere, is not only incredibly sexy but, like an orgy, is a social release, why not make love whilst making war? After all, the young, dumb and sexually stifled are looking for any excuse to expel their angst. I'm afraid if you don't provide one, they may find one on their own and aim their pent-up anger, brought on by their raging hormones, at you. So, whilst they make their way to the battlefield you, as emperor supreme, can skedaddle your way to the bedroom. Remember, it's important to keep disenfranchised peasants warring against each other to keep them from rebelling against you and your associates.

Whilst striving for world dominance, I urge you to tread lightly. A deeply entrenched network of shifty and ruthless operators has been hiding in the shadows whilst secretly controlling everything.[174] Pointing out these hidden orchestrators and their modus operandi will benefit you in a couple of ways. First, it'll stimulate you to mark your territory with esoteric art and architecture that has special meaning to you and your collaborators whilst its true intent remains hidden from the peasants. Keep in mind, when these symbols are rooted in the blood sacrifice and ritualistic history of prosperous civilisations of the past, they hold a special power and energy over the masses. Second, and more importantly, it'll show you how vast and embedded your competitors truly are, which will help you develop your own well-thought-out plan for conquering the planet.

> NOTE: I suggest you join this well-established syndicate and try to rise through its ranks, since nothing short of a miracle will allow you to defeat and replace it. Besides, this carefully layered foundation has taken hundreds, if not thousands, of years to contrive. Rebuilding a new system from scratch is not practical in the interest of time. This handbook provides you with the fundamental knowledge and tactics needed to enslave humanity through any approach, but I'd like to politely remind you that building a world empire doesn't happen overnight. Pardon the cryptic foreshadowing, but the old expression 'Rome wasn't built in a day' aptly applies. I should once again warn you that if you enter this ruthless and deadly game, you do so at your own risk.

For those inquisitive enough to follow the breadcrumbs leading us to the masterminds behind the world's last ancient superpower reemerging from the ashes, I'd like to point out another striking obelisk facing a dome, St. Peters Basilica in Vatican City. No one can deny this is the religious hub of the world. So then, is it a stretch to say there is a connection between this religious epicentre and today's military capital located in Washington DC since they both showcase erect penises pointing toward the sun whilst facing a womb?

When this section is complete, I'll most certainly need a Treasurer Luxury Black cigarette.

What if I reminded you that Vatican City is in Rome and the American system being imposed on the rest of the world just so happens to flaunt the Roman Eagle Aquila as its cultural icon? If you pay attention, you'll see the eagle sitting atop flagpoles in American courtrooms and during presidential speeches just as it appeared on standards carried

---

174.) ODD TV, "American Gods: All Roads Lead to Rome," YouTube video, 14:05, ODD TV, April 21, 2019. https://youtu.be/ltEbCTDGzQ4

by Roman legions.[175] This similarity may not be enough to persuade you that a shrouded Roman cult is conspiring behind the scenes to rule the world, but perhaps recognizing that most *civilised* nations operate under Roman law (a.k.a. civil law, canon law, maritime admiralty law, statutory law or commercial law) will nudge you in that direction. As your awareness sharpens, you may notice that the architecture of many government buildings and courthouses in America is reminiscent of those in ancient Rome, as are the institutions that make up its internal framework such as its Senate, House of Representatives, stock market, big stadium sporting events, public parks and libraries.[176]

Littering the countryside with your deeply inspired erections is one thing, but mysteriously marking your most prevalent and useful tool, the paper money system, is quite another. Decorating these marvellous IOU notes, which are reminders of the extension of credit that's used to enslave future generations, will be your crowning achievement. These art pieces should be imposed on the entire world to bring them under your fraternity's control, since it'll be the worship of these earthly debt notes and acquiring them that'll motivate humanity to blindly do your bidding. Tradition calls for artwork on your mass-produced paper Picassos. Therefore, if your purpose is far-reaching, the designs should be consciously chosen to reinforce your sect's mission whilst remaining stimulating, yet meaningless, to the easily deceived peasants. For example, the Roman Eagle Aquila appears on the reserve currency of the world, the US dollar, along with Roman numerals, a hidden owl, an ancient pyramid, the eye of providence and Latin phrases like 'E Pluribus Unum' (Out of many, one), 'Novus Ordo Seclorum' (New Order of the Ages) and 'Annuit Coeptis' (Favours our undertakings). I'll leave it up to you to decipher the hidden meanings or, better yet, to use your knowledge of ancient languages, religions and esoteric symbols to create your own veiled messages.

There's a minute possibility that this handbook could motivate an outraged reader to form a network of like-minded individuals to assert a drastically different worldview. Such laughable examples could include a matriarchal society run by fembots who plaster the Earth with pink roses and pussy willows. Or a society where technology works in conjunction with nature to serve all living creatures and esoteric

---

175.) Stephanie Schoppert. "Ten Things You Did Not Know About The Roman Legions." History Collection.com. July 28, 2016. https://historycollection.com/ten-things-not-know-roman-legions/7/ and ODD TV, "American Gods," 7:07-8:07.
176.) ODD TV, "American Gods," 8:25

landmarks are bulldozed to the ground because they're no longer relevant. But, to attain such far-fetched utopias, the people must be ready for yet another debt-inducing war fought by the disadvantaged, who will once again spill their blood for their leaders' ideologies.

The insanity of it all provides quite a hearty belly laugh, wouldn't you agree? Will they ever learn?

Because the true profiteers of war are seldom, if ever, singled out for their actions, isn't it better to be the one in charge rather than a peasant in a rat infested bunker next to an unbathed scoundrel with a bayonet? You must realise, if you don't capitalise on the frailties of humanity, someone else will. Even such a revered publication as the Bible acknowledges humans are inherently evil and have descended into sin, so why feel guilty about tapping into mankind's destructive tendencies in order to profit?

As seventeenth century philosopher Baruch Spinoza declared: 'If men were born free, they would, so long as they remained free, form no conception of good and evil.' In short, to rule over others, you must act on instincts and shed any remorse brought on by empathy. Some have argued that empathy is innate in all humans but can be made more sharply pronounced through organised religions. Your belief system, therefore, must strive to eliminate your own guilt whilst working to encourage guilt amongst the peasants.

To maintain a stable society, murder should be made illegal and punished unless, of course, it's done in large numbers to the sound of trumpets or is necessary to protect the ruling actions of you and your associates. When one peasant kills another peasant, it's called murder. When a socially important person is murdered, we call it assassination, which *must* carry a harsher penalty for obvious reasons. And when soldiers kill during a war, they are heroes. Therefore, a **FARM'S** religious teachings must condone killing enemies of its nationally recognised god. Polytheistic religions tend to be less instrumental in this aim since having multiple gods makes one more accepting of other gods and, by default, not as willing to attack other **FARMS** for their different spiritual belief systems. Since nothing comes even remotely close to the amount of bloodshed brought on by opposing monotheistic religions, it'll be in your best interest to assign one to your **FARM** and stick with it.

The drums of war will reach a crescendo when **FARMS** entering a conflict present their ear pleasing manifestos, boasting their superior morality whilst emboldening participants to kill for an invisible entity in the sky. It's also of great benefit to have a **FARM'S** leader appear to be a devout believer in their **FARM'S** god, so peasants not only trust their leader's motives but are willing to go to battle for their god's *chosen leader*. A religious disguise also acts as a deterrent against rebellion since peasants will be much more reluctant to revolt against an authority figure with an all-powerful god on his side.

You may want to put an asterisk next to this one.

It's my guess that only people of means have made it to this point in the book, as the lower echelons of society have been programmed to have an adverse reaction to the tactics presented thus far. Regardless, even if you're one of the few exceptions who has the good fortune to rise above their humble beginnings to the prominent position of lord, you must be willing to accept the fact that all wars are fought not only by disadvantaged commoners, but against them. This is true whether any such war is waged against peasants on your **FARM** or that of another. Yes, you read that right. Some wars will need to be waged against your own subjects. Civil wars are an obvious example. However, we'll discuss more covert wars required to keep your populace manageable, fragmented and engaged in both internal and external conflicts whilst allowing you to prosper.

As you expand your empire and break bread with other lords, your global quest is analogous to a high-stakes poker game; if a member of the game is caught cheating, another player pulls out a gun and shoots them. If an outsider tries to disrupt the game, everyone draws their guns and protects the game. This should be the mindset of all trusted members of your oligarch fraternity. As your global ambitions advance, there may be lords who have a change of heart or are staunchly opposed to your plans and try to empower their own subjects to resist your agenda. *This must not be allowed.*

It's important to recognise that the non-thinking masses are the greatest threat to the stability of your **FARM** and your precious natural resources. Hence, their numbers should be regulated. If they were to *unite*, they would also become a dire threat to your rule. Therefore, the wise lord implements a strategy to manage the threat.

This is hardly a new concept and in more recent centuries has been referred to as the Malthusian Principle. Thomas Malthus (1766-1834) was a professor of history and economics for the beloved East India Company College. He believed that there's a tipping point where human population exceeds available resources, or stated more accurately, the ability for corporations like the former British East India Company to meet consumer demand, putting the social power structure at risk.

This isn't how it's sold to peasants. Induced poverty, starvation and disease help sell the illusion that there isn't enough for everybody, leading many peasants to empathise with their ruler's thinking on the matter.

Psst. The whole human race, over seven billion people, could fit in the state of Texas with a half-acre between each person and if just 10% of the population grew their own food, they could easily provide sustenance for themselves. However, such thinking is a direct threat to any lord's control over their herd and their corporate peasant farm driven by unbridled consumption. Therefore, an economy based on sickness, famine and warfare offers the best means of keeping the flock in line whilst allowing the opportunistic few to enrich themselves on mass suffering.

This leads us to the silent wars you must wage against your own peasants. As much as it pains me to say it, you *must* be able to apply such principles on your own **FARM(S)** before you try to implement them on the rest of the world. If you don't have the *chutzpah* to neutralise those on your own turf, you certainly won't have what it takes to do it on a global scale.

If not already established, one of the first steps should be to have peasants as dependent on you and your corporations (including your government) as possible for all their needs, not to mention all their joyful amenities. In a truly free society, this will be a much more challenging task to achieve, but it can eventually be accomplished with patience, perseverance and lots of influence (financial and otherwise).

For the sake of our discussion, we'll assume peasants are as dependent as possible.

As the Bolsheviks clearly demonstrated in Russia, as did Mao Zedong during his reign in China, taking control of the land gives you control over the food supply which leads to control of the people. World government comrade Henry Kissinger made an even more universal statement by observing: 'If you control the oil, you control entire nations. If you control the food, you control the people. If you control the money, you control the entire world.' This is simply some additional food for thought as you plan your rise to world dominance. Tens of millions, who rejected Mao's, Lenin's and Stalin's leadership, mercilessly met their fate. These bold leaders used a *hard kill programme*. That is, murdering citizens outright either through actions or approval by the **STATE**.[177] War is

---

177.) Joachim Hagopian. "The Globalists' New World Order: Soft and Hard Kill Methods. An Unknown and Uncertain Future: What We Can Do to Counter." Global Research.ca. May 23, 2015. https://www.globalresearch.ca/the-globalists-new-world-order-soft-and-hard-kill-methods-an-unknown-and-uncertain-fuan obvious example of a hard kill programme, which is a great segue into my next point.

In the *free* society of America, a declaration of war invokes a state of national emergency that suspends the *guaranteed* rights of the citizenry. Not only does a declaration of war give you this often-unrecognised advantage of depriving your citizens of their liberties, but you can sprinkle in some Orwellian doublespeak to hide your devilish intentions.

For example, the Ministry of Plenty in George Orwell's utopian classic *Nineteen Eighty-Four* actually brought on starvation as he reversed the names of the various institutions to obscure the agency's true aims from the characters in the story. Let's examine a few real-world examples of America's internal wars against its own citizens, leading off with one dear to my heart, the War on Poverty.

> NOTE: The goal of any war is to obliterate the enemy, thus eliminating both the good and bad of anything found in its crosshairs. The best wars are those prolonged indefinitely, as they provide the largest acquisition of wealth whilst simultaneously more fully destroying the adversary. When aiming a war at your own peasants, you'll want to worsen the stated problem rather than rectify it, as it will not only expand your power but also increase your profits.

Sure, on the surface, it seems noble to give 'a hand up rather than a handout' as the War on Poverty so proudly touts.[178] Please realise such catchy slogans will help sell any misgivings peasants may have regarding similar programmes.

For those in power, what better way to eliminate potential competitors than by drying up the capital they would invest in their own businesses? Those in power eliminate potential competitors by taxing them (gradually at first, of course) to provide a myriad of social services like food stamps, welfare and increased medical care benefits for those deemed impoverished. This will also placate those on the lower rung of society and subdue some of the disruptive actions they might otherwise engage in.

As for those oscillating within the middle tier of your **FARM**, instead of a wider variety of jobs being created by those with an entrepreneurial spirit, the capital is more tightly controlled by those

---

ture/5451356

178.) Robert Rector. "The War on Poverty: 50 years of failure." The Heritage Foundation. September 23, 2014. https://www.heritage.org/marriage-and-family/commentary/the-war-poverty-50-years-failure

in receipt of corporate welfare. Not only does this brilliant scheme transfer a lion's share of the wealth to the politically protected (you and your associates) but it also shifts earnings from the middle class to the poor, thus crippling them both whilst causing resentment and division amongst them. As the money drifts upwards, both the falling middle class and the coddled poor become more dependent on you to remedy the deteriorating situation brought on by your own policies, giving you and your network more power and control. Talk about the fox guarding the hen house. Once again, you must create the problem in order to offer your pre-arranged solution. Don't worry. If done over a long enough period of time, not one in a million will ever figure it out.

The lure of doing nothing to have a decent standard of living can outweigh the burden of toiling on the corporate plantation. By penalising or eliminating welfare allowances for those recipients who marry, you can also perpetuate the disintegration of the family unit and further secure the need for a *War on Poverty* since single-parent households are the biggest reason for childhood destitution. But please don't lose a wink of sleep. The breadwinner (usually the male) can be replaced with a bigger welfare cheque.

Oh, it's such a gloriously vicious cycle, wouldn't you agree? But why stop there?

Programmes such as *Head Start* ensnare young peasants at an early age so they can begin peasant training sooner, thus giving you more influence over them. Since a single, impoverished parent is also less able to provide adequate direction for her offspring, those at peasant training centres should impart the **STATE'S** moral and educational standards on the children. I think you can see where this is going. With the large operating costs for agencies that redistribute wealth (paid for by peasants, naturally) which justify their existence by providing things like more federal funding for each student below the poverty line (also paid for by peasants), the gap between the well-connected and everyone else on the **FARM** opens wider and wider.

Glory be to Beelzebub.

There will come a day when the productive finally realise it's better to sit at home and do nothing rather than go to work. This leads to the advantageous condition of shortages and over time results in malnutrition and civil disorder, causing the use of brute force. Be advised, fear, guilt and violence are the three greatest weapons in your totalitarian toolbox that you can employ effectively. Once all hell breaks loose, peasants will beg you to protect them and restore order.

(You may want to revisit Chapter 10, Enforcement, when applying this technique.) The wise ruler will seize this opportunity to advance their agenda and further clamp down on their subjects. Malnutrition and civil decay lead to sickness, eventually culminating in the desired end goal, death. Since this method of culling the herd can be lengthy and is much more indirect, it's known as a *soft kill*.[179]

If there were an Orwellian doublespeak agency to regulate the War on Cancer and the War on Drugs, it would most certainly be the Ministry of Health. In the novel *Nineteen Eighty-Four*, no such agency exists. But, in real life, since these two wars have been waged against a trusting American populace, the amount of both cancer and drug use has skyrocketed whilst the herd's health has plummeted, thereby supporting this doublespeak name, Ministry of Health. The only thing that has improved dramatically is the enormous profits from these prolific, drug pushing agendas.

May it rain dollar signs!

This is not where their similarities end, however. Both industries lead gullible peasants to believe that a magical pill or potion will cure their ills and end their suffering. This obviously could not be further from the truth. Even those among the scientific community who come to realise the harm done by such things as standardised cancer protocols will not want to disrupt a billion-US$ industry by curtailing the condition. What profitable livelihoods generated from excessive amounts of grant money and donations are to be gained from that? For the medical professionals who suddenly develop a conscience, we've already discussed the proven technique of stripping these Good Samaritans of their licences (Chapter 7) for not using only the treatment methods sanctioned by STATE-approved agencies.

Can you please point me to any prison guards or policemen in favour of losing their job security, pensions and health benefits by eliminating the War on Drugs? How about any clandestine agencies financing their secret operations and private wars through the drug trade? In addition, the War on Drugs gives you free rein to invade all *citizens'* rights in pursuit of finding the harmful substances that you so generously provide. Similarly, the War on Cancer allows you to invade their bodies and use medical agents to destroy not only harmful cells but healthy ones as well. Once you get them hooked on your addictive pharmaceuticals, they'll also become eligible recruits for the illicit War

---

179.) Hagopian, "The Globalists' New World Order."

on Drugs. Remember, the most loyal customers on the planet are those who are addicts, legal or otherwise.

Furthermore, once you hook peasants on the idea that your well-financed research institutions will remedy their poor health habits and intake of toxins, few will question why the prevalence of cancer has increased from 3% in the early 1900s to nearly 50% in men and 39% in women today.[180] It's important to note that coddled peasants expect you to solve their problems and will turn to *authority* to guide them as they've been trained to do. It's up to you to give them solutions. If you can't capitalise on their laziness and lack of knowledge, then ruling the planet may not be for you.

For the sake of our conversation regarding the War on Cancer, we'll entertain a brief discussion on a few important health discoveries along with the biological weapons research that's been used to target peasants' well-being. Even though some of the biggest leaps in eugenics arose from the experiments in Nazi Germany, the heart of this discussion will focus on Fort Detrick, Maryland, home of the National Cancer Institute. Not so coincidentally, this is also the home of America's bioweapon laboratories.

> NOTE: In the early part of the twentieth century, prominent banking family member Dr Otto Warburg discovered the cause of cancer in all cases and therefore, the direction to focus for its cure. Dr Warburg was a meticulous researcher who was awarded a Nobel Prize for his breakthrough findings.[181] Once his cancer-causing discovery was unveiled, it had to be hidden from peasants to create an endless flow of money generated by such heartfelt monikers as Race for the Cure. Whilst peasants threw good money after bad with the hopes of ending their fear of this preventable condition, the path leading to a solution sat right under their noses. Please retain this knowledge for your personal well-being only.

Dr Warburg discovered that when normal cells lose their ability to absorb and utilise oxygen (known as cellular respiration), they lose their *intelligence* and regress to a zombielike state where they rely on the fermentation of sugars to produce energy and stay alive.[182] Put

---

180.) Brian Scott Peskin, B.S.E.E., M.I.T. with Amid Habib, M.D., F.A.A.P., F.A.C.E., *The Hidden Story of Cancer: Find Out Why Cancer has Medical Science on the Run and How a Simple Plan Based on New Science Can Prevent It* (Houston, Texas: Pinnacle Press, 2009), 4, 89

181.) Peskin with Habib, *The Hidden Story of Cancer,* 139-142.

182.) Peskin with Habib, *The Hidden Story of Cancer,* 385.

simply, too little oxygen to the cell is the cause of cancer.[183]

Isn't it miraculous that foods on a shelf spoil due to the absorption of oxygen? Therefore, by incorporating ingredients into foods that block oxygen absorption, profits can be maximised. This is especially true if the same ingested ingredients can also block oxygen absorption in the cells, leading to more cancer treatments.

NOTE: If you're looking to profit from sickness, it's important to understand the root cause of the disease you want to capitalise on. Then, find as many ways as you can to create the condition. Once accomplished, merely provide the remedies to treat the symptoms whilst avoiding the cure. Like any good war, the longer it lasts the more profitable it becomes. As an added benefit, the affected peasant is now compromised physically, mentally, spiritually and financially, leaving them more vulnerable to your domination.

'So, what does Fort Detrick have to do with all of this?' you exclaim. I'm glad your curiosity has finally reached a fever pitch.

In the 1960s, when it looked like cancer's days were numbered because of clinical breakthroughs based on Dr Warburg's findings, a viral goose chase was ordered. Research money was pulled from promising cancer cures and targeted at an undetectable viral enemy funded by Nixon's War on Cancer.[184]

Leading the charge on this viral ghost hunt was tireless glory seeker Dr Robert Gallo, who oversaw Litton Bionetics and directly controlled the National Cancer Institute's research programmes at Fort Detrick.[185] The man was a hack as a thorough inspection of his findings clearly illustrates.[186] But, in the world of Orwellian doublespeak, anyone on the heels of real cures based on genuine science *must* carry the scarlet letter of charlatan whilst useful quacks like Gallo are rewarded handsomely with remuneration and accolades. Even though Gallo's *cancer is caused by a virus* discoveries were rejected for not following the Golden Rule in virology, which calls for the isolation of viral pathogens under an electron microscope,[187] his enthusiasm for faulty science in exchange for prestige

183.) Peskin with Habib, *The Hidden Story of Cancer,* 117.

184.) *Banks, Aids, Opium, Diamonds, and Empire,* 187.

185.) Dr. Len Horowitz, "In Lies We Trust – The CIA, Hollywood, & Bio-terrorism – Dr. Len Horowitz," BitChute video, 2:23:09, MediaGiant, May 31, 2020, https://www.bitchute.com/video/kCOuv9uk9a3f

186.) *Banks, Aids, Opium, Diamonds, and Empire,* 16-22, 303-307.

187.) Guylaine Lanctot, M.D., *The Medical Mafia: How to get out of it alive and take buck our health & wealth* (Miami, FL: Here's the Key Inc., 1995), 157.

eventually paid off. In more ways than one.

Before the big reveal on Gallo's contribution to a very earnest global agenda, we need to take one more leap down a large rabbit hole to give you the background necessary for waging a secret war on human health. As with all brilliant minds working for *the greater good of humanity*, their discoveries must be taken and exploited into lucrative enterprises that also weaken the herd's condition. The benefit is a subclass of worker bees to operate these industries whilst simultaneously indebting themselves to its products and services. If there are a few human sacrifices along the way, it's simply the cost of doing business.

I could kiss the sky!

Back to the matter at hand, in the mid-1800s, just before Thomas Edison and Nikola Tesla began their strained but terse working relationship, another opportunist versus pioneer, Louis Pasteur, plagiarised then vulgarised the work of his rival Andre Béchamp.[188] Like Gallo, Pasteur was an attention seeker who excelled as a tireless self-promoter. (You must watch for those willing to benefit off the backs of others. They can be quite useful toward your end goals.) If Pasteur borrowed a small sliver of Béchamp's research for his own private gain, what of it? He not only had the wits to create a better situation for himself, but he spawned countless ancillary industries that until today serve as a Malthusian dream.

Please do not minimise the importance of the information you're about to receive, as it will dwarf Warburg's findings in comparison. Perhaps I should explain.

Béchamp's in-depth findings centred on his discovery of small corpuscles he named microzymes through the use of his extraordinary (for that time) microscope. It's important to understand that in the mid-1800s, the general thinking was that when meat rotted, milk soured and wine fermented it was due to a process called *spontaneous generation* which, it was believed, basically came from nowhere.[189] But whilst Pasteur and others simply agreed to accept spontaneous generation, Béchamp was hunched over his microscope studying living blood.[190] All his meticulous work finally paid off when it led him to discover fermentation was caused by microzymes.[191] These microzymes were found within human cells as well as outside the body in animals,

---

188.) Guylaine Lanctot, M.D., *The Medical Mafia: How to get out of it alive and take back our health & wealth* (Miami, FL: Here's the Key Inc., 1995), 157.

189.) Lanctot, *The Medical Mafia,* 156-157.

190.) Lanctot, *The Medical Mafia,* 157.

191.) Lanctot, *The Medical Mafia,* 157.

insects, plants and microorganisms.[192] Béchamp observed that these microzymes took on different forms, depending on the conditions surrounding the host cell in which they lived and fed.[193]

> NOTE: Polymorphism is the term used to describe the ability of the germ to exist in multiple forms.[194]

When the health of the host is poor due to malnutrition, toxicity, and mental and physical stress, the microzymes turn into pathogenic germs as a reaction to the imbalance in the cells.[195] I hardly think it's a leap of faith to suggest that the early stages of illness can be viewed as a distress call from the body seeking to restore balance. Béchamp realised that if equilibrium is reestablished, the germ returns to its microzyme state, resumes its peaceful protective function and the ailment vanishes.[196]

Pooey! How's an opportunistic ruler such as yourself supposed to gain an advantage over their subjects if they can resolve their own health issues through less profitable means such as a proper diet and quitting unhealthy habits? The answer is you can't. Therefore, the promotion of Louis Pasteur's limited interpretation of Béchamp's work will serve you well in your aim to make a killing.

In short, Pasteur took Béchamp's germ findings but failed to mention a few, some might say, important details. For instance, when exposed to the air, germs and other abnormal microzymes lose their virulence quite rapidly.[197] Furthermore, he also carefully omitted that an imbalance in the body (illness) creates the germ. Instead, Pasteur gleefully touted the idea that the opposite is true in that the germ causes the illness.[198] If that wasn't useful enough, the icing on the cake had to be when he insisted that these tiny organisms were foreign invaders only.[199]

Not to be insulting, my lord, but you know how we handle foreign invaders, don't you? That's right, we go to war!

If illnesses are seen exclusively as foreign intruders, peasants can be convinced to wage all-out war on sickness by using preventative weapons such as vaccines, strategic manoeuvres like surgeries and the

---

192.) Lanctot, *The Medical Mafia*, 156-157.
193.) Lanctot, *The Medical Mafia*, 156.
194.) Lanctot, *The Medical Mafia*, 156.
195.) Lanctot, *The Medical Mafia*, 156.
196.) Lanctot, *The Medical Mafia*, 156.
197.) Lanctot, *The Medical Mafia*, 157.
198.) Lanctot, *The Medical Mafia*, 158.
199.) Lanctot, *The Medical Mafia*, 157.

consumption of pharmaceutical drugs to attack the invaders. Peasants will put their trust, and health, in the hands of *authority*, giving up faith in themselves and reducing their own inner power.[200]

Pardon me, but we'll take it from here, thank you very much.

It shouldn't be hard to see the difference in revenue generating enterprises that can be formed through the war model as opposed to the peace model. But just to be sure you understand this important concept, let me quickly demonstrate war versus peace profitability through the contemporary process of pasteurisation which continues to make Mr Pasteur a household name.[201]

First, in any war, it's essential that peasants be told the war's being fought to keep them safe whilst also appealing to the majority's moral high ground.

Oh my giddy aunt, is there anything they won't blindly fall for?

A healthy portion of your proceeds will come from services and equipment produced and then paid for by peasants. Generally, it's incredibly important to understand that truth is the first casualty in any war. Truth must be hidden at all costs. Our current example, which we can see as a war on health, is no different.

We'll begin our discussion on pasteurisation with an understanding that the consumption of milk from animals such as aurochs (the forefather of today's cow), yaks, sheep, goats and other animals has been around for roughly ten thousand years.[202] Milk, known as today's virtual queen of the supermarket, is accredited with the development of the modern-day food industry, not only because it's so widely consumed, but because its byproducts such as yogurt, cheese and butter are as well.[203]

Whilst early usage of this nutrient-rich substance was seen as an alternative to starvation, animal milk didn't always agree with the adult human body. Early adult milk drinkers most likely suffered lactose intolerance. The enzyme lactase allowed children under the age of six to digest milk, but lactase didn't occur in adult human bodies until

200.) Lanctot, *The Medical Mafia*, 160.
201.) Lanctot, *The Medical Mafia*, 156.
202.) Bonnie Lavigne. "A Brief History of Milk." homestead.org. July 21, 2020. https://www.homestead.org/homesteading-history/a-brief-history-of-milk/
203.) Lana Valente. "The Origins of Milk: Why Was the First Cow Milked in the First Place?" medium.com. April 23, 2017. https://medium.com/@lanavalente/the-origins-of-milk-why-did-the-first-cow-milker-milk-the-cow-c41e8ef761d6

around 7,500 years ago when a genetic mutation allowed the continual production of lactase.[204]

Milk was a reliable human staple well before refrigeration. In the early 1800s, exposure to cow pox provided immunity to its deadly human cousin, smallpox. Increased demand resulted in increased herd sizes in limited spaces, reduced cows' health and caused a surge in germ-infested milk, justifying pasteurisation in 1895.

In 1917, distilleries began raising cows due to the increased demand for milk and symbiotically, the distilleries need to get rid of excess swill from alcohol production. Because of the cows' poor diet, foodborne illnesses such as tuberculosis, typhoid and coli bacillus swelled. This opened the doors to a wide range of opportunities including the implementation of *mandatory* pasteurisation. Thus, the War on Germs was in full swing in 1917.

Can you hear the triumphant reverberation of till bells?

With a Malthusian playbook in hand (see page 195), the opportunistic ruler must be ready to pounce when the situation presents itself. In this case, peasants were more than willing to accept new *protective measures* to remain safe from an invisible enemy, a.k.a. germs. Solving the cause of the problem, in this case the cows' unsanitary conditions and poor diets, would only disrupt large-scale profits. Instead, dairies launched an all-out assault on the milk, killing everything in it, including a good portion of the nutrients and all the enzymes needed for the body to digest milk's few remaining vitamins and minerals. With nothing left in the milk to spoil, the longer shelf life enhanced revenues. This was a win-win situation for those exploiting it. The exploiters then corralled the mindless, nutritionally deprived consumers into the medical system and pumped them full of drugs, just like the mindless bovine. Once again, avoiding the root of the problem generated an endless flow of cash. It's kind of like playing your favourite song over and over again, isn't it?

Please don't forget about the returns made on the drugs infused into the cows as well. And don't overlook the equipment needed to perform the pasteurisation process. Ka-ching, ka-ching. Agencies staffed with your most loyal and successful associates, from the very industries you're regulating, must be put in place. You'll want motivated insiders not only for their knowledge and commitment to your way of doing things, but because of their willingness to keep small producers

---

204.) Valente, "The Origins of Milk."

and outsiders out. This will allow you to take greater control of the herd's fodder and hence the peasants themselves.

Psst. The hilarious truth is that the temperatures used in pasteurisation are not hot enough to kill the targeted pathogens. Shhh. Even more uproarious is that with the advent of stainless steel tanks, milking machines and refrigerated trucks, not to mention the discontinuation of open pale containers delivered by the farmers, it's no longer necessary to destroy milk's beneficial properties under the guise of protecting public health.[205] But, as you should know, you never let such a wonderful opportunity go to waste.

The War on Germs has intensified so much, peasants spray disinfectant in all directions just upon entering a room. However, as a quick preview, our final internal war for discussion, the War on Terror, has further traumatised peasants to such a degree that they have accepted the irradiation of their food supply, thus allowing the obliteration of everything in, on or around it. You never know when an evil terrorist could be lurking around a loading dock just waiting for the perfect opportunity to contaminate a delivery. Boo! It's better to kill off everything in the food, including the nutrients, than to allow edibles that were tampered with to reach the plates of consumers. Unbeknownst to peasants, they'll be set up for the final blow should you need to reduce their numbers in great quantities.

> NOTE: As a ruler of the planet, culling the herd, unfortunately, is unavoidable. With the rapid evolution and integration of Artificial Intelligence, there will be more and more peasants without a productive role to fulfil on the **FARM**. Coupled with the depletion of natural resources because of an ever-expanding global population, both internal and external wars provide the perfect medium to reduce the planet's numbers whilst also eliminating non-essential peasants. You must realise that by exterminating those who will most likely end up disenfranchised in your system, you're preventing future discontent.

Is there a better agency to regulate the destruction of the herd's slop after processing and growing the crops in such things as depleted, chemically fertilised and overused soil whilst also tainting the food with pesticides, preservatives, *natural* flavours and genetically modified organisms than the Food and Drug Administration (FDA)? Don't food and drugs just go so lovely together, especially since they can both be

---

205.) ProCon.org. "Is Raw Milk More Healthful Than Pasteurized Milk?" Britannica ProCon.org. May 31, 2017. https://milk.procon.org/questions/is-raw-milk-more-healthful-than-pasteurized-milk/

so darn addictive? My goodness, times have changed since Hippocrates first uttered his immortal words: 'Food should be thy medicine and medicine thy food.'

Today, a network news station would pay handsome residuals to the father of the Hippocratic oath every time his commercial aired. 'Put any crap in your body you want. The people you trust to protect you from the damage they create are the same people who approve the drugs you use to correct the problem, even though these *approved* drugs end up causing a myriad of other problems.' Good luck with that. Then you can use the same regulatory agency to wage war against individuals who consume unauthorised substances like nutrient-rich, raw milk. How dare they! Anyone caught buying, selling or running this condemned item across state lines should face the harshest of consequences! When apprehended, their horses and carriages should be impounded![206]

> NOTE: We should promote synthetic drugs that treat symptoms, whilst creating other medical conditions, for mass consumption so that this subtle attack on peasants' health continues. As I previously stated, it'll be the illicit drugs that bring in the highest yields. Therefore, they should be the most widely distributed. Like their pharmaceutical counterparts, illicit drugs will also ripen the herd for treatment in the medical system, which brings us back around to Dr Robert Gallo.

As previously discussed, Dr Gallo claimed he discovered a virus caused cancer. Unfortunately, the scientific community didn't accept his findings as adequate or satisfactory even though they were failing to meet the War on Cancer's demand for a viral enemy. However, like Pasteur, Gallo's pursuit of notoriety and his shoddy science finally served a purpose when there was a need for a new type of viral enemy to hide the underlying causes of a growing health crisis. This crisis had the potential to draw peasants' attention to the silent war being waged against them.

In the late 70s and early 80s, an alarming number of young adults (mostly gay men and drug users) were turning up in clinics and emergency rooms with failing immune systems.[207] This presented quite a dilemma because the condition normally targeted the poor, the old

206.) Michael Tennant. "Amish Farmer Closes Raw Milk Business After Feds Slap Injunction on Him." The New American.com. February 17, 2012. https://the-newamerican.com/amish-farmer-closes-raw-milk-business-after-feds-slap-in-junction-on-him/

207.) *Banks, Aids, Opium, Diamonds, and Empire*, 208.

and the debilitated.

However, before the *official discovery* of HIV by Dr Robert Gallo, in the mid-1970s, two drugs, amyl nitrite and trimethoprim sulfamethoxazole (T/S), sold by the pharmaceutical giant Burroughs Wellcome, were directed at the gay community. Amyl Nitrite (known on the streets as poppers) was an easy sell because it provided a quick high and sent blood to the penis for longer lasting erections whilst relaxing the rectal sphincter muscle, making gay sex even more pleasurable. T/S on the other hand, was ingested just prior to a wild night on the town to help prevent STDs brought on by frolicking with a multitude of anonymous sex partners in dirty bathhouses. Because of their chemical configuration, insiders realized that these two pills, (the same structure as azathioprine, an organ transplant drug, produced and distributed by the same company, Burroughs Wellcome), resulted in immune system suppression.[208]

> NOTE: Azathioprine has been used since the early 1960s to suppress transplant patients' immune systems so their bodies' defences don't attack the new grafts, thereby increasing the amount of successful transplants.

As far as the illicit drug users were concerned, which included adventurous gay males living in the fast lane, the immune suppression qualities of opiates were already well-known and well-documented. However, in the early 1980s, one of the biggest surprises in the new unfurling plot was the damage brought on by crack cocaine. All the other lavishly distributed drugs dumped onto the streets, such as heroin, powdered cocaine, LSD and a slew of other psychotropic drugs, fail in comparison. The lethality of crack in regard to AIDS-related deaths not only helped sell the HIV/AIDS narrative (crack users had a three times higher mortality rate from AIDS-related illnesses than any other non-user demographic including intravenous drug users[209]), but it subdued and thinned out certain American inner cities where growing populations of minorities posed a threat to established order. If families of colour weren't destroyed by addiction to this not so accidentally widely available agent, perhaps harsher sentences and hence longer prison stints for crack users in relation to powdered cocaine users could seal the deal.

During the HIV/AIDS time frame, the clandestine orchestrators of the Vietnam War, the MK Ultra programme and the Iran Contra

---

208.) *Banks, Aids, Opium, Diamonds, and Empire,* 6-7.
209.) *Banks, Aids, Opium, Diamonds, and Empire,* 194.

scandal had masterfully pried open and saturated the American market with illicit drugs and *legal* drugs were being doled out by the pharmaceutical companies.[210] The question is, 'Would anyone in the newly tapped American market start to see a connection to the developing health crisis?'

This is a question you must ask yourself in a similar predicament. Are you beginning to develop a sense of how you would manage such a situation? Well, you must if you're going to outperform all the other hungry aspirants clawing their way to the top of a tall social pyramid.

In addition to the American crisis, on the other side of the world, certain populations on the African continent were being targeted with induced poverty, social disruptions and systemised starvation to allow those with a shrewd entrepreneurial spirit to gain access to the country's rich and abundant resources.[211]

Remember, to rule; only the coldest hearts need apply.

The desperate conditions also spawned an eager workforce willing to toil without adequate protection in the hazardous gold and diamond mines for a meagre day's pay.[212] It sure beats paying grovelling, lazy Americans at their inflated rates. But, then again, a witless consumer base is also required to purchase the products made from the resources a few go-getters had the vision to seize and develop.

Alongside stress and nutritional deficiencies, the poor air quality and inhalation of toxic dust was drawing unnecessary attention to the growing number of immune system disorders rapidly rising on the Dark Continent.[213] Unfortunately, at around this same time, the apartheid government was cracking at the seams, and it appeared as though millions of affected mine workers would run with their palms out demanding remuneration for their work-related diseases.

Can you imagine the horrible duress the mine owners faced?

The one thing these diverse subgroups had in common (miners, gay men, drug users, malnourished poor people) was the oxidative/nitrosative stressors that were causing an imbalance in their immune systems, hampering their ability to fight disease and infection.[214]

Instead of risking profits and attracting attention to what some self-righteous moral do-gooders would label as criminal negligence,

---

210.) *Banks, Aids, Opium, Diamonds, and Empire,* 102-103.
211.) *Banks, Aids, Opium, Diamonds, and Empire,* 5, 284.
212.) *Banks, Aids, Opium, Diamonds, and Empire,* 140-142.
213.) *Banks, Aids, Opium, Diamonds, and Empire,* 144-145.
214.) *Banks, Aids, Opium, Diamonds, and Empire,* 339-347.

collaborators instilled fear in the hearts of the entire world for a much more useful purpose. The quick-witted masters of the corporate plantation devised the idea of a blood-sex plague that would draw attention away from the underlying supply lines and responsible parties involved in all these occurrences, and instead pin blame on an unseen virus that originated from the jungles of Africa that could now attack peasants in their most intimate moments.

This new threat to human race was nothing more than Dr Gallo's rejected cancer virus, renamed HIV.[215]

Brilliant I say!

The story line was also timed perfectly with the rise of the American religious right pushing its way onto the scene. Surely it was the immoral behaviour and wrath of God afflicting certain demographics for their sins and not a few profiteering enterprises fuelling a self-serving agenda.

Wink, wink. There's nothing like a little fire and brimstone to override peasants' critical thinking skills, causing them to quiver in their boots.

> NOTE: Dr Peter Duesberg, once the world's most accomplished retrovirologist, leaked the fact that HIV is a benign passenger virus that is common to high-risk populations who suffer from immune suppression.[216] However, the great Dr Anthony Fauci, who jumpstarted his career on the HIV/AIDS paradox, silenced Duesberg and other critics through his invention of what is known today as cancel culture.[217] By labelling adversaries as *AIDS denialists*, Dr Fauci suppressed the narrative's darkest secret…HIV causes AIDS fails to meet even one of Koch's four postulates, the standard method for proving causation between a pathogen and a disease.[218]

The reckless habits of drug users and hard living gay males played a large part in the HIV/AIDS crisis in America. However, those exploiting the crisis cleverly kept the actual root causes of AIDS secret whilst promoting the blood-sex narrative This finally leads us to one of the major keys to human health. Drugs like amyl nitrite, T/S, heroin and crack cocaine as well as environmental toxicity, tainted food, asbestos

215.) *Banks, Aids, Opium, Diamonds, and Empire*, xvii, 8-11 and Robert F. Kennedy Jr., The Real Anthony Fauci: Bill Gates, Big Pharma, and the Global War on Democracy and Public Health (New York, NY: Skyhorse Publishing, 2021), 182-184.
216.) Kennedy Jr, *The Real Anthony Fauci*, 179.
217.) Kennedy Jr., *The Real Anthony Fauci*, 203.
218.) Kennedy Jr, *The Real Anthony Fauci*, 192-198.

and silicosis all create oxidative/nitrosative stress in the immune system and retard the proper functioning of the mitochondria.[219] The mitochondrias' respiratory/oxygen carrying duties, along with their energy production inside the cells, is one of the key components to good health and resistance to a host of diseases.

Since it would take at least an entire book to explain this process in great detail, I'll leave it to you to do your own research. To save time, however, you may also wish to employ a team of scientists from the eugenics—ah—I mean *reproductive health* movement who specialise in the frailties of the human body to assist you in your endeavours. The advancements in this area have been quite remarkable, and it's now possible to target an individual or a group of people based on their genetic composition using biological methods.

Since one of the most useful tools a leader has at their disposable is the written record, we can continue to build upon previous discoveries whilst past, present and future knowledge is purposefully hidden from the peasants.

The three internal wars (war on drugs, war on health and war on poverty) allowed room for expansion onto other **FARMS**, giving the entire network of lords many opportunities to spread its business of human suffering into new territories whilst increasing its means of control over a larger portion of the global population. However, none of the methods discussed thus far justify a clampdown on day-to-day activities or the use of force against peasants on other **FARMS** quite like the War on Terror.

When assigning a *Nineteen Eighty-Four* Orwellian Ministry to this far-reaching and effective war against the peasants, a delightful combination of both the Ministry of Peace and the Ministry of Love fit the bill quite nicely. For those needing a friendly reminder, the Ministry of Peace handled the creation of continual warfare whilst the Ministry of Love used only the harshest techniques to deal with any perceived dissidence from the *proles*, a.k.a. peasants.

Just the name, War on Terror, should invoke fear, the most effective motivator at your disposal. Here's a quote accredited to the master of this technique, Adolf Hitler: 'Terrorism is the best political weapon, for nothing drives the people harder than the fear of sudden death.'[220] As an added benefit, fear impedes peasants' ability to think

---

219.) *Banks, Aids, Opium, Diamonds, and Empire*, 13.

220.) Jeff Thomas. "The New and Improved Propaganda." LewRockwell.com. April 9, 2020. https://www.lewrockwell.com/2020/04/no_author/the-new-and-im-

critically. Craftily creating an atmosphere of sudden and imminent death, driven by a committed propaganda campaign, will effortlessly lead most peasants in the direction you wish to guide them.

Terror provides the perfect atmosphere, whether you want to invade another **FARM** for its abundant resources or line the masses up for an untried antidote. Since, from our previous examples, we can deduce that a War on Terror creates more terror, let's examine the opportunities that arise naturally or, even more exhilaratingly, with a little nudging.

Like a herd of wildebeests in the Serengeti that cling together for protection against an outside threat such as a lion or a bolt of lightning, the human herd will react in much the same way when given the proper stimuli. In fact, humans may be even more panic-stricken and impressionable due to their ever so fragile collective psyche. You can fully exploit this vulnerability to gain compliance and lead peasants in any direction you see fit. You can use both implicit and explicit fear (see Chapter 10) to not only paralyse the herd's ability to reason, but to amplify or prolong a danger that is real, imaginary or a combination of both.

As a gentle reminder, media outlets can propagate explicit fear, turning it into a direct, in-their-face form of terror in today's world. As previously discussed, in more subtle applications used during the Vietnam War, explicit fear entailed such actions as decapitating a villager accused of aiding and abetting the enemy. They did this in front of the villagers to traumatise them and steer them away from patriotic activity. This technique can now reach mass audiences.

A highly infectious virus that promises an excruciating death for its host, or an event like 9/11, can traumatise the world. Startling reminders and chilling statistics, along with committed authority figures offering their guidance and concern, can all be used to produce the most drastic changes in a society in the least amount of time. Once peasants become invested in their deeply ingrained habits and way of life, it's difficult to pry them away from their familiar routines. This is especially true if you wish to impose stricter controls upon them. They'll more readily accept these new rules if they feel the changes are being implemented for their own protection and the common good. The size and sophistication of the population you wish to affect dictates the amount of trauma you must induce to gain their compliance.

The COVID-19 worldwide pandemic and 9/11 exemplify the results that a horrific and large-scale cataclysmic event can have on reshaping the behavioural patterns of the entire world. With the advent of faster communications and technology, the desired outcomes have never been more satisfying.

History is loaded with examples of this technique in action, clearly illustrated by the cooperation achieved after the 9/11 terrorist attacks. The tone was set when American leader George Bush Jr uttered the words evoking implicit fear: 'You are either with us or against us in the fight against terror.'[221] This very statement coerced America and its coalition partners to invade a **FARM** that not only possessed an extremely valuable resource but refused to accept the current global lords' money system. The audacity! With the world witnessing the devastation caused not only on 11 September 2001, but as a result of the retaliation on *countries* believed to be harbouring *terrorists*, the majority of the world's inhabitants could not comply fast enough.

> NOTE: Once the majority is convinced, they become instrumental in keeping those with doubts in line. Anyone who challenges groupthink will be deemed a danger to the rest of the herd. Oh, and be sure to interrupt your fear campaign with feel good stories and uplifting slogans like 'United we stand' or 'We are all in this together' to placate the sensibilities of those who fully invest themselves in the official stories.

It's incredibly important to misdirect the peasants' energy early in a crisis. This will allow you to impose new controls that are harder to overturn as time goes by. When done over a long enough period, peasants will simply accept their plight as the new normal, forming a fresh set of habits and routines that fall within the most recent restrictions placed on them.

There's really no magic involved when leading your peasants into battle. Famed Nazi, Hermann Goring, said it best: 'Naturally the common people don't want war, neither in Russia, nor in England, nor for that matter in Germany. That is understood. But, after all, it is the leaders of the country who determine the policy, and it is always a simple matter to drag the people along, whether it is a democracy, or a fascist dictatorship, or a parliament, or a communist dictatorship. Voice or no voice, the people can always be brought to the bidding of the leaders. That is easy. All you have to do is tell them they are being attacked and denounce the peacemakers for lack of patriotism and exposing the country to danger. It works the same in any country.'[222]

221.) Washington (CNN). "You are either with us or against us." CNN.com. November 6, 2001. https://edition.cnn.com/2001/US/11/06/gen.attack.on.terror/
222.) Gustave Gilbert, The Nuremberg Diary (New York: The New American Library

Finer words have never been spoken. But, before you shed pity on the peasants and the hardships they'll endure in battle, it's important to recognise the three human needs fulfilled by war.

First, peasants involved in war earn an identity through military rank and glory in battle. Second, wars are fought to maintain or enhance the security of a **FARM**. This is sometimes taken for granted on **FARMS** blessed with security for any reasonable amount of time. Finally, war provides stimulation, giving your vassals something to do outside of organising and rallying against your plans. In short, by launching peasants into a venue where they obliterate each other, you actually provide them with a more stable and purpose-driven society. Furthermore, besides being quite riveting to watch, having peasants kill each other removes any liability from such a clever orchestrator as yourself, who at the same time may simply need to trim a little fat from their plantation. Just be sure the wars are long and drawn out so the social hierarchy on each **FARM** involved isn't disrupted. Well, unless, of course, your objective is to reestablish a new chain of command on one or more of the participating **FARMS**.

> NOTE: You and duelling lords should not be forthright when it comes to naming your external wars. Although more insightful and descriptive language could be used (such as the Opium Wars which occurred back in the mid-19th century), it'll be in everyone's best interest to use more generic terms like that of a World War or the (insert the name of the nation/region here) War, etc. The less peasants know about the root cause of the conflict, the better. If you're at all concerned that engaging in such deceitful practices will impact your respectability, please realise you can buy respectability, but remaining a poor sap only sets you up for failure as a global leader.

It's important to understand that the complete destruction of a **FARM** is no longer the objective in this era of modern-day warfare. With greater collusion amongst lords than ever before, wars can be constructively used to prop each other up economically, especially if one **FARM** has a distinct advantage over another. Therefore, extending wars well beyond a quick victory not only enhances the economic interests of all involved, but the fear and angst a war creates leaves the respective herds hanging onto their leaders' every word.

Historically, wars were fought when one group invaded another group for conquest and plunder. These more basic wars of the past were

of World Literature, Inc., 1961), 255-256.

narrow in scope and were typically launched to acquire a limited supply of resources. These attacks were usually conducted by mercenary armies, reducing the need for popular support since soldiers-for-hire could be placed in and out of battle with no effect on troop or citizen morale.[223] These types of conflicts were generally short-lived, since the goals of these invasions and the resources available to fund them were quite limited. Things took a drastic turn during World War I. This can be attributed to the application of mass citizen armies and the easy to come by cash and credit from the recently formed Federal Reserve Bank. When the dust settled, and humanity was still left standing, critical observers of this quantum leap into modern-day warfare had time to draw some useful conclusions.

> NOTE: Prior to WWI, the primary form of communication was the telegraph, and travel was largely by rail.[224] Although both were great achievements for their time, neither made coordinating mass armies any easier. To make matters worse, these citizen soldiers were spread out across the countryside and were dependent on a signal to launch them into a monolithic logistical campaign that would leave Julius Caesar's mouth agape. These large citizen fighting forces were gathered to wage an attack against an enemy or to defend their homeland against an invading army.

Time was of the essence since the side that could organise and strike the quickest had the best chance of victory. Once the cue was given and the gears of war were set in motion, each soldier had a specific role to play, along with having to gather their equipment and meet at rendezvous points until the assembling groups grew from platoons, companies and regiments into divisions and armies travelling along strategic lines of attack. When on an offensive, it was common for armies to have rallying points deep inside enemy territory.[225] It shouldn't be hard to see how difficult it would be to withdraw such an order once given.

Add to the fact that a dangerous new precedent had been set with multiple entangling alliances pledging to defend one another if a partner entered a conflict. With so many of these pacts in place, one small conflict could pull most of Europe into a glorious form of mass

---

223.) Carroll Quigley, *Tragedy and Hope: A History of the World In Our Time* (New York: The Macmillan Company, 1966), 236.
224.) Quigley, *Tragedy and Hope*, 221.
225.) Quigley, *Tragedy and Hope*, 222.

sacrifice. These pre-arranged agreements added fuel to the fire since weaker nations suddenly exuded a bravado they didn't possess before aligning with a stronger affiliate.[226] Like a drunken mate in a rival town's pub who has to be defended to preserve their friendship and to receive their backup in return, these stronger allies had to honour their commitments for fear that any lack of devotion might be reciprocated one day. All these factors combined to set a hair trigger that put the entire eastern hemisphere on the brink of annihilation.

> NOTE: To run the world effectively, sometimes you need to risk it all to acquire and maintain the global control you desperately crave. If you don't already, you should start taking even the smallest chances in your everyday life to enhance this skill set, as it'll serve you greatly when fully developed.

These alliances made sense to the elite minds forming them. There was always a positive gain for each participant, and they usually came at the expense of their mutual enemy(s), not to mention their own homegrown peasants. With citizens now more fully invested in their *nation's* outcome through their participation in mass armies, their unwavering support was a necessary component to complete this sharp transition into nationalism. These armies soon became the source of domestic pride, and an undisputed victory was now expected instead of the age-old practice of negotiation and compromise to end armed disputes. Flexing military might to overcompensate for internal weaknesses soon became the norm, making any attempts at peace and diplomacy even more difficult once a conflict began.[227]

Even though rulers of that time had their motivations for siding or feuding with certain **FARMS**, commoners didn't always share their rulers' viewpoints. Since England was the perennial power of Europe and had the most to lose, a wonderful invention arose from the pressing need to sway public opinion in favour of the orchestrators of British society. Hence the Tavistock Institute was born out of the Wellington House in 1913.[228] This was essentially the world's first mass brainwashing centre, and it was originally funded by the British Royal Family who was astute enough to recognise the importance of such a concept. Historian and future director of studies at the Royal Institute

---

226.) Quigley, *Tragedy and Hope*, 222.

227.) Quigley, *Tragedy and Hope*, 223.

228.) John Coleman, *The Tavistock Institute of Human Relations: Shaping the Moral, Spiritual, Cultural, and Political and Economic Decline of the United States of America* (Las Vegas, NV: World Intelligence Review Inc. 2006), IX

of International Affairs (RIIA), Arnold Toynbee, once referred to this new propaganda house as both 'a black hole of disinformation' and 'a lie factory'. Oh, what an understatement that would be! The mandate given to Lords Rothermere and Northcliffe was to produce an organisation capable of manipulating British public opinion to garner support for a declaration of war against Germany.[229]

You see, before World War I, the British were quite friendly with the Germans in much the same way the United States is quite chummy with Canada today.[230] As we've already discussed, truth is the first casualty of war as the pioneers of Tavistock clearly understood. Opinion making through a craftily employed smear campaign guided the British public to see Germans as blood sucking monsters rather than congenial neighbours. Posters prompting the casual citizen to 'Don't Stand Looking At This - Go and Help!'[231] littered the English landscape. Horrific stories permeated the public consciousness, accusing the Germans of spearing Belgian babies with bayonets whilst singing war songs, amputating boys' and girls' hands, amputating women's breasts and ripping Belgian women from their homes, stretching them out on tables and gang raping them whilst German soldiers cheered.[232] These stories were not isolated to England and quite purposefully made their way over to the budding economic and military powerhouse, the United States of America, who some clever global planners wanted to bring into the fray.[233]

NOTE: You may remember Nurse Nayirah, who was the daughter of the Kuwait ambassador to the United States, Saud al-Sabah, and her tearful testimony in 1990 before the US Congress reporting the horrors committed by Iraqi soldiers in Kuwait.[234] Her brilliant academy award winning-esque

229.) Coleman, *The Tavistock Institute of Human Relations*, X, 2.

230.) Coleman, *The Tavistock Institute of Human Relations*, 25.

231.) Parliamentary Recruiting Committee. "Don't Stand Looking at This – Go and Help!" Imperial War Museums.org.uk. https://www.iwm.org.uk/collections/item/object/30491

232.) Coleman, *The Tavistock Institute of Human Relations*, 99.

233.) Benjamin Freedman, "Benjamin Freedman's 1961 Speech at the Willard Hotel Complete YouTube," YouTube video, 46:31, Likemuzyk, August 30, 2012, https://youtu.be/-dRd3Ajiu4Q

234.) Russ Winter. "CONSPIRACY FACT: Teenage Kuwaiti Girl Lied to Congress About Iraqi Atrocities to Manipulate Public Support for a Gulf War." Winter Watch.net. November 15, 2021. https://www.winterwatch.net/2021/11/conspiracy-fact-teenage-kuwaiti-girl-lied-to-congress-about-iraqi-atrocities-to-manipulate-public-support-for-a-gulf-war/

performance, with training from the public relations firm Hill and Knowlton, alleged that armed Iraqi soldiers entered the hospital, where she worked as a volunteer, and removed babies from their incubators and placed them on the cold floor to die.[235] Is this sounding eerily familiar? Does the image of Belgian babies on the ends of bayonets come to mind? This appalling statement about the brutality of the Iraqi soldiers was reverberated across America until the United States found itself thrust into the first Gulf War. Furthermore, like the Kaiser of Germany being called the 'Butcher of Berlin' in 1914, Saddam Hussein of Iraq was referred to as the 'Butcher of Baghdad' in 2002.[236] This goes to show, as long as peasants are prevented from understanding their true history, these same storylines can be successfully repeated over and over again.

Two of the best from the west side of the pond, Walter Lippmann and Edward Bernays, represented America as inaugural board members at the Tavistock Institute.[237] You'll see throughout the remainder of this handbook why a think tank like Tavistock is essential to your world domination plans. Well-placed propaganda produces what mass manipulator Edward Bernays referred to as Engineered Consent. Bernays in his own words described this by postulating: 'If we understand the mechanism and motives of the group mind, it is now possible to control and regiment the masses according to our will without them knowing it.'[238]

It's only natural to be quite impressed by the level of sophistication early pioneers like Bernays displayed when shaping and forming public opinion in such subtle ways that peasants thought these manufactured opinions were their own.[239] As I reveal Tavistock's influence, you'll begin to understand how you can utilise this technology to permeate every aspect of your peasants' lives. Examples can be seen in America where these techniques were applied to politics, the media, medicine, art, religion, entertainment and used by intelligence agencies like the former OSS (Office of Strategic Services) and the CIA. I believe former CIA Director William Casey said it best back in 1981 when he

---

235.) Jack Xiong. The Fake News in 1990 That Propelled the US into the First Gulf War." Citizen Truth.org. May 7, 2018. https://citizentruth.org/fake-news-1990-that-ignited-gulf-war-sympathy/

236.) Coleman, *The Tavistock Institute of Human Relations*, XVII.

237.) Coleman, *The Tavistock Institute of Human Relations*, 25.

238.) Coleman, *The Tavistock Institute of Human Relations*, 2.

239.) Coleman, *The Tavistock Institute of Human Relations*, 1.

quipped: 'We'll know our disinformation programme is complete when everything the American public believes is false.'[240]

We'll close out our discussion of World War I by stating that it was the brilliant think-tank at Tavistock Institute that created the term *isolationist* through a technique referred to as *sloganeering*. In order to get elected, Presidential candidate Woodrow Wilson vowed to avoid WWI. However, once in office, sloganeering was cleverly used to guilt trip the American public into joining the fight.[241] What warmongering insider could resist a bloody and expensive conflict upon being called a coward (a.k.a. isolationist) even when most of Wilson's countrymen were opposed to entering the conflict? Here we see the power of guilt at play. Any American with apprehensions about joining this wonderful offering of mass carnage was labelled with this degrading moniker.

Hermann Goring anyone?

Whether these buzzwords spring from the original Tavistock Institute or one of its many tentacles is unimportant. It's their effectiveness that takes precedence when immediate results are required.

Whether waging a silent war against your own peasants or thrusting them into the killing fields against another **FARM**, modern-day weapons come in many shapes and sizes. Some of these murdering mechanisms have been so well-hidden and are so advanced, many peasants refuse to believe they exist. A quick list of these enhanced ordnances includes:

- biological and chemical agents
- energy weapons like lasers and electromagnetic waves
- acoustic devices
- state of the art conventional arms
- legal and illegal drugs
- remote controlled devices
- food
- insects
- unsuspecting human beings
- disinformation centres/outlets

240.) Barbara Honegger, "Did CIA Director William Casey really say, "We'll know our disinformation program is complete when everything the American public believes is false"?" Internet Archive. November 25, 2014. https://archive.org/details/cia-director-william-casey-disinformation-program-quote-soruce/mode/2up

241.) Coleman, *The Tavistock Institute of Human Relations*, 96. And Patricia O'Toole. "How the US Government Used Propaganda to Sell Americans on World War I." History.com. January 26, 2022. https://www.history.com/news/world-war-1-propaganda-woodrow-wilson-fake-news

- household products
- aerial and naval technologies
- cloaking devices
- highly advanced robots
- nuclear weapons
- environmental phenomenon like lightning and storms

In spite of such wonderful breakthroughs in modern warfare, the greatest weapon at your disposal is still the mind of a compartmentalised, frightened and obedient peasant.

Although quite a few of these contemporary weapons are capable of mass destruction, it still takes willing peasants to create, produce, manage and operate them, not to mention tend to other trivial matters on the **FARM** that are far beneath a dignified ruler such as yourself. Can you see the importance of maintaining the illusion of freedom? I mean, who would partake in such madness otherwise?

In addition, even though most *citizens* must buy into your false reality, it's important that your military sees things in a very practical sense because war is a matter of life and death, and there are dire consequences if your military is defeated. Soldiers should also remain compartmentalised and never breach the chain of command, nor should they understand the real purpose of their missions. Hiding your true ambitions keeps them loyal to you and prevents captured or dissenting soldiers from revealing important information. Lead them to believe their assignments are for the greater good even when your ultimate objectives conflict with their best interests which, more times than not, they will.

You'll want your most trusted associates holding various ranks throughout your fighting forces, as an organised military is the greatest threat to your rule. Having many ears to the ground will help prevent acts of rebellion against you. When forced to choose between the citizens and the military, the military should always take precedence.[242] Therefore, you must routinely give glorious speeches praising their efforts even though it's common knowledge that the military is primarily a sanctuary for misfits, giving them one last chance to serve the **FARM** in a productive way.

The type of **FARM** you run will help determine the methods used to fill your combat units. On tightly controlled **FARMS**, mandatory service for all males is usually the norm. Seventeen has become the

---

242.) Niccolo Machiavelli, *The Prince* (London: The Penguin Group, 1999), 62-66.

minimum age considered suitable for military duty for most modern-day **FARMS**, although some rare exceptions exist. Conveniently, this is around the same age when young males are most rebellious against authority.[243] Moulding peasants and instilling discipline in them through military service will turn their destructive angst into constructive aggression that can be used for the good of the **FARM** instead of against your ruling actions.

On less restrictive **FARMS**, drafts are the next form of recruitment used to round up not-so-willing participants. Drafts are usually used in conjunction with voluntary service. If you have the good fortune of running a **FARM** where the military has a favourable public opinion, has reached a high level of success in battle and is able to offer attractive pay and incentives, voluntary enlistment may be used exclusively. Regardless of the techniques applied, you *must* enforce harsh penalties for peasants who shirk their military duty or, worse yet, flee the battlefield. Because death is a very real possibility in combat, the consequence for desertion during a conflict should be capital punishment. Peasants will be less likely to leave the fight if their chances of survival are greater if they remain.

NOTE: Let's use the advanced military **FARM** of the United States of America as an example. During the Vietnam era, heavy backlash resulted when little Billy was ripped out of his home, handed a rifle and instructed to kill or be killed. A stealthier approach was employed after 9/11 by way of a backdoor draft run through the National Guard. Even though Guard troops served multiple tours of combat duty in the Middle East, there was hardly a blip of discontent on the public radar screen.[244] By baiting these soldiers to sign up for service using perks like free university and career training, dropping these weekend warriors off in the combat zone became an acceptable repercussion for their willingness to enlist as professional soldiers. This, despite the fact that Americans once understood the National Guard was to be used for matters promoting, restoring and maintaining domestic tranquillity *within* the United States.[245] Tranquillising peasants with junk food, drugs and entertainment helped ward off any grumblings from the populace which was, and still is,

243.) Griffin, *The Creature from Jekyll Island*, 519.
244.) Rome Neal. "'Back-Door Draft' Raises Questions." CBS News. May 28, 2004. https://www.cbsnews.com/news/back-door-draft-raises-questions/
245.) Jack Spencer and Larry Wortzel. "The Role of the National Guard in Homeland Security." The Heritage Foundation.org April 8, 2002. https://www.heritage.org/homeland-security/report/the-role-the-national-guard-homeland-security

quite pleasantly subdued.

When building your military, hunters and children of veterans provide the best candidates for service. Hunting humans is the ultimate challenge because the hunted fire back, thus adding to the thrill of the chase. You must also keep in mind that not everyone who enlists is going to be a front-line killer. Many will struggle with the moral dilemma of pulling the trigger to take a human life. You can still use these less aggressive soldiers for logistical and operational purposes and as additional targets on the battlefield. Passive participants will be more willing to die as part of a group sacrifice than to kill their adversary.

Those who do kill usually pass through a few predictable phases before reaching a high level of proficiency. Initially, soldiers may feel scared and apprehensive when thrust into battle and abruptly presented with various life-changing moral dilemmas. Once they make a kill, there may be a feeling of remorse along with some personal anguish. As the soldiers become more seasoned, they will grow increasingly desensitised until they achieve the rank of professional soldier. War may not immediately reveal it, but it can actually reverse natural selection by killing stronger soldiers before they have a chance to contribute to the improvement of the gene pool. This does, however, work to your advantage, especially as you age, since the younger and more dominant members of a **FARM** are reduced in numbers, diminishing their threat to your social supremacy.

Peasants who survive their tours of duty and reach a high level of skill in their military disciplines can be quite useful in the private sector or, better yet, as your own personal henchmen. If you wish to protect your world domination franchise, you'll want to surround yourself and key members of your fraternity with the most highly trained and decorated fighting men on the planet. Private military contractors, who draw upon these proven guns for hire, are now very commonplace and can be employed to pursue or defend national, corporate or personal interests. I can't help but smile when-reminiscing about the glory days of the late, great British East India Company. Remember, it was the BEIC that first used private mercenaries to enhance business profits whilst parading behind the guise of a corporate construct.

You should seldom use the most destructive forms of weaponry unless you want to send a powerful message to an enemy or completely destabilise a **FARM**. These devices can destroy all life on this planet but can also reach the sensibilities of even the most radical of madmen. Therefore, their acquisition is quite necessary and is a symbol of supreme military power. However, you'll find that conventional arms provide greater economic benefits and are more practical in most applications.

This is the perfect time to delve into the economic benefits of a long-lasting conventional war. Assuming you have followed this handbook's instructions and have taken over the banking system(s) of the lender nation(s) with your debt-based currency, you can simply sit back and enjoy the show as peasants destroy themselves whilst becoming further indebted and, hence, enslaved to you.

Sure, if you hate a neighbouring *nation* because their industry smoke is clouding your fresh mountain air, the quickest remedy would be to drop a weapon of mass destruction on their unsuspecting civilian population. Once the fallout dissipates, you could expand your **FARM** into the decimated area. Since a nuclear warhead may only cost in the ballpark of twenty to fifty million US\$,[246] just dropping one or two of these devices can bring about a quick peace settlement at a low cost to your peasants.

However, if your network extends the credit and provides the weapons for one or more of the belligerent foes engaged in a conventional conflict, the wealth you can acquire becomes immeasurable.

Financing just a five-year conventional war can cost in the ballpark of trillions. Moreover, the cost of storing and upgrading the nuclear devices far outweighs the price tag of assembling and detonating them.

> NOTE: You must, however, own and control as many weapons of mass destruction as possible, whilst preventing others from doing the same, since these weapons level the playing field for poorer **FARMS** opposed to your will. Besides being a wonderful scare tactic, they can also come in handy if you are, for example, an up-and-coming **FARM** engaged in multiple conflicts and need to quickly dismantle a resilient enemy whilst fighting a broader conventional war against a more surmountable opponent.[247]

Warfare production is an extraneous expense when viewed in terms of basic human needs. However, it would be hard to build up your control grid with profits made on farmers, craftsmen and yarn spinners. By extending the credit for military manufacturing, expansion can occur through the purchase of the large machines necessary to

---

246.) Yoni Blumberg. "Here's how much a nuclear weapon costs." CNBC.com. August 8, 2017. https://www.cnbc.com/2017/08/08/heres-how-much-a-nuclear-weapon-costs.html

247.) Quigley, *Tragedy and Hope*, 817.

mass produce excessive amounts of munitions and equipment. Once the war ends and assuming you're victorious, things like automobiles, aeroplanes, commercial foods and all kinds of trinkets along with my personal favourite, luxury items, can start to share space with armaments on these now higher capacity production lines. This will move you in the direction of total economic dominance.

Advancements in manufacturing along with intelligent focus on technology, brought on the mass production of devices like cameras, computers, televisions and mobile phones. These seemingly innocuous and indispensable items have been secretly used to draw peasants into a carefully contrived false reality splendidly created by their current lords. Not only have these various gadgets mentally programmed peasants, but their every move is being tracked and recorded by them as well.

The standard of living had to be improved for all peasants so they could afford such superfluous goods. Expanding the production of military equipment boosted the purchasing power of peasants without returning any equivalent amount of goods back into the market to compete for their interests.[248] As a result, peasants had more financial capital available for more frivolous yet useful *control tools*—oops—I mean items. By churning out bombs and tanks, even though they have no practical everyday use, their constant production elevates peasants' overall buying power, keeping the other industries operating 24/7. In short, war creates an artificial demand whilst simultaneously balancing surpluses. There's never been a greater economic stabiliser than the warfare system.[249] You're ensuring your peasants' servitude with the production/consumption cycle, driving them continuously on the corporate rat wheel. This leaves them with little leisure time and you with great wealth and power.

If your **FARM'S** able to produce state-of-the-art military equipment, you can make less efficient **FARMS** dependent on you for both your line of credit and your advanced weaponry. Most **FARMS** will need to bolster their arsenals to stay up to date on all the latest killing innovations to remain competitive on the world stage. Should these purchasing **FARMS** be unable to match your level of technical and operational proficiency, they'll also be dependent on you for training, repairing and maintaining these resplendent murderous mechanisms. If you're able to follow the techniques presented in this handbook and

248.) Quigley, *Tragedy and Hope*, 362.
249.) Lewin, *Report from Iron Mountain*, 38.

can further stir up worldwide conflicts whilst bringing multiple nations into the mix, you'll triumphantly create a direct pipeline of revenue into your offshore bank account.

> NOTE: Corporations make the perfect fronts for moving war supplies from one **FARM** to another without opportunistic **FARM** owners having to endure such unfavourable labels as traitors or turncoats. Remember, these legal, fictional entities make the perfect cover for such clandestine activities. Please revisit Chapter 5 for a reminder if it's indeed required.

As initially published but then promptly minimised as a fictional account, *Report from Iron Mountain* dropped the following pearl of wisdom that's worth examination. 'The basic authority of a modern state over its people resides in its war powers. There is, in fact, good reason to believe that codified law had its origins in the rules of conduct established by military victors for dealing with the defeated enemy which were later adapted to apply to all subject populations.'[250] (Didn't we see that with our fine example of the Lieber Code in Chapter 6?) 'On a day-to-day basis, it is represented by the institution of police, armed organisations charged expressly in dealing with *internal enemies* in a military manner. Like the conventional *external* military, the police are also substantially exempt from many civilian legal restraints on their social behaviour. In some countries, the artificial distinction between police and other military forces does not exist. On the long-term basis, a government's emergency war powers—inherent in the structure of even the most libertarian of nations—define the most significant aspect of the relation between state and citizen.'[251]

There are clues everywhere for those willing to look for them. Piecing them together and applying them is an entirely different story and the ultimate aim of this irreplaceable manual.

Back to your publicly funded military. You can minimise its threat to your rule by filling its ranks with only those most loyal to your cause. You should also discreetly afford the lowly grunts subpar healthcare and less than adequate food and lodging. In many cases, these provisions will be an improvement over the conditions from which they came. Additionally, you can use rank and accolades instead of higher pay because you don't want to lift your peasants up too much economically. If you do, they may not see the value in fighting under horrific conditions and may use their

---

250.) Lewin, *Report from Iron Mountain*, 39-40
251.) Lewin, *Report from Iron Mountain*, 39-40.

expertise against your overall desires. Offer them medals as a substitute for substantial pay, as soldiers are mesmerised by decoration.[252]

Because of their conscious or even unconscious participation as disposable commodities in your military machine, these people, by their own choice, are the expendable assets on your **FARM**. Since they're not pitted against you and show up every day, even if begrudgingly, they offer themselves as such. It's your job to utilise them in every way possible for the advancement of your goals and your organisation's overall objectives. Even on the freest **FARM**, once peasants commit to die for your corporation by enlisting, they fully and knowingly offer themselves as its property, lending themselves to many other useful purposes outside of their combat duties.

> NOTE: Have you ever wondered why civilians killed during military operations are known as collateral damage? As we discussed in Chapter 6, citizens are collateral for the public debt—nothing more, nothing less. If the debt is quite large, keeping these losses to a minimum is in the creditor's best interest unless, of course, other types of guarantees like national parks or port cities financially back the debtor nation's more extravagant lifestyle choices.

The battlefield, with its life or death circumstances, provides the perfect testing ground for scientific, medical and agricultural advancements. After their use in combat, these products can be made available to the general public for commercial consumption. Many great discoveries were jolted from the herd's collective fear of death and capacity to destroy, only to arise from the horrors of war to serve humanity in more constructive ways. A few of these major scientific breakthroughs include:

- iron
- weather modification technology
- steel
- atomic particles
- radio relays
- navigation systems
- radar
- wireless communications
- satellites
- drones

252.) General Smedley D. Butler, *War Is A Racket* (United States: Aristeus Books, 2014), 37.

Combat casualties required logistical improvements like centralised medical care units, ambulances and Medivac air transport that improved emergency services on civilian **FARMS** once the fighting ended. Traumatic battle injuries led to the suturing of blood vessels and blood transfusions and gave rise to blood typing and blood banks that eventually resulted in these fluids being held in cold storage for a wide array of **FARM** emergencies. Surgical procedures like debridement for open chest wounds and skin grafts for disfigurement arose from trial and error on the front lines and were then applied to heal hordes of civilians who also suffered from these fatal and life altering afflictions. Widespread infections were first curtailed with penicillin during WWII before reaching large-scale commercial applications. Finally, national fitness standards arose out of the need for a **FARM'S** overall military preparedness, leading to better societal health.

Agriculturally, the most infamous discovery ascended from the defoliation programme known as Operation Ranch Hand during the Vietnam War. The programme ran from 1962-1971.[253] Just remember, 'Only you can prevent a forest!' I joke, just as the pilots of the C123s, nicknamed *Cowboys*, joked during their spraying runs.[254] The test chemicals used in Operation Ranch Hand were identified by a code name referencing the colour of the band wrapped around the fifty-five-gallon barrel containing the agent. These bands came in a rainbow of flavours, the most famous was orange. This was, of course, Agent Orange. The other lesser-known barrel band hues were Green, Pink, Purple, Blue, White, Orange II, Orange III and Super Orange.[255] Much was learned from the effects these various agents had on the vegetation and food crops below. Even more was gained by observing the side effects experienced by both soldiers and Vietnamese villagers. If you thought chemical and biological agents were outlawed by the Geneva Protocol as a result of their use in WWI, you are correct. This will lead us to another invaluable lesson, my aspiring protégé. But first, let us finish our current discussion.

You see, there is, how can I say this…a very dark element involved in warfare. I mean, even the last living combat soldier of World War I, Harry Patch, stated: 'I felt then, as I feel now, that the politicians

253.) History.com Editors. "Operation Ranch Hand initiated." History.com. July 29, 2019. https://www.history.com/this-day-in-history/operation-ranch-hand-initiated

254.) Erin Blakemore. "Agent Orange Wasn't the Only Deadly Chemical Used in Vietnam." History.com August 29, 2018. https://www.history.com/news/agent-or-ange-wasnt-the-only-deadly-chemical-used-in-vietnam

255.) Blakemore, "Agent Orange Wasn't the Only Deadly Chemical Used in Vietnam."

who took us to war should have been given the guns and told to settle their differences themselves, instead of organising nothing better than legalised mass murder.'[256] Well, I mean, he isn't exactly wrong. So, if we're going to legalise mass murder, let's seize the opportunity, shall we? I mean, ah, let me rephrase that. Let's perform maybe a few, well, uh, there's no easy way to convey this so I'll just blurt it out. For the betterment of society, let's perform controversial experiments, which aren't acceptable during times of peace, on living, breathing human beings. Whew! I said it. Now, please let me explain.

Sure cancer, skin diseases and fatigue were observed in subjects exposed to the agents used during Operation Ranch Hand, as were birth defects in their offspring.[257] However, researchers accurately determined the short and long-term effects of exposure to the chemicals involved. For example, dioxins weren't only present in these experimental herbicides but were also common in industrial processes at that time. You see, their use in combat helped raise awareness of the health risks they posed to the general public. Ahem. Since these slow, low-flying aircraft had to dodge enemy fire to avoid being shot down, certain dissemination equipment improvements had to be made so these herbicidal sprayings could cover larger areas with fewer passes. This resulted in larger crop yields at lower costs to consumers back on the corporate FARM and was a genuine victory for our friends in Big Agriculture and the chemical industry, I'll have you know.[258] It's beyond most people's comprehension just how many unnecessary plants and weeds have been eliminated, thus allowing profitable crops to flourish and utility lines to remain unobstructed.

Sorry if I appear a little testy, but I always feel as if this information needs to be defended, which is completely unfair.

Ah, and whilst we're on the topic of quietly observing military test subjects exposed to hazardous conditions, who could forget the Atomic Veteran?[259] These were American Veterans who were purposefully exposed to ionizing radiation in the years 1945-1962 for the sole

256.) Harry Patch with Richard Van Emden, *The Last Fighting Tommy: The Life of Harry Patch, the Only Surviving Veteran of the Trenches* (London, New York, Berlin: Bloomsbury Publishing, 2007), 188-189.

257.) Blakemore, "Agent Orange Wasn't the Only Deadly Chemical Used in Vietnam."

258.) Institute of Medicine (US) Committee to Review the Health Effects in Vietnam Veteran Exposure to Herbicides. "History of the Controversy Over the Use of Herbicides." National Library of Medicine. 1994. https://www.ncbi.nlm.nih.gov/books/NBK236351/

259.) "Atomic Veterans 1946-1962." Atomic Heritage Foundation.org. June 17, 2019. https://ahf.nuclearmuseum.org/ahf/history/atomic-veterans-1946-1962/

purpose of examining its effects on the human body. I'm going to tread lightly here, as I'm aware some of you hoping to conquer the planet may have been conditioned to have nothing but deep respect for our fighting men and women. However, the inconvenient truth is that throughout history select soldiers, as well as citizens and prisoners of war, have been used as human guinea pigs for a plethora of scientific trials.

The most infamous of these took place in the Nazi concentration camps. Although Hitler has become an easy scapegoat for the atrocities that took place during that time, few people are aware of the chemical/pharmaceutical conglomerate, IG Farben, and its lucrative investment in these human laboratories. IG Farben was a willing participant in some experiments, helped finance the Third Reich's rise to power and operated its very own concentration camp.[260]

For your homework, I highly encourage you to read the letters between IG Farben subsidiary Bayer and the Nazi's that detailed the buying and selling of camp refugees. The purpose of these specific negotiations was to set a price for one hundred and fifty female test subjects who, although emaciated, were otherwise in good health. These women were bought at the somewhat reasonable price of 170 Reich marks and were used to test a new sleeping pill. Unfortunately, these unwilling participants never awoke from their slumbers, as evidenced in a follow-up letter from Bayer requesting the purchase of more subjects, since all the female prisoners had died in the trials.[261] Other such medical experiments featured injections, pills, enemas and powders that treated an array of deliberately induced infections like typhus, tuberculosis and diphtheria.[262]

And who could forget the Angel of Death, Dr Josef Mengele's experiments on twins? Typically, studying these identical biological samplings enabled a deeper understanding of nature vs. nurture because two sets of variables could be administered on essentially the same subject. However, it would not be an understatement to suggest Mengele's inquisitiveness pushed the limits of legitimate scientific research, thus giving the eugenics movement a black eye.

260.) Holly Godbey. "Popular Pharmaceutical Company Bayer Bought Concentration Camp Victims in WWII." War History Online. November 28, 2016. https://www.warhistoryonline.com/war-articles/popular-pharmaceutical-company-bayer-bought-concentration-camp-victims-wwii.html?edg-c=1&A1c=1
261.) Godbey. "Bayer Bought Concentration Camp Victims."
262.) United States Holocaust Memorial Museum. "Bayer." Holocaust Encyclopedia. June 13, 2019. https://encyclopedia.ushmm.org/content/en/article/bayer

A few of Mengele's questionable practices involved sewing a set of twins together, injecting chemicals into the eyes of his subjects to change their eye colours and randomly removing organs with no anaesthesia or pain medication.[263] Like other worthwhile pursuits that receive a high degree of public backlash, the eugenics movement had to disappear from the scene for a while and eventually resurfaced under such innocuous names as *Planned Parenthood* and *Reproductive Health* to safely distance itself from the volatile aftermath of World War II. You'll be pleased to know that the atrocities of World War II did lead to a positive outcome by way of the Nuremburg Code, passed in 1947, requiring patients' consent before studies can commence.

> NOTE: As mentioned earlier, there's always a work-around when curiosities must be satisfied and results obtained. However, the questionable human experiments of today must be cleverly packaged and securely executed by carefully selected players to avoid unwelcome suspicions.

Lesser known than Mengele, but equally as cutting-edge, were Japanese microbiologist, Dr Shiro Ishii's human experiments during the same time frame, as part of the Second Sino-Japanese War. In keeping with the tradition of *Nineteen Eighty-Four* Orwellian doublespeak agencies, Dr Ishii's bioweapon's facility was innocuously named 'The Epidemic Prevention and Water Purification Department of the Kwantung Army', in the event you haven't had your daily dose of whimsical irony.[264]

Are you catching onto the pattern here? Do you think I simply make this stuff up?

Test subjects were referred to as *maruta* or *logs* that underwent Dr Ishii and the infamous Unit 731's sometimes *eye-popping* clinical trials.[265] Like Mengele, some of Ishii's curiosities teetered on the threshold of pure sadism. These included replacing human blood with horse or monkey blood, amputating limbs to study blood loss and then reattaching the appendages to opposite sides of the body, spinning a

---

263.) Godbey. "Bayer Bought Concentration Camp Victims."
264.) Paul Iddon. "Unit 731: Japan's Secret Horrifying Human Experiments." The National Interest. December 30, 2020. https://nationalinterest.org/blog/reboot/unit-731-japans-secret-horrifying-human-experiments-175476
265.) Richard Stockton. "Inside Unit 731, Japan's Disturbing Human Experiments Program During World War II." All that's interesting.com. November 11, 2022. https://allthatsinteresting.com/unit-731

subject in a centrifuge until death and placing victims in a low-pressure chamber until their eyeballs popped from their sockets.[266]

> NOTE: Remember from our discussion in Chapter 4, to ease the moral burden on those who carry out your objectives, you'll want to refer to peasants you wish to decimate as subhuman. In our Dr Ishii example, creative ideas like passing a torture chamber off as a lumber mill helped placate local officials. Using the log terminology just added to the effect, as did incinerating the fallen subjects like burning logs in a fireplace. Notice how calling them logs also made these victims subhuman. During war, you can get as innovative as your imagination allows whilst building a dismissive safe place for any questionable practices that would be admonished during times of peace.

Before you begin to form an unfavourable opinion of your mentor extraordinaire, *moi*, I should clarify that I do not raise these ghastly issues for the mere enjoyment of sharing them, although that may play a small part. There are greater teaching lessons in these dark sections of human history.

First, war is messy. As seen from the previous examples, human beings are given a blank cheque to behave as badly as they can get away with as long as it ensures victory for their side whilst also falling in line with their leader's worldview. This leads me to my next point. You must be willing to play outside of the established rules to find success in battle. The consequences involved in losing are too severe to mention and could cost you your life.

Although British citizens are known for being overly apologetic and polite, don't let this cosmetic exterior fool you. Throughout modern history, we've mastered the art of bending the rules for our own gain whilst portraying our enemies as savages.

During our Operation Ranch Hand discussion, I mentioned that chemical and biological agents were outlawed after WWI as a result of the Geneva Protocol. However, it was the British who stood up for their friends from across the pond and argued that the conflict in Vietnam was an *emergency* not a war and that the treaty didn't outlaw chemicals

---

266.) David D. Barrett. "Japan's Hellish Unit 731." Warfare History Network. Fall 2018. https://warfarehistorynetwork.com/article/japans-hellish-unit-731/ and Tracy Dahl. "Japan's Germ Warriors." The Washington Post. May 26, 1983. https://www.washingtonpost.com/archive/politics/1983/05/26/japans-germ-warriors/a0149d21-ba27-460e-a807-d3db942ba507/

during *police actions*.[267] The net effect was that this law breaching operation could continue with barely an eyebrow raised.

> NOTE: Any weapons banned from use in combat under international agreement are most likely incredibly effective. Therefore, these outlawed killing methods should be secretly developed and secured just in case you find yourself in a justifiable situation for their use.

Bending the laws with semantics is not a technique you should try unless you, or those you're aligned with, are in control of the World Court *or* you're certain of victory. The victors write history. I think it's fair to say the World Court also favours the victors. When the time's right, setting up a World Court is in your best interest in much the same way as setting up the laws and courts on your own **FARM**. The major difference is that a World Court will cover a larger jurisdiction and will help any ascending ruler, who could in fact be reading this handbook right now.

To further illustrate the smooth double standard practiced by the British, one must merely rewind the clock to the German occupation of Belgium at the early onset of World War I. Belgian civilians were firing on German soldiers who took citizen hostages and retaliated against Belgian patriots. The Brits trumpeted these German reprisals as *atrocities* and in violation of international law. That would've been the case except for one minor detail. The Belgian civilian snipers fired at the Germans first, an even greater breech of wartime etiquette, thus justifying the Germans' retaliatory actions. But the clever Brits did not stop there. They used these *atrocities* as justification for their own abuses. This included treating food as contraband and seizing neutral shipments on their way to Germany, even when the cargo could not be declared contraband under international law.[268] It shouldn't be hard to see that this was the equivalent of depriving noncombatant German citizens of basic living essentials.

To preserve Britain's own financial, military and natural resources, Prime Minister Neville Chamberlain hatched a clever ploy to shift the German problem onto the Soviet Union just before the outbreak of World War II. To accomplish this, Chamberlain needed to win public opinion to avoid a direct military conflict with Germany. His fear mongering campaign involved exaggerating the threat of a German

---

267.) Blakemore, "Agent Orange Wasn't the Only Deadly Chemical Used in Vietnam."
268.) Quigley, *Tragedy and Hope*, 238.

air raid/gas attack. Public statements were released that severely understated England's ability to defend itself against such an incursion. At the same time, Londoners were asked to dig trenches in the streets and parks whilst *all* citizens were fitted for gas masks, even though they had a better chance of getting hit with bird droppings than a Nazi gas attack. The plan worked. A panic not seen since 1678 ensued. The British public passively accepted the destruction of Czechoslovakia through appeasement just as Chamberlain had hoped.[269]

When America aligned itself with Britain in World War II, as it did in the First World War, they made a joint decision to strategically bomb cities like Freiberg and Dresden but not because they contained key military targets. The Royal Air Force raids were aimed at working-class housing units and were specifically chosen to obliterate citizen morale.[270] Ironically, sometimes these bombings had the opposite effect, speaking volumes about the human spirit. But don't get all sentimental just yet. These planned civilian air raids were the first of their kind and were quite effective in terrorizing German citizens into a state of shock whilst carefully leaving the armament facilities intact. Remember, as much as it may pain you, wars are designed to victimise peasants and not your business associates who invest heavily in the highly profitable yet volatile war industry.

Singling England out in these examples is hardly fair, and it's just as easy to point out an equal number of German and American breaches of wartime pleasantries. In World War II, Germany was able to take on most of the world militarily because of their ruthless exploitation of soldiers and civilians they captured during their early conquests. By starving this enslaved labour force, Germans maintained their pre-war caloric intake per capita, increasing their munitions output whilst barely putting a dent in their nation's food supply.[271] Additionally, wasn't it America that shocked the world by dropping the first atomic bombs on the largely civilian populations of Hiroshima and Nagasaki?

What conclusions can you draw from these slivers of historical controversy? I think it can best be summarised with the old expression, 'All is fair in love and war'. In short, you need to do whatever is required to *win*. As former Oakland Raiders NFL Football Club owner Al Davis used to say, 'Just win, baby'. Since war is the primary driving force of a society and since war also legitimises the entire social hierarchy, there is really no greater task at hand. I'll further expand on the importance of victory

---

269.) Quigley, *Tragedy and Hope*, 584.
270.) Coleman, *The Tavistock Institute of Human Relations*, 185-187.
271.) Quigley, *Tragedy and Hope*, 674.

shortly but, before I do, I'll highlight a few other useful conclusions.

First, you'll want to draw in as much cooperation for your war effort as possible whilst simultaneously depleting your opponent's reputation, morale, supplies, production capacity and fighting forces. This holds true whether you're looking to attract other **FARMS** to your cause or need to incite your own herd to support your desired agenda. You must think creatively to achieve the greatest level of backing even if, at first glance, these methods seem deceptive.

Second, if you're going to enter the fight on behalf of another **FARM**, carefully choose your alliances and stick with them. Third, be certain that there are strategic upsides for your involvement in a conflict. For example, in the early part of the 20th century, Britain dominated the high seas whilst America bordered the British territory of Canada. This was a good alliance, as British naval supremacy saved America the expense of protecting her merchant vessels at sea, whilst America helped monitor Her Majesty's North American province. Letting a highly unpredictable nation like Germany take control of the shipping lanes would have provoked uncertain ramifications in international waters not worth exploring.[272] This Anglo-American alliance forged a friendship that remains incredibly strong today.

Now, we'll focus on the exciting matter of harvesting the spoils of victory. In battle, this is the equivalent of winning the jackpot in a high-stakes poker game. Territories, riches and resources are divided amongst the conquerors, whilst the defeated pay reparations. Tight restrictions placed on vanquished nations can last for decades or even centuries.

However, even more substantial than the perks associated with success in combat is the broadening implementation of your worldview. Each new conquest moves the planet closer to your world vision. As conveyed by the greatest historian in modern times, Professor Carroll Quigley, in his literary masterpiece *Tragedy and Hope*: 'Any war performs two rather contradictory services for the social context in which it occurs. On the one hand, it changes the minds of men, especially the defeated, about the factual power relationship between the combatants. And, on the other hand, it alters the factual situation itself, so that changes which in peacetime might have occurred over decades are brought about in a few years.'[273]

I should also bring to your attention that those who fail on the battlefield will be subject to unflinching scrutiny for any controversial

---

272.) Quigley, *Tragedy and Hope*, 249-250.
273.) Quigley, *Tragedy and Hope*, 831.

actions they pursue whilst in the fog of war. Conversely, any question-able methods employed by the victors will be conveniently dispersed due to the overpowering euphoric feelings of triumph only a winner can exude. Can anyone say, 'Full pardon for the victor'? Again, in case you missed it, the *horrors* committed by the enemy *must* be put on full public display. This will not only support your claim of moral superiority, but will drive the defeated country's world reputation into the ground, giving them yet another obstacle to overcome should they try to rechallenge your supremacy.

Assuming you have reached a high degree of both military and economic proficiency, you can then secretly pardon and recruit valuable human assets from the fallen enemy who will enhance your **FARM'S** killing power. If you're to conquer the planet, you *must* surround yourself with the best and brightest minds. Your only concern should be with those who are dedicated to your worldview and those who are not. Somehow, and for some silly reason, the choice between a cold prison cell or execution versus continuing a lifetime of work can gain allegiance from even the most bitter rivals.

To gain a wealth of knowledge in such areas as rocket propulsion, medicine, biological warfare and chemical weaponry, the World War II victors, the Soviet Union and America, exonerated former Nazi war criminals under Operations' Osoaviakhim and Paperclip, respectively. These defeated but still useful recruits added a level of expertise to their respective **FARMS**, launching the Soviet-American Cold War and Space Race into the stratosphere (quite literally).

> NOTE: If you don't grab these assets when you have the chance, someone else will. Do you really trust that kind of sensitive and highly valued information in someone else's hands?

One of the most controversial, as well as prized, acquisitions of the World War II era was Dr Shiro Ishii. His techniques may have pushed the limits of practical sensibilities, but his covert research and development of lethal microbes such as anthrax, dysentery, typhus, cholera and the Bubonic Plague were innovative as were their modes of distribution. He bred rats and fleas to transmit these diseases, and routinely tested delivery systems such as bombs to enhance the lethality of these potent pathogens. This led to his smashing invention, the *flea-bomb*, that combined two simultaneous modes of transmission to terrorise Chinese villages with Plague (Black Death) delivered by infected fleas dropped from ceramic bombs. Ishii also broke the mould with other, never tried dissemination methods such as aerial spraying and spreading pathogens into Chinese wells, marshes and houses. Like a demented neighbour during Halloween, he inconspicuously infused snacks with germs that were then distributed amongst the locals.[274]

The Chinese weren't the only targets of Dr Ishii's live human test trials. American and Soviet soldiers also fell victim to his wrath. Because Douglas MacArthur, Lt Col Murray Sanders and Dr Edwin Hill deemed his findings absolutely invaluable, America forgave Dr Ishii for his war crimes in exchange for his trade secrets and test data.[275] Dr Ishii was even featured as a guest speaker at Fort Detrick, MD where he captivated an eager team of scientists and military personnel whilst revisiting his glory days in live human experimentation.[276] It turns out his meticulously detailed findings provided little value to the US military but, a deal is a deal, especially when made with those willing to push the limits of human innovation.

The grim realities of war bring yet another lesson to the forefront. Injustice sows anger in the hearts of men and creates the atmosphere for violent retaliation. This is exactly why a fair and just nation will simply be too damn passive to be used as your war surrogate and must be subverted as much as possible to be an effective global enforcement arm. The angst experienced by the herd because of the unfairness bestowed upon them can be constructively aimed at the enemy **FARM** of your choosing. Let's revisit Aristotle's poignant and time-tested observation: 'Anyone can become angry–that is easy; but to be angry with the right person, and to the right degree and at the right time and for the right purpose, and in the right way—that is not within everybody's power and is not easy.' Since the general population on any **FARM** lacks the capacity for such careful discernment, simply rile them up and point them in the direction that serves your interests.

In addition, the bitter resentment taking root on other **FARMS** due to internal and external inequities will push peasants to confront

274.) Andrew Lenoir. "The Twisted Story of Shiro Ishii, The Jozef Mengele of World War 2 Japan." Ati. November 11, 2022. https://allthatsinteresting.com/shiro-ishii-unit-731

275.) Hesper.hu. "US Army Fort Detrick, associated with the 731 Unit." Medium.com. May 15, 2020. https://medium.com/@hesperhu/u-s-army-fort-detrick-associated-with-the-731-unit-9259575749a6 and Wikipedia. "Shiro Ishii." Wikipedia. December 7, 2022. https://en.wikipedia.org/wiki/Shiro_Ishii

276.) GT staff reporters. "US pardoned Japan's war criminals in exchange for Unit 731 chemical weapons – how trustworthy is its clarification on Ukraine labs?" Global Times. March 22, 2022. https://www.globaltimes.cn/page/202203/1256557.shtml

those deemed responsible for their hardships, further promoting the continuous warfare model. Common sense tells us that bombing a wedding party in a foreign land or blaming a horrific event on a rogue group of religious zealots will stir up animosity. Once violence is unleashed, even the fear of retaliation can drive the initial bloodshed to constantly escalate.

We learned an important principle from the art of sloganeering and advertising (see page 219): 'A truth is forgotten while a lie lives on.' It should be easy to see that the truth dies the moment the first propaganda wave starts, and a lie can be extended almost indefinitely. Did they ever find those weapons of mass destruction in Iraq? Anyone? You can use falsehoods like a cattle prod to guide the gullible herd in the direction you choose. To sell a massive lie, just move an audience to accept the lies without understanding the issues behind their perception of the event. The following will clearly and metaphorically illustrate this technique.

I will refer you to a page out of early 20th century American history and the quaint scene of Woodrow Wilson admiring the sheep grazing in his front garden. The real reason Wilson plopped the flock on the White House lawn is because it served as a healthy reminder how gullible the American public was in believing the propaganda used to commit the United States to World War I.[277] Of course, they cleverly hid this outward sign of disrespect behind a propaganda campaign used to sell the Wilsons as a model American family supporting the war effort by saving taxpayer money on groundskeepers and by auctioning off the wool to donate $52,000 to the American Red Cross.[278] That was fine and dandy until these ghastly creatures began wreaking havoc on the White House grounds requiring fencing and other costs.[279] Clearly, the taxpayer money saved by these grass grubbing beasts wouldn't change the amount owed by peasants by even a penny. Baa! However, Americans ate it up more voraciously than a cud chewing lamb and, as a result, were more effortlessly led to the slaughter.

In Chapter 11, Training Your Peasants, I stressed the importance of distorting history in education centres to give groomed peasants-in-the-making a limited and agenda friendly worldview to win their allegiance. Whether they choose to enter the fighting ranks or the corporate plantation,

---

277.) Coleman, *The Tavistock Institute of Human Relations*, 87.

278.) Brian Resnick and National Journal. "White House Sheep, a History." The Atlantic. October 17, 2014. https://www.theatlantic.com/politics/archive/2014/10/white-house-sheep-a-history/453405/ and Coleman, *The Tavistock Institute of Human Relations*, 87.

279.) Resnik and National Journal, "White House Sheep."

fill them with a sense of duty to advance your **FARM'S** noblest ambitions.

In days gone by, dissenters were handled by methods such as imprisonment and execution. This was especially true on more repressive **FARMS** like the Soviet Union, where even a loyalist could find himself in front of a firing squad because of a ruler's paranoid delusions. However, in today's modern world, one must eliminate a legitimate threat in one of two ways. Either by attacking his character to discredit him completely, making him ineffective as a staunch opponent, or by eliminating him from the face of the planet. The latter is especially true if you conquer another **FARM** outright. Rooting out the previous ruler's loyalists is necessary if you want to take that **FARM** in your deeply inspired direction. Since the heads of many **FARMS** today are part of an elite network, more times than not a leader can be given amnesty in some far away land as long as they promise not to meddle in your affairs and remain out of public view. The repercussions for resurfacing should be made quite clear to those who wish to abuse this generously granted privilege.

A couple of historical examples will provide a template for managing the rabble rousers who discourage military participation or expose your ruling actions. To paraphrase Hermann Goering, *Dragging the people into war is easy, no matter how you govern your* **FARM**. *Convince the herd that they are under some sort of attack and denounce the peacemakers for lack of patriotism and for exposing the* **FARM** *to danger. It works the same on any* **FARM**. As evidenced time and time again, sometimes condemnation is simply not enough to silence the loudmouths opposed to your ambitions, therefore more proactive measures must be taken.

Even in the United States of America, once considered the freest plantation on Earth, the Sedition Acts of 1798 and 1918 and the Espionage Act of 1917 had to be instituted to limit patriotic dissent.[280] Even when ruling according to the most liberal herd management styles, you must execute caution when dealing with those opposed to your objectives and narratives. If dissenters are openly allowed to voice their opinions on vital policies and military actions, whether foreign or domestic, others may begin to see validity in their point of view and undermine your efforts. I'm sure you can imagine the trickle-down effect this could inspire.

280.) Dave Roos. "The Sedition and Espionage Acts Were Designed to Quash Dissent During WWI." History.com. September 21, 2020 and Peter McNamara. "Sedition Act of 1798 (1798)." The First Amendment Encyclopedia. 2009. https://mtsu.edu/first-amendment/article/1238/sedition-act-of-1798

These three acts, which were clear constitutional violations of both free speech and freedom of the press, threatened violators with fines, deportation and imprisonment and were especially aimed at those who wished to impede the war effort or incite disloyalty within the military. Although the Sedition Acts met their fate soon after their passage, many portions of the Espionage Act are still active law today. This serves as a stark reminder as to the parameters you must lock into place to protect your organisation's agenda.

Edward Snowden attempted to expose the level of surveillance imposed on the American population. The government accused him of violating the Espionage Act. Although I'm sure even the unenlightened masses were not the least bit surprised by Mr Snowden's reports of unwarranted government prying, it's important to make an example out of anyone who dares to defy his commitment to the **STATE**.

Julian Assange's seventeen violations of the Espionage Act illustrate how the guise of National Security can cover up you and your associates' more savoury indulgences. Using his platform Wikileaks, Mr Assange carelessly leaked scores of classified emails and documents, revealing the identities, key buzzwords and other confidentialities of some very influential people whose ritualistic practices are none of the peasants' business.[281] What could have been extremely detrimental turned into a positive. This breach of national security was used to set a new precedent against any media professional who dares publish such sensitive documents.[282]

I am losing my cool with these audacious ingrates!

Whilst the foolish American **FARM** still uses the more archaic term of *espionage* to name a law that should be used to string up as many instigators as possible, other **FARMS** around the globe such as Hong Kong, India, Ireland, Myanmar, Malaysia, Singapore and the UK call the act what it is, The Official Secrets Act.[283] And it's of the utmost importance that peasants do not violate it! Sure, in a cutesy, feel-good Hollywood film, British whistleblower, Katharine Gun, leaked a top-secret US National Security Agency (NSA) request

281.) Alan Ewart. "Pizzagate Summary: What Is Spirit Cooking And Who Is Marina Abramovic?" Inquisitr. November 29, 2016. https://www.inquisitr.com/3754020/ pizzagate-summary-what-is-spirit-cooking-who-is-marina-abramovic-news

282.) David Asp (Updated by Deborah Fisher). "Espionage Act of 1917 (1917)." Middle Tennessee State University, The First Amendment Encyclopedia. August 2022. www.mtsu.edu/first-amendment/article/1045/espionage -act-of-1917

283.) Wikipedia. 2003. "Official Secrets Act." Last modified March 7, 2023. https:// en.wikipedia.org/wiki/Official_Secrets_Act

to its equivalent, UK's Government Communications Headquarters (GCHQ), to monitor the private communications of UN delegates for scraps of information, personal or otherwise, that could blackmail smaller, undecided member states into voting for the Iraq invasion in 2003.[284] But so what? The invasion went on as planned, and the peasants got a film allowing them to think there are those on the inside who will do the right thing and fight for their interests.

I'm confident that if a trusted associate, like Ms Gun, were to release information of a much more sensitive nature, a true budding lord would know exactly what to do. Of course, I mean they would prosecute such a reprehensible misfit to the fullest extent of the law. A law put into place to act as a deterrent so that much more drastic measures are unnecessary.

I'm trying to be a gentleman here, but these acts of insubordination make it difficult, if not impossible! Good Lord of the underworld! My blood has reached its boiling point! Okay—Breathe—Happy place— Happy place. Let's end this chapter on a more uplifting note, shall we?

Assuming you've enjoyed success on the battlefield and have aptly applied the key principles provided in this handbook, there will come a day when you need to elevate your war-making tactics for the ultimate crowning achievement of uniting the whole world under your rule. However, you may need to create a cataclysmic event (if one does not naturally occur) that poses a dire risk to civilised society to nudge humanity into joining forces and making the personal sacrifices necessary to defeat this universal threat.

I pose the questions, 'Is there a common enemy (real, imaginary or a combination of both) that can generate enough fear and imminent danger to bring about an authoritarian world government? If so, would this same unifying foe be daunting enough to direct humanity's productive energy toward the eradication of this enemy whilst further enslaving the entire planet under an ever-expanding surveillance state?'

Oh, please do read on as we near the apex of this insightful manual.

284.) Katharine Gun interviewed by Tim Adams. "Iraq war whistleblower Katharine Gun: 'Truth always matters.'" The Guardian. September 22, 2019. https://www.theguardian.com/film/2019/sep/22/katharine-gun-whistleblower-iraq-official-secrets-film-keira-knightley and "Official Secrets." IMDB. August 30, 2019. https://www.imdb.com/title/tt5431890/

Chapter 15

PSYCHOLOGICAL/FALSE FLAG OPERATIONS

Those who can make you believe absurdities can make you commit atrocities.
— Voltaire

Before I divulge the priceless information in this chapter, I'd like to remind you that running a world empire is not for the faint of heart. The beauty in this is that those with a soft spot for their fellow man will laugh off the idea that one would consciously use the following tactics to incite the herd into a war or any other knee-jerk reaction because they themselves could never resort to such underhanded techniques and, therefore, neither could anyone else. This is to the ignorant peasants' detriment and being able to carry out such bold actions will truly separate you from the pack.

It's also important to recognise that the end justifies the means. If you're serious about becoming world emperor, you'll need to make stern, courageous decisions that go against the best overall interests of even those who conduct your most passionate objectives. To conquer and enslave the entire planet, the ultimate goal of every ruler-in-the-making, you'll need to dig into a deep, dark, secretive bag of tricks in order to cunningly manipulate the masses into courses of action they might not otherwise take.

If the following techniques disturb you, it may comfort you to know that by betraying the commoners so deeply, you're actually building an extra layer of protection between you and them. From simple observation of the herd, it's clearly much easier to fool most people than it is to convince them they were fooled. Therefore, anyone who attempts to point out your shifty techniques will receive a hostile backlash from those who blindly trust what they were led to believe. Just commit to whatever lie you choose and repeat it often enough that it becomes truth. This is where total control over the media and other information outlets proves invaluable.

> NOTE: Should you decide to use the following time-tested techniques, you *must* fully understand the content contained in the rest of this handbook and, above all, you *must* use it to deflect attention away from your nefarious actions. If your peasants have been trained correctly, they'll revert to their embedded programming and obey authority (see Chapter 11).

Fear is the most powerful motivating weapon at your disposal. You can use it against an individual, a group of people, an entire **FARM** and, when applicable, the entire world. You must strictly observe one general rule. The presumed power of an enemy causing allegiance to a society must be proportionate to the size and complexity of that society.[285] A couple of examples will conveniently illustrate this point.

In the early 1950s, a squadron of communist guerillas (Huks), who believed in vampires, occupied a hillside in the Philippines. Colonel Edward Lansdale of the United States decided the best way to remove their threat and influence on a nearby village was to perpetuate a rumour that a vampire was roaming the jungle.

In his autobiography, *In the Midst of Wars,* Lansdale details how his *psy*chological *war*fare (PSYWAR) squad set up an ambush along a trail used by Huks.[286] They planted a myth amongst the villagers and gave it a couple of days to circulate.

'When a Huk patrol came along the trail, the ambushers silently snatched the last man of the patrol, their move unseen in the dark night. They punctured his neck with two holes vampire fashion, drained his blood and put the corpse back on the trail. When the Huks found their bloodless comrade, every member of the patrol believed that a vampire had killed him and that one of them would be next if they remained on the hill. When daylight came, the whole Huk squadron moved out of the vicinity.'[287]

If only it were always this easy.

Our next example, in the 1980s, politicians selling the American dream were losing their credibility and authority. Since citizens were becoming sceptical of false promises, those seeking political offices hatched an alternative approach; the selling of nightmares[288] By tapping

---

285.) Lewin, *Report from Iron Mountain*, 44.
286.) Valentine, *The Phoenix Program*, 25-26.
287.) Edward Lansdale, *In the Midst of Wars* (New York: Harper and Row, 1972), 70-72.
288.) Adam Curtis, "The Power of Nightmares: The Rise of the Politics of Fear," You-

into citizens' darkest fears, candidates would be elected to protect citizens from their own imaginations. Of course, promotion and repetition of harrowing details would be necessary to drive the hysteria into every corner of American culture. This is when the CIA's Team B was commissioned, headed by Harvard Russian Historian Richard Pipes, a staunch opponent of both communism and the Soviet Union,[289] and the perfect candidate to lead Team B.

Since America was, and still is, a very advanced society, the looming threat had to reach epic proportions to match the magnitude and intricacy of America's state-of-the art militaristic FARM. Team B affiliates like Donald Rumsfeld and Paul Wolfowitz made sure that it did. The looming Soviet threat may have been slightly, or should I say largely, exaggerated, but that's a minor detail when a formidable bogeyman is needed to unite a society.[290]

A group of outside experts (Team B) gained access to CIA intelligence. Although they knew that the Soviet Union was in a state of economic despair, they used a little creativity to promote a different conclusion.[291] According to Team B, Soviet submarines were so advanced they could not be detected, even though the intelligence community saw no proof of an upgrade to the Soviet submarine fleet.[292]

Can you feel the horror a multitude of invisible enemy submarines lurking off your shoreline could create? If so, excellent.

You must adapt this style of thinking if you're to provoke something as unnatural, yet as advantageous as an escalating arms race. An arms race not only produces enormous profits through government borrowing and weapons sales but generates enough firepower to fully advance a world domination agenda. In this example, the forward thinkers behind Team B drummed up a threat that rivalled, if not exceeded, America's high-tech capabilities, which motivated its citizens to get behind its cause.

NOTE: The Cold War lasted decades to the tune of over five trillion in adjusted 1990s US$ even though neither enemy fired a single shot.[293]

Tube video, 2:58:21, Nix Bee, April 4, 2019, https://youtu.be/yK3wz-OyR1U

289.) Curtis, "The Power of Nightmares," 27:30-28:35.

290.) Curtis, "The Power of Nightmares," 25:26-27:30.

291.) Curtis, "The Power of Nightmares," 27:54-31:20.

292.) Curtis, "The Power of Nightmares," 28:55-30:29.

293.) Stephen I. Schwartz (Publisher of The Bulletin of the Atomic Scientists). "Cold War's Heavy Cost." The New York Times. May 20, 1999. https://www.nytimes.com/1999/05/20/opinion/1-cold-war-s-heavy-cost-770728.html

The second example illustrates another important concept in today's modern world. The superiority of a society's war-making potential over its other characteristics is not the result of a threat presumed to exist. It's the reverse. Threats against the national interests are usually created or accelerated to meet the challenging needs of the war system.[294] In laymen's terms, this means that when striving to conquer the planet and enslave humanity, you must maintain an unrelenting effort if you're to continue expanding your empire whilst broadening your war-making abilities. It's the equivalent of building a house. Once you begin the project, you must keep going or lose momentum, and you will never finish your home. The same can be said of subjecting the entire planet to your rule.

We can categorise these two classic, historical examples as Psychological Operations. PSYOPS can be incredibly useful in achieving overt and covert political and military objectives. Sometimes you'll need to persuade, change and influence those on your **FARM**, those on other **FARMS** or a combination thereof. PSYOP exercises can range from honest and factual programmes designed to benefit a society to exercises requiring anonymity and misdirection due to the objectionable tactics and hidden agendas involved.

In today's highly sophisticated world, you'll need a person or group to commit some sort of deplorable act to justify political, economic and military responses to accelerate your agenda. Whilst such an event may occur organically, an all-out internal orchestration from within your trusted group of associates may be needed. The methods and depths of violence required will depend on the level of threat that actually exists or needs to appear to exist. If your **FARM** requires more drastic and permanent changes, create an incident with a high degree of shock value. This will allow you to establish a long-lasting psychological trigger that can be repeatedly activated to win predictable responses from your herd.

Any outstanding intelligence officer's work goes unrecognised by the general populace, whilst those on the inside fully understand the agent's contributions. Classified information should always be on a need-to-know basis whether it's a clandestine operation designed to bring about your world empire or a hefty dose of disinformation fed to the masses to keep them off your tail. I can't think of a more fitting time to introduce psychologist Kurt Lewin. Credited and seen through the eyes of the herd as a pioneer in social behaviour and an innovator in the corporate

---

294.) Lewin, *Report from Iron Mountain*, 30.

climate, this publicly palatable version of Dr Lewin is only scratching the surface. The man was an absolute genius when it came to the inception commonly known as the Tavistock Shock Doctrine. Although a thorough Google search will omit it, a close inspection of his work will help us deduce his game-changing contributions to this useful social phenomenon.

The mass killing power displayed in World War I was far beyond that of any war previously experienced.[295] The trauma induced on the common citizen was impressive enough, but it was the brutality witnessed by the combatants that produced the most profound effects. This was especially true for a young soldier named Kurt Lewin.

It was Lewin's participation in this grisly conflict that inspired his first published article entitled *Kriegslandschaft* or *The War Landscape*. This insightful piece offered a sneak peek into the foundation for his later works that would eventually earn him the title, *The father of modern-day social psychology*.

Recovering from an injury sustained on the battlefield allowed him time to reflect on how a soldier's immediate needs can alter his perception of the world around him.[296] Certainly one can clearly understand how a tree in a forest can turn from a living symbol of beauty that perhaps provides a perch for a cackling bird to a source of concealment whilst waiting to massacre an opponent. An explosion or flurry of machine gun fire can change the physical form of a tree, but the soldier's imagination can alter its purpose.

Not all soldiers escaping the horrors of World War I were as inspired by their afflicted mental perceptions as Kurt Lewin. Mental stress during World War I made otherwise healthy individuals unable to function, and develop physical symptoms such as fatigue, tremors, confusion, nightmares, and impaired sight and hearing that often lingered long after the fighting ended, a condition known as *shell shock*.

Some of these subjects, ironically, were studied at the Tavistock Clinic that opened in 1920 because of the experiences of World War I.[297] But it wasn't long before probing them for their breaking points became more important than treating their psychosomatic illnesses.

295.) Quigley, *Tragedy and Hope*, 27, 255-256.

296.) "Lewin, Kurt." Encyclopedia.com May 23, 2018. https://www.encyclopedia.com/people/medicine/psychology-and-psychiatry-biographies/kurt-lewin

297.) "The Founding and Early History of the Tavistock Clinic." NHS. The Tavistock and Portman. https://100years.tavistockandportman.nhs.uk/the-founding-and-early-history-of-the-tavistock-clinic/ and "Tavistock Clinic." Encyclopedia.com. December 21, 2022. https://www.encyclopedia.com then search Tavistock Clinic

This work resulted in the genesis of psychological warfare.[298] Hanging around in the background and playing a much larger role than curious observer was none other than our good friend, Dr Kurt Lewin.[299]

By looking carefully at the more generic versions of Dr Lewin's theories, his resounding impact on modern-day PSYOPS becomes glaringly obvious.

For example, his *Life Space Theory* suggesting that one's behaviour and perception of the world is shaped by past, present and future events and experiences.[300] Although this appears to be a dulled down version of his *War Landscape Theory*, this hypothesis more broadly covers the psychological function of the average human mind and gives us a glimpse into how it can be cunningly influenced. On the other hand, his *Force Field Analysis* concentrates on the environmental forces acting on an individual, specifically through social situations that shape goals, behaviours and needs.[301] These two fundamental principles provide the framework for the shock doctrine.

Whilst Dr Lewin outwardly generalised the psychological lessons learned from the grim realities of battle and neatly applied them to the social problems of the day, he was also working behind the scenes as advisor to the Office of Strategic Services' (OSS) psychological warfare programme. Although this beast of a man died in 1947, some of his contributions to the PSYWAR effort were still considered classified in the 1980s.[302] Talk about leaving a legacy. This may seem insignificant, but it gets even better. The OSS, formed in 1942 as an intelligence gathering service for America during WWII, was the predecessor of the CIA. The CIA was established through the National Security Act of 1947. It was at that time that the CIA became, and remains, the United States' premier foreign intelligence and clandestine operations agency.

298.) "Tavistock Institute: An Ongoing Social Engineering Project to Mind Control Humanity." The Millennium Report. December 1, 2018. https://themillennium-report.com/2018/12/tavistock-institute-an-ongoing-social-engineering-project-to-mind-control-humanity/

299.) Coleman, *The Tavistock Institute of Human Relations*, 173.

300.) "Kurt Lewin's Psychological Field Theory." The Psychological Notes HQ. February 13, 2020. https://www.psychologynoteshq.com/psychological-field-theory/ and Britannica, T. Editors of Encyclopaedia. "field theory." Encyclopedia Britannica, May 3, 2016. https://www.britannica.com/science/field-theory-psychology

301.) Brandon Gaille. "Force Field Analysis Explained with Examples." BrandonGaille Small Business & Marketing Advice. September 6, 2021. https://brandongaille.com/force-field-analysis-explained/

302.) Encyclopedia.com, "Lewin, Kurt." and Coleman, *The Tavistock Institute of Human Relations*, 186, 262.

'So what?' you cry out to the heavens.

I suppose it's time to direct your attention to the *CIA KUBARK Counterintelligence Interrogation Manual of 1963* and the *Human Resource Exploitation Training Manual of 1983*.

There's little doubt that the creators of these riveting manuals, working off the real-world findings of Kurt Lewin and his exuberant gang of colleagues, were gaining a firm understanding of the internal and external stimuli required to manipulate the human psyche. One of the most significant conclusions drawn from these dynamic manuals is that deliberately applied physical and mental duress causes recipients to regress into a childlike state, opening a window of suggestibility that, in a controlled environment, can easily be recognised by a trained interrogator. At this point, the interrogatee's will is weakened and cooperation can be attained.

NOTE: As an aspiring ruler-in-the-making, take time to delve into these practical yet insightful manuals to more fully understand the art of achieving compliance.

One last widely known Kurt Lewin theory is CATS (Change As Three Steps). This not only serves as further proof of Dr Lewin's creative genius, but also provides deeper insight. A metaphor of melting ice is commonly used to simplify Lewin's CATS Theory; Unfreeze-Change-Refreeze must take place to firmly establish transformation. In terms of real-world behavioural patterns, you must first interrupt an individual's current behaviour (unfreeze). Next, you must encourage the new behaviour (change). Last, you must lock the new behaviour in place (refreeze). Let's confidently place the theory in your expanding world ruler *bag of tricks*.

Before we reach the heart of our discussion on the Tavistock Shock Doctrine, I need to make a quick, subtle point. Shell shock, mental illness brought on by trauma on the battlefield, can be reversed by a process known as electroshock therapy, first performed on a live human in 1938.[303] Simply stated, you can shock someone into mental illness or shock them out of it. During shock therapy, *routine* behaviour stops or unfreezes.

303.) Mark L. Ruffalo. "A Brief History of Electroconvulsive Therapy: The story of a misunderstood but effective treatment." Psychology Today. November 3, 2018. https://www.psychologytoday.com/us/blog/freud-fluoxetine/201811/brief-history-electroconvulsive-therapy and "The Disturbing Story of the First Use of Electroconvulsive Therapy." Neuroscientifically Challenged. https://neuroscientifically-challenged.com/posts/first-use-electroconvulsive-therapy

We can also recognise from our brief summary of the 1963 and 1983 CIA interrogation manuals that when individuals are subjected to shock/trauma they regress to a childlike state, providing a window of suggestibility that allows an authority figure (you) to offer a recommended change.

'During the process of regression, the subject may experience feelings of guilt, and it is usually useful to intensify these.'[304]

Of course, it is!

You can play on the two big emotions of fear and guilt so strongly that you lead peasants to believe the recommended *change* is for their own good. Peasants will change their behaviour if the external pressures, such as those found in a *Force Field Analysis* or induced by the CIA's methods (sleep deprivation, phobias, isolation, etc.) are compelling enough. By encouraging a new behaviour with rewards for cooperation and continued shock/trauma if necessary, peasants can discover for themselves the need to voluntarily *change*.

To refreeze this necessary change, you must maintain it over an extended period of time and reinforce it with reminders of old trauma whilst enhancing it with new means of jarring the subjects into a deeper state of compliance. Remember from our discussion in Chapter 4, the best way to undermine peasants' freedom is by gradual usurpations.

The magnificence of Kurt Lewin's Tavistock Shock Doctrine is that, through real world experimentation, he applied his observations to the collective group mind and perfected his technique for manipulating the masses. This tactic has evolved to a societal phenomenon that, with the advent of technology and communications, has the ability to reshape the behavioural patterns of the entire world.

Feel free to let out the devilish snarl emanating from the depths of your bowels.

Can you think of any examples in today's finely integrated world where a collective shock disoriented the public so much that a more restrictive, radical and profit-driven agenda was slipped past the paralysed populace almost overnight? Do events like wars, coups, terrorist attacks, market crashes, natural disasters or even pandemics have the ability to unfreeze-change-refreeze major behavioural patterns on a **FARM**?

Excellent my budding pupil. Now that you're thinking like an elite global planner, let's raise the level of discussion.

304.) CIA. "Kubark Counterintelligence Interrogation." (July 1963), 103.

We'll revisit the insightful words of Rahm Emanuel (see Chapter 12), who so eloquently reminded us, 'You never want a serious crisis to go to waste.' In today's high tech, tightly controlled society, a major natural upheaval in the peasants' day-to-day affairs may not occur when it's most urgently needed. Therefore, for the right crisis to unfurl at the right time, a staged incident may conveniently suit your fancy.

> NOTE: Creating your own disaster grants you control of the magnitude and finer details of the incident and allows you to precisely craft its narrative. You should broadcast stories with high emotional impact to divert peasants' attention away from obvious holes in your narrative so blame is not placed on an event's orchestrators.
>
> You can also exploit a naturally occurring tragedy by having your embedded media agents react spontaneously in your favour. Having a prefabricated script on standby to suit such an unexpected convenience will be to your advantage. The stronger your worldview and the more prepared you are to seize any catastrophic event with predetermined contingency plans, the better your chances are of ruling the entire planet.
>
> The word crisis in Chinese is composed of two characters, danger and opportunity.

A False Flag Operation is a delightful way to achieve a spectacular event that will jar peasants from their doldrums whilst bending them to your will.

'But what exactly is a False Flag Operation?' you curiously ponder.

First, let's explore its history. The term *false flag* originates from the former practice of pirate ships flying the colours of a neutral nation to deceive merchant ships into thinking they were dealing with friendly vessels. Although the pirates would often reveal their true colours (i.e. the skull and crossbones) just before an attack, they would, at times, continue to fly the phony flag during an assault. This was known as an attack under a false flag. Eventually, a *False Flag Operation* became the definition of any covert action that sought to shift responsibility to a different party.[305]

The US Department of Defense and Joint Chiefs of Staff proposed Operation Northwoods in 1962, a now-declassified False Flag operation created to justify an invasion of Cuba. It's one of the few publicly

---

305.) BP Perry. "The Truth About 'False Flags' From Nazi Germany To The Vietnam War." Sky History. https://www.history.co.uk/article/the-truth-about-false-flags-from-nazi-germany-to-the-vietnam-war

accessible records providing the details on how to lead a nation to war via an internally staged event.

Operation Northwoods proposed a list of deliberately concocted ideas that could be used as pretexts for war with Cuba, including:

- Blaming Cuba for blowing up a US ship in Guantanamo Bay.
- Using *friendly* Cubans to stage attacks on US military bases.
- Sinking a ship near the harbour entrance and holding funerals for non-existent victims.
- Developing a Communist Cuban terror campaign in Miami, other Florida cities or Washington, DC.
- Shooting down US drones disguised as civilian airliners.
- Using properly painted MIG-type planes posing as Cuban fighter planes to harass, hijack and shoot down real civilian aircraft.

In keeping with the theme of creating a narrative that packs a heavy emotional wallop, one storyline considered in the *detonated drone posing as a civilian aircraft* scenario included the contrived tale of a plane full of college girls on their way to South America to help feed the poor.

Awww. Can you imagine the outpouring of emotion, including anger, swelling amongst the herd after being presented with such a tragedy? Peasants would run through a wall of fire to avenge such a dastardly deed. Be advised that the more innocent the victims, the more susceptible your herd will be to your ingenious persuasion.

Whilst Operation Northwoods offers valuable insights, it's crucial to avoid leaving behind such an incriminating paper trail. This is especially true when your **FARM'S** leader refuses to approve the plan and meets their untimely demise by taking a long convertible ride in the light of day.

Psst. President Kennedy's defiance may or may not have been the reason such a shocking national tragedy occurred. However, I believe his assassination sends a resounding message to any future leader who thinks they can step in the way of a lucrative global agenda. Wouldn't you agree? I'll let you read between the lines on that statement.

I suppose the unfortunate occurrence of a public assassination also sends a paralysing shock wave through the herd, stymieing their enthusiasm for the newly slain leader's rallying cries. Like the old saying goes, 'Cut off the head of a snake and the body dies'.

I should mention that waiving certain conspiratorial truths in the face of your herd can also serve as a benchmark to gauge your grip on the masses. A magnificent control measure, CIA's 1967 Document 1035-960, was used to promote the term *conspiracy theory* whilst also providing specific instructions on how to downplay any critics of the Warren investigation. Your media contacts can use the term *conspiracy theory* to discredit faultfinders of your narratives.[306] Since the use of this term is already commonplace on most modern-day peasant farms, simply encourage your news agents to continue ridiculing and mocking anyone who questions your fabrications, and the herd, if properly trained, will imitate the ridiculing behaviour. Again, you can judge the effectiveness of your PSYOP efforts by monitoring public opinion and by watching for outward signs of rebellion.

> NOTE: Psychological Operations that use symbols such as words, gestures, banners, monuments, music, clothing, television programmes, films, insignia, photographs, hairstyles, designs on coins and postage stamps, etc. to manipulate a target group's beliefs, attitudes or actions is known as propaganda. Propaganda is often used in conjunction with a False Flag Operation to help promote an event and assist in achieving its desired outcome. These activities can be militaristic, ideological, environmental, political, technological, biological, personal and economic (or any combination thereof) and used to accomplish a variety of objectives. It's important for an aspiring global lord to recognise that the desired end goal justifies the methods used. Your ability to effectively use these techniques at the right time and for the right reasons will determine just how high you will rise as CEO of Planet Earth.

There are too many examples of False Flag Operations to cover in this compelling manual. Therefore, I ask for your due diligence and implore you to personally research the following shortlist of agenda-serving provocations:

- The Burning of the Reichstag
- Nero and the Great Fire of Rome
- The sinking of both the USS Maine and RMS Lusitania
- Operation Himmler
- Various US mass shootings
- The Gulf of Tonkin
- Pearl Harbor
- The Mukden incident

306.) CIA. "Countering Criticism of the Warren Report." Archive.org. April 1, 1967. https://archive.org/details/CIADOC1035960

- The Lavon Affair
- Marble Framework

Even though each event was shrouded with propaganda devised to protect its orchestrators and their true aims, aspiring rulers of humanity should be able to uncover the hidden objectives behind these *shocking* events and appreciate the intricacies involved in their deceptive executions.

Keep in mind that for the continuity of this manual, the use of underhanded tactics to bait a victim into a desired course of action also fits into the category of False Flag Operation.

One incredibly top-secret affair worth exploring is Operation Gladio. (Gladio is an Italian form of the word Gladius which was the short sword used by Roman Gladiators to make a kill in the arena.)[307]

However, it would be both irresponsible and reprehensible of me to encourage anyone, let alone a naïve apprentice with wholesome ambitions of ruling the entire planet, to commit acts of violence against innocent people for the sake of achieving political and military objectives.

That was Operation Gladio. I will not condone such a practice although the killing of innocent people has been a form of societal sacrifice since the days of early civilisation and was the dominant theme in Greek and Roman art and literature for over a millennium.

Come on, we're all familiar with the concept of a sacrificial virgin being tossed into the mouth of a volcano to appease the gods, but I will not encourage such barbaric behaviour.

However, I suppose if your competition is using barbaric tactics, you and your team may also consider it. If you want to ascend to the top of a global empire and rule all humanity, targeting the vulnerable population strikes a sensitive nerve in the herd, cascading into a flurry of negative emotions such as fear, anger, contempt, and sorrow, making peasants prime targets for the unfreeze-change-refreeze technique. If you so desire, this is also the perfect time to suggest your subjects give up all their perks and privileges to receive protection from your governmental apparatus. Unbeknownst to the peasants, the STATE may have orchestrated the violence.

For your historical knowledge only, my lord, Operation Gladio was a top-secret paramilitary operation that began after World War II

307.) Paul L. Williams interviewed by George Noory, "Paul L. Williams OPERATION GLADIO," YouTube video, 1:55:17, Aretha Boudreaux, September 25, 2017, https://youtu.be/w06uX0rXuPg

and comprised what are now known as *stay-behind armies*.[308] To better understand the moniker, function and purpose of these underground guerilla divisions, let's look at their humble beginnings during the Great War. Whilst the Anglo-American Alliance (England and America) was quite formidable with their traditional militaries alone, it was the unorthodox fighting methods of their clandestine agencies, the MI6 and OSS, behind enemy lines that helped defeat the Axis Powers (i.e. Germany, Italy and Japan).

I apologise if I'm jostling your memory unnecessarily, but the United States created the Office of Strategic Services (OSS) (1942-1945) as a foreign intelligence and covert operations agency for World War II only. Its English counterpart, the MI6, on the other hand, formed in 1909 and is still active today.

I know I can be pesky, but I'm a stickler for details when instructing an emerging ruler of humanity.

Due to the Axis Powers' reign of terror throughout Europe against anyone who disagreed with *fascist* ideology, the OSS and MI6 became quite adept at forming alliances with anyone willing to use subversive techniques. Therefore, any country looking to defy a hostile takeover had to establish an underground resistance network.

Once the threats of Mussolini and Hitler were vanquished, these useful agitators needed a purpose. To the meticulous global planner, any new aim would be for naught if it didn't constructively use such a network to help expand said planner's world empire.

The CIA was created in 1947 through the National Securities Act to replace the OSS, terminated in 1945 after World War II. Interestingly, and not so coincidentally, 1947 was the same year the *Cold War* began with the Soviet Union. It lasted over four decades into the early 1990s. A unifying purpose was born, not only to keep these secret armies in place, but to keep them active and prepared for any impending Soviet/Communist Bloc invasion. Since this vast network of surviving World War II clandestine operators would stay behind enemy lines to disrupt Soviet control should it occur, they were known as *stay-behind armies*.

NOTE: If it's not glaringly obvious, the key to uniting a **FARM**, a series of **FARMS**, and eventually the entire world, is to rally

308.) Andrea Angelini. "Gladio Stay-Behind Operation: An Italian Noir in Wartime." italics Magazine. May 1, 2020. https://italicsmag.com/2020/05/01/gladio-stay-be-hind-operation-an-italian-noir-in-wartime/

your minions against a common enemy. The more ominous and threatening the adversary, the more cooperation and active participation you'll receive. In our current example of Operation Gladio, the looming common enemy was communism. It may seem quite silly now, since the nation out to remove communism from the face of the Earth, the USA, has since embraced all ten planks of the Communist Manifesto.

It just goes to show, the gullible herd will eventually accept any worldview you slyly impose on them.

Now, where were we? Oh yes…

Given the opportunity to reveal the key ingredients for success, anyone in the game of world takeover would include merging as many standing armies as possible under one umbrella. Historically, this was done in 1949 by an organisation known as NATO (North Atlantic Treaty Organisation). Initially made up of western European countries, the US, the UK and Canada, NATO's goal was to form an intergovernmental military alliance that calls all its members to act in mutual defence of one another if attacked by an external threat. Just like all its member states, NATO not only possessed publicly recognised, conventional fighting forces but also maintained a deep-seated secret intelligence network whose offshoots carried out super-secret covert operations throughout Europe.

It wasn't until 1990 that Gladio's tightly held secret operations, carried out by a special branch of the Italian secret service, was made known to the public by a meddling Italian magistrate, Felice Casson.

All European NATO countries had similar stay-behind armies that functioned under different names but shared a common purpose—to defeat the dastardly communists. These other sects, however, were kept secret. Since it was the discovery of Operation Gladio in Italy that led to the unravelling of this entire tight-lipped affair, the whole brilliant but risky undertaking throughout Europe is commonly referred to as Operation Gladio.

NOTE: Refusing to confirm or deny accusations for national security purposes must be applied when covert activities that breach the public trust are questioned. This will remind peasants that their safety and comfort comes with a price not worthy of further investigation. Is that point clear to you? This is one of the most effective modern-day methods to ensure matters violating peasants' blind faith in your **FARM'S** institutions remain hidden.

No one can deny that the original purpose of *preparing for a Soviet invasion* was a palatable justification for NATO, the CIA and the MI6 to bankroll and train these deeply entrenched stay-behind armies.[309] However, like any Trojan horse operation needed to further a world domination agenda, there must be a turning point when the original inception of a programme transforms into a more pliable version of its original self to address any burgeoning needs and challenges. For Operation Gladio, this steep transition took place in 1963, the same year Lyman Lemnitzer moved from the Chairman of the Joint Chiefs of Staff in the United States to Supreme Allied Commander Europe of NATO.[310]

As a friendly reminder, this was also the same year the Kubark Counterintelligence Interrogation Manual was released. Was this an odd coincidence or simply a wave of fresh ideas bursting onto the scene?

I'll let you be the judge.

However, before you decide either way, I must bring a few details to your immediate attention. First, General Lemnitzer was the chairman of the Joint Chiefs of Staff (JCS) from 1960 to 1962. Second, the chairman of the JCS is the top General in the United States military and the principle military advisor to the president. Third, General Lemnitzer was the chairman of the JCS during the inception of Operation Northwoods, rejected by President Kennedy. Fourth, Lyman Lemnitzer was laterally moved in 1963 from chairman of the JCS to NATO as Supreme Allied Commander Europe, the second-highest military position within NATO.

As the character Howard Beale exclaimed during one of his climatic diatribes in the 1976 Academy Award-winning film *Network*, 'What has that got to do with the price of rice?' Well, if you have the penchant for conquering the planet that you think you do, the penny will soon drop.

You see, it was right after this change in leadership in 1963 when Operation Gladio not only concerned itself with preparing NATO members for a communist bloc invasion but also expanded to seek and destroy domestic enemies who didn't share the Anglo-American worldview.[311] Until you try implementing an economic or political system on a *nation* that has no interest in adopting it, you won't understand how irksome

---

309.) "Dr. Daniele Ganser Interview: NATO's Secret Armies – Operation GLADIO," YouTube video, 1:20:55, The Mind Renewed, February 3, 2015, https://youtu.be/coIJWITJWCs

310.) Dr. Daniele Ganser interviewed by Julian Charles.TMR 097: Transcript: Dr. Daniele Ganser: Operation GLADIO & The Strategy of Tension." The Mind Renewed. January 4, 2016. https://www.themindrenewed.com/transcripts/792-int-70t

311.) Ganser interviewed by Charles, "TMR 097."

these opposition groups can be. Therefore, the primary method used to effectively achieve these Operation Gladio objectives became known as a false flag strategy of tension.[312] Has the flash gone off yet? If not, nothing shall hinder it after this next section.

As we know, a Soviet invasion into a NATO-backed country never took place, despite all the planning and preparations to resist it. To be fair, there were a few NATO countries whose networks went dormant due to the lack of a perceived threat. However, the ones with the most strategic value had discreet elements of their intelligence services working under the direction of *officially non-existent* agents from NATO, the CIA and the MI6. It was these rogue groups in the host countries that carried out acts of violence including bombings, kidnappings and assassinations.[313] The basic idea was to commit false flag terror attacks that shocked the populace and then blame the enemy of one's choosing. Sound familiar? Tavistock Shock Doctrine anyone? Take my word for it, the best way to discredit an adversary is to blame them for a horrific act of terror. If your enemy is the Soviet Union or any group supporting its communist ideology, is there no better way to suppress its momentum?

> NOTE: Media control and advanced propaganda techniques are crucial in achieving optimum results whilst your stunned adversaries passionately attempt to deny their involvement in a horrific plot they had no part of.

Another useful tactic successfully carried out by the instigators behind the short sword militia was to infiltrate non-violent opposition groups and push them into acts of violence and murder. Regardless of the technique used to create the mayhem that sends the petrified herd into a state of shock, this is the opportune time to seek more funding from a **FARM'S** inhabitants. A domestic national emergency fully justifies a steep hike in taxes that are redistributed by the **FARM'S** political structure to its enforcement arms. What cannot be taken from the *citizens* directly can be extracted from them indirectly through borrowing. Not only is this form of fundraising more discreet, it's also more profitable for a lord who receives interest payments on the appropriated money whilst creating the favourable condition known as inflation. Additional policing powers are also necessary to protect the

312.) Ganser Interview, "NATO's Secret Armies – Operation GLADIO," 22:00-23:08
313.) Andrew Gavin Marshall. "Operation Gladio: CIA Network of "Stay Behind" Secret Armies." Global Research. July 17, 2008. https://www.globalresearch.ca/operation-gladio-cia-network-of-stay-behind-secret-armies/9556

populace from the evil enemy.

Did you see what I did there? By taking the peasants' money to enhance your policing powers, peasants will have little choice but to make good on the payments needed to guarantee their own protection, or else!

If you remember from our Kurt Lewin discussion, by applying an external force on a populace through a strategy of tension, one can change the behavioural patterns of those under its influence. Over time, you'll bend even the most resilient target groups to your will. Your patience and perseverance are necessary to reach your goals. In the case of Operation Gladio, the Soviet Union collapsed at the end of the four-decade-long Cold War, and even China has since adapted its economy to fit into the Anglo-American model, thus showcasing the success of long-term planning.

> NOTE: Building a rival farm into a superpower can only be done by following something similar to its predecessor's economic blueprint. However, this new superpower must out produce and exceed the previous military's technological advances. Remember, most empires will implode naturally after roughly two hundred and fifty years. Isn't it better to stay one step ahead? By developing a farm with a totalitarian political system already in place, the final stage of your takeover will simply involve granting this new tyrannical policing nation the authority to bring the entire planet under your total control.

Because communism is now embraced by its once biggest adversary, the United States of America, it's no longer a viable trigger to spring the herd into action. Is there a new enemy to help you take a step toward world domination? This dark, menacing force would have to be hiding in every *country* to justify enhanced policing, restrictions on peasant privileges, a union of the world's militaries and a more aggressive war policy used against those harbouring such an enemy or who fail to participate in the enemy's extermination. Please feel free to have some fun and stretch your thinking when conjuring up such a looming threat. This adversary would also unite all peasants for the common purpose of ensuring their survival. Of course, this could only be achieved by following all edicts handed down by the **STATE** under the direction of its knowledgeable and brave leaders (i.e. carefully selected members of your fraternity).

Your nails won't require any trimming until well after our chilling yet breathtaking climax. I can hardly stand the anticipation of our titillating reveal!

I would be amiss if I didn't share some additional deflection methods that can be employed to prevent you from worrying yourself into a tizzy when carrying out some of the more controversial tactics presented in this handbook. Of course, we've already mentioned the gold standard of stonewalling techniques used to protect your biggest secrets and most controversial actions, withholding the details of an operation *for national security purposes*. This will be your ultimate advantage when dealing with a relentless public looking to expose your governmental structure's most guarded vulnerabilities. For total control of your **FARM**, it'll be necessary for your **STATE** apparatus to maintain all its confidential activities whilst your peasants possess none of their own. The following will also help divert peasants' attention or stall their inquisitiveness long enough to render them insignificant.

One of the most enjoyable diversion methods because of its disheartening effect on peasants is that of a government investigation. Its conclusions should then be brought before the equivalent of a kangaroo court, where carefully selected insiders control the verdicts of these high-profile public trials along with all their cherry-picked revelations. There should, however, be plenty of chest-thumping from authority figures complimented with a memorable number of biting remarks that give the impression there is a genuine attempt to reveal the truth.

> NOTE: A window into the truth is mandatory to relieve high-level perpetrators from karmic retribution and legal repercussions. Remember the maxim, 'Silence is consent'? You'll need your herd's silent approval if you want to remain unscathed in these two areas of cosmic justice. Therefore, never hide an event when you can use it to deliver the most paralysing shock value achievable. Providing small doses of reality amongst a fine blend of lies is an art that allows you to tuck away the details of incrimination whilst hiding the truth in plain sight.

Another nice touch to a government inquiry is utter dismay from government officials when they're unable to get straight answers from those called into question or when these same officials experience frustration with the legal process. Tough questions can be asked, and insinuations made that shed light on the facts, but there's a line that should not be crossed when protecting **STATE** secrets. This holds true regardless of political affiliation or rank within the corporate government structure. For those who violate this unspoken rule, things like demotion, character and physical assassination, and the unearthing of criminal activity (actual or falsified) remind perpetrators and future agitators that there are consequences for breaching this sacred rule. You can also use these retaliation methods on persistent civilians or legal professionals who don't know when to quit. Before exacting your revenge, however, it would behove you to allow a little time to elapse before launching your retribution, so the action and reaction are far enough apart to appear completely unrelated.

> NOTE: If you need to re-establish credibility to your government and its legal processes, opening an investigation into trivial matters such as steroid use amongst baseball players can reassure peasants that there can be serious consequences when one is called before your legislative body and found guilty. Public humiliation and the stripping of accolades can send a ripple effect through the herd that can gnaw at them for years. The majority will be consumed by such an inquiry, provided they're kept in a perpetual state of adolescence. It'll provide much more digestible tea break chat than the weighty matters that are best managed by your **FARM'S** top political and corporate leaders.

Another good defence is a great offence. You can accomplish this through your media outlets. By hitting peasants with a steady stream of both manufactured and real-world traumatic events, you can further divide their time and energy and reduce their ability to focus on just one affair. Add other distracting stories in fields such as sports, business, health, politics and entertainment to give peasants a plethora of avenues to focus on rather than on your **STATE'S** transgressions.

Gaining peasants' trust in your official information outlets is a fine art and the most useful tool available for achieving cooperation from your herd. The main gist is to subtly condition peasants to believe official narratives as the absolute truth whilst simultaneously building an entire false reality that's delivered right into their living rooms. Healthy doses of fear and distress are excellent feelings to invoke since they create a state of dependency. By tossing in a dash of feel-good stories, you can pluck peasants' emotions in a way that their day-to-day affairs seldom can.

Once you have control of the media outlets, your *presstitutes* can mock and ridicule anyone who raises objections to your narrative. This prevents open discussion and damages the credibility of the agitator along with anyone sharing a similar viewpoint. When performed effectively, your peasants will mimic the thought patterns they observe through your dissemination outlets rather than break free from groupthink and risk being attacked by the herd. Even before radios, television, films and the Internet, there were few willing to leave the safety of the pack, giving the opinion-makers the power to sway the public in their favour.

NOTE: History has not favourably treated those who challenged the ruling authority's narrative. The level of devotion you exude in forcing your worldview upon others is related to the lengths you'll go to silence those who oppose your directives.

Once you gain trust, you can influence a target group even before a natural or skilfully orchestrated event occurs. Films, music, books and news stories can lay the groundwork for any new reality you'd like to introduce.

Once peasants start becoming reliant on authority and its indoctrination outlets, they hand over their will. Over time, you can eagerly convince your herd of just about anything. For instance, because of the pressing issue of over-expanding **FARM** populations, slowing peasants' reproductive rates became an urgent undertaking. By purposefully confusing peasants' sexual identities and by encouraging them to surgically transform themselves into their gender of choice, their ability to procreate is truncated. By distorting moral behaviour, you can further corrupt peasants into accepting new norms which may include your majesty's more sordid whims and desires.

Weakening peasants' wills, whilst simultaneously exerting meticulously constructed external forces upon them, makes the problems peasants face appear too large and too complex to solve, discouraging unity and the desire to change their fate. In times of hardship, the downtrodden masses will look for ways to self-medicate and wallow in their misery rather than strengthen their resolve. The structure and comfort you and your associates provide will allow you to gently guide your vassals into any suggested course of action you propose. By tirelessly promoting your established order as trustworthy, peasants will be much too terrified when confronted with the idea that it's you and your associates who are working against their best interest. This is an additional safeguard built into this strategy should you need to dismantle a **FARM** or reduce its numbers. This is also an excellent reason to leave an existing structure in place should you wish to seize it through subversion. It provides the perfect guise whilst you completely disarm your enemy.

Due to vast improvements in technology, mass production and communications, the ability to reach a worldwide target audience has never been easier. High-speed information is yet another Trojan horse now readily available to promote your fraternity's agenda to a hypnotised global population. Surveillance devices are currently embedded in just about every home, office and business and in every peasant's hand. You can use these devices to distract, misinform and promote any course of action paramount to fulfilling your needs.

Because you're reading this manual at a time when you can conveniently slip into power with the mechanisms of global control already in place, it'll behove you to understand their gradual evolution.

Although slightly more primitive, some past methods may still apply and, at the very least, will provide valuable insight into the fundamental principles required to firmly grasp the larger, more awe-inspiring ideas required to unite the entire world under your rule.

Although it may not be the first thing you think of, there are many instances when PSYOPS might become quite necessary for enhancing your economic interests. To understand the economic motive more clearly, simply revisit 1947 postwar France, when dockworkers in the port city of Marseille began striking due to increased tram fares. This ignited a cascade of nationwide protests that nearly paralysed the entire French economy.[314] Although one may see the immediate need to reverse such a potentially devastating situation, from a lord's point of view, let's look at the intricate layers of perspective needed to fully grasp the importance of troubleshooting such an occurrence.

However, first I'll paint a clear picture of the situation.

In Chapter 4, I clearly spelled out a comprehensive list of political and economic systems, but these are not your only options. If you can create others that more effectively suit your end goals, then please do so. However, the two political/economical ideologies needed for our current example are Eastern Communism versus Western Democracy. The same fraternity of architects behind today's blueprint for global enslavement devised both ideologies.[315]

Communism is a ruler-friendly system that immediately subjugates its people. Because of communism's high demand on the productive members to provide for the *greater good*, it eventually leads to a lack of effort from the prolific since they no longer see the point in personal sacrifice. This ultimately leads to shortages that can lead to hardships for its people and thus the spreading of great misery. Well, all except for, of course, its daring leaders who redistribute the forcefully

---

314.) Alfred W. McCoy, The Politics of Heroin: CIA Complicity in the Global Drug Trade Revised Edition (Chicago: Lawrence Hill Books, 2003), 54-57.
315.) Carr, *Pawns In The Game*, 191.

derived wealth first to themselves and their allies before evenly spreading the crumbs to the pleading masses.

Western Democracy, on the other hand, as we discussed in Chapter
4, is assigned the bad rap of *capitalism* even though reaching your full
potential for the betterment of yourself and your society would be the
crowning achievement of any living being and those fortunate enough to
derive the benefits of such a system. However, if done correctly, democracy
can also lead to enslavement. A prolific, unbridled, corporate peasant farm
provides a more bountiful lifestyle for its members at the expense of other
FARMS who cannot be as resourceful.

> NOTE: The wise aspiring planetary ruler will cleverly pit two
> opposing **FARMS** against each other whilst using them to attain
> said ruler's ultimate plans. In 1947 France, Western Democracy
> was the preferable system to enslave humanity. However, once
> that structure was in place, the more restrictive system, Eastern
> Communism, could later be craftily inserted since it was much
> more applicable in regard to regulating human production,
> ingenuity and freedom.

Although each method of rule has its merits and drawbacks,
even as far as peasants are concerned, it's much easier to demonise one
ideology from the viewpoint of the other if each is labelled with a term
that ends in 'ism' and is further vilified with disparaging words like
evil for communism or *greed* for capitalism. Branding these governing
systems with derogatory buzzwords will steer peasants away from
utilising their intellect and help prevent any meaningful sharing of
ideas. These much more useful and emotionally charged generalities
can cunningly induce unconscious reactions from the herd. Whilst
the clever global oligarchy fully understands the importance of all
diametrically opposed governing philosophies, it's best if individuals,
groups and nations are dutifully bound to just one. This will keep the
commoners fighting against opposing **FARMS** rather than turning
against you and your global agenda.

Before returning to the port city of Marseille, I beg for your
leniency, as a few remaining details must be brought to your ever so
tolerant attention.

These will be rattled off as historical points, so they can more
easily be added to our flavourful talk soup. To begin, the major criminal
syndicates of the 1920s were all synonymous with the world's great ports
and transportation hubs such as New York, Chicago, Hong Kong, Saigon

and, of course, Marseille.[316] Also in the 1920s, opium and its byproducts were driven from two hundred years of legal commerce into the black market and assigned the new nomenclature of *illegal substance*.[317] Making something harder to acquire without reducing its demand increases its market value and hence the price users are willing to pay.

On a national level, France was an area of great interest to the two leading adversaries of the Cold War, i.e. the United States and the Soviet Union. The United States signed the Marshall Plan into law in 1948 to provide financial assistance to her western European allies (NATO countries) to help rebuild their infrastructure and economies whilst also seeking to deter the spread of communism.

> NOTE: The astute emperor-in-the-making will sense a connection to our discussion on Operation Gladio. If this describes you my shooting eastern star, I'm so proud of you I could squeeze your cheeks.

Marseille was not only known for its long history of gangsters but for its powerful labour unions that, at the time, were under the direct influence of the communists.[318]

Communist societies don't have excessive amounts of discretionary funds available for expensive habits like high-end drug use. Furthermore, these more rigidly run societies show much less tolerance for such undermining habits.

As an interesting historical footnote, the communist elements of French labour played a significant role in resisting the Nazi occupation during the Second World War, whereas the right leaning underworld was a willing collaborator for the right price. The most ruthless and cold-blooded criminals make the best allies when fear, force and intimidation are required to achieve your objectives. These organisations come well-armed, well-funded and prepared to use violence to protect their interests. Another fun little fact reveals that if one is looking to supply transatlantic arms and supplies to Western European NATO allies, Marseille is a key port from which to do so.

Even if you're in control of a major harbour, the expansion of drug production requires financing, logistics and protection. Criminal networks, unbeknownst to most peasants, share a commonality with

---

316.) McCoy, *The Politics of Heroin*, 11.
317.) "History of Heroin and Opium Use and Abuse." Narconon. https://www.narconon.org/drug-information/heroin-timeline.html
318.) McCoy, *The Politics of Heroin*, 46.

covert government agencies because they are the only two organisations in the world that specialise in the *clandestine arts*. This should make sense intuitively, since both perform nefarious activities that operate outside of the normal channels of civil society and must remain undetected.[319]

I believe that includes all the talking points required to resume our conversation.

Two years after the war, French cities like Marseille were still climbing out of the rubble. Unemployment was high, wages were low and basic commodities were in short supply. Those with jobs had to put in long hours to help boost production *for the good of the nation* whilst being offered little compensation. Inflation was also running rampant, and the working class was expected to shoulder the brunt of the national tax burden to pay the ingenious creditors of the war against Hitler. The tramways were the last thread of civilised order remaining in Marseille. When the recently elected socialist mayor raised tramway fares, the communist-dominated workforce of Marseille launched the nationwide strike of 1947.[320]

There were only three major political parties in France: the (a) communists and (b) socialists on the left, and the (c) Gaullists somewhere out in right field.[321] The communists included the largest party, with 28% of the vote, due to its firm grip on the most powerful labour union in France: the Confédération Générale du Travail (CGT).[322] After the war, the communists were gaining the greatest momentum, and if they continued to win elections in Marseille, the second largest city in France, there was concern the momentum could encourage them to form their own national government, replacing the Fourth Republic. By winning Marseille, they would also seize control of one of the most important ports in all of Europe.[323]

With General de Gaulle too autonomous to be consistently relied upon and the socialists losing ground to the communists politically, there seemed to be one obvious choice for an alliance. It should be cautiously noted, however, that influential socialists had been filling the void left by the treasonous right-wing elements of the Marseille underground, and collusion with certain socialists would mean forming a partnership with those involved in organised crime.

319.) McCoy, *The Politics of Heroin*, 16.
320.) McCoy, *The Politics of Heroin*, 54-55.
321.) McCoy, *The Politics of Heroin*, 58.
322.) McCoy, *The Politics of Heroin*, 58-59.
323.) McCoy, *The Politics of Heroin*, 59.

I'm going to stop here and give you a second to think about how you would manage such a precarious situation as a rising world emperor given the historical points and the situation at hand.

Are you ready to give your answer? The history of the entire modern world is riding on your decision. If you answered anything but align yourself with the socialists, the purchase of this handbook was not a complete waste of money. If you made it this far in the manual, I'm certain you have the mental fortitude to reign supreme over the entire human race, but you'll need to sharpen your focus and shed your reluctance to work with nefarious elements.

In retrospect, we can see that the decision by previous global planners to aid and support the socialists has played out well when considering all the worldwide control mechanisms now in place.

When inspecting the situation from the French national perspective, we can accurately understand its leaders' thinking based on their postwar decisions and by perusing many detailed public archives. If the French had allowed the communists to impose their worldview on its citizens, it would have meant submission to the dogma of the Soviet Union that considers personal achievement the scourge of the Earth and demands that all personal gain and sacrifice benefit the **STATE**. Ultimately, this would lead to the surrender of the French people and her resources to an inefficient economic system run by Russians. Any wealth generated would end up in the hands of the Russian power structure whilst simultaneously lowering the standard of living for French countrymen.

Likewise, by accepting financial assistance and political influence from the US, France would be placed in a similar position regarding the submission of its national sovereignty. The big difference, however, is the healthy amount of development money and consultation it would receive by cooperating with the west, not to mention, the enhanced security a partnership with other western European nations would provide. Despite the concessions France would be pressured to make, it meant a way out of economic hardship and a boost to the morale of its citizens.

This proposition was not without flaws from the French point of view, however. The French detested the idea of a strong and rearmed (West) Germany fostered by the Anglo-American Alliance. France saw this as a betrayal meant to serve the British and their quest for hegemony in Europe. They felt that a fortified Germany could neutralise a rebuilt France if she became a threat to British rule.

Regardless of her postwar leanings, France wasn't crazy about being the linchpin caught between two jockeying superpowers, the USA and the USSR. Both were striving for world domination, and French decision makers feared that this high-stakes-tug-of-war put them in the crosshairs of nuclear annihilation or, at the very least, made their country prime real estate for a conventional war between these two rising giants. Despite suspicions that American support was more about the influx of American goods for the benefit of America's economy, siding with the US was still the more sensible option if France was to have any chance of restoring her industries as well as her autonomy.

> NOTE: As shown by France's resistance to follow all American directives whilst receiving Marshall Plan support, it's noteworthy for any aspiring lord in a similar situation to properly pick and choose certain obligatory policies to resist. If done properly, this will help strengthen your **FARM'S** overall global position without losing much needed foreign aid. It takes some *chutzpah* to defend your sovereignty, but each move is vital in what amounts to a long, drawn-out game of chess.

From the Soviet national perspective, war torn Eastern Europe was already firmly in her clutches whilst communism was also enjoying immense popularity in Italy and France. Most of France's collectivist adoration came from the French's most esteemed national treasure, its workforce. The most powerful labour union in France, the CGT, had long prided itself on communist ideals. The communists were also held in high regard by patriotic French citizens because of their fierce resistance during the Nazi occupation.

As tensions grew between the two emerging Cold War giants, they both showed great interest in the port city of Marseille. Both sides understood this port could serve as a vital artery used to pump American weapons and supplies into the heart of every NATO country in Western Europe. Blocking this crucial corridor with elected loyalists and blue-collar comrades would stave off American efforts to empower its alliances in order to counteract the hard-earned Soviet gains achieved after the fall of Hitler.

Sounds like a wonderful title for a Mel Brooke's musical, does it not? The *Fall of Hitler*?

Obviously, from the American national perspective, this is exactly why it needed to obtain the port of Marseille, to move US arms and supplies to NATO members to stop the expansion of the communist ideology. Since the US mainland did not experience the structural damage suffered on the European continent, its industries simply shifted focus away from wartime manufacturing to producing goods that made peacetime living more enjoyable. This created a sudden surge in wealth that not only put America in a position to assist the rebuilding efforts of her NATO partners but could exemplify the benefits of implementing such a system over the one being touted by the Russians. The American economy was thriving and had the potential to soar even higher if it could continue to expand into new markets.

It was just after World War II when the top thinkers behind the ascending American empire realised that to ensure victory, the ideological war against the Soviets would have to be fought on four strategic fronts.[324] Of course, the most gentlemanly of these four areas and the one most in line with the finer aspects of Anglo-American congeniality was diplomacy. This involved solidifying relationships with already friendly countries and gently guiding them in the direction of freedom without forcing the American political system or way of life upon them.

I mean, who needs to be convinced when such an evil enemy is lurking in the midst. Next, and perhaps my favourite, is the militaristic aspect.[325] There is simply no other way to defeat a looming threat than by fully arming yourself and your allies.

Military strength is a close cousin of economic superiority.[326] What good is an ally (or an enemy for that matter) if their **FARM** is in ruins and they can barely afford or produce the most basic of supplies?

Can you see the greater good involved in helping amiable markets stand on their own two feet?

Without the proper weapons to defiantly boast, 'I'm sorry, your totalitarian principles of enslavement are not welcome here', the words will carry little weight against an ambitious and ruthless opponent such as the communists.

Finally, let's ignite our discussion on the fourth and final strategic front necessary for victory, psychological operations, by returning to the loading docks of Marseille during the strike of 1947.[327]

324.) Susan M. Perlman, "Shock Therapy: The United States Anti-Communist Psychological Campaign in the Fourth Republic France" (Electronic Thesis, Treatises, and Dissertations, Florida State University, 2006), 26, www.diginole.lib.fsu. edu/islandora/object/fsu:180272/datastream/PDF/view /Florida State University Libraries (180272).

325.) Perlman, "Shock Therapy", 26.

326.) Perlman, "Shock Therapy", 26.

327.) Perlman, "Shock Therapy", 26.

Global planners believed PSYOPS could enhance and neatly tie together the diplomatic, military and economic dimensions needed to combat the influence of communism on vulnerable populations. A crumbling economy presents the perfect opportunity for a totalitarian regime to step in and assert its will. This does not mean that strong-arm tactics should be above a liberator's means of averting such a calamity. By making the wise decision to align with the socialists and hence form an indirect partnership with the criminal underworld, US arms and money could be funnelled to the Corsican gangs in Marseille to launch assaults on Communist picket lines and to harass important union officials. The focus of this intervention was to avert a societal collapse and a potential communist takeover.[328] Tagging along with US special operatives was the US psychological warfare team that applied additional pressure through pamphlets, radio broadcasts and posters that discouraged workers from continuing the strike.

> NOTE: The US developed three types of propaganda known by the colour codes of White, Grey and Black. I'll assign each to an example to show their application. Pamphlets, radio broadcasts and posters fall under the category of Grey since the origins of the messages had to be ambiguous.[329] The French were proud colonisers leery of American intervention. The source of the message or action had to appear to be coming from another source. Here, it appeared to originate from within France itself. If revealed, Grey propaganda would not devastate its source.

If you can understand the desperation of a pack of ravenous dogs placed in deplorable conditions, you can imagine the social pressure placed on the purpose-driven dock workers when the American government threatened to ship sixty-five thousand sacks of flour back to the United States. Well, unless the generous supply of food, meant to end the violence and help the hunger-stricken Marseille population, was immediately unloaded.[330]

Because of this clever ploy, I imagine a more efficient workday has never been seen. Never underestimate the persuasive effect subtle PSYOP instruments like pamphlets, posters and radio ads can have when panic sets in on a starving population. Heroes can quickly turn into villains when reason is lost and well-planted seeds begin to sprout.

328.) McCoy, *The Politics of Heroin*, 60.
329.) American Foreign Relations. "Propaganda –Types of propaganda." American Foreign Relations. https://www.americanforeignrelations.com/O-W/Propaganda-Types-of-propaganda.html
330.) McCoy, *The Politics of Heroin*, 61.

After less than a month on the picket lines, workers in Marseille, and throughout France, returned to work on 9 December 1947, officially ending the nationwide strike. This intervention in France was a historical first for US foreign policy. Never before had America intervened in the internal affairs of a traditional and long-standing western ally until the Cold War gave it justification.

Fear is such a wonderful motivator, wouldn't you agree?

To add a beautiful finishing touch to America's newly gained influence on the French economy and political system, eighty-seven boxcars arrived at the Marseille train station on Christmas Eve, 1947. They were carrying flour, milk, sugar and fruit as gifts from the American people amidst cheers from hundreds of schoolchildren waving tiny American flags.[331]

My eyes well up at the thought of this endearing moment that uplifted the French commoners and aroused a sense of patriotism and goodwill in the average American citizen. It's nice to end on a pleasant note for once after discussing such hardship and misery.

Oh, and by the way, the boxcars that arrived on Christmas Eve along with the warm reception from the French youth was all staged propaganda.[332] Sorry to burst your bubble, but it's imperative to understand the task at hand and not be burdened by silly feelings.

> NOTE: This Christmas Eve surprise is classified as White Propaganda since the operation's intent is to truthfully reveal the originator of the message or action to positively affect, and therefore, strongly influence the target audience in the source's direction.[333]

The actual aim of the previous passages was to provide various viewpoints on a real-world scenario and to illustrate ways to influence a critical target audience in your favour. We investigated varying outlooks from directly involved nations (the US, the USSR and France), groups (dock workers, socialists, Gaullists and communists) and individuals (from the children waving American flags to Americans reading about it in the newspaper to the citizens of France swayed by radio programmes and leaflet campaigns).

It's my great pleasure to say, 'I've saved the best for last'. Such a wonderful global opportunity will now be presented through the

---

331.) McCoy, *The Politics of Heroin,* 61.
332.) McCoy, *The Politics of Heroin,* 61.
333.) American Foreign Relations, "Propaganda."

majestic eyes of a world ruler. I'll unveil some of the thought processes involved during this critical flash point in history.

As I hope you understand by now, human societies, as well as individuals, are most useful/productive when they're working toward a common purpose, usually driven by some sort of outside threat. Some forward thinkers looking to unite the planet into one tightly controlled network conceived the conflicting systems in this example, capitalism and communism. However, in 1947, world rulers lacked the firepower, technological systems and other control mechanisms necessary to gently merge all nations on Earth under one uniform umbrella. Therefore, an ideological war of epic proportions would prove to be an important step in achieving this long-term goal. Of course, western capitalism was the preferred vehicle to bring about the innovations necessary to accelerate this plan. Many **FARMS** played a part in contributing to this goal whether or not they realised it. In this new modern era, some **FARMS** had no choice but to produce and acquire modern capabilities or perish in their attempt to survive.

Although he was no longer leading the masses with fiery speeches whilst triumphantly yelling into a microphone, Adolf Hitler's spirit transported his immortalised words from the great beyond by reminding us: 'The great strength of the totalitarian state is that it causes those who fear it to imitate it.' By emulating either of these two superpowers, those playing the role of jittery pawns were unwittingly contributing to a great leap in the emerging global super state.

The Cold War played a significant role in not only forcing the production and advancement of the weapons necessary for a world takeover, but it also simultaneously empowered and enriched those with the vision to orchestrate it. To fight this war of one-upmanship, the best scientists, forward thinkers, military advisors, media pundits, intelligence agents and lawbreakers were given the freedom and funding to operate in the best interest of those seeking world dominance.

We discovered during our Operation Gladio discussion, that secret stay-behind armies were used in NATO countries to shock populations into compliance in order to satisfy specific political, military and economic objectives. In many instances, these underground operatives thrived in industries such as the drug trade, racketeering and murder. Once conjoined with American, British and NATO intelligence networks, they had protection to run their operations on a global stage. All they needed in exchange for their rise in prestige was their willingness to commit acts that would promote the wealth-creating ideals of western capitalism for the purpose of undermining and eventually enslaving all **FARMS** that embraced it. Little did these gangsters know, nor I'm certain did they care, about the long-term effects of their actions. All it takes is allowing those with an aptitude for a certain function (like distributing drugs) to thrive in their area of expertise, and they'll be so consumed with their own undertakings they'll fail to recognise their role in the bigger picture.

> NOTE: The disinformation used in Operation Gladio is the most secretive of the three and is known as Black propaganda. Black propaganda supports PSYOPS which are clandestine in nature and usually carried out by a government agency, a military unit or paramilitary organisation. However, they can also include activities by private companies and groups. These operations are politically sensitive due to the deceptive tactics involved and require a high level of compartmentalisation since they're meant to disparage a hostile government, party, group, organisation or individual.[334] If confronted, responsibility is denied at all costs for obvious reasons.

Of course, we saw that a communist/totalitarian system is best equipped to regulate human behaviour, including that of drug dealing and the illegal flow of arms used to protect it. Despite this minor glitch, authoritarianism should, however, be seen as an ideal system to rule from once your global takeover is complete. Otherwise, how are your directives supposed to reach the commoners without the watered-down interpretations of middlemen? Since drugs (legal and illegal) were the most profitable and subversive tools available to begin the transformation of a prosperous, open society to that of a morally depleted wasteland, they were allowed to freely flow into some of these pivotal *nations.* Not only did the onslaught of addictive and mind-altering substances justify more policing power and hence financing from the citizens to the **STATE** for their protection (well, that's what you should tell them anyway), but the lucrative drug revenues helped bankroll the special operations needed to steer the herd into the welcoming arms of the broadening international syndicate.

A *big brother,* if you will. It's such an endearing term for such a wonderfully menacing entity, isn't it?

I hate to use the word criminal for valuable wartime assets since

---

334.) Wikipedia. 2006. "Psychological Operations (United States)." Last modified December 30, 2022. https://en.wikipedia.org/wiki/Psychological_operations_(United_States).

that term only pertains to those who are captured and on the losing side of a conflict. However, former Nazis and various defectors from hostile nations proved invaluable for their selfless contributions to a new world order. Dr Shiro Ishii and Josef Mengele (page 230) are proof that human brutality should, occasionally, be given the opportunity to flourish in order to learn, observe and build upon the discoveries gained from such callous experimentation.

Can you give me one good reason, as a potential Emperor of the planet, man should not be as cruel as nature? Should those who refuse to think be spared?

In the wild, if animals cannot act on their instincts, they perish. Mankind's greatest gift is the mind. If we cannot use it with our instincts to provide sustenance and protection for ourselves, is it up to someone else to supply it for us?

Yes! For the good of society, some may say. But, even in that, for advancements to be made and for the entire human race to reach a higher plateau, sacrifices must be made. I see no reason the most burdensome, who refuse to innovate, take risks or simply stand on their own two feet, are not the first to be offered. Any grub can eke out an existence and live off the productive efforts of others. However, it's the builders of society you want to associate with, for they are the true architects of your worldview.

The others be damned!

Now where were we? Oh yes.

I'll conclude this section with some final thoughts on the red scare or, in plain words, the communist movement. It's my assumption that we agree that a communist-type system is the most advantageous to rule from. However, it was the unbridled capitalistic system, driven by a healthy pinch of fear, that could most expeditiously provide the worldwide surveillance and weapons systems needed for complete world domination.

What a pity the adversary may have been much closer than the unthinking masses realised.

Like in most of Europe, the two opposing Cold War ideologies, American capitalism and Soviet communism, were as equally at odds in South America over the same four decades. This may seem like a long time for a newcomer such as yourself, but those forty years passed by quite unassumingly and with great result. That is, until the early 1990s, when a new ruse was needed to expand this highly effective strategy into additional regions such as the Middle East and Africa.

It should be clear to see the win-at-any-cost arms race mentality pushed both superpowers to cross boundaries they wouldn't have otherwise breached. The end result of the Cold War was a merging of nations on the European and South American continents that, little by little, implemented the most enslaving elements of both dogmas. The once free America, along with her allies, began morphing into the most exalted, propagandised versions of their enemy, the communists, giving even deeper meaning to Mein Fuhrer's prophetic statement: 'The great strength of the totalitarian state is that it causes those who fear it to imitate it.'

In today's high-tech world, the idea of an airborne leaflet campaign seems rather preposterous. However, this couldn't be further from the truth. Remember, for every action, there's an equal and opposite reaction. High-tech devices aren't foolproof. Signals can be jammed and transmission stations obliterated. You may be invading a poor **FARM** where advanced technologies are unavailable or, at the very least, hard to find.

You can use leaflets in quite a few ways when conducting psychological operations, especially in a war zone. Perhaps you're about to flatten an area and wish to limit collateral damage of non-combatants involved in wartime production. Dropping leaflets could encourage them to abandon their duties, reducing the target areas' casualties. Brochures can also be a helpful way to encourage an enemy to surrender. In the Persian Gulf War, an estimated one third of Iraqi troops surrendered due to leaflet drops providing instructions on how to do so.[335]

Perhaps you want to offer your adversaries a reward for defecting or for providing important strategic information. For example, by dropping pamphlets as part of the Korean War's Operation Moolah, the United States offered financial rewards to North Korean pilots flying the new, high-performance Soviet MIG-15s to land in South Korea.[336]

In addition, you may wish to use propaganda to diminish enemy morale, neutralise enemy propaganda, encourage the enemy to dial into your radio frequencies or convince the enemy you have noble intentions by creating a friendly atmosphere and listing the selling points of your **FARM'S** ideology. Either inside a war zone or in areas of humanitarian crisis, you may wish to provide information on how to access air dropped

335.) Ed Rouse. "Gulf War Facts on the Effectiveness of PSYOP." Psywarrior. https://www.psywarrior.com/gulfwar.html

336.) Caleb Larson. "Operation Moolah: The Secret Plan to Get a Russian Fighter Jet out of North Korea." The National Interest. April 22, 2020. https://nationalinterest.org/blog/buzz/operation-moolah-secret-plan-get-russian-fighter-jet-out-north-korea-147036

supplies and how to open and consume them once they arrive.[337] Airborne leaflet campaigns provide the most reliable way to reach these objectives.

Finally, as with mass media propaganda, the most efficient way to gauge your leaflet campaigns' success is by interviewing and polling the intended recipients. From there, you'll know who to sack for their ineptitude and who to promote for their competence, as there's little room for error in these high-stakes affairs.

Now it's time to tuck those boring leaflets in a corner whilst we discuss more inventive ways to inflict psychological advantages over your prey. The first is Project Blue Beam; technology that projects three-dimensional, holographic, real-looking images into the sky or other open spaces. Coupled with audio projection, imagine the possibility of a religious **FARM'S** god hovering above the battlefield, instructing their soldiers to surrender. How about paralysing the world with fear by creating a seemingly real alien invasion that drives the people of every country into the arms of the **STATE** for protection? Does this sound crazy? Perhaps you should investigate the advancements in this area.

In combat zones, army battalions typically travel with a tactical PSYOP team (TPT) including a team chief, an assistant team chief and a gunner who also operates the loudspeaker. A local translator in an occupied territory also becomes a key member of the squad and can be quite useful in certain situations, for instance, providing instructions to the adversary on how to surrender in order to save the lives of both enemy and friendly troops. Conversely, the PSYOP unit can also diminish enemy morale or coax an opponent into a dangerous battlefield position.

For example, in Afghanistan during the War on Terror, a PSYOP sergeant used the burning of two Taliban fighters killed in a firefight to lure the Taliban into a location where the US had a distinct tactical advantage.[338] Since Islamic law forbids cremation, the American PSYOP sergeant broadcasted insulting and abrasive messages, regarding the incinerated bodies, to taunt the soldiers into an ambush.

Once the flaming bodies' story leaked from the front lines, damage control had to be initiated. US military personnel were ordered to undergo Afghan sensitivity training.[339] Yes, public perception

337.) Wikipedia. 2005. "Airborne leaflet propaganda." Last modified December 8, 2022. https://en.wikipedia.org/wiki/Airborne_leaflet_propaganda

338.) James Sturcke. "US soldiers 'desecrated Taliban bodies.'" The Guardian. October 20, 2005. https://www.theguardian.com/world/2005/oct/20/usa.afghanistan

339.) Kathleen T. Rhem. "Burning Afghan Bodies Resulted From Poor Judgment, Not War Crimes." Global Security.org. November 29, 2005 https://www.globalsecurity.org/military/library/news/2005/11/mil-051129-afps04.htm and Wikipedia,

is always a valid concern in today's modern world, and you should try to appease even your herd's frailest sensibilities. This is in your best interest, despite the brilliant decision-making and execution of such a controversial tactic.

If your herd needs an additional jolt of fear, perhaps an example from the Canadian province of Nova Scotia during the COVID-19 pandemic can spark some ideas. The Canadian Armed Forces sent letters to residents warning them that bloodthirsty grey wolves had migrated into their area. They coupled the warning with howling sounds echoing from loudspeakers hidden in a nearby forest. You can almost feel the rise in panic that must have spread through the already stressed-out populace. After an investigation into the incident, the whole affair was ascribed to a military training exercise.[340]

On the opposite end of the spectrum, suppose you would like to boost the morale on your **FARM** and its fighting forces, so they continue to labour and risk their lives to support your global ambitions.

May I suggest a staged photo opportunity? Despite the controversy over whether the image of US Marines raising an American flag at Iwo Jima was meticulously arranged or impulsive in the moment, one cannot dispute its effectiveness. It's the most famous image of World War II and widely recognised around the world even today. The image has been turned into a monument, depicted in several films, appeared on a postage stamp and on commemorative coins. Most importantly, the US Treasury Department adopted the image to serve as the symbol for a massive war-bond campaign and plastered it on millions of posters.

When looking to raise an enthusiastic surge in patriotism along with a substantial amount of funds, never underestimate the value of a powerful image and its impact on the human psyche.

Similar to the success of photographer Joe Rosenthal's iconic Iwo Jima snapshot is the more highly criticised, but equally impactful, toppling of Saddam Hussein's statue in Firdos Square in 2003. At first glance, the collapsing sculpture repeatedly televised across the globe appeared to feature liberated citizens rejoicing at the fall of the wacky Iraqi's regime. Upon closer inspection, however, you can clearly see that most exuberant participants were journalists and US Marines blessed by a small dash of

---

"Psychological Operations."

340.) Ben Makuch. "Military Incompetence Unleashed a Wolf Psyop on Unsuspecting Canadians." Vice. October 16, 2020. https://www.vice.com/en/article/m7aqgp/military-incompetence-unleashed-a-wolf-psyop-on-unsuspecting-canadians

unenthused Iraqi citizens playing the bit part of indifferent onlookers.[341]

As they say, it's nothing a little movie magic can't fix.

Likewise, with assistance and inspiration from Hollywood, the Jessica Lynch story of capture and rescue in the same year provided even more pro invasion propaganda. A heavy dose of dramatic licence was required to enhance her story and fuel support for a war that some armchair critics were boisterously calling into question. Even though Ms Lynch committed nothing less than treason for openly admitting that the details of her capture/rescue didn't match the more heroic version promoted by the Pentagon, it doesn't lessen the impact it had on the gullible public yearning for a gallant hero story.[342] The lesson here is that embedded journalists and PSYOP teams, in collusion with your mass media outlets, should strive to identify the opportune moments you can use to sway the masses and the war in your favour. These efforts will write, record and further promote the winning side of history in a way that you and your daring associates most honourably deserve.

If these flubs in promotion for the Iraq War planted some seeds of doubt in the American public's mind, it was nothing that couldn't be fixed by handing out school supplies to needy Iraqi children. This feel-good exercise was brought to you by the 345th PSYOP Company and just goes to show, you must not get too up or down whilst having the audacity to move forward with your plans.[343] Simply keep chugging along.

Regarding breaking the will of captured enemies, persistent blaring music, sleep deprivation, intimidation with military working dogs and a wide variety of humiliating sexual acts were used at Abu Ghraib prison to weaken the will of detainees in order to obtain vital information.[344] Twenty-four hours of ear crunching riffs from the heavy metal band Metallica, along with theme songs from Sesame Street and Barney the Dinosaur worked particularly well.[345]

It makes you see that purple lump of useless mass in a whole different light, doesn't it?

341.) Patrick Martin. "The stage-managed events in Baghdad's Firdos Square: image-making, lies and the "liberation" of Iraq." World Socialist Web Site. April 12, 2003. https://www.wsws.org/en/articles/2003/04/fird-a12.html

342.) Abigail Pesta. "I'm Jessica Lynch and Here's My Real Story." Glamour. June 3, 2007. https://www.glamour.com/story/jessica-lynch

343.) Wikipedia, "Psychological Operations."

344.) Seymour M. Hersh. "Torture At Abu Ghraib." The New Yorker. April 30, 2004. https://www.newyorker.com/magazine/2004/05/10/torture-at-abu-ghraib

345.) BBC. "Sesame Street Breaks Iraqi POWs." BBC News. May 20, 2003. https://news.bbc.co.uk/2/hi/middle_east/3042907.stm

To employ the next tactic, all you need is a large gathering of people and a few agent provocateurs. Then, depending on the situation and the desired outcome, have your agitators provoke acts of violence that appear to be coming from the peacefully gathered crowd. Forceful responses from the police against sizable crowds will escalate a situation rather than ease it.

This essential technique must be included in every world emperor's arsenal. Global planners have used it around the world to:

- Ignite spontaneous uprisings against uncooperative regimes
- Deepen racial tensions
- Discredit peaceful protests
- Justify tighter restrictions on citizens
- Substantiate enhanced policing techniques
- Militarise police departments

Suppose you need to clear the way for an important gathering of world leaders, and the demonstrators are blocking limousine access to important entry points. By inciting violence, your enforcement arm is now authorised to use force to get these demonstrators out of the damn way!

Or, similar to Operation Gladio, perhaps you need to discredit a growing movement that's opposed to your world domination plans. Maybe you'd like to spark a race war or rein in those who dare to break away from your **STATE** construct. Having them appear to be enemies of the people and a threat to public order is an excellent strategy. Whether encouraging a crowd to participate in a staged insurrection or pitting countrymen against countrymen, the applications of this shifty technique are limitless and only restricted by the creativity of its planner.

A wonderful tool for planting the seeds of blind obedience is the constant repetition of emergency drills. Not only does this actively engage peasants in the promotion of widespread fear, but it also conditions the masses to rely on authority for protection should a crisis unfurl. By including your vassals in the practice of a specific ritual, you're garnering their unconscious consent for a societal sacrifice. Also, leading peasants to believe authority is looking out for their best interest will allow you to slip in your underlying agenda. As we uncovered in our discussion of World War II, England's Prime Minister Chamberlain used a campaign of fear to build the threat of a German airstrike. Fitting citizens with gas masks and having them digging trenches along roadways and public parks intensified British citizens' fear of a German air attack. Chamberlain's appeasement policy

was eagerly embraced with barely a whimper.[346]

To sell the Cold War in the United States, children and adults were repeatedly reminded to duck and cover in the event of an atomic blast. Classroom drills, usually preceded by such stimulating mediums as filmstrips, instructed trembling students to curl into a ball under their desks for protection. These traumatised youngsters grew into adults embedded with fear of nuclear annihilation who then leapt into the welcoming hands of the **STATE** for protection. Certainly, a small part of the scarred adult's labour to support an arms race is a fair trade-off for safety. Obviously, if a school desk made of cheap particle board would adequately safeguard any living creature from an atomic blast, perhaps a well-constructed bridge made of steel and cement would also suffice. I happen to have a few for sale if you, or someone you know, are in the market. I don't mean to tease but, on the other hand, I do hope you enjoy the silliness of it all.

If disarming your peasants is of utmost importance, attacking your **FARM'S** most vulnerable members with weapons you wish to seize will effectively rally support for this worthy cause. One idea is to run drills in your peasant training centres that condition the children to fear a gun-toting assailant hell-bent on blasting them to smithereens with whatever weapon(s) you wish to confiscate. Once again, entrusting authority to execute these drills gives those in charge full consent to manage such a scenario should it occur. You're developing trust and reliance on those in positions of power and, in this case, encouraging your young producers-in-the-making to submit to authority. By inundating your herd with these grizzly scenarios, it creates an acceptance of this new normal but will also spark outrage and cries from the irate masses that something must be done about it.

Well, if they insist.

The designated victims aren't the only ones conditioned by these drills. First responders are also trained to react in predictable ways that can move your clandestine operatives in and out without detection. Dictating the standard operating procedures will allow you to exploit implanted vulnerabilities as you develop your operation. Remember, a headline crisis can be real, staged or a combination of both. The more controlled an event is, the more precisely you can manage its outcome and narrative.

You can buy yourself some valuable time if the actual response teams are entrenched in a training exercise at a reasonable distance

---

346.) Quigley, *Tragedy and Hope*, 584.

from the event site. The last thing anyone needs is a real-life hero impeding a vital and meticulously planned black operation.

Whether it's a school shooter, an evil terrorist or a maniacal leader looking to take over the entire planet, it's important to understand that every good crime boss has a fall guy. The advice I'm about to give you is absolutely priceless whether you're coaxing your FARM into war, protecting your *national security* assets, concealing the details of subversive activities, implementing new restrictions on your FARM or suppressing historical facts to control your flock more easily. A lone madman committing horrific acts of evil against the herd will achieve your objectives and much more.

I'm not a psychologist nor do I handsomely portray one on television, but perhaps the reason the idea of a sole maniac at large is so terrifying is because it forces peasants to intimately identify with that part of themselves that's capable of such an act or helps them see that part of themselves who dreads being at the mercy of such a monster. Not so ironically, the 1963 Bronx Zoo exhibit, *The Most Dangerous Animal on the Planet*, displaying only a mirror, strikes a deep chord.[347]

Alternatively or conjunctively, the rogue lunatic myth may allow peasants to easily dismiss the act(s) as an anomaly in one person rather than a flaw in humanity, allowing them to take a righteous stand filled with moral indignation. Intellectually, it could also lead peasants to believe that if they can stop that one person, the wickedness will disappear. This gives them a much simpler goal to attain than stomping out the mindset of many.

Placing culpability on one person also directs the peasants' focus in a single direction making it much easier to lead them toward your underlying objective. Identifying a single *evil* person also removes the tendency for your marauders to question why legions of people agree with your adversary's position, thus preventing objectivity in those you're trying to persuade.

Having a single target that can be removed is important if you wish to continue the unscrupulous operation after the poster boy for malevolence has been eliminated. This was done at the end of World War II under the notorious Operation Paperclip when Nazi scientists were recruited by the United States to resume their work for the *good guys* under assumed identities. Hitler's demise let the world breathe a

---

347.) Mayukh Saha. "Exhibit Called "The Most Dangerous Animal In The World." Truththeory.com. April 11, 2022. https://truththeory.com/new-york-zoo-exhibit-the-most-dangerous-animal/

little easier whilst the back door was pried wide open, enabling these highly debatable weapons and scientific research programmes to continue.

Finally, by declaring certain beliefs to be dangerous and then by associating those convictions with an infamous villain, you obtain greater control over your herd's thoughts and, under certain conditions, can apply more aggressive surveillance and policing actions against those with similar views. George Orwell beautifully portrayed this technique in *Nineteen Eighty-Four* through the character of Emmanuel Goldstein, a fabricated terrorist and public enemy number one.

For two minutes every day, known as the *Two Minutes Hate*, Outer Party and Inner Party members of Oceania were required to gather in a public viewing area to watch a film depicting the top adversaries of the day. If the secretly embedded Thought Police were monitoring anyone, they had to openly and loudly express contempt for Goldstein and his cohorts; otherwise, they were deemed sympathetic to his cause and dealt with appropriately. The aim of these daily gatherings was to psychologically excite the crowds into an emotional frenzy filled with hatred, fear and loathing for Oceania's enemy of the moment. This behaviour allowed citizens of Oceania to vent their anguish and personal hatred toward politically expedient enemies. In directing members' subconscious feelings away from the Party's government of Oceania, and toward non-existent external enemies, the Party minimised *thought-crime* and its subsequent, subversive behaviours.[348]

By giving evil a face, you can direct outrage at the scapegoat of your choosing and away from the actual perpetrators, a.k.a. you and your associates. By blaming an evil empire, a heartless terrorist or even a deadly semi-automatic weapon, you can readily sway the herd toward the outcome of your choosing.

The far-reaching impact of these large-scale psychological operations would be severely limited if not for the calculated collusion between global planners and corporate media outlets.

In today's information age, censoring, controlling and discrediting anyone with unsanctioned viewpoints is important; establishing peasants' trust in your **FARM'S** *official sources* is essential. Since America's media giants have mastered the art of manipulation, their techniques are important in our conversation.

The most important media tip for any ruler-in-the-making requires

348.) Wikipedia. 2004. "Two Minutes Hate." Last modified December 18, 2022. https://en.wikipedia.org/w/index.php?title=Two_Minutes_Hate

telling a big lie and then repeating it often through all media outlets so that people eventually come to believe it. And when I say repeat it, I mean incessantly drive it into their bloody skulls. Adolf Hitler detailed this technique in his compelling memoir *Mein Kampf* (*My Struggle*). I believe Herr Hitler knew a thing or two about the subject matter. In his ground breaking chronicle, he theorises: 'In the big lie there is always a certain force of credibility; because the broad masses of a nation are always more easily corrupted in the deeper strata of their emotional nature than consciously or voluntarily; and thus in the primitive simplicity of their minds they more readily fall victims to the big lie than the small lie, since they themselves often tell small lies in little matters but would be ashamed to resort to large-scale falsehoods. It would never come into their heads to fabricate colossal untruths, and they would not believe that others could have the impudence to distort the truth so infamously. Even though the facts which prove this to be so may be brought clearly to their minds, they will still doubt and waver and will continue to think that there may be some other explanation. For the grossly impudent lie always leaves traces behind it, even after it has been nailed down, a fact which is known to all expert liars in this world and to all who conspire together in the art of lying. These people know only too well how to use falsehood for the basest purposes.'[349]

My final thought on this matter is…so should you.

The second point works with the first. You must remember to oversensationalise every newsworthy headline, especially an orchestrated tragedy. This will allow you to inflict the most jarring effect possible on your herd. Startling them opens them to suggestion and creates a nearly unchangeable first impression of an event. Be prepared to take advantage of the opportunity.

The third tip for our discussion is a subtle hint rather than a suggested course of action. When creating a narrative meant to misinform your herd, what you don't disclose is often more important than what you do. Remember, you want to provide just enough information for the masses to form a basic understanding of an event. Nothing more, nothing less. By controlling the amount of information they receive, you can more easily control their thinking and responses. With the amount of powerful communication mediums now in place, we're reaching the defining moment in history when the entire planet can be brought under the cunning direction of a sprouting world emperor such as yourself.

349.) Adolf Hitler, *Mein Kampf* (White Wolf, 2014), 104.

However, it may require one or several more cataclysmic events to merge the world's peasant farms into one tightly supervised human plantation.

As many students of history have learned, humanity seems to be at its best when united for one common purpose, and especially when endangered by some sort of formidable opponent. To survive, the majority must sacrifice many things for the promise of safety and security. Many seemingly farfetched but encouraging ideas could aptly unite the world for one purpose…to fulfil your every wish and desire.

Perhaps an environmental calamity (already well underway) will prompt peasant farms of the world to trade in their cushy lifestyles for more *sustainable living*, which could also involve harnessing peasants' energy for cleaning up the oceans or putting a freeze on a warming trend. Or maybe a fabricated alien invasion can cause a panic large enough to send citizens scurrying to their respective national governments, hoping the regimes of the world join forces to battle this celestial invader. Even a nuclear/biological/chemical weapon disarmament effort could bring plantations around the globe together to create the foolish notion of everlasting peace and prosperity for the masses.

I'll end this manual with two recent, well-conceived crises that have traumatised the world and sent the flock into immediate compliance with their respective leaders' every directive. These catastrophes have helped guide Earth's inhabitants toward an iron fisted reign of terror, the likes of which has never been seen.

Hopefully, these two life-changing events will tie together many of the concepts presented in this handbook and will reveal similarities in their details and execution that you can apply when mustering the grit to initiate such a Herculean effort. I say grit because, unfortunately, to gain control of the entire planet, it's necessary to scale down the world's population to a more manageable size. Besides, to create the level of fear required to unite humanity against a common enemy, a substantial number of human offerings must be made.

Please keep in mind that something as monumental as enslaving humanity cannot be achieved without direction and planning. You must build upon the accomplishments of lords before you, and meticulously plan years in advance if you're to move all peasants into your web of control.

Chapter 16

THE NEW PEARL HARBOR

I remember getting a call from the fire department commander telling me that they were not sure they were going to be able to contain the fire...and I said, 'Well, you know, we've had such terrible loss of life...maybe the smartest thing to do is "pull" it (Building 7)'...and they made that decision to "pull" (Building 7) uh, and we watched the building collapse.
— Larry Silverstein

Since all humans love a good story, a myth is an incredibly powerful tool that plays a fundamental role in society.[350] Whilst the red scare versus the evils of western capitalism propaganda inspired sizable changes, built and fortified underground networks and justified the meddling in other **FARMS**' affairs, its impact was on the decline after four decades of use. Therefore, a new tale was needed to pry into inaccessible **FARMS** in regions like the Middle East and Africa that remained impervious to the Cold War hoopla. Such an expansion would bring the world one step closer to unification under one giant, far-reaching, monolithic canopy.

Like any great mythical character, a larger-than-life villain to some and liberator to others must be presented. In terms of a worldwide conflict, such a daunting figure can help provide the catalyst needed to spark a battle of epic proportions, providing the cover needed to install your framework for global enslavement whilst empowering your operatives.

One crucial instrument used in the transition from Evil Empire bogeyman to Islamic radical bugaboo was the Pakistan Inter-Services Intelligence (ISI). With American funding, of course, this clandestine Pakistani agency became an empowered and willing conspirator in dismantling what was left of the Soviet threat in its final decade,

350.) Wikipedia. 2018. "Myth." Last modified December 15, 2022. https://en.wikipedia.org/wiki/Myth

spanning the late 1970s to the end of the 1980s. They did this by facilitating the construction of a Gladio-type network in central Asia that would, in the years to come, present one of the latest and greatest threats to humanity: terrorism.

The architects deserve an award for perfectly crafting the transitional game plan. The entire premise of this reshuffling of arch enemies was based on a few basic principles. Without a valid outside threat to seize America's attention, such a prosperous and productive society could easily find itself in a state of moral decay that could knock it from its position on the world stage. Remember, a state of decadence is fine when the time is right to deconstruct a **FARM**. However, when the worldwide agenda needs a **FARM'S** high tech and military contributions, such an industrious **FARM** must be given an honourable and collective task to keep it focused.

With the Soviet Union economically depleted from trying to keep up with the US in an arms race that produced enough firepower to knock Earth from its orbit, a small straw placed ever so gently on the proverbial camel's back would bring this mighty red adversary to its knees. Once accomplished, the once great Soviet Empire would no longer serve as a credible threat to American hegemony. With the 1990s' equivalent of five trillion US$ spent and Operation Gladio's underhanded tactics leaking into public view, it was time to shift the public's focus toward an emerging rival.

The rise of the Christian religious right instantly appeared in America during the AIDS/drug crisis of the late 70s and early 80s, but was this merely a coincidence? To the casual observer, it may appear so. But what if some very enlightened social planners were building the pretext for an upcoming religious conflict capable of fulfilling biblical prophecies whilst serving many ancillary needs?

What if unleashing a squadron of evangelists capable of stirring up the country's *moral majority* could help divert attention away from the root cause of America's growing dependency on extremely addictive substances? By outwardly chastising victims of new, readily available narcotics (whether victims were suffering from addiction or infected with HIV), would the improper placement of blame help add another layer of protection for the drug trade operatives and their motives?

This is just food for thought to quench your ravenous hunger for spiritual nourishment, Oh Pious One.

Hold on to your bible for this next idea. What if the ultimate purpose for this upsurge in fundamental Christian values reminded

Americans of their core religious principles so that an attack by an outside monotheistic religion, for instance, radical Islam, would shake the foundation of the country and launch its God-fearing members into the front lines of battle? Of course, any good modern-day crusade needs two larger-than-life deities to preside over the bloodshed in a 'my god is better than your god' grudge match. But with the stigma of the Cold War still hanging around like a bad penny, and no other real serious threat to global peace to speak of, some laborious work was in order.

May I present to you, Operation Cyclone?

This programme, brilliantly conceived by the CIA, served a dual purpose. On one hand, it was to destabilise the Soviet Union by spreading militant Islamic doctrine inside the Russian controlled Central Asian Republics, namely Afghanistan. Jimmy Carter's National Security Advisor, Zbigniew Brzezinski, could not have said it better when, in 1988, he told an interviewer with *Le Nouvel Observateur*: 'We didn't push the Russians to intervene, but we knowingly increased the probability they would.... The secret operation was an excellent idea. It had the effect of drawing the Russians into the Afghan trap.... The day the Soviets officially crossed the border, I wrote to President Carter, essentially, "We now have the opportunity of giving to the USSR its Vietnam War."' Indeed, for almost ten years, Moscow had to continue a war that was unsustainable for the regime, a conflict that brought about the demoralisation and finally the breakup of the Soviet empire.[351]

As mentioned earlier, it was the Pakistani ISI that served as the conduit for funding, training and supplying arms to the ISI's specially handpicked Afghan resistance fighters. Not so coincidentally, the leaders of these Afghan guerilla groups were immersed in the drug trade with a large portion of US funding ending up in the hands of the brutal, incompetent and corrupt drug lord Gulbuddin Hekmatyar.[352] With the CIA's vast arsenal of funds and highly advanced weaponry, the ISI's once meagre budget of several million US$ became a deeply funded, powerful covert unit and strong arm of Pakistan President General Zia ul-Haq's martial law regime. The ISI became a mere extension of British and American intelligence networks.[353] In fact, they were nearly identical to the NATO underground networks in Europe.

Can you see the bigger picture coming into view? Before we get into the second of the two-fold purpose of Operation Cyclone, let's add a couple

---

351.) McCoy, *The Politics of Heroin*, 475.
352.) McCoy, *The Politics of Heroin*, 475.
353.) McCoy, *The Politics of Heroin*, 474.

of general principles regarding the changing of the ghastly ghouls of evil.

Much like the western world, what better way to create the immense fortunes necessary to fund a world empire than the incredibly prosperous drug trade? With illicit underground networks firmly established in NATO countries and Southeast Asia, opening the Golden Crescent area of Afghanistan, Pakistan and Iran would provide the financial bump necessary to build, fund and supply an ever-expanding group of nefarious players and operations. A lesson any aspiring global lord can certainly learn from. Also, by setting up a war zone in Afghanistan, clandestine agents constructed a cloak of secrecy around any unlawful activities necessary to achieve their stated objectives.

Returning to the second half of Cyclone's purpose, we find that it's identical to the first half…to spread radical Islam throughout Central Asia. Are you confused? Didn't I say that the objective was to end the Cold War and develop a new threat to world peace? This is exactly what Operation Cyclone ultimately achieved.

So, what would a long-term strategist such as yourself call these multipurpose Islamic warriors? To perhaps spark an idea, what if you knew these radical guerilla fighters would work with your democratic government which needed the financial and moral support of its citizenry to help bring down an evil empire that despised freedom? On the other hand, unbeknownst to disillusioned peasants, what if you also knew these very same jihadists would be attacking the *free* world one day? I don't know about you, but the double entendre moniker of freedom fighters seems to compliment these opposing mission statements quite nicely.

Regardless of which assigned task we concentrate on, secretly trained Mujahideen mercenaries received the best unconventional warfare preparation western intelligence offered. Most of it took place in CIA training camps that ran along the Pakistani border.[354] However, some of the more notorious and world-renowned names associated with the jihadist movement even visited military bases on US soil, including the pinup boy for the War on Terror, CIA operative Tim Osman, also known to the world as Osama Bin Laden.[355]

To help facilitate this transition into *a new era of terror*, as I like to call it, The Project for a New American Century (PNAC) committee

---

354.) McCoy, *The Politics of Heroin*, 477.

355.) J. Orlin Grabbe. "When Osama Bin Ladin Was 'Tim Osman.'" What Really Happened. November 8, 2001. https://www.whatreallyhappened.com/WRHAR-TICLES/bin_laden_osman.html

was formed in the United States in 1997. This esteemed military minded think tank was a heavenly blend of brilliant minds able to draw upon the successful experience of Team B orchestrators like Donald Rumsfeld and Paul Wolfowitz and merge it with visionaries like Dick Cheney, Steve Forbes, John Bolton and Scooter Libby, who had fresh, new, bold ideas.

Because we've been riding on a principal theme and because I also get a little weepy every time I read it, I'm going to present excerpts from PNAC's Statement of Principles written on 3 June 1997. Please apply your ever so sharpening reading between the lines skills to draw out what is truly being said by superimposing these eloquent words over the backdrop of our current discussion:

> As the 20th century draws to a close, the United States stands as the world's preeminent power. Having led the West to victory in the Cold War, America faces an opportunity and a challenge: Does the United States have the vision to build upon the achievements of the past decades? Does the United States have the resolve to shape a new century favorable to American principles and interests? We are in danger of squandering the opportunity and failing the challenge. We are living off the capital – both the military investments and the foreign policy achievements – built up by past administrations. Cuts in foreign affairs and defense spending, inattention to the tools of statecraft, and inconsistent leadership are making it increasingly difficult to sustain American influence around the world. And the promise of short-term commercial benefits threatens to override strategic considerations. As a consequence, we are jeopardizing the nation's ability to meet present threats and to deal with potentially greater challenges that lie ahead.... We need to accept responsibility for America's unique role in preserving and extending an international order friendly to OUR security, OUR prosperity, and OUR principles.[356] [I added capital letters for emphasis.]

When you too have your own team of willing collaborators and associates, please realise, OUR will be an important term. Just refrain from bringing it to the public's attention.

356.) PNAC. "PNAC ---- Statement of Principles." SCRIBD. June 3, 1997. https://www.scribd.com/document/445100175/PNAC-statement-of-principles-pdf

Now, I admit, I may be a tad bit odd in that I'm probably only one of a handful of inquisitors who might find enjoyment perusing such periodicals as the September 2000 PNAC document entitled, *Rebuilding Americas Defenses: Strategies, Forces, and Resources For a New Century*. This is especially true when the big game is on or perhaps when the herd's favourite musician is receiving an accolade. However, what I'm about to reveal will undoubtedly scale back the fluff exhibited in PNAC's Statement of Principles, or any other writings these spirited government administrators circulated. Instead, they neatly tucked the following into this ninety-page report. Keep in mind, this organisation was open to public scrutiny and goes along with the unspoken policy of *qui tacet consentit* or silence gives consent.

> *The process of transformation, even if it brings revolutionary change, is likely to be a long one, absent some catastrophic and catalysing event–like a new Pearl Harbor.*[357]

For the sake of expediency, I would also like to point out the not-so-subtle fact that since its inception in 1997, the PNAC committee obsessively focused on removing Saddam Hussein from power. This is evident from articles published in the New York Times in 1998, written by PNAC founders William Kristol and Robert Kagan, along with other obvious gestures such as sending an open letter to sitting President Bill Clinton from core PNAC members, calling for the removal of the butcher of Baghdad in the same year. As an astute conquistador-in-the-making, I'm sure even if some of this information is new to you, you're seeing the world from an evolving perspective. To complete the picture, however, I must bring a few more pieces of the puzzle to the forefront.

PNAC's Statement of Principles mentioned: 'We are living off the capital–both the military investments and the foreign policy achievements–built up by past administrations.' As the ruler reins are passed to future generations, magnificent ideas of the past must never be discarded. Alternatively, they should be studied, absorbed and, when appropriate, put to good use, as there may be a more suitable time and purpose for even the most seemingly implausible of strategies.

I'll leave it up to you to do the math. In 2001, as PNAC members

357.) Project for a New American Century. "Project for a New American Century: "Rebuilding Americas Defenses."" Internet Archive. 51. https://archive.org/details/ProjectForANewAmericanCenturyRebuildingAmericasDefenses/page/n61/mode/2up

shuffled into prominent Bush administration positions, I imagine a catastrophic and catalysing event–*like a new Pearl Harbor,* seemed as if it would never happen. When it did, it came with a vengeance on 11 September 2001 and had an eerily similar feel to two previous, well-conceived covert actions, the Burning of the Reichstag and Operation Northwoods. As a quick reminder, *The Burning of the Reichstag* was a fire that was set to Germany's parliament building (the Reichstag) which was cleverly blamed on a communist infiltrator. Oh, those pesky pinkos. This allowed the Nazis to seize absolute power and suspend the citizen's liberties for the safety of the nation whilst also steering public anger toward anyone labelled a communist.

Operation Northwoods, on the other hand, was rejected by President Kennedy due to the avant-garde scenarios that would've been used to justify a military invasion of Cuba, a.k.a. a false flag attack. Some suggestions, which at the time seemed preposterous to Kennedy, included:

- Developing a Cuban terror campaign in American cities
- Blowing up an unmanned vessel anywhere in Cuban waters and listing non-existent American casualties in US newspapers, creating a wave of national indignation
- Blowing up a US ship in Havana and blaming it on Cuba
- Sinking a boatload of Cubans enroute to Florida (real or simulated)
- Hijacking US civil air and surface craft
- Shooting down a chartered US passenger airliner and blaming it on a Cuban aircraft[358]

Surely, the resemblance of 9/11 to the Burning of the Reichstag meets Operation Northwoods could've been just one strange coincidence. However, when one follows the logic of invading Iraq after fifteen Saudi Arabians hijacked aeroplanes and flew them into the World Trade Center and the Pentagon, well, the dots don't quite connect. Keep in mind, the network calling itself Al Qaeda, formerly known as the Mujahideen, which had absolutely no presence in Iraq, took responsibility for the attack. However, it's the job of your handpicked conspirators to ensure peasants believe otherwise. If you ran a **FARM** that no one would dare attack nor could they because they lacked the technological sophistication to do so, could you create an incident that would motivate your peasants to commit to a long-desired military objective? How would you go about doing it and how would

358.) "Operation Northwoods." The Black Vault. September 10, 2016. https://www. theblackvault.com/documentaries/operation-northwoods/

you sell it to your herd? As an aspiring world conqueror, would you have the courage to orchestrate an attack on the symbol of economic power and the headquarters of the most imposing military humanity has ever known? If so, would you have the framework in place to unite the peasant farms of the world into one giant global plantation once you set the plan in motion?

As a layperson, there's no shame in admitting that you'd be in over your head with this type of planning and decision making. The confidence needed to pull off such a massive undertaking usually comes with time and real-world experience. But, quite honestly, you're born with it or you aren't. If you're frightened or repulsed by such a burden, please bear in mind that all **FARMS** build up aggression that needs a release. As a modern-day lord, it's up to you to pull the trigger. The capable ruler will manage this responsibility with pinpoint precision and will direct the bloodthirsty herd in an appropriate direction to best suit his needs.

For those with the wits to capitalise on such an earth-shattering event, wasn't it incredibly brilliant of these forward thinkers to immediately declare War on Terror?

Whether global planners sat back and waited for such a distinct opportunity or pulled the levers from behind the scenes is trivial. A lurking enemy that can resurface in any country creates a perpetual adversary, justifying unlimited invasions of unlimited countries until we purge such an evil monstrosity from the Earth. Can you feel the hysteria such a boundless threat produces? Not only will most peasants clamour for their state's protection, but such an adversary will justify whatever precautionary measures you implement to ensure the herd's safety. The wise words of William Pitt state it best: 'Necessity is the plea for every infringement of human liberty; it is the argument of tyrants; it is the creed of slaves.'[359] Although tyrant is not a word I would use to describe a courageous leader who realises the importance of bearing down on their peasants, you must convince the vassals the control measures instated are necessary for their own safety and well-being. Or who knows what kind of large-scale atrocities could occur!

With former Gladio networks accessible and additional radical Islamic syndicates established as the new menace to human freedom, the infrastructure was now in place to ramp up strategic tension just about

---

359.) "William Pitt" In *Oxford Essential Quotations*, edited by Ratcliffe, Susan.: Oxford University Press, https://www.oxfordreference.com/display/10.1093/acref/9780191826719.001.0001/q-oro-ed4-00008337

everywhere across the globe. Explicit fear, using this more expansive Gladio nexus, could be achieved with additional acts of terror executed by newly entrenched agents. These random and sudden acts of violence would keep the impending danger fresh in peasants' minds, thereby lengthening the duration of the campaign to meet all its objectives.

Further acts of violence can also be realised by provoking individuals and target populations prone to retaliatory responses. To be more specific, I should reference a quote by Peter Ustinov: 'Terrorism is the war of the poor and war is the terrorism of the rich.' If you wage war on a poor country, convince the world that the enemies' retaliatory responses are acts of terror. Obviously, such desperate measures, in many instances, will be an impoverished **FARM'S** only means of defending its homeland. You should widely disseminate propaganda insinuating otherwise. Barbaric injustices like the bombings of weddings in hostile countries attended by innocent bystanders can incite hatred and fuel the desire for retribution for decades and even centuries to come. This will fan the flames of war and drive profits to unprecedented heights. But remember, to profit most handsomely, you must first secure the world's banking system.

> NOTE: If looking to bring more **FARMS** into a conflict, you must inundate these target *nations* with reports of horrible atrocities (real, imaginary or both) occurring in the war. This will cause fear that such brutalities can spread to their **FARM** and motivate those on the outside looking in to join the fight.

Equally as important as *explicit fear* is the less shocking but more ominous *implicit fear* that also plays a vital role in selling any long-term terror campaign. As discussed in Chapters 10 and 14, simple words like 'You are either with us or against us' will make objectors of military actions or emergency power abuses think twice about voicing their concerns. In the meantime, a looming terror threat is an excellent way to justify the militarisation of a **FARM'S** police forces that, not so inadvertently, cause concern amongst the herd that those same weapon upgrades could be used against them. Of course, this may be necessary should the herd develop a collective epiphany. Although it's not likely, you must never rule out this unflattering possibility. As I like to say, prepare for the worst and hope for the best.

You can ramp up implicit and explicit fear by using the most advanced weapon known to date—the mainstream media. The ways to use this powerful medium are nearly unlimited and the following examples should give you a few ideas. First, repeated coverage of a traumatic event will dominate peasants' thoughts, creating whatever new reality you wish to impart. Colour coded charts and graphs can serve as constant reminders of the level of danger the new enemy poses at any time. Keep in mind that any announced threat level (low or high) achieves the same goal, because it reminds peasants that a threat exists.

You can aim outrage and mockery at those with dissenting viewpoints to intimidate the masses into remaining attached to *official* narratives. Feel-good stories of heroism shown on news broadcasts, television shows and films can help sell the new reality and strengthen the herd's resolve to remain committed to this evolving paradigm. Powerful slogans like *United We Stand,* and *We Remember* after 9/11 conjured up mixed feelings of togetherness, outrage and sorrow and inspired Americans to buy into the new American agenda on a deeper and more personal level.

Politicians' passionate speeches on how to cope with grim possibilities that lie ahead promote confidence in their leadership and the emergency actions they take for the safety of the *citizens.* Gaining mass trust early on makes the prospect of peasants becoming wise to any deception less likely, especially once a compelling myth is culturally accepted. A small amount of truth, carefully apportioned, and craftily delivered through media outlets during a crisis, will divide your peasants into a small camp of truth seekers and pit them against the larger majority of obedient subjects. This will serve to further divide and conquer your **FARM** into yet more subdivisions based on the differing perceptions of a traumatic event.

Please also be aware that some slipups will occur. As long as you stand firm and incessantly repeat your version of the events, most peasants, with their short-term memories, will cling to your official explanations. As Mayer Amschel Rothschild once remarked: 'When you assume the appearance of power, people soon give it to you.'[360] Therefore, continue the guise of authority whilst repeating official narratives and not one in a thousand will question you.

Accidentally on purpose, interviews with firefighters and other witnesses who heard explosions in the buildings before and after the planes hit, or announcing the collapse of Building 7 on live television whilst it's standing in the background, only to suddenly transition to a lost signal as it begins its implosion, are the type of mishaps that can

---

360.) "Silent Weapons for Quiet Wars" (San Diego, CA: The Book Tree, 2018), 11.

and should occur. Just be sure to avoid the repetition of these glitches on mainstream media outlets and certainly do not draw unnecessary attention to their existence. If peasants wish to bicker about such revelations, let them. It will serve as divisive fodder, encouraging them to attack one another rather than you and your hidden network. Turning them on each other, of course, is much simpler to achieve and will distract them from any meaningful pursuit of justice.

By traumatising peasants to such a magnificent degree and constantly reminding constituents of the devastation witnessed in the US on 9/11, politicians used fear of terrorism as a grim warning of the type of scenario that could happen if no governmental action is taken. This allowed for the easy passage of new laws that placed tighter controls on all peasants and remain in place.

This is the perfect segue into the ultimate control apparatus, taking us a step closer to the undisputed, grand unification of the world's peasant farms. Throughout the Cold War, the Phoenix Program, a template for profiling and collecting information on citizens, underwent continuous development, similar to Operation Gladio. After experiencing messy growing pains in Vietnam, Phoenix quietly expanded its operations to other countries like El Salvador and Nicaragua, where it was developed to near perfection. Phoenix was a first of its kind collaboration between police, intelligence agencies and the military. The primary purpose was to disrupt citizen unity and eliminate cooperation with the resistance.

Are you drawing any parallels?

An enemy, seen as a threat to world tranquillity, who might act alone or inspire others to join their cause, could justify implementing the Phoenix Program across the entire globe.

Hmm. Now who could that enemy be? Oh, I know. How about a war against anyone with a dissident thought or, in layman's terms, a terrorist? Are you beginning to see the enormous flexibility such a sweeping manhunt can provide?

Before an intrusive and large-scale operation like Phoenix can be instated (especially on a *free* FARM like America), a few laws must be passed to strip the citizens of their rights, making these illegal government infringements, legal. Remember, this was the first step taken by the Nazis when they seized absolute power after the Burning of the Reichstag. Your transgressions are not illegal if the laws are rewritten to allow them.

As the old saying goes, 'He who has the gold makes the rules'.

In America, three major law changes will illustrate the way to tweak and pass legislation so that it can establish an aggressive system of control, like the Phoenix Program.

For our first case, let's examine the Foreign Intelligence Surveillance Act of 1978 (FISA). This act originally provided procedures for the physical and electronic surveillance and collection of foreign intelligence information between foreign powers and agents of foreign powers suspected of espionage or terrorism. It also established a Foreign Intelligence Surveillance Court (FISC) to oversee requests for surveillance warrants by federal law enforcement and intelligence agencies gathering foreign intelligence.[361]

Did I mention the word *foreign*?

However, after such a life-changing event as 9/11, the federal government easily persuaded the court to allow domestic mass surveillance along with warrantless and indiscriminate searches on private American citizens, for the purpose of keeping them safe, of course. This led to many more safety measures, such as capturing all fibre optic and cable data, including all mobile and landline telephone calls, and the recording of every keystroke on every American computer, including Internet searches, social media posts and emails.[362] Such ingenious formats hardly make enhanced interrogation necessary. Most modern-day peasants will boastfully offer their innermost thoughts and personal information if they're simply offered a platform.

Some pouting US analysts may gripe that this is information overload, and I would normally agree if not for one thing. The collection of this data is not meant to prevent an attack against their *nation*, it's intended to do something much more important. It's meant to flush out threats to you and your associates' international world order. As Joseph Stalin's head of Secret Police, Lavrentiy Beria, once brilliantly proclaimed: 'Show me the man and I'll show you the crime.'[363] If you dig deep enough, you'll eventually find something on every peasant.

361.) Wikipedia. 2004. "Foreign Intelligence Surveillance Act." Last modified December 3, 2022. https://en.wikipedia.org/wiki/Foreign_Intelligence_Surveillance_Act

362.) Judge Andrew Napolitano, "Napolitano: Why FISA is the loss of our privacy," YouTube video, 3:16, Fox News, January 18, 2018, https://youtu.be/vo6yNw-BIEuo and "Foreign Intelligence Surveillance Act (FISA): An Overview." Congressional Research Service.gov. April 6, 2021. https://crsreports.congress.gov/product/pdf/IF/IF11451 and Violet Blue. "Keyloggers: Beware this hidden threat." PCWorld.com. June 28, 2017. https://www.pcworld.com/article/406909/keyloggers-what-you-need-to-know-about-this-hidden-threat.html

363.) Michael Henry. "Show me the man and I'll show you the crime." The Oxford Eagle.com. May 9, 2018. https://www.oxfordeagle.com/2018/05/09/show-me-the-man-and-ill-show-you-the-crime/

Authorities can use this information against anyone with a dissident outlook and bring them up on charges.

> NOTE: As a firm reminder, the origin of and reasons for these encroachments should remain behind closed doors and, when questioned, should be withheld for national security. Certainly, you would never deprive peasants of their liberty for your own benefit, but only for their own. That's all they need to know. Anyone who questions the intent is clearly up to no good and can serve as a shining example to others who question your **STATE'S** authority. Most peasants will interpret the targeted dissident's actions as harmful to the rest of the **FARM**. As a result, they'll support enhanced policing measures when your tightly run media outlets announce rebellious actions.

The second law worth discussing is the Patriot Act. Unlike FISA, the Patriot Act was enacted after that tragic day in American history, 11 September 2001. It was, however, in its final form, conveniently waiting for passage long before the attacks occurred. It never hurts to have a piece of legislation lying around that conveniently compliments an agenda that you wish to impose, just in case the right opportunity for widespread acceptance presents itself.

As you may have discovered from our discussion regarding the *Freedom Fighters* of Afghanistan, I simply adore the use of a double entendre, especially when applied to a shadowy government activity. Although most shocked and petrified Americans were willing to embrace any enactment with the word Patriot in its title, can you see the possible dual meaning? What if the Patriot Act's actual intention was to identify those who remained patriotic to the pre-9/11 America and its freedom protecting constitution? That would present an eerily similar situation to the VC sympathisers who were simply fighting for their right of self-determination. And who has time for that nonsense when there's a world empire to build?

The Patriot Act was really just an extension of FISA with a few useful bells and whistles attached. Its three main provisions expanded law enforcement's ability to spy on citizens through domestic and international phone taps, eased interagency communication, allowing federal agencies to more effectively use all available enforcement resources in counterterrorism efforts, and the act increased penalties for terroristic crimes, including an expanded list of activities that qualified as terrorism.[364]

364.) Wikipedia. 2001. "Patriot Act." Last modified November 14, 2022. https://en.wikipedia.org/Patriot_Act

Comrade Stalin would be fervently rejoicing in his grave at just the mention of such enhanced policing actions. Similarly, those looking to conjure up more terrorists for a global crusade against these menaces to society would be equally satisfied.

Like the PICs (Provincial Interrogation Centers) in Vietnam, each state in America has a fusion centre where all profiling information on citizens is stored. Whilst FISA obtained data can be pumped directly into these electronic information warehouses, the Patriot Act accommodates the more old-school intelligence gathering methods like granting powers to snoop through homes, and even seize property, without notifying the owners. Who could leave out the more inconspicuous inspection of an individual's records held by third parties? Of course, to really get inside the mind of a terrorist, perusing their reading list or observing their supermarket shopping tendencies can provide wonderful insights into their thinking and behavioural patterns. Pay close attention to anyone reading books similar to this one or making large purchases of chemical fertiliser, for example. These could be telltale signs someone is looking to unseat you or, better yet, ready to play into your cleverly set trap.

Until every peasant is under your control, one effective method used to divide and conquer your **FARM** is by lumping your peasants into groups. This long-established technique has many useful purposes, but is most effective in a *national emergency* when there's not enough time to sort through every member of society to determine their allegiance. By sorting peasants into groups, you can easily target them based on your parameters. Just be sure to include their group affiliations in their profiles. This will come in handy when it's time to move in for the kill.

When thinning the herd, you have a limited window of opportunity to achieve maximum results before you can expect some sort of retaliation against you. During initial periods of establishing your authority, expect things to get messy. Mass bloodshed is an imperfect science, and innocent bystanders will be caught in the fray. You must be ready to accept it.

The wise ruler realises that liberators and their supporters will grant sympathies to groups on the receiving end of wartime injustices. An artful and advanced global planner will skilfully blend this knowledge with false flag strategies to incite terror for fulfilling an underlying agenda not readily understood by the common observer. As always, your media outlets will play a crucial role in selling the narrative you wish your target audience to believe.

As you consolidate the planet's **FARMS**, you might terrorise a large group of people whilst offering a safe haven they can retreat to, thus dividing the world into larger, more generalised territories. This tactic was executed by Zionist leaders, before and after World War II, to create the state of Israel.[365]

Global planners also proposed a similar sanctuary for Muslims who were persecuted after 9/11. One scenario envisioned an Islamic super state spanning from Indonesia, Malaysia and Singapore to parts of the Philippines, Thailand and Myanmar.[366]

> NOTE: One of the suggested names for this new Islamic mega nation was Eurabia.[367] Coincidentally, the nation of Oceania in Orwell's *Nineteen Eighty-Four* had two other super state rivals, Eurasia and Eastasia. Hmm. I can't help but notice the striking phonetic resemblance of Eurabia to these two fictionalised states that battled Oceania for world supremacy.

It's quite intriguing to watch art imitate life and vice versa, wouldn't you agree?

An outpouring of official support toward an established enemy of the **FARM** (like Muslims living in America post 9/11) can add further chaos and confusion, thus making **FARM** inhabitants more vulnerable to the rules you implement.

Although such a method may seem counterintuitive, you are agitating both groups and further pitting them against one another. Not only can you justify increased surveillance on those in the enemy group, but you can also impose increased surveillance on those opposed to this foreign element for trumped up reasons such as potential *hate* crimes. By allowing the enemy group to freely immigrate into a targeted society, you not only increase the implicit fear their presence brings, but you also increase the likelihood of an internal conflict, requiring an authoritarian resolution only a capable ruler such as yourself can provide. This internal strife will provide a clever diversion and minimise the probability that either side will recognise the role you and your associates are playing in their demise. By empowering an antagonistic foreign culture over the host **FARM**, you'll have a much easier time

---

365.) Freedman, "1961 Speech at the Willard Hotel," 0:-46:31.

366.) Maria Ressa. "The quest for SE Asia's Islamic 'super' state." CNN.com. August 29, 2002. https://edition.cnn.com/2002/WORLD/asiapcf/southeast/07/30/seasia. state/

367.) Thomas A. Salo. "Eurabia: Strategic Implications for the United States." Defense Technical Information Center. March 1, 2010. https://apps.dtic.mil/sti/citations/ ADA520029

dismantling previous societal norms and replacing them with norms that are more compatible with your end goals.

Remember: unfreeze, change, refreeze.

If experience has taught most modern-day lords anything, it's watching for revolutionary groups fighting for *freedom*. This should be obvious since it'll be your goal to expand your independence whilst stripping peasants of theirs.

A group fighting for its *freedom*, in most cases, translates to the group wanting to run the society according to its own ideals, not yours. Again, as seen from Operation Gladio, there are ways to discredit legitimate movements to stymie competition and impede momentum. Implicit fear is an effective tool against patriotic activity and will require propaganda and public denouncement to sway public opinion against anyone tied to rebellious factions. By controlling the mainstream media narrative, a ruling class can create great leverage over a **FARM'S** highly fixated and obedient disciples.

As an example of the type of censorship necessary to quell any spontaneous uprisings, after 9/11, a songwriter named Aimee Allen was on the rise and was the 2000s' meaner and leaner version of 1980s' bad girl of rock n roll, Joan Jett. That was, of course, until her album entitled *I'd Start A Revolution* was set for release just after the 9/11 attacks. This incendiary anthem, coupled with her radical political views of a constitutionally limited American government, forced her record label to silence her dissentious voice.

Shelving her album's release and locking her into a seven-year recording contract, with no hope of her music reaching the outside world until her indenture expired, proved to be one of the many keen preventative measures taken by the entertainment industry to censor such inflammatory art. These precautionary measures played a pivotal role in preventing peasants from *uniting* against those responsible for the mayhem whilst diverting their attention elsewhere.

On a human level, lumping peasants into groups forces them to focus on their group's attributes whilst simultaneously excluding others for their differences. This removes peasants from their common bond, their innate desire to be free, respected and, dare I say, loved. Disrupting peasants' connection to others due to their whims and fancies, skin colours, religions and the like, serves as a great divider and will prevent them from connecting on a deeper and more substantial level.

I must admit, it's a personal joy of mine to watch the little ingrates bicker over matters of little significance whilst they're robbed blind of their wealth and personal dignity. Just remember, as emperor supreme, it's your job to create the issues for the hordes to haggle over. In today's fast-paced world, you can cunningly achieve this through your corporate news outlets and their parroting subsidiaries.

The danger of encouraging group behaviour is that those with more serious aspirations might draw attention to your methods and attract others into their ranks, thus becoming a threat to your rule. For this, and a plethora of other reasons, the third and final law change used to subtly implement the legal framework of the Phoenix Program was the Authorization for Use of Military Force of 2001 (AUMF). This measure gave the President of the United States authorisation for the unspecified use of force against nations, organisations or people they determine planned, authorised, committed or aided the terrorists on 9/11. This authorised use of force also includes nations, organisations or people the president feels can carry out future acts of international terrorism against the United States.

I would like to point out a few of the many splendid concessions this simple piece of legislation provides. First, this ultimate killing power falls within the discretion of one individual, i.e. the President of the United States. Under this condition, the wise and savvy global architect must land this one powerful leader in their back pocket so they can instruct this sole figurehead on whom to neutralise and when. Second, the type of force to be used in the AUMF is nondescript as are the type of acts and specific locations that deem one a *terrorist*. In other words, from the scanty language presented in the AUMF, those organisations or persons capable of *international terrorism* can be from any country and operating anywhere in the world, including in the United States of America, whilst committing undefined offences. Washington DC, the military capital of the world, has declared war against a global enemy that encompasses the entire Earth, including in its own jurisdiction, and can use the guise of 9/11 to justify military force against any person or group capable of any random act of terror.

Wonderful! The stage has been set.

Of course, it'll be necessary to profile every citizen and form a more cohesive collaboration between the police, the military and intelligence services or, in short, to implement the Phoenix Program in America and across the planet to ensure the chattel are safe from any harm they may cause themselves. People who see this new form of rule as a threat and perhaps want to do something about it, will elevate themselves above their normal status of *enemy combatant* to *terrorist*. When the time is right, you have the legal grounds to eliminate them. By continually expanding the definition of terrorist, you can further cast a net over the undesirables and resistors on any **FARM**, including those on an unrestricted **FARM** like the US, who wish to defend their dwindling freedoms.

Gradually introducing criminal offences such as *terroristic threats* for abusive language against a wife, neighbour or even a police officer, adds a nice touch when selling a new narrative to the general public. Please take note that, by reusing the root word *terror* on television and in local law enforcement actions, many more years were added onto this fabricated war against an ever-elusive enemy.

Since it's the global lord's bold worldview that creates the industries occupying the landscape and, as mentioned in earlier chapters, because all businesses have become subsidiaries of their corporate governments, thus forming an intricate nexus, it makes sense that anyone who poses a risk to its basic operation should be classified as a terrorist. This will allow one to cast a much larger dragnet over the herd and aggressively sort out those who insist on disrupting lucrative business practices. Examples of disruption include damaging and interfering with the operations of animal testing centres, abortion clinics and environmentally hazardous job sites like oil pipelines and mountaintop removal mines. Known more broadly as Ecoterrorism, the Animal Enterprise Terrorism Act was passed in 2006 and once again used brilliantly vague language to impose ever-tightening restrictions on peasants rather than on controversial but fruitful enterprises. For instance, *interfering with* could include someone urging others to boycott eggs from a producer that uses battery cages for their hens, or someone who videotapes the cruel treatment of horses at a slaughterhouse, since both can be used to discourage profits even if conducted through something as benign as an email campaign. If labelling someone a terrorist for such seemingly minor infractions bothers you, just remember that these same social warriors will be the first ones to rebel against any perceived *injustices* imposed on your **FARM**.

Trust me, it's better to target them sooner rather than later.

To elevate the stakes a few notches higher, if you have the good fortune of overseeing a productive and wealthy **FARM**, protect the delicate infrastructure you, or at least those you seized it from, had the vision to build. In America, this is done through a programme known as InfraGard.

Since corporations make the perfect Trojan Horses for infiltration on a **FARM**, and since your associates fill the ranks of your **FARM'S** most important industries, it makes absolute sense that these profit-driven entities should be included in a Phoenix-like intelligence-gathering programme. We learned during the Vietnam War and in Nazi Germany that, if you're looking to collect information on members of the community, who better to gather that information than respected members of that same community?

> NOTE: Currently over 400 of the top Fortune 500 companies have active members in InfraGard, whose secretive membership status rivals the CIA. It's interesting to know that the inaugural members of the Central Intelligence Agency were predominantly Wall Street investment bankers and savvy international corporate lawyers much like the core members of InfraGard today.[368]

By promoting such fabulous campaigns as 'If you see something, say something', these corporate stiffs might actually be given permission to fulfil their darkest fantasies during periods of civil unrest. Although leaks of members having full authority to use lethal force against peasants who attempt to destroy infrastructure during declarations of martial law have come to light, it's nothing a little damage control can't contain. To see this effective public relations work in action, please review the 'Big Brother' episode of *Conspiracy Theory with Jesse Ventura*. Even though a member, who I'm sure won't make this same mistake again, leaked this unspoken perk to a reporter, there's no harm done in leaving such an imposing proposition loom in the public consciousness.

It's an example of what kind of fear?

Good. Implicit fear. Well done my burgeoning czar!

Since we're on the topic of business, a catastrophic event such as 9/11 not only delivers a physical, spiritual and emotional jolt to the stunned witnesses, it can also bring on quite an economic shock. Having insider knowledge that a large scale, life-changing event is about to occur will allow the savvy business minded ruler to reshape the economy to best suit their overall plans whilst stuffing their pockets full of delectable, green bills.

A few examples will illustrate the practicality of such thinking in today's modern world.

The current consumption rate of the Earth's seven billion plus inhabitants poses a dire threat to the continuation of not only the human

368.) Burton Hersh. "Banking CIA-Style: How the Money Moves Under The Table to Fund Covert Operations." Los Angeles Times. August 4, 1991. https://www.latimes.com/archives/la-xpm-1991-08-04-op-453-story.html

species, but most life on this tiny blue planet. Humans have overfished the oceans by over 50% and global wildlife has decreased by over 40% since the 1970s.[369] Improving technology has not only produced the control grid necessary to rule over the entire world whilst supporting the large population necessary to create and implement it, but it has exhausted many of the Earth's natural resources in the process. Being that progress is often an inaccurate, messy and inefficient undertaking, despite noble efforts to reduce its hazardous effects on the environment, the toll it's taken on the world's ecosystems is reaching a crescendo. Therefore, toward the latter part of the twentieth century, the global elite had to face the grim reality that growing populations coupled with excessive consumption rates would need to undergo some sort of controlled demolition to reel in humanity from the brink of extinction. The event on 11 September provided the perfect guise to begin this subtle yet steady descent into a more manageable and sustainable society.

If you remember that chilling day and the days immediately following, much of the industrial world shut down; commercial flights were grounded, important landmarks were closed, sporting events were cancelled and downtown Manhattan, the epicentre of global economic power, was buried under a pile of rubble.

Although this lag in commercial activity wasn't as prolonged as some would have liked, a new type of reality began to emerge. A myriad of new laws started shooting out of the US Congress like midgets out of a circus cannon. A new economy, based on heightened security amid a worldwide fear of terrorism, also emerged. For example, new and invasive nude body scanners were installed in airports across the globe and, in America, complimented the Transportation Security Administration's (TSA's) enhanced groping procedures.

NOTE: As a friendly reminder, long-term mass subjugation requires gradual usurpations. As Aldous Huxley pointed out to George Orwell, a jackboot to the face will result in an unwelcome backlash where a subtle conditioning strategy will gain your

---

369.) Erin Blakemore. "Some Ocean Populations Declined by Nearly 50 Percent Between 1970 and 2012." Smithsonian Magazine. September 17, 2015. https://www.smithsonianmag.com/smart-news/ocean-populations-declined-nearly-50-percent-between-1970-and-2012-180956660/ and Damian Carrington. "Earth has lost half of its wildlife in the past 40 years, says WWF: Species across land, rivers and seas decimated as humans kill for food in unsustainable numbers and destroy habitats." The Guardian. September 30, 2014. https://www.theguardian.com/environment/2014/sep/29/earth-lost-50-wildlife-in-40-years-wwf

subjects' compliance without them ever realising it. Like the witch in Hansel and Gretel, some finesse should be used when fattening them up before you deliver the final blow.

Another big winner in this more tightly controlled, post 9/11 economy was the now quite commonplace RFID (Radio Frequency Identification) technology. Again, following legislative acts demanding its implementation, businesses began popping up everywhere that prudently supplied this emerging technology. Remember, it's incredibly important to identify all potential threats as early as possible, giving the **STATE** ample time to extinguish them. In America, this meant tightening the clamps on US CITIZENS, leaving them no choice but to comply or face losing things like their farms, their ability to travel, their jobs and even their freedom (what little they still had). For instance, the Food Modernization Safety Act takes a page from the Lenin/Stalin playbook by gradually taking control of first the farms, then the food and eventually the people. RFID compliance is just one of the many tools available to achieve this monolithic but necessary goal.

Of course, to be sure a chicken or spear of broccoli hasn't been compromised by a terrorist sneaking around a pasture in a pair of dungarees and a cowboy hat, each animal, fruit and vegetable *must* contain a microchip with a barcode to track the consumable food product from farm to fork. If farmers lose track of these potential bioweapons at any stage of the process, they risk audits, fines and confiscation of their property. As always, to help support this expanded security for the farmers' own good, they're charged a modest fee to ensure their cooperation and to be sure their products meet all the latest *safety* standards.

The cost of compliance for the major food providers, hopefully managed by your most trusted associates, should be miniscule compared to the local, smaller-scale farmers filled with high hopes of feeding their communities. Based on the mass quantities produced on the larger industrial lots, this will mostly occur quite naturally. You can always make up the difference by subsidising the major food manufacturers for the *well-being* of the peasants, of course.

NOTE: The best way to protect the herd from widespread poisoning is to have many localised **FARMS** distributing to smaller areas. In the event of a contamination scenario, the affected area is minimised, and the cause is easily traced back to its origin. I hope you're realising, gaining power and control becomes much harder when wealth and the ability to produce are evenly distributed to others. Since food is necessary, you must establish your network's control over this essential resource. A wonderfully orchestrated crisis, like the War on Terror, provides the ideal scenario to ensure this happens.

By burdening the insignificant producers over a long enough period, you'll drive them from the **FARM**, into perhaps retail, passing more and more ownership of the peasants' rations over to you. Perhaps you can build a warehouse or strip mall over the once fertile land to ensure peasants don't revitalise the property, thus keeping them dependent on your distribution of fodder. This will allow you to manage your subjects more fully and, when the time is right, to tighten the reins, so you can restrict their access to this basic human need through price control and limiting supply.

After 9/11, Lancaster, PA became the most heavily surveilled city in America because it produced the best homegrown, free range, pesticide, chemical and anti-biotic-free food. Those pesky Amish with their traditional agricultural practices and consumption of non-processed, nutritionally rich foods needed to be watched and stopped at all costs. These daring criminals were running raw milk across state lines! Their horse-drawn carriages outmanoeuvred authorities and provided wholesome foods to invigorate peasants above their normal levels. Strengthening peasants' bodies and minds robs a ruler of their profits by promoting good health instead of sickness, thus depleting a ruler of a revenue stream generated by their treatments.

Notice, I used the word *treatment* instead of *cure*.

The TSA, Homeland Security and the ever-expanding FDA were created by farm leaders to grab more governmental power. Besides the obvious tax increases required to protect the **FARM**, there are other creative ways to fund a terrorscape. A few quick examples will hopefully spark some ideas.

Perhaps a fee can be applied to any item that can be used as a *weapon of mass destruction*. A CO_2 tank heading to a local beer distributorship, for instance, may or may not need to pass some sort of inspection before being purchased for Suzie's birthday bash. Obviously, if you want pure profit, don't bother to inspect the items but still charge the fee. To further bilk the peasants, begin a tax funded agency responsible for this tedious task. This will help justify the surcharge whilst also allowing those in the new department to feel like they're earning their lucrative salaries. Roving agents strapped with firearms and pinned with government badges will present a show of force, guaranteeing the herd's cooperation and, hence, **STATE** revenues.

Of course, to help pay for enhanced security measures like new airport scanners, RFID chips in passports and licences, and food safety equipment, it'll be necessary for both private and public enterprises to increase their prices and licensing fees to cover these additional costs. For those who fail to comply, additional revenue can be generated through penalties and fines. If those in the private sector refuse to drink the Kool-Aid, so to speak, they can have their property seized, sold at an auction and thus converted into a profit. During such a dire time when anyone, anywhere can suddenly become an evil terrorist, tools like the Food Safety Modernization Act and the Patriot Act have legalised forfeitures of property and bank accounts for even the slightest infraction since either could be used for quite nefarious purposes.

Indeed, local farmers unwilling to play along may have hopes of funding a terrorist group that will run drills on their property. To be safe, and during a time of national emergency, such confiscations are not only encouraged but required.

To allow your other lucrative industries to thrive, tighter surveillance also provides opportunities. Say, for example, gluttonous peasants fill their grocery carts with Twinkies, fizzy drinks and other delectable peasant favourites due to their depressed state during a national tragedy. Since all their purchases can be recorded and stored in their profiles, when these same subjects are diagnosed with blocked arteries, isn't it the overweight and overindulgent peasants' fault for jamming these comfort foods into their cake holes?

Due to your shopping habits, Mr Fatso, your insurance claim is denied! Thank you, sir, and have a good day!

If necessary, you can always borrow against the collateral of the nation, i.e. the peasants and everything they own, to fund your enhanced security state. Simply charge future generations for the protection you so generously offer today by nonchalantly adding it to their ever-expanding bill. Their great, great grandchildren will pay for it when the hidden inflation tax drops on their head like a Hellfire missile dropped from a Predator drone.

NOTE: I just love Predator drone jokes by the way. Nothing tops the one told by former president Barack Obama with the Jonas Brothers in attendance. Though his daughters are big fans, Mr Obama advised the boys not to get any ideas because of two words…Predator drones.[370] I suppose you had to be there. Let's move on, shall we?

Along the lines of lethal aircraft, war preparation is the driving force of any modern-day economy, and not only will it create more tax revenue through ramped up military production, but it will provide more purchasing power for its determined workforce. This can then be used to purchase products from a plethora of other industries. Remember, extraneous expenditures in areas such as warfare, welfare and space travel drive the **FARM'S** businesses 24/7, thus committing most peasants to the corporate plantation.

Once again, a diligent media apparatus is required to sell any new agenda to the masses to gain their loyal obedience. When shock from the initial inciting incident wanes, offshoot stories spreading additional fear can prolong mass trauma for years and even decades. Since you not only opened your wallet to purchase this pragmatic guide, but because you've shown extreme dedication by making it to this point in the text, I'll give you a rare, behind-the-scenes look at actual reality versus the post 9/11 illusionary world carefully configured for peasants.

By receiving this information, you're no longer one of them but one of us. Please act accordingly!

Post 9/11 scare tactics were created by slapping together some of the most benign circumstances and puffing them up with ingenious flair. Your presentation of these otherwise trivial matters will prove your prowess in this area.

If you lived through the 9/11 era and its residual media fallout, you'll remember news segments that initially spoke of elaborate, multi-tiered caves in Afghanistan, used by Osama Bin Laden and his fellow conspirators, that contained bedrooms and offices, secret exits, ventilation systems, entrances large enough to allow entry of trucks and tanks, all run on hydroelectric power stations capable of powering computer and telephone systems.[371]

HA! This was done to promote the myth of a sophisticated, operational and elusive enemy who was plotting further death and

---

370.) Barack Obama, "Obama Jokes About Killing Jonas Brothers With Predator Drones," YouTube video, 0:29, Michael Moore, May 2, 2010, https://youtu.be/WWKG6ZmgAX4

371.) The Week Staff. "The Caves of Afghanistan." The Week. January 8, 2015. https://theweek.com/articles/528956/caves-afghanistan and Curtis, "The Power of Nightmares," 2:19:35-2:20:15.

destruction inside these highly strategic mountain fortresses.

Also, enter into the picture the Northern Alliance (an Afghan militia that fought against the Taliban) who was, quite intentionally, on the American payroll. To not only propel the Al Qaeda mystique to blistering new heights, but to also cash in on it, the Northern Alliance provided a tip that Bin Laden was hiding in the mountains of Tora Bora. For this helpful intelligence, and as proof the entire world was on the side of bringing these dastardly fugitives to justice, the Northern Alliance was paid the healthy sum of one million US$ for their generous input. As a result, the American military blew the region's mountaintops to smithereens and began searching for Bin Laden and his secret Al Qaeda network. The most they found were a few, small, naturally occurring caves that contained modest amounts of ammunition.[372]

This is where the art of deception quite splendidly came into play.

Rather than broadcast these anticlimactic findings, a simple mention that Bin Laden was still at large, proved to be much more menacing. To ramp up the search efforts, the British, who pride themselves on their superior ability to flush out terrorists, gallantly arrived on the scene. As discussed earlier, the third media point needed for our current topic is controlling the narrative through what you don't say. The British, with nothing but a few confused goat herders to show for their efforts, would most certainly fall into that category.[373]

The lack of an existing Al Qaeda network is a moot point when fear needs to grip the world and palms of willing collaborators need to be greased. Even though the Northern Alliance wasn't able to provide one credible lead when it came to the elusive Al Qaeda command centre's whereabouts, they did hand over quite a few Al Qaeda fighters. The fact that these prisoners included anyone who simply looked Arabic with no proven ties to any terrorist organisations is beside the point.

War is a dirty business.

So is selling and promoting it. If a few innocent bystanders get swept up in the haste to produce a few enemy combatants, it's a simple mistake anyone could make under the fog of war. *Capisce*?

Can you remember from an earlier discussion when a similar quota was placed on captured and slain enemies to justify a controversial programme to the American people that would eventually be used to fulfil a far-reaching global agenda? If you recalled the early days

---

372.) Curtis, "The Power of Nightmares," 2:18:00-2:21:45.
373.) Curtis, "The Power of Nightmares," 2:21:45 2:22:53.

of the Phoenix Program, your ability to absorb information and implement it into a working worldview is sharpening and will serve you well in your aim to enslave humanity.

Even though these *sleeper* cells were proving harder and harder to conjure up in the Middle East doesn't mean they weren't quietly blending into American towns and cities just waiting for the opportune time to strike.

Well, to ratchet up the fear in the US, that's what the masses needed to believe anyway.

One quick example, taken from the first major trial in the War on Terror, will help illustrate this technique in action. This pristine opportunity began when FBI Agents approached a house in Detroit, Michigan looking for a Yemen man who suffered from mental illness and believed he was the Minister of Defence for the entire Middle East.[374] Though the person of interest had committed suicide one year prior, the agents took the time to shake down his previous residence. This, despite the four new occupants insisting they didn't know who this past tenant was. Regardless, during the raid, the agents uncovered a day planner left behind by the former occupant. It contained scribblings and doodles of what appeared to be a military base.[375]

In addition to the day planner, they also found a tourist tape and some false documents. One of the forged documents belonged to an international conman named Youssef Hmimssa who knew the four residents but didn't live there. To bring a case against the four Middle Eastern men now living in Terror Manor with what could, at best, be described as circumstantial evidence, prosecutors quickly cut a deal with Mr Hmimssa in exchange for a scathing testimony against the residents in the house.[376] I mean, what conman wouldn't take a sweet offer that included a reduced prison sentence along with a promise that no additional charges would be filed against him? The sleeper cell investigation was later dropped because Mr Hmimssa was running off at the mouth whilst incarcerated and admitted to a fellow prisoner he made the whole thing up.[377]

I know, I know. The behind-the-scenes activities of a fear campaign can be uproariously comical compared to the terror-driven gobbledygook peasants are led to believe.

374.) Curtis, "The Power of Nightmares," 2:26:00-2:31:43.
375.) Curtis, "The Power of Nightmares," 2:26:00-2:31:43.
376.) Curtis, "The Power of Nightmares," 2:26:00-2:31:43.
377.) Curtis, "The Power of Nightmares," 2:31:00-2:31:19.

But wait, it gets better.

The video tape that featured the four men in question at your run of the mill tourist destinations such as Disney World and Las Vegas would seem like any other holiday tape to the casual observer. However, when sweeping new reforms and a totalitarian police state needs urgent justification, a heavy dose of creative licence is required. Specialists were called in and the recorded innocent moments were turned into riveting, heart pounding assumptions. For example, a brief pan over to a rubbish bin whilst the teenagers were waiting in line for a ride was interpreted as a hidden message to place a bomb in the bin. Olympic Village, anyone?

An *expert* confirmed that loud voices dominating the soundtrack were hiding secret messages buried more silently below the teen angst. A quick camera sweep down a tree that ran from their hotel room to a car park next to an adjoining motorway was clearly pointing out a concealed spot to hide a sniper that could then fire upon oncoming traffic. Finally, on what appears to be a running camera that was accidentally turned on whilst facing the ground as the videographer was walking to a new arrival point, was most certainly a measurement counted in paces, again detailing the proper placement of an explosive device.[378]

Can you feel the tension mounting?

Whilst the thought of a random detonation planted by a hidden sleeper cell added a haunting touch of panic to the already fear-driven American society, the next scare tactic took the hysteria to the next level.

Are you sure you're ready? It could kill you instantly with barely a second to realise it.

Alright, if you insist.

It was (cue the eerie organ music) a dirty bomb. Assisting the mainstream media in this scare-a-thon was the entire entertainment industry, as this new phenomenon appeared as the central plot in films, television shows, magazine articles, video games and books.

'What exactly is a dirty bomb?' you ponder as you scratch your head in bewilderment. I'm glad the question pushed its way to the forefront of your cerebral cortex.

In theory, a dirty bomb is a poor man's nuclear weapon. The idea is to combine radioactive material with a conventional explosive device so that the detonation contaminates the neighbouring area of

---

378.) Curtis, "The Power of Nightmares," 2:29:03-2:29:44.

the blast site. Sounds horrific, doesn't it? The dirty secret, however, is that tests conducted by the US Department of Energy and the US Army discovered that, as long as proper cleanup ensues and those in the area do not remain in the affected area for an entire year straight, the health effects resulting from exposure to the radiation are negligible and far from life-threatening.[379] However, and as I'm sure you'll agree, the herd is much more malleable when fear is constantly pumping through their veins.

'So, what or who brought on this elevated state of public delirium?' you ecstatically clamour.

Well, if you thought our last batch of *inoperatives* was hysterical, this next one will have you rolling inside a small coffin-like box.

Costing the United States a mere ten million US$ to acquire from Pakistan, Abu Zubaydah, was definitely *a bang for the buck*.[380] Taken into captivity on 1 August 2002, whilst suffering from severe gunshot wounds, this former Afghan Civil War veteran soon became the first test subject for the CIA's newly developed, enhanced interrogation programme. The resilient Mr Zubaydah's questioning began immediately after awaking from his coma in a Pakistani hospital whilst strapped to a bed with a sheet. Announcing publicly that he was the third-highest-ranking member of Al-Qaeda, policy makers now had the justification needed to set up secret prisons in foreign countries around the world, where they would be removed from US law and able to test some new and, dare I say, *controversial* torture methods. Abu Zubaydah was first taken to a detention site in Thailand prepared especially for him, which inconspicuously operated under the pseudonym of Detention Site Green (as in green light, perhaps?).[381]

The inside scoop, however, was that Mr Zubaydah was not a member of Al-Qaeda, let alone a high-ranking operative. He did,

379.) Joseph Trevithick. "The US Army Tested Its Own 'Dirty Bombs." War is Boring. October 13, 2015. https://warisboring.com/the-u-s-army-tested-its-own-dirty/bombs/ and Wikipedia. 2002. "Dirty Bomb." Last modified January 2, 2023. https://en.wikipedia.org/wiki/Dirty_bomb and United States Nuclear Regulatory Commission. "Background on Dirty Bombs." U.S.N.R.C. February 23, 2022. https://www.nrc.gov/reading-rm/doc-collections/fact-sheets/fs-dirty-bombs.html and Curtis, "The Power of Nightmares," 2:42:00-2:45:00.

380.) Jim W. Dean and Gordon Duff. "Blockbuster: The Story of Abu Zubaydah, Brain Damaged CIA Hero Still at Gitmo." Veterans Today, February 7, 2022. AND Wikipedia. 2002. "Abu Zubaydah." Last modified December 31, 2022. https://en.wikipedia.org/wiki/Abu_Zubaydah AND Ismael Loutfi "Abu Zubaydah: The Fake Terrorist America Tortured," YouTube video, 10:38, The Gravel Institute, February 4, 2022, https://youtu.be/3xAFv7LQ_bY

381.) Rendition Research Team. "Abu Zubaydah." The Rendition Project. March 28, 2002. https://www.therenditionproject.org.uk/prisoners/zubaydah.html

however, suffer from head trauma because of a mortar shell blast in Afghanistan in 1992 that lodged shrapnel in his skull, leaving him with a few mental incapacities, to say the least.[382] He was perfect! All that was required to give the government credibility for apprehending a plotter of 9/11, as well as more fear-driven scenarios to frighten the world into a tizzy, was his complete isolation and utter silence throughout the remainder of his life.

Well, what do you think these secret prisons that bypass the need for evidence and a speedy and public trial are for? Answer this I demand of you!

We'll bypass the minor details of the 24/7 torture he endured and fast forward to Mr Zubaydah murmuring something about a dirty bomb plot sometime after being water boarded just over 83 times in one month.[383] Whether or not a Godzilla film inspired his startling yet delirious revelation is inconsequential. A new scare tactic had been born after probing the limits of human pain tolerance. This illustrates that once the herd is hit with a big jolt of fear, you can justify any type of egregious actions taken by continually building upon their initial trauma.

However, to achieve maximum results between waves of terror and periods of calm, you *must* supply a steady stream of propaganda along with conflicting messages that stymie the herd's ability to think clearly or draw rational conclusions. Such examples from the War on Terror can include making the desperate defensive actions of an inferior FARM appear cowardly. Whilst I admit it takes a certain degree of courage for any bloke to risk their life for their society, what battle scenario do you think is more heroic: stave off an occupying army in your homeland by wiring yourself with an explosive that will detonate at the next checkpoint or fuelling fighter jets on a floating fortress hundreds of nautical miles from the battlefield?

Of course, the person blending in as a civilian to catch the more advanced military off guard is the more chicken-hearted action to take when promoting your world enforcement arm.

Breathe. Breathe. You're melting into warm sand on a beach in Southern France.

Ah. Where was I? Oh yes.

382.) Jason Leopold. "Why Did US Medical Personnel Remove High-Value Detainee Abu Zubaydah's Eye? truthout. https://truthout.org/articles/why-did-us-medical-personnel-remove-highvalue-detainee-abu-zubaydahs-eye/ and Loutfi, "The Fake Terrorist Tortured," 2:29-3:10.
383.) Loutfi, "The Fake Terrorist Tortured," 6:40-6:47.

Whatever common threat you select to rattle your herd should be so terrifying that the politicians and authority figures promising to protect the populace from their worst nightmares can most easily waltz into positions of leadership. As we'll soon discover, a doomsday scenario prompting mass psychosis is not limited to one caused by a predetermined group of *evil* humans.

In the case of 9/11, the shock value was so magnificent that an official investigation of the crime scene was conveniently overlooked. Blame was quickly placed on expedient enemies and predetermined agendas were hastily launched into action. However, after 441 days of grovelling, the pesky family members of those slain in the attacks finally got their wish, and an *official* inquiry was begrudgingly set in motion. Like any situation where criminal accusations can be directed inward and careers of associates ruined, it's vitally important to precisely manage every aspect of such a probe. This involves carefully controlling things like subject areas of examination, all briefing materials, topics for the hearings, witnesses and lines of questioning for those testifying.[384] The obvious advantage to dragging one's feet early on is that it allows you to form the outline and narrative of the investigation before it begins whilst also buying you valuable time to cover your tracks.

The National Commission on Terrorist Attacks Upon the United States, more commonly known as the 9/11 Commission, experienced a few early growing pains until the tricky balance between citizen approval and bureaucratic cover up could be reached. For example, well-known world government loyalist, Henry Kissinger, had to step down as the committee's first Executive Director and control turned over to a lesser known but equally trustworthy, Phillip D. Zelikow, due to some mutterings about Mr Kissinger's personal business relations with the Bin Ladens and other Saudi oil tycoons.[385] Even the normally reliable state dissemination outlet, i.e. the *New York Times,* couldn't hide its shock and dismay over Kissinger's

---

384.) James Corbett, "9/11 Suspects (Full Documentary | 2016)," BitChute video, 1:13:20, Corbett Report Extras, September 4, 2020, https://www.bitchute.com/video/5zvQtc0k9U8/ and James Corbett, "9/11 Suspects (Full Documentary | 2016)," Corbett Report.com, 1:13:20, August 9, 2020, https://www.corbettreport.com/911suspects/

385.) William Walters. "The 9/11 Commission: Secrecy and public inquiry." Ebrary. net. May 3, 2021. https://ebrary.net/139011/political_science_/commission_se-crecy_public_inquiry and Corbett, "9/11 Suspects," 26:19-29:44.

appointment.[386] However, I suppose a group of four intrusive 9/11 widows, who affectionately referred to themselves as the Jersey Girls, left this monolithic news agency no choice but to express apprehension to ole Hank's appointment or risk exposing the entire plot.[387] Their pointed questions forced Mr Kissinger's hand, leaving him no choice but to distance himself from the investigation.

This difficult early inception of the bipartisan study group also produced another alarming setback when patriotic American, Vietnam Veteran and triple amputee, Max Cleland, excused himself from the ten-person panel because he, like six of the final ten members, felt the commission was set up to fail.[388]

Just because the commission may have been slightly underfunded, gently urged along and denied access to certain documents and testimony, there was no need for Mr Cleland to scuttle about yelling the investigation was a scam for crying out loud! The nerve of that feeble-minded double-crosser!

Similarly, former Counter-terrorism Coordinator and warm-hearted apologist, Richard Clarke, didn't have to state 'the fix is in' just because Mr Zelikow graciously stepped in for Mr Kissinger during the committee's dire time of need.[389] This may or may not have incited other barely acknowledged rumblings that Mr Zelikow himself should have been investigated since he was part of the Bush transition team briefed by the Clinton Administration upon entering the White House. Or, that Mr Zelikow should have been a person of interest because he authored the Bush administration's 2002 National Security Strategy that outlined the pre-emptive war doctrine that would be used against Iraq.[390]

Quite successfully, I might add.

'A conflict of interest?' they bemoan. Just beware. There will always be those who'll look to foil a well-thought-out strategy by drawing attention to trivial matters. It's your job as an aspiring ruler over these nettlesome ingrates to ensure they do not succeed.

Anyway, all this finger pointing made absolutely wonderful political theatre. Not only did the real architects behind 9/11 avoid criminal

386.) Corbett, "9/11 Suspects," 27:53-28:17.
387.) Corbett, "9/11 Suspects," 27:20-29:20.
388.) "9/11 Commissioner Sen. Max Cleland on The 9/11 Commission: "It's a scam" (CNN 2003)." The Lawyers' Committee for 9/11 Inquiry. https://www.lawyerscommitteefor9-11inquiry.org/9-11-commissioner-sen-max-cleland-on-the-9-11-commission-its-a-scam-cnn-2003/
389.) Corbett, "9/11 Suspects," 32:33-32:47.
390.) Corbett, "9/11 Suspects," 30:20-33:05.

prosecution due to private, behind-closed-doors, oathless testimonies used with stringent stonewalling, but their peripheral accomplices assisting in the cover-up sidestepped criminal indictments as well.

If this isn't a prime example of showing the world who's boss, I don't know what is. Not only were no government officials arrested because of this star chamber proceeding, not a single one lost their job or was even reprimanded.[391]

That's quite impressive considering the large-scale failure that day and the many following it.

Take, for example, Christine Todd Whitman, who was Administrator of the Environmental Protection Agency (EPA) from 31 January 2001 to 27 June 2003. To exemplify the type of loyalty that's required when completely revising the landscape of not just the most dominant **FARM** on the globe but the entire world itself, look no further than Ms Whitman.

Naturally, when such a tall order is placed, a few casualties must regrettably occur. In the same way, when conducted with a Malthusian mindset, additional pain and suffering should be doled out to bolster a ruling team's wealth and power whilst also reducing an oversized population, if indeed it's necessary. Lingering death, illness and destruction following a national tragedy not only elevates a ruler's strength over their herd but serves as a constant trigger to reignite the initial trauma as well.

The air contained crime scene evidence that emergency personnel, first responders, cleanup crews, downtown workers and residents breathed for days, weeks and months. Unfortunately, two independent, glory seeking researchers covertly gathered some World Trade Center dust for testing that revealed military grade nano-thermite in its contents.[392] Other than that well-suppressed fact, the hazardous residue blanketing the city and its perilous repercussions on those in the vicinity remained secret for a substantial amount of time, thanks to the dependable Ms Whitman.

Despite hazardous levels of toxins like fibreglass, asbestos, mercury, benzene, lead, cadmium, sulphur dioxide and other particulates filling the city air (as discovered by industrial hygienists, USGS scientists and local labs), the EPA, led by Ms Whitman, persevered and convinced the terror-

---

391.) Star chamber: characterized by secrecy and often being irresponsibly arbitrary and oppressive

392.) Editor. "Interview with Dr. Niels Harrit on Discovery of Nano-Thermite in WTC Dust." Foreign Policy Journal. March 7, 2011. https://www.foreignpolicy-journal.com/2011/03/07/interview-with-dr-niels-harrit-on-discovery-of-nano-thermite-in-wtc-dust/

stricken inhabitants to go about their business.[393] The trickiest time for first responders was at the start of the cleanup. Even though they reported health problems such as coughing, wheezing, eye irritation and headaches, team member Whitman calmly stood her ground and helped prevent many from abandoning the area or, at the very least, from taking precautionary measures as they were lured into toxic piles of rubble.[394]

For instance, on 13 September 2001, during an on-camera interview, Ms Whitman vowed: 'We know asbestos was in there. It's in those buildings. Lead is in those buildings. There are the VOC's [Volatile Organic Compounds]. However, the concentrations are such that they don't pose a health hazard.'[395] On 18 September 2001, whilst the EPA and Ms Whitman confidently encouraged the entire city to return to work, including the New York Yankees taking the field for the first time since the attacks, the EPA also detected sulphur dioxide levels in the air so high that, according to one industrial hygienist, they exceeded the EPA's standard for a classification of *hazardous*.[396] Ms Whitman willingly took one for the team that day by confidently stating: 'I am glad to reassure the people of New York that their air is safe to breathe.'[397]

> NOTE: If long-term health problems are expected from any pre-planned or catastrophic event, just be sure to invest and control the industries that will care for the victims. Please revisit Chapter 14 to review how to conceal your involvement in what the pitiful whimpers of the weak may suggest is profiteering.

To further bury the grim atmospheric reality of what New Yorkers were inhaling, when a local lab tested dust samples from near the WTC site and reported the dangerous concentrations of fibreglass and asbestos found in them, the NY State Department of Health warned all local testing centres they'd lose their licences if they processed any more independent samplings.[398] Stripping peasants of their licences is a useful tactic to ensure cooperation and to keep a tight rein on a well-constructed narrative. Remember, rescinding peasants' permission to

393.) Corbett, "9/11 Suspects," 14:47-15:14 and 18:21-19:20.
394.) Corbett, "9/11 Suspects," 17:47-17:55.
395.) Corbett, "9/11 Suspects," 16:31-17:07.
396.) Corbett, "9/11 Suspects," 17:28- 17:47.
397.) Joanna Walters. "Former EPA head admits she was wrong to tell New Yorkers post-9/11 air was safe." The Guardian. September 10, 2016. https://www.theguardian.com/us-news/2016/sep/10/epa-head-wrong-911-air-safe-new-york-christine-todd-whitman
398.) Corbett, "9/11 Suspects," 18:05-18:21.

participate in commerce will leave them economically powerless as well as unable to retrieve all the years of experience and tuition money spent investing in a chosen profession. You'll know you have them when they're more concerned with their own petty self-interests than they are with their fellow man and community. In that regard, perhaps I do share one similarity with these less than fortunate creatures.

Anyway, no matter how many potential health risks were brewing beneath the surface, much like the gold under the Twin Towers,[399] the herd was kept oblivious whilst a literal smokescreen hovered above the city skyline, thanks to the calculated efforts of Ms Whitman and her highly capable team. As an added layer of protection, it's hard for crime scene witnesses to share their personal testimonies when wheezing toxic particulates out of their lungs and struggling with monumental health care costs. As should be quite self-explanatory, especially if you've ever watched a good gangster film or an old spaghetti western, dead men don't talk. It would be quite unfortunate if innocent bystanders had seen something they shouldn't have and met their untimely fate.

Any don worth their weight in gold bars will have a team on standby ready to tie up any loose ends. Quite literally, I might add, for your sadistic pleasure.

The safe air quality facade was successfully carried out until it ran its course and could no longer be upheld. This is when the EPA's own Inspector General, in order to take some heat off of the now fully exposed Ms Whitman, announced in the EPA Evaluation Report on 21 August 2003 that: 'The White House Council on Environmental Quality influenced, through the collaboration process, the information that the EPA communicated to the public through its early press releases when it convinced the EPA *to add reassuring statements and delete cautionary ones.*'[400]

Well, well, well if that's not a startling revelation, I don't know what is.

Fortunately, all necessary precautions were taken by inserting loyal accomplices, who weren't afraid to assert their *authority*, into key damage control roles. Although there were a few setbacks, these accomplices protected the narrative and furthered the plan toward world dominance.

As one sitting on top of the hierarchal pyramid, you must establish a firm chain of command all the way down to the local level. From our

399.) Geoffrey Gray. "Gold, Recovery of." New York Magazine.com. August 26, 2011. https://nymag.com/news/9-11/10th-anniversary/gold/

400.) John Heilprin. "EPA Pressed to Call Air Safe After 9/11, Report Says." The Washington Post. August 23, 2003. https://www.washingtonpost.com/archive/politics/2003/08/23/epa-pressed-to-call-air-safe-after-911-report-says/18553efb-fb3d-47ac-8b7d-fc8b259d7a70/

current discussion, you can see this finely tuned mechanism in action when a seemingly random act by the New York State Department of Health issued its warning to meddling laboratories that were disrupting the handy work of the professionals. Please be forewarned. Unless you have achieved a high position within a well-established and extensive network of closely connected individuals, you should not attempt this type of large-scale operation. However, playing the part of a willing collaborator may be a good starting point for any aspiring ruling class member looking to get their feet wet and their hands dirty.

> NOTE: Clever rulers understand they don't need everyone in on the fix, just the right accomplices in the most suitable positions. As shown by the admission in the EPA Evaluation Report, you must remain appreciative of those willing to do your bidding. We must fully protect these uniquely dark and power-thirsty souls, as they are quite scarce. For if they are not protected, who will stick their neck out for such insidious schemes? A simple act such as vaguely admitting the orders were passed down is the least one could do to shift some of the blame away from an associate under duress. With the government investigation under complete control and no specific names mentioned in the release, who cares if some report reveals a small hint of truth? The ignorant masses would never in a million years read it anyway.

Ms Whitman was not free from difficulties after this EPA report, however. Upset by the innocent but deceptive statements that put their lives in danger, a few agitated residents and workers in the Lower Manhattan and Brooklyn area had the audacity to file a tedious and attention-stirring class action lawsuit in 2004.

An example of a peasant empathiser who attained a prominent position, Deborah A. Batts of the Federal District Court in Manhattan, found that the EPA did, in fact, make 'misleading statements of safety' that 'increased, and may have in fact, created the danger.' By unflinchingly delivering her final bleeding-heart judgment: 'The allegations in this case of Ms Whitman's reassuring and misleading statements of safety after the 11 September 2001 attacks are without question conscience-shocking.'[401] Judge Batts lit the fuse prompting these newly emboldened claimants to stay on the attack. This time they were looking to override Ms Whitman's immunity from prosecution as a federal agent.

401.) Corbett, "9/11 Suspects," 21:12-22:01 and "Judge Blasts EPA Ground Zero Appraisal." CBS News. February 2, 2006. https://www.cbsnews.com/news/judge-blasts-epa-ground-zero-appraisal/

By selecting a panel of less conscionable and exponentially more dependable justices to handle this revolting appeal, these howling pleas were finally laid to rest in 2008 and Ms Whitman's good name rightfully restored.[402]

Whew!

This was quite a feat on its own. However, it was even more refreshing to see the vision predicted by Mr Zelikow, in a 1998 Council on Foreign Relations document, brought to fruition whilst the herd was too startled and shell-shocked to notice the cover-up in the congressional probe and the glaring holes in the official story. For instance, there was the curtailing of all information showing ties between the 9/11 attacks and Saudi Arabia despite the most obvious being that fifteen of the nineteen alleged hijackers were Saudi citizens.

Two more fringe players will lead us to our final talking point regarding what Mr Phillip Zelikow described in 'Catastrophic Terrorism: Tackling the New Danger', a Council on Foreign Relations article published in November 1998.

For a euphoric morale boost to show that even the most sinister of dreams can indeed become reality, I'll present a passage after Phillip, if I may be so bold as to call him Phillip, asked readers to imagine a catastrophic act of terrorism: 'Like Pearl Harbor, the event would divide our past and future into a before and after. The United States might respond with draconian measures scaling back civil liberties, allowing wider surveillance of citizens, detention of suspects and use of deadly force. More violence could follow, either future terrorist attacks or US counterattacks. Belatedly, Americans would judge their leaders negligent for not addressing terrorism more urgently.'[403]

It's interesting to note that Mr Zelikow's grim talk about such a future dystopia bears a striking resemblance to one that the Phoenix Program could graciously accommodate. Fortunately, for today's global lords, the programme was ready for service and all its kinks worked out.

402.) Corbett, "9/11 Suspects," 22:01-22:19 and Anthony DePalma. "Judge Dismisses 9/11 Suit Against Former Head of E.P.A.." The New York Times. April 23, 2008. https://www.nytimes.com/2008/04/23/nyregion/23whitman.html#:~:text=A%20 federal%20appeals%20court%20dismissed%20a%20lawsuit%20against,to%20 breathe%20after%20the%20terrorist%20attack%20in%202001.

403.) Ash Carter, John M. Deutch, Phillip D. Zelikow. "Catastrophic Terrorism: Tackling the New Danger." Harvard Kennedy School: Belfer Center for Science and International Affairs. November/December 1998. https://www.belfercenter.org/ publication/catastrophic-terrorism-tackling-new-danger

Can you think of any greater travesty than to let such an expansive system of control go to waste?

I think any burgeoning ruler would find this clever little snippet from the article incredibly insightful since the post-apocalyptic world that was described with pinpoint accuracy happened just three years later. One worthy of running an entire world empire would, of course, fully utilise such a well-known, myth-creating talent to spearhead any important policies needed to fulfil such a bold vision. If this same originator also possessed the stamina and willingness, why not allow them to run a lopsided investigation to handle any scepticism? Let's explore some slivers of truth so we know what to cover up with unreliable jibber-jabber.

One fringe player was masterfully painted as a treasured American hero because of his courage throughout the 9/11 crisis, but he has a much darker edge than publicly meets the eye. Touting him as a hero in the media made it nearly impossible to accuse him of being a willing collaborator in any treasonous plot to change the American landscape. Mayor Ghouliani, as I like to call him, exquisitely played a brave, compassionate leader for the camera whilst coolly removing the crime scene evidence in plain sight and with open admission. Besides moving 1.5 million tons of debris with 120 dump trucks to the Fresh Kills Landfill on the same night of the attacks whilst selling the steel to Chinese company BaoSteel at friendly, bottom floor prices, the mayor let an even dirtier secret slip out during an ABC News interview with Peter Jennings.[404] The revelation had him candidly admitting he evacuated his temporary headquarters at 75 Barclay Street after being told, 'the World Trade Center was going to collapse.'[405] Being the consummate professional Mr Ghouliani is, he never revealed the source of his *tip* and simply denied the accusation when confronted by a pesky citizen's group, *We Are Change,* after his slip of the tongue.[406] I surely hope that you, as comandante supreme, would see that members of such a brazen outfit as *We Are Change*, whose members questioned officials with blatant indignation, would be tracked and data based for the rest of their pathetic lives. The mayor's honest live media

404.) Corbett, "9/11 Suspects," 4:00-7:32.

405.) Rudy Giuliani interviewed by Peter Jennings, "Rudy Giuliani to Peter Jennings: "We were told the WTC was going to collapse," YouTube video, 4:59, Lawyers' Committee for 9/11 Inquiry, May 3, 2019, https://youtu.be/oCRVovnzD5A

406.) Rudy Giuliani interviewed by Luke Rudowski, Sabrina Rivero and Tom Foti, "WeAreChange Confronts Giuliani on 911 Collapse Lies," YouTube video, 1:47, urWURLDnow, May 29, 2007, https://youtu.be/4n7uJnKGTGg

flub, which contradicted his later testimony at the 9/11 Commission hearing, was never pursued thanks to a tightly monitored investigation with no intent other than to arrive at an agenda serving conclusion. If you need any surer proof, please refer to the excellently composed 9/11 Commission's Final Report.

Please keep in mind, however, when developing a narrative based on a few falsehoods, it's sometimes necessary to reveal a small lie in order to conceal an even bigger one. This is where we'll discuss our last tool for a controlled Tavistock Shock Doctrine event, as it relates to 9/11. To introduce this element, I pose the question, 'What false flag operation would be complete without a cleverly implanted Emergency Exercise?' To understand how this useful and sometimes convenient tactic was uniquely applied on 11 September 2001, a little backstory is necessary.

Whilst there are many excruciating details I could bore you with, I'll cut directly to the chase. In 1999, the Office of Emergency Management (OEM) was moved to the 23rd Floor of World Trade Center Building 7 and was nicknamed *The Bunker* due to the $13 million invested to equip this fortified command centre with its own air and water supply, emergency generators and blast-resistant glass, amongst a plethora of other terrorist-thwarting amenities. A problem arose when one vocal and dearly departed emergency management personnel member, Barry Jennings, arrived at the bunker after the first plane hit the North Tower at 8.46 a.m. Appearing at the bunker just before the second plane hit, Mr Jennings quickly realised that the Operations Center was empty when it should have been bustling with government officials and high-ranking rescue personnel operating their command posts.

Whether America's Mayor was actually at the bunker that memorable morning and was advised to slip out the backdoor or was truly diverted to 75 Barclay Street on his way there is irrelevant. He acknowledged he knew the World Trade Center was going to collapse. Well, of course, you don't want a key associate and his immediate staff in harm's way during such a large-scale humanitarian crisis. Whether Mr Giuliani had an accidental slip of the tongue or if he was, quite ingeniously, delivering a clever misdirection to divert the herd's attention, could indeed spark a lively debate. However, cleverly causing a stir over such a self-incriminating statement, and then coyly retracting it, left the clumsy obviousness of the emergency exercise named Operation Tripod virtually ignored.

A simulated chemical/biological terrorist attack drill based in downtown New York, named Operation Tripod, was conveniently scheduled for 12 September 2001. The gist of the exercise was to simulate a chemical and biological terrorist attack that was to use Pier 92 as its makeshift command centre. Well, especially since the communication equipment and other ever-so-conveniently placed supplies were already situated and at a safe distance from the mayhem, it was only natural that it replaced the then fallen Building 7 as OEM's backup logistical nexus.[407]

Since the explanation of how a building drops to the ground at free fall acceleration is difficult enough, let alone one that was not even struck by an aeroplane, an analysis on the demise of the home of *the Bunker,* Building 7, was also omitted from the final 9/11 Commission Report.[408] Because Building 7 raises more questions than it answers, a healthy dose of grandiose plot ideas from those tortured in captivity mixed with some trumped-up Iraqi involvement in the attacks were ingeniously inserted into the report instead.

I tip my hat to you Mr Zelikow, you crafty old fox. Not one in a million could have masterfully sold it so well.

The second and final fringe player needed for our last talking point, which is that of using emergency drills to accompany a false flag attack, is Commander in Chief of both NORAD and US Space Command, General Ralph Eberhart.[409] To set the tense stage regarding the hijacked airliners on 9/11, we must first mention that in his role as Commander in Chief of US Space Command, General Eberhart was responsible for setting the INFOCON threat level.[410]

Established in March 1999, INFOCON was designed as a measure of threat (1 through 5) to Defense Department computer systems and networks, whereby elevated warning levels required enhanced protocols for securing Department of Defense communications and information

407.) Corbett, "9/11 Suspects," 11:45-12:52 and "Biochemical attack drill scheduled in New York for 12 September." Aldeilis.net. December 29, 2005. https://aldeilis.net/english/biochemical-attack-drill-scheduled-in-new-york-for-12-september/

408.) "The 9/11 Commission Report." https://www.9-11commission.gov/report/911Report.pdf

409.) Kevin Ryan. "The Case Against Ralph Eberhart, NORAD's 9/11 Commander." Foreign Policy Journal. January 16, 2013. https://www.foreignpolicyjournal.com/2013/01/16/the-case-against-ralph-eberhart-norads-911-commander/ and "2015, General Ralph E. "Ed" Eberhart, USAF (ret.)." The American College. https://militaryaffairs.theamericancollege.edu/soldier-citizen-award/award/recipients/2015-general-ralph-e-ed-eberhart-usaf-ret

410.) Elizabeth Woodworth. "General Ralph Eberhart during the 9/11 Attacks." 911Truth.org. February 15, 2015. https://911truth.org/general-ralph-eberhart-911-attacks/ and Corbett, "9/11 Suspects," 53:00-53:40.

systems.[411] Roughly twelve hours before the 9/11 attacks, team member Eberhart set the INFOCON threat level to INFOCON 5 which is the lowest available threat level, giving any would-be *hackers* the best chance of compromising Defense Department systems and controls.[412] Not that anybody could have foreseen such a grisly scenario unravelling as the good General stated during a City Club of Portland speaking engagement on 23 April 2004 when he emphatically declared: 'Many people will talk about that they, they knew that there was going to be an attack. They knew people were going to take over an aircraft and fly it into a building. I can tell ya that there was no credible intelligence, at that time, to go build a defence against that type of an attack. Tragically we were wrong.'[413]

Thankfully, it wasn't only General Eberhart's active role that helped bring this New Pearl Harbor event to fruition, but it was his smooth tongue that helped deflect public criticism in the tumultuous climate that followed. You see, leading up to the 9/11 attacks, NORAD had conducted twenty-eight exercise events involving hijackings between October 1998 and September 2001.[414] At least five of them involved a suicide crash into a high value target and at least six of the exercises took place in American airspace.[415] Such a public declaration obviously, when compared to these active preparations, would nullify the general's position that nobody could have foreseen such a world-changing event unfurling. However, what it did illustrate was the general's unwavering commitment to the *official storyline* of complete surprise.

Speaking of surprises, those from the military and NORAD who were about to take part in Operation Northern Vigilance (part simulation, part real-world activities) and the exercises Global Guardian and Vigilant Guardian, all scheduled on 11 September 2001, were equally confused when reports of a hijacking were first relayed by the FAA's Boston Center.[416] New York Air National Guardsman, Major

411.) Department of Defense. "Information Operations Condition (INFOCON)." public intelligence. July 25, 2009. https://publicintelligence.net/information-operations-condition-infocon/

412.) Woodworth, "General Eberhart during the 9/11 Attacks." and Corbett, "9/11 Suspects," 53:00-53:40.

413.) General Ralph E. "Ed" Eberhart. "Homeland Defense in the Global War on Terrorism." YouTube video, 1:02:45, City Club of Portland, March 2, 2015, https://youtu.be/91WAUorgWVU

414.) Corbett, "9/11 Suspects," 53:00-53:22.

415.) Corbett, "9/11 Suspects," 53:00-53:40.

416.) Katie Lange. "9/11 Air Defense Stories You Might Not Know." Military.com. https://www.military.com/history/911-air-defense-stories-know and Fandom.

Jeremy Powell, was the first person from the military to receive that dreaded call from the Boston Center. Since the hijacking drill to be conducted as part of Vigilant Guardian wasn't supposed to start for another hour, it prompted Major Powell to pose the question: 'Is this real world or exercise?' This ripple effect of ambiguity spread throughout the chain of command, allowing the orchestrators of the real-world event a small amount of extra time to ensure they struck their targets.

The inability to properly track the seized aircraft and generate a valid position for an intercept, along with a few other communication problems, added to the haze of uncertainty and caused crucial delays. I'm not saying that tinkering with computer systems and communication networks regulated under INFOCON threat levels could achieve this, but as an unspoken rule, no one should open this line of questioning, if they know what's good for them. On the other hand, grounding all fighter jets by ordering them to battle stations, rather than ordering them to scramble, certainly provides an advantage to those in unprotected airspace attempting to uninhibitedly reach their targets.[417]

Rather than accept responsibility, and to purposefully confuse those looking to assign blame, General Eberhart did what any smooth conspirator would do. He gave four conflicting versions of his story. If that wasn't clever enough, the good general also pushed responsibility for the delay onto the Federal Aviation Administration, stating it was their reluctance to ask for assistance that prompted the setback.[418] However, in actuality, it's not some obscure policy but official standard operating procedure of NORAD to escort errant, unresponsive and skyjacked aircraft as they did 129 times under General Eberhart in the year 2000 alone.[419]

I hope you're seeing that the ends justify the means, and if you want to build your world empire, you and those you recruit must lie, cheat and steal to do so. Instead of a court martial and subsequent death penalty, Eberhart was given positions in the private sector as chairman and board member of several companies making healthy sums of money from the War on Terror.[420] You'll know you're in your full power when you can achieve a similar level of mastery by pulling off such clean and immeasurable results.

"Global Guardian." Military Wiki. November 2014. https://military-history.fandom.com/wiki/Global_Guardian
417.) Corbett, "9/11 Suspects," 54:54-55:02.
418.) Corbett, "9/11 Suspects," 49:54-50:34.
419.) Corbett, "9/11 Suspects," 50:46-50:57.
420.) Corbett, "9/11 Suspects," 55:25-55:44 and "General Ralph E. "Ed" Eberhart, USAF (Ret.)." SFA. https://ussfa.org/team/general-ralph-e-ed-eberhart-usaf-ret/

To lighten the mood and put the finishing touches on what amounts to a very bleak real-world example, here are a few final suggestions. For one, a false flag attack doesn't have to include only innocent bystanders. If you have a nemesis or someone nipping at your heels from within a government agency, for instance, why not place such a rival in the crosshairs of an attack? As this applies to 9/11, a certain FBI agent named John P. O'Neill became quite the nuisance…a nuisance who had the potential to compromise the entire New Pearl Harbor plot. However, it's nothing a career change and reassignment couldn't fix. Tragically, Mr O'Neill never made it out of his new post and was killed in the North Tower whilst helping others evacuate.[421]

The lessee of the three buildings that collapsed on 9/11, Larry Silverstein, had the divine inspiration to take out an insurance policy that included acts of terrorism just weeks before the attacks.[422] This was also just shortly after being awarded a 99-year lease on the WTC complex for a minimum investment of roughly $15 million.[423] To date, Mr Silverstein, as a token of appreciation for his generous contributions to the cause, has received over $4 billion in insurance settlement money for the three buildings that miraculously collapsed into their own footprint at free fall acceleration.[424]

Valuable and highly visible fluff pieces like the one distributed by Popular Mechanics, *Debunking 9/11 Myths*,[425] are used to conceal these

421.) Frontline. "The Man Who Knew." PBS. October 3, 2002 https://www.pbs.org/wgbh/pages/frontline/shows/knew/ and Stephanie Merry. "He hunted bin Laden – then died in 9/11. Now the FBI legend is the center of a new TV show." The Washington Post. February 23, 2018.
https://www.washingtonpost.com/lifetyle/style/he-hunted-bin-laden--then-died-in-911-now-the-fbi-legend-is-the-center-of-a-new-tv-show/2018/02/22/518f1ec4-1335-11e8-9065-e55346f6de81_story.html
422.) Phil Hirschkorn and Jonathan Wald. "Verdict in 9/11 insurance battle." CNN.com. April 30, 2004. https://www.cnn.com/2004/LAW/04/29/attacks.insurance/index.html
423.) Sean Adl-Tabatabai. "9/11: Larry Silverstein Designed New WTC-7 One Year Before Attacks." September 11, 2001 Research and Archives. August 6, 2017. https://911researcharchives.org/the-luckiest-investor--alive/larry-silverstein-designed-new-wtc-7-one-year-before-attacks/ and Kevin Barrett. "Larry Silverstein, Lewis Eisenberg made billions from destruction of Twin Towers." Veterans Today. January 7, 2019. https://www.veteranstoday.com/2019/01/07/larrys/
424.) Jen Chung. "WTC Insurance Payout Totals $4.55 Billion." Gothamist. March 7, 2008. https://gothamist.com/news/wtc-insurance-payout-totals-455-billion
425.) Popular Mechanics Editors. "Debunking the 9/11 Conspiracy Theories: Special Report – The World Trade Center." Popular Mechanics. September 9, 2022. https://www.popularmechanics.com/military/a6384/debunking-911-myths-world-trade-center/

back door dealings.

Providing peasants with *reasonable* explanations why the laws of physics were suspended that fateful day adds an additional layer of protection for the orchestrators and peripheral accomplices involved. By establishing these types of periodicals as the leading voices in the sciences, peasants will learn to trust whatever paid advertisements are promoted as legitimate investigative research in these highly controlled sources of information.

If you're able to sway all major publications of a *free society* in your favour, you'll also wield enough influence to grant a leader the coveted Nobel Peace Prize, even when this person's first military act as president was to send unmanned drones into the Swat region of Pakistan, where many poor villagers, including four children, were decisively eliminated.[426]

Awarding this esteemed honour to a willing *figurehead* is also a convenient way to provide a hearty chuckle for all the people behind the scenes pulling the levers for this awesome display of power.

By adhering to the principles outlined in this handbook, you too may become one of these deeply influential masters of mayhem.

Well, naturally, with such a looming threat striking fear into the hearts of the populace, the governments of the world had to join forces to protect the innocent civilians who hoot and holler for their overlords to keep them safe. To accomplish this, however, you must know what each peasant is doing at every minute of the day to make sure one of them is not an evil terrorist about to unleash their wrath on humanity. A more than fair compromise, one might say.

Anyway, losing rights, like that of privacy, is a price society must pay to stay safe from some fanatic's heinous actions, wouldn't you agree? Shouldn't governments be granted the authority, even on *free* **FARMS**, to imprison or terminate individuals based on their affiliations and threats to established order? I thought you might like this proposal, especially since you may need to sift out some agitators of your own one day.

History has shown that you can get roughly twenty years' use out

---

426.) Spencer Ackerman. "Interview: Victim of Obama's first drone strike: 'I am the living example of what drones are.'" The Guardian. January 23, 2016. https://www.theguardian.com/world/2016/jan/23/drone-strike-victim-barack-obama and Micah Zenko. "Obama's Final Drone Strike Data." Council on Foreign Relations. January 20, 2017. https://www.cfr.org/blog/obamas-final-drone-strike-data and Muhammad Idress Ahmad. "Death from Above, Remotely Controlled: Obama's Drone Wars." In These Times. July 9, 2015. https://inthesetimes.com/article/drones-andrew-cockburn-kill-chain-chris-woods-sudden-justice

of any deeply traumatising historical event. This also means you must move quickly to implement all your new programmes and policies before the subduing effects of such a life-changing catastrophe wear off. The 11th of September attacks were the perfect ruse to allow the implementation of the Phoenix Program in the United States and in other unchartered areas, but are now a couple of decades behind us. Can you think of an even more sinister enemy that can strike fear at any moment as it mercilessly rips through society, leaving a trail of victims in its wake?

To unite the world into one giant technocratic society run by elite minds like yours, this new foe must be a global threat that endangers the entire human race. This new danger doesn't even have to be a radicalised ideologist or an out-of-control superpower nation. It must, however, deliver a strong enough jolt to the herd that they become more deeply ensnared in the control mechanisms firmly established during the War on Terror. Well, if they want to stay safe, that is.

If you suggested a weaponised virus that can effortlessly move from person to person and nation to nation, you are way ahead of the game and may very well rule the planet one day.

May I propose a toast to your merciless reign!

Chapter 17

THE NEW NORMAL

When a well-packaged web of lies has been sold gradually to the masses over generations, the truth will seem utterly preposterous, and the speaker a raving lunatic.

— Donald James Wheal

As we reach the zenith of this meticulously crafted handbook, I'll attempt to illustrate the transition from a terrorscape to a bioscape using the many techniques presented throughout this tutorial. As we examine the *live exercise* currently taking place, you'll need to view these historic changes with a Malthusian mindset to fully appreciate the consolidation of world power into the hands of a courageous few.

There will be six major human compulsion techniques used in this quiet war against the peasants: fear, flattery, bribery, shame, guilt and force. Each comes with a few effective and sometimes comical examples to illustrate their resounding impact on societal behavioural patterns that have been magnificently sculpted into a *new normal*. Other well-conceived Tavistock terms critical to selling this new narrative include such phrases as social distancing, mask up, contact tracing, fake news, essential worker, flatten the curve, herd immunity, asymptomatic, quarantine, isolation, lockdown, shelter-in-place/stay-at-home, follow the science, super spreader, delta variant, vaccinate, Omicron (a hilarious anagram for moronic) and we're all in this together.

Whether most global citizens are still jittery because of the War on Terror, the threat of Global Warming or any other induced frenzy that's repeatedly broadcast through every media outlet and information network across the globe, the results have never been more astounding. A carefully developed but relatively harmless (in most people) biological pathogen has garnered an inspiring amount of compliance in its inaugural test run. Not only have most peasants overlooked the gain-of-function research admittedly performed in both the US and China, but they have obediently followed all directives issued by authority figures worldwide.

> NOTE: Although it will be discussed in further detail, gain-of-function research means to scientifically alter an organism to gain a function it didn't already have.

First, let's quickly examine the most important part of a panic-inducing phenomenon…the enemy, Covid-19. To delve into the pandemic's origins, we must first revisit America's predominant bioweapon's laboratory, Fort Detrick, Maryland. Despite the 1925 Geneva Protocol prohibiting the use of chemical and biological weapons in war, Camp Detrick, as it was originally known, began offensive bioweapon development in 1943. By 1969, Fort Detrick had around seven germs (publicly admitted to anyway) that were weaponised for warfare.[427]

As I mentioned previously, if certain types of weapons are banned from use in combat, it speaks volumes as to their effectiveness. Of course, if a potential enemy is developing such nefarious agents, you must be prepared to have them at your disposal as well. Or so the peasants should be told.

In 1969, despite eight years of America's use of chemical compounds in Vietnam (an emergency police action) as part of Operation Ranch Hand, President Nixon had a brilliant idea that would ease the American public's disfavour with not just their involvement in Vietnam but with warfare in general. On 25 November 1969, he announced the end of all US offensive biological and chemical weapons programmes via the National Security Decision Memorandum (NSDM 35).[428] Nixon's *Statement on Chemical and Biological Defense Policies and Programs* speech boldly renounced any form of bioweapon that could incapacitate or kill. The speech also promised the easily smitten citizenry that his administration would submit the 1925 Geneva Protocol to the Senate for ratification.[429] This was all a public display meant to demonstrate America's commitment to an atmosphere of peace and understanding between nations.[430]

427.) Dr. Len Horowitz. "In Lies We Trust." 31:02-31:30.

428.) Jonathan B. Tucker and Erin R. Mahan. "President Nixon's Decision to Renounce the US Offensive Biological Weapons Program." NDU Press. https://ndu-press.ndu.edu/Portals/68/Documents/casestudies/CSWMD_CaseStudy-1.pdf

429.) Richard Nixon. "Statement on Chemical and Biological Defense Policies and Programs." 2001-2009 state gov November 25, 1969. https://2001-2009.state.gov/documents/organization/90920.pdf

430.) Nixon. "Statement on Chemical and Biological Defense Policies and Programs."

Just the thought of it makes me want to drink a warm glass of milk, how about you?

However, Mr Nixon earned the nickname Tricky Dick for good reason. Hidden up this ambitious politician's sleeve was not only the wilful intent to continue the programme under a new name, but also to expand it. He cleverly accomplished this by ending all US offensive biological and chemical weapons programmes and, instead, continued research aimed at defending against any foreign nation's biological warfare threats, regardless of their actual existence or likelihood of development.

Can you see the wiggle room this provides?

So, in essence, the change was in name only. The Department of Defense increased the annual budget in biological warfare funding from $21.9 million to $23.2 million the following fiscal year, instead of cutting it. The transition of Fort Detrick from a bioweapon testing facility to a solely defensive NIH run health research lab, which Nixon pledged, never occurred, and the biological weapons remained intact in Pine Bluff, Arkansas.[431]

Instead, advancements in biotechnology were used to clone, mutate and mass produce viruses and other germs and open up the field of retrovirology for such necessary applications as germ warfare and population control.[432]

Although you don't have to possess a doctorate degree in microbiology to rule the world, familiarity with these cutting-edge technologies is important. You must aggressively pursue leading researchers in these highly sought-after specialties.

As a quick synopsis HIV, MERS, EBOLA, SARS-CoV-1, SARS-CoV-2 (the virus that produces the disease known as COVID-19) and certain viruses linked to various cancers (like HTLV-1) all fall under the category of retroviruses because of their RNA as opposed to DNA composition.[433] These retroviruses contain an enzyme called reverse transcriptase that allows the RNA, once it invades a host cell, to produce its own viral DNA and replicate itself inside the gracious suitor whilst often transforming the original host cell's DNA to include

---

431.) Dr. Len Horowitz. "In Lies We Trust." 43:00-43:50.

432.) Dr. Len Horowitz. "In Lies We Trust." 40:03-41:49 and 46:00-46:45.

433.) Mark E.J. Woolhouse and Liam Brierley. "Epidemiological characteristics of human-infective RNA viruses." Nature. February 20, 2018. https://www.nature.com/articles/sdata201817/ and The American Cancer Society medical and editorial content team. "Viruses that Can Lead to Cancer." American Cancer Society. March 31, 2022. https://www.cancer.org/health/cancer-causes/infectious-agents/infections-that-can-lead-to-cancer/viruses.html

its viral intruder.[434] This process occurs more quickly than typical DNA to RNA replication and can overwhelm a victim's immune system, severely disabling or killing him.

It's kind of like launching a microscopic army into a foreign enemy, isn't it?

> NOTE: Some agents strike quickly whilst others wait inside the host until the right biological conditions are met or the right chemical components are introduced, then they launch an attack on an unsuspecting victim.

Is it any surprise the War on Cancer was declared through the National Cancer Act in 1971 just as the defensive biological weapons programme was kicking into high gear? Did Mr Nixon and big industry know something the rest of the world didn't? Mainly, that there would be an avalanche of new cancer cases, thus inspiring his seemingly clairvoyant call for a war on this emerging health crisis.

If you're quick to link the HIV/AIDS outbreak at the end of the 1970s to the burgeoning field of retrovirology enabled in that same decade, you're just some whacky conspiracy theorist starving for attention.

Wink, wink. Of course, this is the type of scarlet lettering that can discredit those challenging your official narratives.

Should you decide to apply a similar extermination method, you can always take comfort in the closely guarded CIA principle of *plausible deniability* or, as I like to say, 'Good luck proving it'.

Plausible deniability is an impeccable defence strategy in cases of biological malfeasance. With the public's attention misdirected after the announcement of NSDM 35, potentially lethal pathogens were revisited, tinkered with and enhanced. Antidotes like vaccines were developed and marketed to *defend* innocent citizens against these viral assailants.[435]

> NOTE: During a health crisis, properly conditioned peasants will readily accept any highly recommended treatment offered to

---

434.) Ian M. Mackay, PhD (EIC). "Human T-Lymphotropic Virus type 1 (HTLV-1): a primer." Virology Down Under." May 17, 2018. https://virologydownunder.com/human-t-lymphotropic-virus-type-1-htlv-1/ and Prabarna Ganguly, PhD.. "Retrovirus." NIH: National Human Genome Institute. January 18, 2023. https://www.genome.gov/genetics-glossary/Retrovirus

435.) Henry A. Kissinger. "NDSM 35." Nixonlibrary.gov. November 25, 1969. https://www.nixonlibrary.gov/sites/default/files/virtuallibrary/documents/nsdm/nsdm_035.pdf

> avoid a horrible fate. An inoculation makes the perfect delivery system to catch the target population off guard and further debilitate them without their knowledge.

A few quick examples will illustrate these Malthusian treatments in action that address one problem whilst creating several others. You'll accumulate wealth through the additional medical services that you and your associates gladly provide whilst also weakening and further reducing your herd.

The first example is the polio vaccine, currently promoted as one of the key justifications for inoculations. The unspoken truth regarding the polio vaccine is that it contained a tumour-causing virus, Simian Virus 40 or SV40. This virus came from infected monkey kidneys that were used to nurture the polio virus for the vaccine.[436] The modest projected years of infection from SV40 via the polio jab are 1955 to 1963, although some estimates go back as far as 1952. A mother can pass this tumour-inducing virus through childbirth as once commonly admitted by even the American Center for Disease Control and Prevention (CDC) on their website.[437] However, with all the accusation pointed at such agenda-friendly institutions, a wise ruler must demand that such incriminating statements be immediately withdrawn from public view.

Additionally, forty thousand inoculated children were sickened with polio through the Cutter Incident. This occurred in 1955 when Cutter Laboratories failed to inactivate the poliovirus, leaving two hundred children paralysed and ten dead. As a result, Albert Sabin's

---

436.) Tam Dang-Tan, Salaheddin M. Mahmud, Ricardo Puntoni, Eduardo L. Franco. "Polio vaccines, Simian Virus 40, and human cancer: the epidemiologic evidence for a casual association." Nature. August 23, 2004. https://www.nature.com/articles/1207877 and Michael E. Horwin, M.A., J.D.. Simian Virus 40 (SV40): A Cancer Causing Monkey Virus from FDA-Approved Vaccines." SV40 Cancer Foundation. 2003. https://www.sv40foundation.org/cpv-link/

437.) Elisa Mazzoni, Elena Pellegrinelli, Chiara Mazziotta, Carmen Lanzillotti, John Charles Rotondo, Illaria Bononi, Maria Rosa Iaquinta, Marco Manfrini, Fortunato Vesce, Mauro Tognon, Fernanda Martini. "Mother-to-child transmission of oncogenic polyomaviruses BKPyV, JCPyV and SV40." PubMed.gov. February 22, 2020. https://pubmed.ncbi.nlm.nih.gov/32097686/ and "CDC Admits 98 Million Americans Were Given Cancer Virus Via The Polio Shot." TigerDroppings. February 11, 2021. https://www.tigerdroppings.com/rant/politics/cdc-admits-98-million-americans-were-given-cancer-virus-via-the-polio-shot/95051818/ and CDC. Cancer, Simian Virus 40 (SV40), and Polio Vaccine Fact Sheet." Internet Archive Wayback Machine. March 7, 2011-January 6, 2023 https://web.archive.org/web/20120508130224/https://www.cdc.gov/vaccinesafety/updates/archive/polio_and_cancer_factsheet.htm

even more dangerous ingestible vaccine, which reactivated the virus whilst passing through the stomach, replaced Jonas Salk's injection. Sabin's oral vaccine continued to infect recipients into the 1990s.[438]

That's what I call progress.

> NOTE: When looking to introduce a vaccine for an established disease, be sure that the illness is rapidly declining within the human herd if not at its tail end. This will help provide the illusion that the vaccine is the reason for the eradication of the disease.

This next well-kept secret is surely one you don't want to go blabbering on about at social gatherings with the common folk, as it will raise gut wrenching cries of disbelief followed by contempt from devout Big Pharma disciples. Such a reckless act would certainly forfeit your hard-earned control over the herd's compromised health and well-being.

Anyhow, let me ask you this. How did Africa end up with strictly heterosexual cases of HIV whilst America witnessed predominantly homosexuals and drug users as the infected demographic? What if I implied that someone deliberately targeted these populations with the disease? Once again, by sneaking a positive-test-producing agent into smallpox injections in Africa, and Hepatitis B vaccines in the major American cities of New York, Los Angeles and San Francisco, two different targeted populations were adversely affected by the same stigma.[439] If you, my aspiring emperor-in-the-making, are new to this privileged information, it may be difficult to accept. However, for more proof of this bold claim, simply consider the contaminated haemophilia factor VIII blood-clotting agents that were manufactured by Bayer AG.

When the company was caught peddling tainted medicine that was discreetly spreading HIV to haemophiliacs, the company simply pushed the factor VIII agent on to poorer countries, unloaded their stockpiles and recouped some of their production costs whilst spreading the disease related microbes to more unsuspecting victims.[440] Of course, a neatly packaged statement announcing reassuring words to the world that the

---

438.) Michael Fitzpatrick. "The Cutter Incident: How America's First Polio Vaccine Led to a Growing Vaccine Crisis." Journal of the Royal Society of Medicine. March 2006. https://www.ncbi.nlm.nih.gov/pmc/articles/PMC1383764/

439.) Dr. Alan Cantwell, "Dr. Alan Cantwell – AIDS and the Doctors of Death – Part 1," YouTube video, 21:41, Yipppe, February 25, 2017, https://youtu.be/6-BIE9d-WqWU

440.) Suzanne Goldenberg. "Bayer division 'knowingly sold' HIV-infected protein." The Guardian. May 23, 2003. https://www.theguardian.com/world/2003/may/23/aids.suzannegoldenberg

company had 'always behaved responsibly, ethically, and humanely' was all peasants required to keep them from prying into the matter any further.

It really is that easy once you have attained absolute power.

> NOTE: If you can gently lead your herd into accepting that drug companies and their ancillary arms such as pharmacies, hospitals and well-trained practitioners may induce iatrogenic deaths amongst the populace in order to *save lives,* you'll eliminate suspicion. Using the *health care system* to profit whilst providing lifesaving and beneficial services will help establish a benevolent front. This compassionate veneer will allow you to dole out even more suffering and casualties through *treatment options* that inconspicuously conceal your more mischievous intentions.

Our last grand but, unfortunately, short-lived delivery system example took place during the 1976 Swine Flu outbreak. Private David Lewis died on a military base at Fort Dix, New Jersey when he was ordered to participate in a forced march despite feeling ill. Thirteen others were hospitalised which kicked off a fear-driven propaganda campaign that propelled forty-six million Americans to roll up their sleeves and take a wonderfully devious experimental vaccine.[441] Regrettably, the well-established side effects, known to some researchers even before the vaccinations were administered, quickly became public knowledge after five hundred known cases of Guillain-Barré Syndrome quickly surfaced and resulted in at least twenty-five deaths.[442]

Sadly, the vaccination campaign was abruptly ended after only ten short weeks, and as many as four thousand Americans filed claims for vaccine damages against the federal government.[443] As a historical footnote, this pesky liability issue would need to be fully flushed out to protect future pandemic orchestrators and their creatively earned profits.

441.) Mike Wallace, "60 Minutes: Swine Flu (1976)," YouTube video, 15:45, The University, March 12, 2020, https://youtu.be/4bOHYZhL0WQ

442.) Shari Roan. "Swine Flu 'debacle' of 1976 is recalled." Los Angeles Times. April 27, 2009. https://www.latimes/archives/la-xpm-2009-apr-27-sci-swine-history27-story.html

443.) Roan, "Swine Flu 'debacle.'" And Wallace, "60 Minutes: Swine Flu (1976)," 0:00-0:47.

NOTE: Before the first official shipments of Swine Flu vaccines were delivered to state health departments in late September of 1976, someone purposefully spread an unnamed bacteria through the vents of the Bellevue-Stratford Hotel in Philadelphia on 21 July 1976, adding to the Swine Flu hysteria.

I beg you don't breathe a word of this to anyone. Russian defector Sergei Popov developed this unknown biological agent. When he exposed rabbits to this mysterious pathogen, the cause of death could not be determined.[444] It was perfect! The goal was to trick investigators into thinking the dreaded Swine Flu caused the atypical pneumonia that developed a few days after inhaling this bioweapon. Unfortunately, no link to the Swine Flu could be established. However, since the one hundred and eighty-two cases resulting in twenty-nine deaths were traced back to the Bellevue-Stratford in Philadelphia where the American Legion member victims were attending a three-day bicentennial conference, the new illness became known as Legionnaires' disease. If these early trial runs were to prove one thing, it's that much more work needed to be done to successfully pull off a global pandemic with as few glitches as possible.

I should add that there's a critical connection between the 1976 Swine Flu outbreak and our next biological false flag operation tip, i.e. releasing an agent on a military base or near a biological research facility. This strategy will ensure the disease's release whilst also giving you total control over the narrative of its origin.

In our Swine Flu example, the virus first appeared at the Fort Dix Army Post near Trenton, New Jersey. Other noteworthy leaks include the Spanish Flu of 1918, the anthrax mailings in 2001 and early cases of tick-borne Lyme disease first identified around Long Island Sound, where the US military's Plum Island animal research lab is cozily nestled.[445].

We must take a hard look at gain-of-function research. As a buildup to the current *live exercise* taking place, we'll focus on this advanced form of experimentation as it pertains to retroviruses like HIV, SARS,

444.) Dr. Len Horowitz. "In Lies We Trust." 1:06:09-1:07:52.

445.) History.com Editors. "First Cases reported in deadly 1918 Flu Pandemic." History.com. March 3, 2021. https://www.history.com/this-day-in-history/first-cases-reported-in-deadly-influenza-epidemic and Dr. Len Horowitz. "In Lies We Trust." 1:26:07-1:29:54 and Melissa Dykes. "The Officially Ignored Connection Between Lyme Disease and Plum Island." Truth Comes to Light. September 9, 2017. https://truthcomestolight.com/the-officially-ignored-connection-between-lyme-disease-and-plum-island/

MERS, EBOLA and SARS-CoV-2 that have all come into existence since the enactment of NSDM 35. To the common, uninformed peasant, the emergence of these lethal animal viruses making a deadly leap into their unsuspecting human hosts can seem like a random occurrence. However, to the expert virologist these things just don't happen, they're made to happen. This is where gain-of-function research comes into play.

So that the definition is understandable to even the least scientific-minded oppressor of humanity-in-the-making, gain-of-function research can be described as genetically altering microorganisms (such as bat, monkey or pangolin viruses) to increase certain biological functions like transmissibility, virulence and host tropism (the type of host or host tissue a pathogen can infect).[446] Some of this can be accomplished by applying *selective pressure* to a culture.

HA! It appears the malleable peasant is not the only lower life form able to be manipulated by outside pressures. Science has now found a way to do it on a microscopic level!

I'm so excited I could belt out a scream eerily reminiscent of a young child stuffed inside of a small crate filled with snakes and insects![447]

Oh! Well, ah, oh my. Um…ah. Pardon me whilst I compose myself for a moment.

Ah. Where were we? Ah, yes.

Let's return once again to the Dark Continent to discuss this popular experimental germ release destination where deadly pathogens can be released, studied and hopes for a cure explored. Where else could you conduct controversial test runs of potentially fatal microorganisms and their often harmful but somewhat medicinal and profitable treatments if not on an uncivilised society that can't get out of its own way? I trust this information will remain between us, of course.

If you feel buyer's remorse for the purchase of this handbook, let me shed some light on the African population's enduring history as human guinea pigs.

446.) Neha Mathur. "What is Gain-of-Function Research?" Medical.net. September 4, 2022. https://www.news-medical.net/health/What-is-Gain-of-Function-Research.aspx#:~:text=Gain-of-function%20research%20%28GOFR%29%20refers%20to%20the%20serial%20passaging.tropism%20by%20applying%20selective%20pressure%20to%20a%20culture .

447.) Ian Leslie, "Teresa's escape from brutal 'satanic cult' and bizarre rituals (1989) | 60 Minutes Australia," YouTube video, 18:33, 60 Minutes Australia, August 4, 2020, https://youtu.be/c2ioRBNriG8

As far back as 1906, when a vector-borne parasitic disease called Trypanosomiasis (a.k.a. sleeping sickness) caused apathy, slow movement, speech disorders, physical weakness, and death in its victims, and threatened to cripple both the European and African workforces, immediate action was required. There were great profits at risk, I'll have you know. That's when 1905 Nobel Prize winner Robert Koch made his way to the German colonies of East Africa to set up his Bugula sleeping sickness research camp. At the Bugula camp, he lined up one thousand test subjects each day and administered a concoction called Atoxyl, a reagent containing arsenic. Early test runs achieved little success in taming the parasite, but did cause pain, blindness and death in his test subjects.[448]

Similarly, we can fast forward to 1981 when the apartheid government launched Project Coast in South Africa as part of its newly established biological and chemical weapons programme. Besides such common objectives as assassination and suppression of internal dissent, Project Coast's more secretive purpose was racial warfare with an emphasis on the sterilisation of Blacks.[449] Project Coast's history is quite interesting and well worth your own further study. The purpose in bringing all this up, however, is to drive home the point that there's a need for societal sacrifices when it comes to the overall benefit of humanity. Vulnerable, undeveloped and defenceless sectors of the population make the perfect offerings.

It's the same for a herd of wildebeests, for crying out loud. The weak are discarded for the good of the whole. We're not monsters; we're men of reason.

Finally, if I don't keel over from a stroke after having to passionately justify and defend a standard ruling class position, I have set the stage for the Ebola outbreak of 2014.

A few noteworthy details demand your full attention. The first, and no surprise, is that US government agencies have a long history of carrying out *defensive biological research* at laboratories in Liberia and

---

448.) Edna Bonhomme. "When Africa was a German laboratory: Western scientists transformed Africa into a living laboratory during the sleeping sickness epidemics of the early 20th century. They should not be allowed to do the same now." Aljazeera. October 6, 2020. https://www.aljazeera.com/opinions/2020/10/6/when-africa-was-a-german-laboratory

449.) Miles Jackson. "A Conspiracy to Commit Genocide: Anti-Fertility Research in Apartheid's Chemical and Biological Weapons Programme." Journal of International Criminal Justice. November 14, 2015. https://academic.oup.com/jicj/article/13/5/933/2411996

Sierra Leone. Liberia, Sierra Leone and neighbouring Guinea were at the epicentre of the deadliest Ebola outbreak in recorded history where over ten thousand Africans lost their lives.[450]

Thankfully, the Department of Defense had awarded a $140 million contract to the Canadian pharmaceutical company, Tekmira, to conduct Ebola research just weeks before the fatal West African outbreak. This initial clinical trial included injecting healthy humans with the deadly Ebola virus, who could then be treated with an experimental medicine called TKM-Ebola.[451] Ah. What perfect timing in a world of seemingly random events. By cooking up a slightly modified version of the drug (affectionately named TKM-Ebola-Guinea and funded by our altruistic friends at Wellcome Trust) to specifically target this new strain of the virus, the emerging pharmaceutical got to prove its worth in a real-world crisis and increased its market value.[452]

I'm astounded by how closely the sound of ringing tills resembles the blast of a mighty trumpet.

Fiercely trusted associate from the world of disease, Dr Anthony Fauci, in his speech entitled, *The Ebola Outbreak 2014-2015: The Perfect Storm*, presented at the American Society for Microbiology Biodefense Meeting on 11 February 2015, was an exquisite slideshow master class. The gifted orator passionately covered the outbreak from A to Z, including the first case, when he sympathetically acknowledged the young boy who contracted the disease by touching an infected fruit bat.[453]

450.) Clement Kpeklitsu. "US Bio-Warfare Work in Africa." Modern Ghana. July 18, 2017. https://www.modernghana.com/news/788788/us-bio-warfare-work-in-africa.html

451.) Kpeklitsu, US Bio-Warfare Work in Africa." And Miles Udland. "Tekmira Shares Turn Negative After Rallying On Hopes For Ebola Drug." Insider. August 4, 2014. https://www.businessinsider.com/tekmira-pharmaceuticals-ebola-treatment-2014-8?op=1

452.) Kate Kelland. "Trial of Tekmira's TKM-Ebola treatment starts in Sierra Leone." Reuters. March 11, 2015. https://www.reuters.com/article/us-health-ebola-tekmira-idUSKBN0M71JV20150311 and Gretchen Vogel. "In setback for potential Ebola drug, company halts trial: Human tests of TKM-Ebola-Guinea stopped early." Science. June 19, 2015. https://www.science.org/content/article/setback-potential-ebola-drug-company-halts-trial and Matt Egan. "As Ebola spreads, drug stocks surge." CNN Business. October 1, 2014. https://money.cnn.com/2014/10/01/investing/ebola-drug-stocks-pharmaceuticals-outbreak-tekmira/index.html and CBS/AP. "FDA lifts hold on experimental Ebola drug from Tekmira." CBS News. August 8, 2014. https://www.cbsnews.com/news/fda-lifts-hold-on-experimental-ebola-drug-tekmira/

453.) Dr. Anthony S. Fauci, "The Ebola Outbreak of 2014-2015: A Perfect Storm." YouTube video, 27:11, American Society for Microbiology, March 15, 2016, https://youtu.be/hB9DLmmKRs8

Ha! Not one person in the modern world would dare question such a farfetched story that allegedly takes place in an area where people are cleverly depicted as primal savages.

The good doctor also clarified that the retrovirus could only be spread by bodily fluids like vomit and diarrhoea and also during the traditional burial procedures, which he lovingly described as a beautiful local tradition but the perfect storm for spreading infection.[454] He even slipped in a clownish picture of himself in a biohazard suit to add a bit of laughter to his otherwise daunting speech.[455]

Now for the truth of the matter.

If the doctor of death were to give it to you straight, he'd tell you that Africa, with its rich history of human experimentation and careful placement of American bioweapons laboratories along the Ebola beltway, was the real perfect storm. A perfect storm that allowed a test run of an outbreak that coincided with the development of a new drug by a Wellcome-backed company to treat this same doomsday virus. The African continent makes the perfect human laboratory, as its primitive people are accustomed to suffering, civil strife and disease.

If a plague of biblical proportions were to empty this resource-rich paradise of its inhabitants, proper Anglo-American empire expansion, necessary for the well-being of any dominant society, could effectively take place. Three thousand plus US troops were dispatched to perform command and control logistics and engineering operations, which included constructing Ebola treatment facilities as well as identifying and tracking potential contagious carriers through contact tracing.[456]

Practice makes perfect as we shall soon see.

> NOTE: Please remember, there should be valid clinical trials to test the efficacy of all potential remedies in the event you, your offspring, your loved ones or your trusted associates accidentally become infected. Once a countermeasure for a disease is firmly secured, you can consider spreading the pathogen through a purposeful or accidental release, a recommended treatment, a purposeful mishandling of the situation or any combination thereof. Remember, when you create a problem, you can then offer the solution which, if you've understood this handbook correctly, further weakens the peasants' condition whilst generously padding your heavily guarded underground vault.

454.) Fauci, "The Ebola Outbreak: A Perfect Storm." 5:20-6:27 and 15:00-15:21.
455.) Fauci, "The Ebola Outbreak: A Perfect Storm." 19:43-20:17.
456.) Fauci, "The Ebola Outbreak: A Perfect Storm." 15:20-16:19.

The AIDS epidemic, as discussed in Chapter 14, was part of a PPP (Potential Pandemic Pathogen) operation in which Dr Fauci, as head of the National Institute of Allergy and Infectious Disease (NIAID), got his feet wet as a dependable front man in the growing field of drug assisted suicide. By pushing the Burroughs Wellcome immunosuppressant drug AZT on those with compromised immune systems,[457] Dr Fauci showed he could brush off criticism whilst offering a lethal treatment with a hearty dose of sincerity and reassurance. This, whilst never revealing the true nature or origins of the developing retroviruses threatening the existence of much of humanity. In the world of organised crime, they refer to this as loyalty. It's a rare trait, and individuals who demonstrate it for the overarching goals of World Empire should be reassigned to similar roles when necessary. It's obvious that they should also be highly rewarded and protected at all costs.

It's now time to tie a few crucial pieces of the puzzle together so we can finally leapfrog into today's fear inducing, compliance gaining and wealth transferring *live exercise*. The Ebola release in 2014 coincides with the exact time period that helps shape our current state of affairs.

You see, the original SARS-CoV-1 virus that appeared suddenly in China in 2002 sent a bit of a shock wave through the modern world. It firmly established that severe respiratory viruses like SARS-CoV-1 have short-lived transmission periods (eight months in 2002-2003). This is because lethal pathogens efficiently kill their hosts and after enough instances, prevents further passage. The trail of bodies also makes their path easier to identify and hence contain. A respiratory virus will linger longer if it's milder, as the same host who is not incapacitated can pass it multiple times. Since this is a disease axiom, I ask you, aspiring-ruler-of-all-humanity, is there a way to strengthen the impact of a mild disease if, indeed, a lethal disease cannot be developed to competently incapacitate a large enough percentage of the entire world?

I pose this question simply to challenge you to constantly think outside the box.

A mysterious outbreak of SARS-CoV-1 first appeared in 2002 and again in April 2004 when two careless graduate students working with the virus at China's National Institute of Virology in Beijing became infected. For a decade after these leaks—oops—I mean occurrences, there was a frenzied effort to create a vaccine to stop this deadly respiratory disease in case it should ever again slip past the confines

457.) *Banks, Aids, Opium, Diamonds, and Empire*, 255.

of a highly secure and extremely well-regulated bioweapons research facility.[458]

Truly, I jest.

So, in 2012, a clinical trial was finally set up to test a highly anticipated vaccine for SARS-CoV-1. The results seemed promising… at first. But, like another respiratory vaccination experiment on fragile living creatures gone awry, things went a little bonkers after antibody production was achieved on the test subjects. I'm referring to the 1966 Respiratory Syncytial Virus (RSV) vaccine that was tested on a small group of children and caused quite an embarrassment when 80% of the thirty-five participating youngsters were hospitalised and two toddlers died from the aftereffects of the jab.[459]

Unlike the RSV vaccine, the SARS-CoV-1 vaccine was first tested on animals for obvious reasons. Unfortunately, the results were the same. Antibodies formed and stopped the infection of SARS-CoV-1, but hypersensitivity to the wild virus caused an immune system imbalance leaving it vulnerable to certain components of the pathogen that wreaked havoc on the test subjects. Due to this disappointing discovery, caution in proceeding to the application of a SARS-CoV-1 vaccine in humans was advised.[460]

It's natural to feel a healthy dose of empathy for the microbiologists who felt they finally had it right. However, to the World Conqueror, these results could not have been more satisfying. We shall soon discover why.

Ferrets are an excellent choice when pursuing gain-of-function research in respiratory diseases because of similarities between ferrets' and humans' lung physiology, viral transmission methods and cellular receptor distribution. Also, like humans, these weaselly creatures emit a foul stench when excited or afraid, come in a variety of colours and are known to kill their own babies.[461] However, even though ferrets

458.) Robert Roos. "China confirms two more SARS cases." CIDRAP. April 29, 2004. https://www.cidrap.umn.edu/sars/china-confirms-two-more-sars-cases

459.) Patricio L. Acosta, Mauricio T. Caballero, Fernando P. Polak. "Brief History and Characterization of Enhanced Respiratory Syncytial Virus Disease." ASM Journals. March 7, 2016. https://journals.asm.org/doi/10.1128/CVI.00609-15

460.) Chien-Te Tseng, Elena Sbrana, Naoko Iwata-Yoshikawa, Patrick C. Newman, Tania Garron, Robert L. Atmar, Clarence J. Peters, Robert B. Couch. "Immunization with SARS coronavirus vaccines leads to pulmonary immunopathology on challenge with the SARS virus." PubMed.gov. April 20, 2012. https://pubmed.ncbi.nlm.nih.gov/22536382/

461.) Karin Lehnardt. "45 Furry Ferret Facts." Fact Retriever. December 8, 2016. https://www.factretriever.com/ferret-facts

were one of the animal species enlisted for their honourable role in the SARS-CoV-1 vaccine experiments, they were at the centre of controversy during a 2012 research project. It was years of committed exploration that led to the creation of highly pathogenic, H5N1 (avian) influenza virus strains that became airborne transmissible between these furry varmints who take great pleasure in stealing and hiding things. Perhaps it was all the critter mischief wreaking havoc in the laboratory that prompted the National Science Advisory Board for Biosecurity (NSABB) to launch their cautionary report entitled 'White Paper Gain-of-Function Research: Ethical Analysis' citing instances of biosafety mishaps involving anthrax, smallpox and H5N1 in government research centres. Whether it was out-of-control lab animals or lackadaisical scientists, this scathing review points out the Obama administration's pause in funding for gain-of-function (gof) experiments involving influenza, SARS, and MERS viruses in particular.[462] However, it's a global leader's responsibility to turn a setback into an even greater opportunity.

Since the controversial gain-of-function experiments were no longer welcome in the United States, it was time to find a more suitable host country that would overlook human rights concerns and Convention on Biological Weapons' regulations. The People's Republic of Communist China fit perfectly, providing a template for the ideal totalitarian *technocratic society* to be imposed upon the rest of the world.

'But what is a technocratic society?' you eagerly ponder.

A technocratic society abolishes old democratic pricing mechanisms like supply and demand and turns over resource allocation to self-appointed rulers (like you and your team) who've mastered the art of engineering societies for personal profit. Imagine a world where artificial intelligence replaces unnecessary humans whilst high-speed data is exchanged, gathered and stored in real time for the remaining workers who are carefully monitored by digital surveillance. As overlord of this system, you can then dictate which resources companies may use, at what times and for what purposes, whilst the spared peasants are told what to buy and when.[463] With the Earth's resources under your control, the need for elected bureaucratic middlemen would be outdated. If the peasants don't like it, you can simply shut them off or deny them access to basic living essentials.

462.) Professor Michael Selgelid. "White-Paper Gain-Of-Function Research: Ethical Analysis." NIH.gov. 2016. https://osp.od.nih.gov/wp-content/uploads/2016/09/Gain-of-Function_Research_Ethical_Analysis.pdf
463.) Mercola and Cummins, The Truth About COVID-19, 45.

Remember, he who has the gold (and all the planet's resources) makes the rules.

If you're at all upset that a trustworthy world leader like America handed over its gain-of-function research to its alleged enemy, Communist China, you're still thinking like a peasant. If you recall from Chapter 5, orchestrators can use corporations as clever disguises to mask illicit activity. This allows them to not only operate a laboratory or any other legal fiction in a foreign land, but also to shroud cartel members, including private, hidden board of directors of the incorporated foreign land itself. With China's oppressive and monolithic power structure already firmly established, it makes the perfect location to launch a full-scale Trojan horse attack on humanity. Boisterous whistleblowers can more easily disappear, and its iron fisted government, universally accepted for its authoritarian actions, can bring investigations to an abrupt end. Can you imagine an investigative team sent to the Middle Kingdom to uncover the details of a laboratory leak? They'd be lucky to make it out alive. Certainly, a government investigation initiated by any inquisitive nation would lead to nowhere with no apologies or excuses.

There are other practical reasons to launch a widespread biological attack on such a fertile human breeding ground. China's oversized and tightly packed population centres create the perfect environment for deadly contagions to spread amongst the weaker and less desirable portions of the global population. Although the 2002-2004 SARS-CoV-1 outbreaks in China appear to be a failed dress rehearsal compared to today's wonderfully synchronised pandemic, that early trial run provided valuable insight into what it takes to conduct a successful worldwide biological warfare campaign. China, with its marvellous top-to-bottom oppressive command structure, proved to be an excellent ground zero despite some early hitches.

By judiciously applying the State Secrets Law as it pertains to the handling of public health related information, media outlets and local officials had to be careful about what they could say and not say regarding the atypical pneumonia first appearing in Guangdong, China in November 2002. Using the National People's Congress session due to convene in March 2003 as an excuse to underplay the emerging situation, the disease was given every opportunity to catch fire until the World Health Organization finally felt enough time had passed to hit the global panic button on 15 March 2003. This is when the presence of a fatal respiratory disease known as SARS was hauntingly announced to the world.[464]

464.) Yanzhong Huang. "The SARS Epidemic and its Aftermath in China: A Political Perspective." NIH National Library of Medicine. 2004. https://www.ncbi.nlm.nih.

If only the pathogen had been contagious enough to infect others more efficiently and virulently. What in evil's name would it take?

Also stalling as much as possible was the Chinese Center for Disease Control and Prevention.

Hmm, sounds quite similar to the US Centers for Disease Control and Prevention, doesn't it? Perhaps it was their intimate and longtime collaboration that inspired the name.

The Chinese Center for Disease Control and Prevention did not issue a nationwide bulletin to hospitals on how to prevent the ailment from spreading until 3 April 2003, nearly five months after the initial case. Finally, in mid-April, the government listed SARS as a disease to be closely monitored and reported on daily.[465]

Of course, it was also around that time when about a thousand government officials were reprimanded or removed from their posts because of their blatant mishandling of the crisis. This, despite being put in a position where if they initially spoke about the outbreak, they could've been arrested for violating the State Secrets Law.

Remember, when it's a lose-lose situation for peasants, it's a win-win for their ruler.

Not wanting to appear complacent once disciplinary actions started, local administrators began enforcing every Draconian measure imaginable to prove to their overlords they could execute the will of the **STATE**. The possibility of imposing strict medical protocols on the entire world sparked a firestorm of determination amongst global lords that continues to this day.

'But could these measures be imposed on the global level and, most importantly, on a *free society* like America?'

It's funny you should ask. Along with all the Project For A New American Century legislation rushed through Congress after 9/11 was the Model State Emergency Health Powers Act, passionately promoted by the Bush administration.[466] This legislation was drafted at the request of the US Centers for Disease Control and Prevention and was distributed to US state legislatures for review and approval on 21 December 2001, only three months after 9/11.[467]

---

gov/books/NBK92479/

465.) Huang. "The SARS Epidemic and its Aftermath in China."

466.) Twila Brase, R.N.. "A Model for Medical Tyranny." Foundation for Economic Education. August 1, 2002. https://fee.org/articles/a-model-for-medical-tyranny/

467.) Faith Lagay, PhD. "The Proposed Model State Emergency Health Powers Act." AMA Journal of Ethics. May 2004. https://journalofethics.ama-assn.org/article/proposed-model-state-emergency-health-powers-act/2004-05

Of course, there were a few nosy parkers whinging that the act was prime for abuse due to the tremendous power this new law granted individual states. They also rambled on about how it went beyond the scope of addressing bioterrorism whilst disregarding the medical privacy standards they had grown accustomed to. All because it permitted state governors in any health crisis to impose quarantines, limit people's movements and ration medicine whilst granting them full authority to seize anything from dead bodies to private hospitals.[468]

Well, truth be told, they weren't exactly wrong. But regardless, it's just a small price to pay for, well...ah...safety? If they knew what was good for them.

Are you beginning to see the pattern here? With all the unfathomable horror paralysing the publics' sensibilities, in hindsight, there could not have been a more ideal time to slip these stringent new health guidelines past the knee knocking herd.

You know, just in case they were ever needed. Like, for instance, in the event of a pandemic that coincidentally materialised less than a year after these strongly encouraged changes began circulating or maybe, at some later time, after people had long forgotten the legislation had been enacted in the first place.

> NOTE: Please remember from our Burning of the Reichstag conversation in Chapter 10 that, if you don't want to break the law as a ruler, you must change the laws prior to your corrective actions so that your necessary but controversial deeds are justifiable and legal. You can always use a state of emergency to your advantage and, as part of the refreeze process, you'll want to legislate your new normal into existence whilst society is still at the mercy of authority due to heightened fear levels.

Since the NIH website explains China's overreaction to the SARS outbreak of the early 2000s much better than I ever could, I'll affectionately hand over the microphone. 'Driven by political zeal, they sealed off villages, apartment complexes and university campuses, quarantined tens of thousands of people and set up checkpoints to take temperatures. By 7 May 2003, eighteen thousand people had been quarantined in Beijing. The Maoist *Patriotic Hygiene Campaign* was

---

468.) Sue Blevins. "The Model State Emergency Health Powers Act: An Assault on Civil Liberties in the Name of Homeland Security." The Heritage Foundation. June 10, 2002. https://www.heritage.org/homeland-security/report/the-model-state-emergency-health-powers-act-assault-civil-liberties-the and Lagay, "The Proposed Model State Emergency Health Powers Act."

revitalised. In Guangdong, eighty million people were mobilised to clean houses and streets. In the countryside, virtually every village was on SARS alert, with roadside booths installed to examine all those who entered or left.'[469]

However, their strict emphasis on *science*[470] made government officials in the twenty-first century much more effective in executing authoritarian policies than the late Yale protégé, Mao Zedong.

'Increasing pressure from higher authorities easily created a results-orientation structure that made non-scientific, heavy-handed measures more appealing to local government officials. They found it safer to be overzealous than to be seen as *soft*. Until 2 June 2003, for example, Shanghai was quarantining people from the regions hard hit by SARS (such as Beijing) for ten days even if they had no symptoms.'[471]

Can you feel my elation building? I'm so excited, I could shed deadly pathogens everywhere!

Finally, and the last positive to be retrieved from what I'm sure will ring bells of familiarity in your ears, was the *Beijing Morning News* article run on 12 May 2003. This public notice served as a dire warning to people spreading rumours about SARS, informing them they could be jailed for up to five years for delivering misinformation, even though these Chinese citizens were simply relaying mainstream news received through the Internet. Indeed, an immediate follow up speech by Vice Premier, Wu Yi, reiterated the **STATE'S** control over the media to 'strictly prohibit the spread of rumours and other harmful information.'[472]

Surely, if even a few of these overbearing tactics could be imposed on a *free* **FARM** like America during a deadly, highly infectious pandemic, a great reduction in personal liberties could be attained.

To rule humanity with an iron fist, you must be willing to risk it all to reach your ultimate goal.

But first, the promising SARS-CoV-1 virus would need an upgrade to live up to its lethal and contagious potential. All the successes and failures of past pandemics would have to be evaluated before a detailed plan could be devised, then devoutly executed to engulf the entire world in a microbial hysteria. Deadly outbreaks quickly turn

469.) Huang. "The SARS Epidemic and its Aftermath in China."
470.) Federico Soldani. "The political career of Mao, Yale and the "reorientation of thought." PsyPolitics. July 28, 2020. https://psypolitics.org/2020/07/05/the-political-career-of-mao-yale-and-the-reorientation-of-thought/ and Huang. "The SARS Epidemic and its Aftermath in China."
471.) Huang. "The SARS Epidemic and its Aftermath in China."
472.) Huang. "The SARS Epidemic and its Aftermath in China."

local and manageable since potential *super spreaders* rapidly die long before they're able to widely infect others, lowering the pathogens' transmissibility. To enhance the promising SARS respiratory virus as an untraceable weapon of mass destruction that seems to have appeared out of nowhere, scientists would have to return to their gain-of-function laboratories to upgrade the 2004 SARS-CoV model 1 whilst orchestrators shuffled back to their meeting rooms to reorganise their plans.

Before we explore the nuances of this new and improved strategy, I feel a few words of inspiration are necessary. A plague launched on humanity, along with its recommended cures, can also serve as an excellent diversion to usher in any state-of-the-art technological developments you wish to impose on your herd. Less personally infringing computerised advances such as contact tracing applications in mobile phones, digital passports and smart helmets that read body temperatures from a distance (as well as other personal information)[473] can be implemented along with more invasive breakthroughs such as direct injections of highly advanced nanotechnology and the use of radio-frequency electromagnetic fields to influence human health and behaviour. Remember, the more technologically advanced a **FARM** is, the less need you have for excess peasants. A lethal and infectious disease is just one way to eliminate the surplus without destroying infrastructure whilst providing the perfect cover for implementing these imprisoning devices.

In the way of biotechnology, I pose the question, 'What if an antidote could actually instruct the body to produce a more lethal offshoot of a virus or, at the very least, could weaken the body's immune system to the prevailing pathogen-of-the-day as we saw in the RSV vaccine and the ferret experiments?' This would be a wonderful challenge to present to the engineers and scientists on your payroll, would it not?

However, by placing blame on those who refuse to submit to the treatment, overall panic can be amplified, and additional societal pressure placed on the resistors. By cutting off social activities, wage-earning opportunities and even the ability to shop for basic living essentials, you can achieve their compliance or significantly weaken the disobedient peasants' positions. The stress they endure under such

---

473.) The Associated Press. "'Smart helmet' can check your temperature from a safe distance: Rome's airport is testing it as a way to scan passengers for potential signs of coronavirus." 13 WTHR.com. May 13, 2020. https://www.wthr.com/article/news/world/smart-helmet-can-check-your-temperature-safe-distance/531-2ad45df5-e337-4a26-9340-de9034cadfcd

trying conditions is enough to put them in a plastic FEMA coffin.

By Jove, I'm just pulling your leg.

One can never laugh too much at the expense of these prophetic yet highly ignored Good Samaritans. Alright, let's explore the genius behind the remarkable yet fairly innocuous, fear-instilling, power-and-wealth-accumulating SARS-CoV-2 virus.

Our study picks back up with the SARS gain-of-function research moving to China after funding was ceased in the United States in 2014. There are many particulars to cover, so please focus your attention. Although there are quite a few key players in this planetary saga, none have boldly stepped into the limelight, whilst performing the role of one part hero and one part villain, more gallantly than the great Dr Anthony Fauci. Serving as director of the National Institute of Allergy and Infectious Disease, the good doctor became the poster boy for the COVID-19 pandemic after serving as an advisor to every US president (both republican and democrat) since Ronald Reagan. For this type of large-scale operation, it's best to have a front man obedient peasants sing praises for and at whom suspicious agitators direct their anger. As we have mentioned before, Dr Fauci has more than earned his overseers' trust in this recurring role.

Also starring in this worldwide calamity and acting as a liaison between Dr Fauci, the NIH and China, is British zoologist, disease ecology expert and president of EcoHealth Alliance, Dr Peter Daszak. It's less important to remember the names of the key players in these examples than it is to understand their contributions to the overall plan. Please also pay close attention to their adherence to the steadfast principles presented in this handbook, which has allowed these principal actors to shape the world to the liking of their masters.

The SARS-CoV-2 story had to be adjusted quite a few times because of inquisitive troublemakers. This made for TV dramedy boldly flashed stomach-churning images of Chinese wet markets where bats, pangolins (sometimes described as scaly anteaters) and other exotic animals were allegedly sold, killed and then eaten as a light afternoon snack. It was the Huanan Seafood Wholesale Market, in particular, that was officially named 'ground zero' of the COVID-19 pandemic and where 'patient zero' was formally declared infected. Dr Peter Daszak of EcoHealth Alliance drove the narrative in this nightmarish scenario where an enhanced bat corona virus skipped decades of evolution and suddenly jumped species to become highly infectious in humans.[474]

474.) Mercola and Cummins, The Truth About COVID-19, 19-23.

NOTE: Please remember to make your official story as grandiose as possible. Then repeatedly bash it into the peasants' permeable brains. Your authorised narratives should be simple yet daunting whilst appearing so unfathomable that they startle peasants senseless. This will help eliminate any doubts those meticulously groomed to trust and obey might have, since their relatively low comprehension levels would never allow them to believe that their ruler could make up such a monumental yet misleading claim.

Even though the *official* wet market story regarding the origin of the SARS-CoV-2 outbreak still traumatises those with a daily staple of beef, chicken and pork, the *Beijing News* initially leaked a dangerous truth bomb that required immediate redaction. Thank all that is evil and wretched for a nation willing to impose prompt censorship. This was all because the truth was disclosed when Huang Yanling, a scientist at the Wuhan Institute of Virology, was embarrassingly revealed as *patient zero* in the widely circulated Beijing publication.[475]

Is it me or does the Wuhan Institute of Virology have an Orwellian ring to it, similar to, say Dr Shiro Ishii's Epidemic Prevention and Water Purification Department discussed in Chapter 14? Well, of course it does, as you never want a name to divulge the enormity of what you're secretly working on, including the work of a two-bit, half-brained scientist that's weaponising hundreds of bat viruses in their lab!

I'm sweating and shaking profusely. I could choke the life out of the imbeciles responsible for publishing that article! Perhaps it's best for me to avoid caffeine for a few days.

To deal with the *Beijing News'* blunder I ask you, dear budding-owner-of-humanity, what steps would you take to overcome a similar obstacle that's certain to arise? Since there are so many routes you could take, let's explore the scenario where peasants are demanding a proper investigation into the matter.

Did someone say, '*Proper investigation*'? Aha! Don't believe the official story? Perhaps the person with vested interest in the *official story* would suffice. In the case of COVID-19, this was none other than Peter Daszak who created the zoonotic origin story.

These techniques must become reflexive. To ensure a firm handle

475.) Nina Lloyd. "'World's first Covid patient' who vanished from Wuhan a year ago still missing." Mirror. January 17, 2021. https://www.mirror.co.uk/news/world-news/worlds-first-covid-patient-who-23334046 Mercola and Cummins, The Truth About COVID-19, 21-22.

on the situation, it was of the utmost importance to use Dr Daszak in not just one but two authority-driven inquiries, the Lancets COVID-19 Commission and the World Health Organization's investigative committee.[476]

But wait, there's more. As we saw with Mr Zelikow, those with the highest stake in the game will work most passionately to see that their brainchild survives public ridicule and opposition. With coronavirus gain-of-function research, Dr Daszak's EcoHealth Alliance played an active role in weaponising such viruses. And it served as an indirect pipeline for US money coming from Dr Fauci's NIAID, including $3.7 million that went to scientists at the Wuhan lab, like the Batwoman, a.k.a. Dr Shi Zhengli, who collected, analysed and experimented with hundreds of live bat viruses.[477]

> NOTE: Chinese scientists worked intimately with US scientists and military virologists to observe the evolution of virulent strains of bat viruses in human tissues. Through a gain-of-function process called *accelerated evolution*, they turned these wild corona viruses into more lethal and more transmissible pandemic inducing *superbugs*.[478] This proves that despite our differences, we really can all get along, especially when working toward the common goal of enslaving humanity.

The adjustments made to the SARS-CoV-1 virus provided the upgrade needed to turn a short-term local killer (SARS-CoV-1) into a global phenomenon. It's not that the delicately engineered enhancements made SARS-CoV-2 more lethal than SARS-CoV-1, but it made it more infectious. However, to spread it across the planet, the new offshoot would have to unlock human cell defences more efficiently. To do this, it was found that by perfectly placing a unique four-amino-acid segment

---

476.) Mercola and Cummins, The Truth About COVID-19, 21.

477.) Fred Guterl. "Dr. Fauci Backed Controversial Wuhan Lab with US Dollars for Risky Coronavirus Research." Newsweek. April 28, 2020. https://www.newsweek.com/dr-fauci-backed-controversial-wuhan-lab-millions-us-dollars-risky-corona-virus-research-1500741

478.) Ed Browne. "Wuhan, US Scientists Planned to Make Coronaviruses, Documents Leaked by DRASTIC Show." Newsweek. October 8, 2021. https://www.newsweek.com/wuhan-us-scientists-make-coronaviruses-ecohealth-wiv-drastic-docu-ments-1636532 and Rowan Jacobsen. "Inside the risky bat-virus engineering that links America to Wuhan: China emulated US techniques to construct novel coronaviruses in unsafe conditions." MIT Technology Review. June 29, 2021. https://www.technologyreview.com/2021/06/29/1027290/gain-of-function-risky-bat-virus-engineering-links-america-to-wuhan/ and Mercola and Cummins, The Truth About COVID-19, 23.

in the SARS-CoV-1 genome, this new coronavirus could more readily penetrate and infect human cells in order to replicate and reproduce.[479]

As a word of caution, you must become reasonably informed through your specialised team in any area of mischief you would like to partake in. Whether you're creating a macroscopic event like 9/11 or a microscopic one like a viral pandemic, it's pertinent that you leave no evidence that could lead back to you and your team. You may fool the average peasant, but top professionals working with advanced technology like electron microscopes could, for example, examine a genetically manipulated organism and detect traces or scars on the genome where insertion of a foreign material occurred.[480] This is the type of detail that you must consider when trying to achieve such a world-changing event.

In this case, much like sending millions of pounds of crime scene steel to China before crime scene investigators could inspect the evidence, modern genetic engineering procedures can actually create new viral constructs using *seamless techniques* that leave absolutely no indications of tampering.[481] Therefore, by having this kind of advanced knowledge before releasing a biologically engineered weapon, you can more comfortably move ahead with your plans knowing a link leading to you and your associates will very hard to prove.

If indeed you're prepared to launch the ultimate *end game* false flag offensive on the entire planet to unite it into one significantly downsized peasant farm, you must be ready to launch an especially memorable and noteworthy psychological campaign. To implement your plans fluidly, you must be fully committed whilst acquiring and applying as much knowledge as possible from previously staged events.

If you choose a drastic *end-of-life-as-peasants-know-it* super

---

479.) Mercola and Cummins, The Truth About COVID-19, 25-26 and Alla Katsnelson. "What do we know about the novel coronavirus's 29 proteins?" Chemical and Engineering News. April 1, 2020. https://cen.acs.org/biological-chemistry/infectious-disease/know-novel-coronaviruss-29-proteins/98/web/2020/04

480.) Mercola and Cummins, The Truth About COVID-19, 25.

481.) Mercola and Cummins, The Truth About COVID-19, 25 and Xiquan Liang, Jason Potter, Shantanu Kumar, Namritha Ravinder, and Jonathan D. Chestnut. "Enhanced CRISPR/Cas9-mediated precise genome editing by improved design and delivery of gRNA, Cas9 nuclease, and donor DNA." NIH: National Library of Medicine. January 10, 2017. https://pubmed.ncbi.nlm.nih.gov/27845164/ and Ding Zhou, Zhennan, Qingxiao Pang, Yuan Zhu, Qian Wang, and Qingsheng Qi. "CRISPR/Cas9-Assisted Seamless Genome Editing in Lactobacillus plantarum and Its Application in N-Acetylglucosamine Production." NIH: National Library of Medicine. October 16, 2019. https://pubmed.ncbi.nlm.nih.gov/31444197/

event, drills, simulations and round table discussions can help sharpen your strategies and allow you to manage obstacles more casually.

In the case of COVID-19, there were a few simulations hosted by the quite cooperative think tank known as the Johns Hopkins Center for Health Security. This is the same organisation that had the *chutzpah* to orchestrate syphilis experiments in Guatemala and the Baltimore lead paint study.[482] The Johns Hopkins School of Hygiene and Public Health (the most highly awarded university in terms of federal research grants) was initially funded by the Rockefeller Foundation, and more recently the Gates Foundation. This shows that the old principle, *if-you-scratch-my-back-I'll-scratch-yours,* has long been at play.[483]

The first notable pandemic simulation hosted by Johns Hopkins and friends was Operation Dark Winter conducted on 22-23 June 2001. It was a mock version of a covert and widespread smallpox attack on the United States. The conclusion reached at the end of this dry run was that current organisational structures and capabilities are not well-suited for the management of a biowarfare attack.[484]

Well, I must say, this is important information to retain when looking to reinvent human society. It seems, to effectively live in this *new normal* of lethal microscopic pathogens, a *Climate Change* is in order, as I'm sure you enthusiastically concur.

The second and more recent test trial was Clade X, held on 15 May 2018 in Washington DC. This tabletop exercise aimed to illustrate the high-level strategic decisions and policies that the United States, and the world, would need to pursue in order to prevent a pandemic, or mitigate its consequences, if it were mysteriously unleashed on the unhealthy and hence vulnerable general population. [485]

482.) Jonathan Stempel. "Johns Hopkins, Bristol-Myers must face $1 billion syphilis infections suit." Reuters. January 4, 2019. https:// www.reuters.com/article/us-maryland-lawsuit-infections/johns-hopkins-bristol-meyers-must-face-1-billion-syphillis-infections-suit-idUSKCN1OY1N3

483.) Rachel Wimpee and Barbara Shubinski. "Timeline: American Foundations and the History of Public Health." Rockefeller Archive Center. December 11, 2020. https://resource.rockarch.org/story/timeline-american-foundations-and-the-history-of-public-health/ and https://hub.jhu.edu/2021/02/09/nsf-research-development-funding-rankings-2019/

484.) Johns Hopkins Center for Health Security. "Dark Winter." Johns Hopkins Bloomberg School of Public Health. https://www.centerforhealthsecurity.org/our-work/exercises/2001_dark-winter/

485.) Johns Hopkins Center for Health Security. "Clade X: A Pandemic Exercise." Johns Hopkins Bloomberg School of Public Health. https://www.centerforhealthsecurity.org/our-work/exercises/2018_clade_x_exercise/

Indeed, offering a Malthusian minded solution is a most noble and merciful cause.

Many useful concepts arose from the one-day simulation, including quite a few Tavistock-type terms that helped sell today's COVID-19 live exercise. Dr Eric Toner, starring in the role of Senior Director for Global Health Security, NSC, masterfully stole the show during a mock press release when he announced that: 'Global markets have plummeted. The Dow Jones is down 60% from its high five months ago and the Fed is now projecting a deep economic recession. Many domestic hospitals are failing due to lack of staff and supplies. Telework and social distancing measures are being encouraged by the CDC. Schools across the country are closed and many public gatherings have been cancelled. Public demand for surgical masks and respirators far exceeds the available supply....'[486]

> NOTE: Once you're in control of just about every facet of human society, you can create such a dismal reality almost without a panic-inducing micro villain. By offering a few startling statistics along with anxiety inducing 24/7 news coverage through information distribution outlets and institutions of authority, fear will grip the herd and they will be more than willing to follow any lifesaving suggestions you provide. As brethren Adolf Hitler wisely concluded: 'Terrorism is the best political weapon, for nothing drives people harder than a fear of sudden death.'

As far as last-minute preparations are concerned, it was the gathering on 18 October 2019, known as Event 201, sponsored by the great technocratic minds of our day, including the John Hopkins Center for Health Security, the World Economic Forum, and the Bill and Melinda Gates Foundation (less than three months before the first SARS-CoV-2 infection), that simulated the aftermath of a fictional pandemic featuring a not-so-coincidental coronavirus that originated in bats and passed to humans through those filthy animals that lie in their own slop.[487] In this case, I refer to those foul, gamey animals known as pigs, not peasants.

Event 201 predicted the all too familiar scenarios seen in the live

486.) Johns Hopkins Center for Health Security, "Clade X Pandemic Exercise: Segment 4," YouTube video, 1:18:54, centerforhealthsecurity, May 18,2018, https://youtu.be/tqa7NHq73xM

487.) B. David Zarley. "The next pandemic is out there. Is the private sector ready? With Event 201, Johns Hopkins turns an eye toward the private sector's global pandemic preparedness." Freethink. November 8, 2019. https://www.freethink.com/health/global-pandemic-preparedness-plan

exercise such as patients with mild symptoms quickly spreading the virus to more susceptible portions of the population, deathly ill victims overwhelming healthcare facilities, travel bans, economic breakdowns, hording scenarios, lockdowns and political pandering from public figures adding to the confusion, etc.[488]

However, some of these situations had to be deliberately induced when the pathogen fell short in real life. For example, the *USNS Comfort* (a floating Naval hospital) was brought into New York Harbor to provide additional support for flooded infirmaries that never quite materialised during the height of the pandemic. Instead, this buoyant sick bay was dismissed from duty after a month of minimal service.[489] Despite this bump in the road, the fearmongering continued, and New York City became one of America's most progressive cities when forcing government recommended mandates on its citizens. This truly demonstrates that if one stays the course, the most egregious plans can be craftily implemented.

The true hidden gems in this brilliantly designed dress rehearsal of Event 201, however, were the detailed plans discussed to combat misinformation and disinformation.

For your own personal wealth of knowledge, Your Greatness, misinformation is false information that is spread regardless of whether or not there's intent to mislead others. Disinformation, on the other hand, is information that's deliberately designed to deceive its target audience.[490]

The relevant subject matters covered in this area of grave concern included ways to deal with those who have the gall to suggest that the virus at the centre of the crisis is manmade or that there's some sort of collusion between governments and pharmaceutical companies to fast-track an unsafe vaccine for the sake of profit.

488.) Johns Hopkins Center for Health Security in partnership with the World Economic Forum and the Bill and Melinda Gates Foundation, "Event 201 Pandemic Exercise: Segment 2, Trade and Travel Discussion." YouTube video, 34:24, centerforhealthsecurity, November 4, 2019, https://youtu.be/QkGNvWflCNM

489.) Jon Simkins. "Hospital Ship Comfort departs NYC, having treated fewer than 200 patients." NavyTimes. April 30, 2020. https://www.navytimes.com/news/your-navy/2020/04/30/hospital-ship-comfort-departs-nyc-having-treated-fewer-than-200-patients/#:~:text=The%20Military%20Sealift%20Command%20hospital%20ship%20USNS%20Comfort,the%20last%20month%20supporting%20the%20region's%20COVID-19%20efforts.

490.) UW Bothell and Cascadia College. "News: Fake News, Misinformation & Disinformation." Campus Library. December 29, 2022. https://guides.lib.uw.edu/c.php?g=345925&p=7772376

The audacity of these peasants is reaching unprecedented heights, I tell you!

Suggestions to manage this type of insolence ranged from issuing prison sentences for those creating *Fake News* on obedient **FARMS** like China to fact-checking and censoring websites and social media content in more Anglo-American friendly countries.[491] Algorithms that monitor suspicious speech are a way for big data companies to sort through the online chatter and effectively target those challenging the official narrative.

Also, touched upon was a concept known as *soft power*.[492] When fully realised, this technique would feature a steady stream of celebrities and other recognizable public and social media figures behaving in a way that all *good citizens* should emulate. A short list of Tavistock objectives included masking up, social distancing, self-quarantining and following all CDC guidelines and directives. After all, a lovable celebrity or an extraordinary athlete would never lead the masses astray, unless, of course, their career and affluent lifestyle depended on it.

Finally, I should mention that forums like Event 201, are idea sharing seminars bringing together people who support or, at the very least, are paid handsomely to advance the current global sustainable development agenda. As a world emperor attentively listening from behind the scenes, these insightful discussions construct the framework for the live exercise and allow you to pick the brains of the chosen few brought in to offer their expert opinions. It's best if the participants are leaders in their respective fields, as this will bring forth the brightest ideas to work with. Even if it's only a drill or roundtable discussion, the element of fear should be ominously present, and the possibility of an unsolvable crisis left lingering in the air to haunt even the most trusted of associates. This will help ensure their continued participation when a potential pandemic pathogen (PPP) is ultimately released.

Where SARS-CoV-2 picked up its enhanced feature can only be explained by the beautiful minds that gave it this tremendous quality that otherwise would've taken centuries to evolve naturally. What makes this leap into human beings so extraordinary is that SARS-CoV-2 could bind to human ACE2 cells more readily than was ever possible with the

---

491.) Johns Hopkins Center for Health Security in partnership with the World Economic Forum and the Bill and Melinda Gates Foundation, "Event 201 Pandemic Exercise: Segment 4, Communications, Discussion, and Epilogue Video." YouTube video, 36:09, centerforhealthsecurity, November 4, 2019, https://youtu.be/LBuP40H4Tko

492.) Mercola and Cummins, The Truth About COVID-19, 39.

cells of the pathogen's first carrier, the horseshoe bat, thus turning a rudimentary law of nature on its head. This universally accepted axiom has long proved that a virus will cling to its original host more so than any subsequent conveyors.[493]

Well, until now, that is.

You haven't lived until you've broken the laws of both nature and physics for the entire world to see. Then, in turn, to witness humanity so stunned by an event's magnificence that you barely hear a cry of opposition. I apologise for the slight detour, but it's wonderful to bask in the beauty of pure brilliance every now and then.

Now, where were we? Ah, yes.

To be honest, as a modern-day lord, all this microbiology shoptalk is quite fascinating, but it's completely irrelevant. Now that a virus capable of inducing a global pandemic had finally been brought into existence, there was just one more giant piece of the puzzle that had to be introduced to fully enact the plan.

> NOTE: Please be aware that when defying natural evolution so blatantly, you'll likely activate an army of glory seeking researchers hoping to be the first to confirm a famous virus's biological and epidemiological trail. As already shown during the COVID-19 pandemic, this type of wild goose chase can be used to your advantage. By constantly changing the state approved plot lines surrounding the pathogen's origin, you can consume valuable time and resources of those tracking the phantom virus back to its murky beginnings. With scientists unable to produce any concrete findings whilst squabbling over an array of ever-changing theories and conflicting reports, the chaos and confusion created will help overshadow any gaping holes in your official story. Even if serious concerns are raised that your front men are not being forthright, there are an endless number of unnamed and undiscovered viruses roaming the planet and disguising a microscopic weapon's true origin should be a fairly straightforward task.

Does this not present the perfect opportunity to apply the old standby of plausible deniability? Indeed, my astute disciple, I believe it does.

To reach the levels of hysteria necessary to throw humanity into a complete and utter frenzy, a lord must make the problem appear much larger than it truly is. Again, no disrespect to the good doctor and his international team who created a biological masterpiece, but when

---

493.) Mercola and Cummins, The Truth About COVID-19, 25-26.

going for broke, you must be absolutely certain the plan is foolproof.

So, I ask you, up-and-coming-czar-of-humanity, how can you give the illusion the virus is everywhere and infecting everyone, requiring a complete reorganisation of human society?

If you could have just one tool to persuade humanity to fall in line with your plan, what would it be? Perhaps you answered complete control over television programming or a naval medical vessel that you could pull into a major port to give the illusion there's much more widespread death and destruction than there really is. A vast network of authority figures ready to fall in line with the edicts of the day would also be an excellent choice. However, to fully convince even those in positions of influence that the problem is much more dire and widespread than it truly is, I think most upper echelon lords would agree that the test used to convince peasants they're stricken with the fatal pathogen, whether or not they actually are, is an orchestrator's most prized possession. In this case, it's none other than the RT-PCR test.

RT-PCR stands for Reverse Transcriptase Polymerase Chain Reaction, and the technique was invented by American biochemist Dr Kary Mullis in 1985 for which he was awarded the Nobel Prize in 1993.[494] Unfortunately, after being awarded this high honour, Dr Mullis began voicing his opinion in a way that was detrimental to World Empire. Because of this, his untimely death a few months before the COVID-19 pandemic couldn't have come at a more suitable time. You see, Dr Mullis was one of those HIV causes AIDS deniers and thus jeopardised what even he realised was 'billions of dollars spent to make up some great mysteries about HIV'.[495] The late Dr Mullis began exposing the fact that HIV is actually an innocuous passenger virus, thus threatening to expose an industry that was built upon the world community believing HIV is a deadly pathogen that leads to AIDS. Obviously, you should never tolerate this type of inflammatory language under any circumstances. That's why you, as a modern-day lord, must work to build a new social order to ensure that it isn't.

In the meantime, I can't emphasise enough how important it is to absorb every little detail a great mind expresses, especially if they are a pioneer in their field. This is a universal truth that you must adhere

494.) "Kary B. Mullis – Facts." NobelPrize.org. February 4, 2023. https://www.nobel-prize.org/prizes/chemistry/1993/mullis/facts/

495.) Celia Farber. "Was the COVID-19 Test Meant to Detect a Virus?" uncoverdc. com. April 7, 2020. https://www.uncoverdc.com/2020/04/07/was-the-covid-19-test-meant-to-detect-a-virus/

to despite petty grievances and differences in opinion with the world's most highly regarded thinkers. In fact, the less you like a particular innovator, the more justified you'll feel in ripping their work from their soul and putting it to use for your own personal gain. Remember, as the ruler of humanity, there simply isn't enough time to come up with every detail for every pursuit you wish to embark on. Let the peasants figure out the intricacies whilst you siphon their ideas and put them into action. Please understand, the masses will be quite eager to build the cage for their own enslavement if you make it appealing enough.

As this applies to Kary Mullis and his revolutionary RT-PCR test, right from the inventor's mouth came forth the words: 'If you do it well, you can find almost anything in anybody.'[496]

To the rare medical professional with scientific integrity, there may be some reluctance to misuse such an avant-garde technology designed 'to find almost anything in anybody'. To the World Emperor looking to *make a killing* convincing panic-stricken test takers they're carrying a deadly virus, the importance of misapplying such an analytical tool is immeasurable. If you tense up at the thought of manipulating the masses so boldly, you can ease your mind knowing that most commoners are incapable of sorting out good science from bad. As long as authority figures sell such large-scale deception with conviction and demonise those who oppose it, the herd will be none the wiser. As Plato once said: 'Those who can see beyond the shadows and lies of their culture will never be understood, let alone believed by the masses.'

Truer words have never been spoken.

RT-PCR and RT-qPCR tests were the centrepiece of the entire operation. Their sole purpose is to detect, amplify and replicate DNA molecules, however, they have no controls to measure the amount of human DNA present in a sample. The tests were never designed to determine an accurate viral load in a subject, the key factor in predicting how the disease has and will advance in a patient, if at all.[497] Again, the inventor's intent for the PCR test was for situations where small amounts of DNA were available and amplification, replication or

---

496.) Lee Harding. "PCR Test is Flimsy, Say Inventor and Courts." Frontier Centre For Public Policy. February 27, 2021. https://fcpp.org/2021/02/27/pcr-test-is-flimsy-say-inventor-and-courts/

497.) Kevin McKernan and Bobby Malhotra interviewed by Naomi Wolf. "PCR lab visit: whistle-blowers Kevin McKernan, Bobby Malhotra explain why COVID tests are garbage." A State of Truth. February 7, 2021. https://mrtrueman. posthaven.com/pcr-lab-visit-whistle-blowers-kevin-mckernan-bobby-malhotra-explain-why-covid-tests-are-garbage

both were required for comparative observation or research purposes. For example, a more suitable application would include a crime scene where tiny traces of DNA could identify or exonerate a crime suspect, or a prehistoric fossil containing a smidgeon of DNA from a forty-thousand-year-old woolly mammoth could be studied. If the latter scenario rings a bell, it was Dr Mullis' discovery that indeed inspired the Hollywood blockbuster film, *Jurassic Park*.[498]

Who said science was boring?

Being the perceptive world emperor-in-the-making that you are, I'm sure the letter q in the RT-qPCR nomenclature piqued your interest. If so, I'm quite pleased that it did, as it's yet another opportunity for you to learn how even the slightest of subtleties can help pull off the largest deceptions. In this case, you must not miss your *cue*. Yes, that's a play on words but so is the intentional misrepresentation of the two types of RT-PCR tests that both begin with the letter Q: qualitative (RT-PCR) and quantitative (RT-qPCR also known as real-time PCR).[499] To understand this ingenious scheme, you must first know that it's widely accepted in the medical and scientific community that the q in RT-qPCR means quantitative exclusively.[500] Quantitative testing is used to approximate how much of a sought after DNA fragment is present in the sample. Once determined, a reasonable, although far from perfect, conjecture can be made regarding the viral load. In theory, this estimated viral load can then indicate the possibility of illness from a detected pathogen.

Well, it sounds pleasing to the ear anyway. I'm sure you understand why the quantitative RT-qPCR would be the best choice of PCR tests when trying to determine the level and severity of infection throughout a population.

However, since viruses like HIV and SARS-CoV-2 are retroviruses (RNA viruses), the targeted pathogens must first be converted to complimentary DNA with the enzyme reverse transcriptase before starting the actual PCR process. Unfortunately, peasants were too

---

498.) Celia Farber. "Interview Kary Mullis. AIDS: Words from the Front." VirusMyth. July 1994. https://virusmyth.com/aids/hiv/cfmullis.htm

499.) Lab Tests Guide. "Difference Between PCR, RT-PCR and qPCR." Labtestsguide.com. October 21, 2022. https://www.labtestsguide.com/difference-between-pcr-rt-pcr-and-qpcr and Mi Seon Han, Jung-Hyun Byun, Yonggeun Cho, John Hoon Rim. "RT-PCR for SARS-CoV-2: quantitative versus qualitative.» The Lancet. May 20, 2020. https://www.thelancet.com/journals/laninf/article/PIIS1473-3099(20)30424-2/fulltext

500.) NIH. "Real-Time qRT-PCR." National Library of Medicine. November 9, 2017. https://www.ncbi.nlm.nih.gov/probe/docs/techqpcr/

traumatised and too busy listening to insiders reading pre-approved scripts to realise the startling truth muttered by Dr Stephen A. Bustin. Bustin is the professor of molecular medicine who assisted in developing the actual MIQE (Minimum Information for Publication of Quantitative Real Time PCR Experiments) guidelines to standardise PCR protocols. Whilst the herd was parroting the phrase 'Trust the science', they had no idea what science to trust. This was glaringly evident when hardly a peep was uttered after Dr Bustin's startling admission that: '[…] in the course of this conversion process the amount of DNA obtained can vary widely, even by a factor of ten.'[501] If that wasn't telling enough, the bar of incrimination was raised to the colonised moon when Dr Bustin had the gall to state: 'We demonstrate that elementary protocol errors, inappropriate data analysis and inadequate reporting continue to be rife and conclude that the majority of published RT-qPCR data are likely to represent technical noise.'[502] I think what Dr Bustin was saying was that when attempting to diagnose every human being on the planet during a worldwide *pandemic*, the results of the RT-qPCR test would lead to an utter fiasco. I'm sure the doctor is extremely grateful that nothing was made of his careless choice of words.

To lessen the odds of accuracy, whilst increasing the amount of false positives, the other q, known as qualitative testing, was substituted in its place.[503] I mean they both begin with the letter q, and who in their

501.) David Crowe interviews Stephen Bustin. "The Infectious Myth – Stephen Bustin on Challenges with RT-PCR." PodBean. April 14, 2020. https://infectiousmyth. podbean.com/e/the-infectious-myth-stephen-bustin-on-challenges-with-rt-pcr/ and Torsten Engelbrecht and Konstantin Demeter. "COVID19 PCR Tests are Scientifically Meaningless. Though the whole world relies on RT-PCR to "diagnose" Sars-Cov-2 infection, the science is clear: they are not fit for that purpose." OffGuardian. June 27, 2020. https://off-guardian.org/2020/06/27/covid19-pcr-tests-are-scientifically-meaningless/

502.) Stephen Bustin, Tania Nolan. "Talking the talk, but not walking the walk: RT-qPCR as a paradigm for the lack of reproducibility in molecular research." PubMed.gov. September 2, 2017 https://pubmed.ncbi.nlm.nih.gov/28796277/

503.) Xiamen Zeesan Biotech Co., Ltd. "SARS-CoV-2 Test Kit (Real-time PCR). FDA.gov. https://www.fda.gov/media/140717/download and Shin Jie Yong. "Is the Coronavirus PCR Test a Fraud? An Objective Look Into Why People Insist So." Medium.com. February 14, 2021. https://medium.com/microbial-instincts/is-coronavirus-pcr-test-a-fraud-an-objective-look-into-why-people-insist-so-fba67dd70fc3 and UW Medicine. "SARS-CoV-2 (COVID-19) Qualitative PCR." Department of Laboratory Medicine and Pathology. January 12, 2023. https://testguide.labmed.uw.edu/view/NCVQLT?tabs=no and Nan Pazdernik and Martin Whitman. "Meaning or definition of common qPCR terms." IDT: Integrated DNA Technologies. June 15, 2013. https://www.idtdna.com/pages/education/decoded/article/qpcr-terminology-what-does-it-mean-

right mind reads the fine print on a tiny pamphlet enclosed in a box of test kits when there are lives to be saved?[504] If the reason for this cunning move is not jumping off the page, let me make it abundantly clear. Qualitative testing is a traditional technique used to determine whether or not a DNA fragment is present. That's it!

Now we'll learn why simply detecting a suspected microorganism is of little significance.

> NOTE: Because acquiring positive test results was of the utmost importance at the height of the COVID-19 pandemic, and qualitative RT-PCR tests were substituted for quantitative RT-qPCR tests to achieve this aim, both tests will hereafter be referred to as RT-PCR tests.[505]

When it comes to spotting an infectious disease, some might say that the PCR test has a few slight drawbacks. The biggest and most important secret is that the process has no way of distinguishing between an inactive virus and a live or reproductive virus, thus meaning the mere detection of a presence is no cause for alarm.[506]

Well, I mean, of course it is!

Another shortcoming that has instead become the RT-PCR test's greatest characteristic is cycle threshold or CT. A cycle threshold refers to the number of times the DNA is magnified and replicated.

I'll use a fingerprint analogy to illustrate how the CT setting can control an entire pandemic. When observing fingerprint marks to be compared side by side, a close inspection of the whole pattern will quickly reveal a match. However, as the images are reproduced and blown up, the likelihood that a fragment, perhaps a curve of a line on one print, will match a similar bend somewhere randomly found on the other increases. This, of course, is a basic analogy and the actual standard will not be an established fingerprint but a fragment of genetic material from a properly classified virus.

However, once again, the game must be rigged even further to guarantee a victory. SARS-CoV-2 initially failed to meet the gold standard in microbiology which is a photograph of a purified viral

504.) Gnomegen. "COVID-19 RT-qPCR Detection Kit. Instructions for Use." FDA. gov. https://www.fda.gov/media/137895/download

505.) Han, Byun, Cho, Rim, "RT-PCR for SARS-CoV-2: quanative versus qualitative."

506.) News Wire. "COVID: 'Every Scary Thing You're Being Told Depends on the Unreliable PCR Test.'" 21st Century Wire. December 30, 2020. https://21stcentury-wire.com/2020/12/30/covid-every-scary-thing-youre-being-told-depends-on-the-unreliable-pcr-test/

isolate captured under an electron microscope.[507] Nonetheless, with a team of highly loyal scientists in place and the world's most important international health agency ready to rubber stamp any directives barked at it, the fix was firmly in place. All they required was a report; in this case the Corman-Drosten paper and some creative scientific deception, and an end of days plague was ready for the world stage.

Sure, once the scientific community realised the World Health Organization (WHO) published the paper within 24 hours and without peer review, outlining the details of the original RT-PCR test used to diagnose COVID-19, this back door approval may have made a few principled members a tad bit cranky but, by then, it was too late.[508] The world had already taken the bait.

> NOTE: When Victor Corman was assembling the standard for his original RT-PCR test as defined in his co-authored paper, he was nabbing viral sequences stored in a computer database as opposed to possessing an actual purified viral isolate to more accurately base the test on.[509] My question is, why on the plague-ridden Earth would anyone want to limit oneself to the rigid results produced by a viral isolate when the opportunity existed to mix and match some of the same genetic sequences found in both the SARS-CoV-2 engineered lab weapon and typical everyday corona viruses? Keep in mind, there are thousands of corona viruses that affect humans resulting in diseases that range from the common cold to COVID-19.[510]

Did a light bulb just switch on? Yes, that's why those with common cold symptoms also tested positive for SARS-CoV-2. This was even

---

507.) Engelbrecht and Demeter. "COVID19 PCR Tests are Scientifically Meaningless."

508.) Mercola and Cummins, The Truth About COVID-19, 80 and Pieter Borger, Rajesh K. Malhotra, Michael Yeadon, Clare Elizabeth Honor Craig, Kevin McKernan, Klaus Steger, Paul Mcsheehy, Lidiya Angelova, Fabio Franchi, Thomas Binder, Henrik Ullrich, Makoto Ohashi, Stefano Scoglio, Marjolein Doesburg-van Kleffens, Dorothea Gilbert, Rainer J. Klement, Ruth Schruefer, Berber W. Pieksma, Jan Bonte, Bruno H. Dalle Carbonara, Kevin P. Corbett, and Ulrike Kammerer. "External peer review of the RTPCR test to detect SARS-CoV-2 reveals 10 major scientific flaws at the molecular and methodological level: consequences for false positive results." ResearchGate.net. November 2020. https://www.researchgate.net/publication/346483715_External_peer_review_of_the_RTPCR_test_to_detect_SARS-CoV-2_reveals_10_major_scientific_flaws_at_the_molecular_and_methodological_level_consequences_for_false_positive_results

509.) Mercola and Cummins, The Truth About COVID-19, 80.

510.) McKernan and Malhotra interviewed by Wolf, "PCR lab visit," 8:32-17:00. And Mercola and Cummins, The Truth About COVID-19, 80-81.

admitted by the authors of the Corman-Drosten papers who confessed the test would also pick up 'other Asian corona viruses'.[511] This includes the first Asian man with cold symptoms who tested positive on the prototype PCR test but was never confirmed to be carrying the actual SARS-CoV-2 virus through proper genetic sequencing.[512] Even more hilarious is the fact that those at the CDC later claimed they possessed the viral isolate from a man experiencing routine sickness who was swabbed after returning from China and who tested positive for SARS-CoV-2 on an RT-PCR test.[513] However, DNA sequencing was again overlooked and the PCR test, which was never standardised with a proper purified isolate to begin with, once again served as the only means to supposedly identify the viral isolate. Can you feel the hysteria building, not to mention the sheer comedy of it all? Also of interest, there are well over two hundred and fifty RT-PCR tests approved by the FDA, as listed on their website, adding another level of confusion for anyone trying to sort out which test is based on the viral isolate and which isn't.[514]

To further tilt the tables in our beloved orchestrators' favour, when amplifying a sample of SARS-CoV-2 past 35 cycles (35 cycles results in 3% reliability and anything above 35 is considered indefensible) to, say, 45 as recommended by the WHO and 40 for the FDA and CDC, more positive readings can be masterfully acquired since you're more likely to find what you're looking for.[515] Remember, Mr Mullis once exclaimed: 'If you do it well, you can find almost anything in anybody.' To reduce the number of positive test results, simply lower the CT to a more accurate level of 17 cycles, and more reasonable outcomes will be obtained.[516]

The applications of such widespread manipulation are endless, but I'll provide a few examples just for a lark. Suppose you wish to ruin a political rival that is disobeying your directives, or you want to amplify the herd's fear level, justify lockdown procedures, have the

---

511.) McKernan and Malhotra interviewed by Wolf, "PCR lab visit," 9:33-10:00.

512.) McKernan and Malhotra interviewed by Wolf, "PCR lab visit," 8:32-17:00.

513.) Centers for Disease Control and Prevention. "First Travel-related Case of 2019 Novel Coronavirus Detected in United States." CDC.gov. January 21, 2020. https://www.cdc.gov/media/releases/2020/p0121-novel-coronavirus-travel-case.html and Beatrice Dupuy. "Posts falsely claim COVID-19 virus has not yet been isolated." AP News. December 8, 2020. https://apnews.com/article/fact-checking-afs:Content:9847920299 and Mercola and Cummins, The Truth About COVID-19, 81.

514.) "COVID-19 Test Basics." FDA.gov. January 4, 2023. https://www.fda.gov/consumers/consumer-updates/covid-19-test-basics

515.) Mercola and Cummins, The Truth About COVID-19, 78.

516.) Mercola and Cummins, The Truth About COVID-19, 78-79.

petrified masses run to your medical establishment for experimental genetic therapy or sway the economy in your favour by shutting down certain segments of the business sector. Ramping up the cycle threshold, thus resulting in a higher number of positive cases, can help achieve these goals. On the other hand, if you desire to make it appear that a favourable politician's policies are curbing the spread or that a certain treatment is working, lowering the CT can lower the number of positive test results, and if it's lowered enough, can even bring the entire outbreak to a close. That is, of course, when it benefits a world ruler to do so.

Hence, the power of the test. This is why the slogan 'Test, test, test' was echoed throughout the world at the beginning of the pandemic.[517] It allowed otherwise healthy individuals to believe they had the deadly virus, causing them to disrupt their daily routines.

The moral of the story is that if you can get the herd to willingly submit to such a whimsical biological probe, you can not only collect their DNA for your own world domination objectives but also put the fear of God in them through positive test results. Once they willingly submit, it's a simple matter to gain their consent to undergo just about any procedure you recommend in order to 'keep them safe and alleviate their suffering'.

Oh, if they only knew.

More positive test results will fuel the desire for more testing, meaning even more positive test results, raising the pandemic hysteria to insurmountable heights.

Hooray for moral indecency and the vast amount of treasure it consistently yields!

There's one last thing to note as we close our discussion on the RT-PCR test. Hopefully, by now, you've learned that it's important to keep marching toward your end goals, despite any obstacles that arise. As the old adage goes: 'You can fool all the people some of the time, and some of the people all the time, but you can't fool all the people all the time.' Why should the RT-PCR test be any different?

There were a small number of smart alecks keen on exposing some of the vulnerabilities inherent in the RT-PCR test.[518] As mentioned previously, without control standards in place to measure the amount

517.) Engelbrecht and Demeter, "COVID19 PCR Tests are Scientifically Meaningless."
518.) TLB Staff. "Flawed Paper Behind Mass PCR Testing Faces Retraction After Exposure." The Liberty Beacon.com. December 11, 2020. https://www.thelibertybeacon.com/flawed-paper-behind-mass-pcr-testing-faces-retraction-after-exposure/

of human DNA present in test samples, all sorts of mischief can occur.

Take for instance that buffoon of a president, John Magufuli, in the East African country of Tanzania who tried to earn his fifteen minutes of fame on the world stage by claiming that some of his nation's RT-PCR test results came back positive on samples taken from goats and pawpaws. As you may have guessed, it's nothing a little negative press featuring the horrendous conditions brought on by his government's lack of concern during a serious worldwide health crisis couldn't handle.[519]

On the other hand, some college kids found that flushing their nostrils with neti pots just before testing reduced their likelihood of a positive lab result, thus allowing them into the classroom and out of self-quarantining.[520] Although these debt slaves in training may not have fully understood why this method worked, the removal of their DNA from the swab site allowed those who were contagious to test negative due to the flushing of genetic material from their snouts and to go about their daily lives and infect others. Obviously, their attendance was welcome in the classroom, so the transmittal of the virus could be blamed on the healthy. As evidenced by the material presented thus far, you must be ready to manage any serious situations that emerge whilst being able to look past more trivial matters.

A lord worthy of planetary domination will be more than capable of making these distinctions.

It's now time to reiterate why China was chosen as the launching pad for this worldwide technocratic makeover. This will, hopefully, give you insight into the decision-making process should you need to pick a suitable plague release point of your own one day.

The first order of business when kick-starting a worldwide pandemic is to pick a viral launch site in a tightly packed metropolitan area; for instance, an overcrowded Chinese city where people travel internationally for business. Aeroplanes' recirculated air and intimate seating arrangements provide the perfect environment for transmission, but you can also consider releasing the agent in the aircraft once they depart a pandemic's ground zero. As the crisis grows, so can the number of release points.

519.) Nolan Quinn. "Tanzania's COVID Denialism Harms its Economic Future." Council on Foreign Relations.org. February 23, 2021. https://www.cfr.org/blog/tanzanias-covid-denialism-harms-its-economic-future and Laura Smith-Spark. "The countries making dubious claims over Covid-19 – and what that means for the world." CNN.com. March 5, 2021. https://www.cnn.com/2021/03/05/world/covid-tanzania-turkmenistan-north-korea-intl/index.html

520.) McKernan and Malhotra interviewed by Wolf, "PCR lab visit," 33:26-34:00.

We have discussed discharging the agent on a military base or near a bioweapons' facility. In the case of SARS-CoV-2, the Wuhan Institute of Virology is the Chinese equivalent of the United States germ mecca, Fort Detrick, Maryland. With China's lax government oversight when it comes to policies and procedures at their bioweapons' labs, whilst at the same time being incredibly vigilant when it comes to protecting state secrets and *accidental* mishaps, a world ruler could not find a more ideal location to kick off a world altering cataclysmic event. Besides, as we saw with the 2002 SARS outbreak, the **STATE** framework is firmly in place to give the virus ample time to spread and, with the right microorganism, bring on a widespread calamity.

Although you may want to review this entire chapter before committing to a manmade plague of your own, it's important to remember how the repeated reference to science seemed to bring out the most barbaric cruelty from faithful adherents to the **STATE** versus those who, although I cringe to say it, think for themselves. Looking back at the SARS outbreak in China in 2002, you can see those who were incapable of understanding the intricate details of the situation resorted to their inherent brutality to make up for their mental shortcomings and thus heavy-handedly imposed the **STATE'S** will on others.[521] This knee-jerk reactionary behaviour once again demonstrates that people most certainly fear what they don't understand. Fortunately, for any aspiring world emperor, this proves to be a recurring theme throughout human history and one that shows no signs of ending anytime soon. A skilled despot will capitalise on this human frailty to further widen the divide. When possible, this should be done to the point of violence, justifying the need for even greater governmental force.

Whenever peasants demonstrate they are incapable of civil behaviour, it's the duty of their overlord to curtail their freedoms for the mere sake of restoring tranquillity. Once in place, peasants must adapt to their new parameters which must never be revoked.

I do hope you're following along with this train of thought.

We'll splinter off shortly to show how you can turn anyone opposed to *science* into a terrorist, further legitimising the Phoenix framework already in place on a majority of the world's **FARMS**.

Since a few beautiful minds in the global lord movement understood the lifespan of empires and had the foresight to develop a **FARM** that could be used to usher in a worldwide totalitarian

---

521.) Huang. "The SARS Epidemic and its Aftermath in China."

governmental system, China became the prototype for global enslavement.

Let's take a quick look at some of this cooperative government's most dynamic features so that superior thinkers like yourself can cut and paste these lord friendly attributes across the planet.

> NOTE: Please be advised that the use of the expression cut and paste is not simply a modern catchphrase inserted into this manuscript without purpose. It is a deliberate choice of words that comes with insider knowledge that the physical world and its virtual equivalent are about to be merged for a new human existence on Planet Earth and beyond. The more you can purposefully use language and images to pre-programme your peasants for any changes you're about to impose, the better your results will be. Every finger must point, and every toe must curl with the intent of enslaving humanity if you're to succeed in this highly ambitious undertaking. May the power of darkness drive every fibre of your being toward this gratifying and enchanting outcome.

As previously discussed, China has received an ample boost of American investment since the early 1970s, which began turning this heavily populated *human resource factory* into the workshop of the world. With all the industrialised nations now dependent on China's cheap and efficient production capabilities, pulling the plug on this international supply hub can freeze the global economy in its tracks. Besides, by shifting the world's resources and wealth over to such a disciplinarian style government, the planet's best and brightest can now be seduced financially into lending their talents to a **FARM** whose stated goal is *biological dominance.*[522]

Is this not remarkably similar to Operation Paperclip and Operation Osoaviakhim used by the US and USSR, respectively, to dominate the world by way of conventional and nuclear weapons that, in turn, led to an arms race?

Just thought I'd provokingly ask.

Take, for instance, Harvard's Dr Charles Lieber who was

522.) Overwatch. "Chinese Government Attempts to Collect American DNA Data." Echo Analytics Group.com. June 23, 2022. https://echoanalyticsgroup.com/overwatch/chinese-attempts-to-collect-american-dna-data-the-threat-of-ge-netic-warfare/ and "'Warfare beyond rules': Chinese officers envisioned combat by non-military means." World Tribune.com. April 1, 2020. https://www.worldtribune.com/warfare-beyond-rules-chinese-officers-envisioned-com-bat-by-non-military-means/

recruited into China's Thousand Talents Plan for his particular skill with nanotechnology. The central government of China established the Thousand Talents Plan in 2008 to recognise and recruit leading international experts in scientific research, innovation and entrepreneurship or, in simpler terms, to steal American technology.[523] The ego is a magnificent human component that you can manipulate to achieve astonishing results. I mean, what emerging scientist wouldn't want to work in an environment where his most life-altering creations are allowed to blossom into their full potential? Please name me one competent modern-day lord who wouldn't want to capitalise on the spoils of these developments. Although there may be many examples of comparable *national security* compromises, this one is relevant to our discussion.

After years of struggle to slip a micro transistor into a human cell to send it signals to manipulate its innate biological responses, in 2011, Dr Lieber created a transistor so small (the size of a virus) that it could penetrate cell membranes and probe their interiors without disrupting function.[524] The trick was to coat this miniscule electronic device with a phospholipid bilayer, the same genetic material as a cell membrane, so that it could easily enter into a cell without adversely affecting it. This process, known as membrane fusion, replicates the way cells engulf viruses and bacteria since both are also enclosed with this outer fatty lipid bilayer.[525]

Once again, a wise ruler must pay close attention to every utterance from the great minds of their time, as they cannot afford to miss even the smallest detail. For instance, when Dr Lieber precisely revealed: 'Digital electronics are so powerful that they dominate our daily lives. When scaled down, the difference between digital and living systems blurs, so that you have an opportunity to do things that sound like science fiction—things that people have only dreamed about.'[526]

Point well taken, Dr Lieber.

Unfortunately, at times, one knows a little too much for their own good, and when lips start flapping, federal charges start stacking. It's

523.) Geoff Brumfiel. "Harvard Professor's Arrest Raises Questions About Scientific Openness." NPR.org. February 19, 2020. https://www.npr.org./2020/02/14/806128410/harvard-professors-arrest-raises-questions-about-scientific-openness

524.) Jonathan Shaw. "Virus-Sized Transistors." Harvard Magazine.com. January-February 2011. https://www.harvardmagazine.com/2011/01/virus-sized-transistors

525.) Shaw, "Virus-Sized Transistors."

526.) Shaw, "Virus-Sized Transistors."

funny how one can openly sign an agreement between Harvard and the Wuhan Institute of Technology with US government awareness as Dr Lieber did, only to be treated more harshly than those who were selling nuclear secrets to the Soviets during the height of the Cold War.[527] Let that be a lesson to others who might think of violating their non-disclosure agreements. These damn fools will conjure up all sorts of conspiracy babble when they should be thankful for the opportunities they're provided. We'll return to the nanotransistor topic shortly when it is once again relevant to our conversation.

After a relaxing stroll on the grounds of your private estate, you could probably come up with a few more enticing reasons why China should be the focal point of this life altering pandemic. However, I'll cover one last consideration that's simply too big to be ignored. Plainly stated, the leap in technological advances and production capability in the Sleeping Giant has not only increased its GNP, but it has also opened the door for a trial run of the world's very first Social Credit System. This promising new surveillance society, being predominantly run by Artificial Intelligence, currently includes over 200 million video cameras that monitor everything Chinese citizens do.[528] This includes all human activities, ranging from what a person buys, to their credit history, to how they behave in social settings. These closely observed behaviours are then run through various algorithms to create a social credit score. Scores range from 350 to 950, and are also influenced by reports from private citizens who are paid to spy, and then file reports, on their neighbours.[529]

I must take a second to catch my breath as I reflect on how precisely Orwell's dystopian society has been recreated in real life. This is truly an incredible homage to the Big Brother/Big Data technocrats whose industries covertly extracted the talents of those who toiled and shared their ideas to create the tools for their own enslavement.

It is quite awe-inspiring to witness it all come to fruition. Is it not?

Finally, as a last point for this quick summation of China's social credit system, a low social credit score blacklists all the dog-faced scoundrels who fail to be *good citizens* and attaches a social stigma

527.) Pam Barker. "Alleged Chinese Agent Charles Lieber & His Virus Transmitters." Europe Reloaded.com. April 22, 2020. https://www.europereloaded.com/alleged-chinese-agent-charles-lieber-his-virus-transmitters/

528.) NBC Nightly News, "Social Credit System Coming To China, With Citizens Scored On Behavior | NBC Nightly News," YouTube video, 2:33, NBC News, May 11, 2019, https://youtu.be/NOk27I2EBac

529.) NBC Nightly News, "Social Credit System Coming to China," 0:00-1:47.

that follows them everywhere they go. Once this happens, these now targeted individuals are excluded from many permitted privileges like good jobs, good schools for their children and low-interest-rate loans.[530] On the other hand, a high social credit score rewards those who are compliant with the aims of their hidden overseers, thus allowing them full access to a long list of perks in exchange for their model behaviour. This can include good deals on holidays, low-interest-rate loans and invites to the best social gatherings.[531]

Who in a million years would want to miss a popular mixer where getting drunk in public or gossiping will immediately lower one's social credit score?[532] It's a pity that peasants can never seem to catch a break. Those poor little darlings.

> NOTE: A society run by Artificial Intelligence will make it nearly impossible for peasants to figure out who is truly in control of their lives. Remember, ruling from the shadows is greatly encouraged for your long-term survivability as a global lord. A technocratic society permits this type of obscurity and much more.

Alright. So, the virus has been released within this ultimate totalitarian template for the rest of the world to follow. Now what? Well, this is where the fun begins. All the years of trials and tribulations, as well as hard work and planning, are now complete. It's finally time to capitalise on all the suffering that's been induced over the past century in the name of progress. To reiterate, the six silent weapons used in this quiet viral war against peasants are fear, flattery, bribery, shame, guilt and force. Each will be highlighted with a few real-world examples to stimulate your creativity. Keep in mind, these methods were used to gain compliance and urge peasants to volunteer for what can only be viewed as one giant social and medical experiment. Please remember, each societal norm replaced and every submission of will obtained moves our elite fraternity another step closer to dominating every mind, body and spirit on the planet.

Go ahead. Let out a primal scream. It's good for your darkening soul.

As I've emphasised many times throughout this handbook, fear is the most powerful motivator at your disposal. This is especially

530.) NBC Nightly News, "Social Credit System Coming to China," 1:43-2:02.
531.) NBC Nightly News, "Social Credit System Coming to China," 1:33-1:43 and NBC News, "A Look Inside China's Social Credit System | NBC News Now," You-Tube video, 8:06, NBC News, June 4, 2019, https://youtu.be/0cGB8dCDf3c
532.) NBC Nightly News, "Social Credit System Coming to China," 1:05-1:20.

true in the early stages of an orchestrated crisis. You must stun the herd into a submissive state and then bombard them with horrifying reports of death and destruction. Once this early trauma is induced, you can then judiciously coerce them in the direction of your choosing. A worldwide, false flag attack like the COVID-19 pandemic should have several, multi-layered aspirations deeply woven into its fabric. If played properly, a shock doctrine event of this magnitude can bring its organisers more wealth and power whilst, at the same time, restricting generously granted peasant privileges.

The success of any operation will depend on how traumatic your Tavistock Shock Doctrine event is, along with how convincingly you sell your official narrative, how prepared you are to implement the desired changes, and how far you're willing to go to see your plan through to completion. Having a strong and reliable clandestine network in place is absolutely critical to reach your stated aims. Equally important is having complete control over all *respected* information outlets, allowing you to tightly regulate exactly how peasants perceive your planned crisis.

There's no better way to amplify fear, manipulate a herd's emotions and achieve widespread complicity than through a skilfully run media empire. Featured *experts* from a **FARM'S** relevant centres of power can serve as useful mouthpieces to gain trust whilst getting the herd to accept new protocols and make necessary sacrifices for *the good of the* **FARM**. For example, businessmen, politicians, military leaders, health care professionals and scientists can cleverly establish certain *facts*, defend narratives, divide opinion, create a strategy of tension, deliver small doses of truth or any other purpose that tickles your fancy.

If you're experiencing slight anxiety, please be advised that you don't need everyone in on your scheme, just the biggest influencers. For instance, the empty-headed news presenter reading the cue card at the local news station does not need to know the deep, dark particulars of a plot. In fact, even if they were to figure them out, more times than not, they won't want to stir the pot and lose their job and will blissfully recite whatever gibberish is flashed on the teleprompter.

The more prominent and skilful newsreaders can be recruited and brought into the fold to consciously set the standard for those aspiring to the same level of professional stature. Just be sure to handsomely reward your media insiders whilst protecting them at all costs. They're instrumental to your plans.

In regard to staging a worldwide pandemic, please remember that every crisis needs a face. Whether it's that of an authority figure, a lone gunman, a fugitive from justice, a terrorist or a leader of a rogue nation, a visible person is required to absorb the criticism and, at times, the occasional praise of the easily befuddled masses. Like the character Emmanuel Goldstein in *1984,* who became a convenient outlet for the proletariats to place blame for their anguish, a proven insider, a patsy, or even a carefully groomed statesman can be thrust into the public eye to serve as a proverbial punching bag for peasants and their misguided energies. It's better than peasants sitting with their own thoughts and reflecting on who is truly responsible for their declining plight.

Hero to some, villain to others, Dr Anthony Fauci was once again featured in his recurring role as a *public health expert* whilst making moves behind the scenes that proved his loyalty to a technocratic and Malthusian depopulation agenda. Similar to Josef Mengele and Dr Shiro Ishii, a certain callousness was needed for the advancement of *science.*

Although directed at canines and not humans, the $1.68 million provided by the NIH under Dr Fauci for a study on beagle puppies, whose vocal cords were severed to silence barks of pain whilst being eaten alive by diseased sand flies, spoke volumes.[533]

> NOTE: Many successful serial killers got their start by maiming helpless animals. Therefore, it stood to reason that if Dr Fauci could fund the torment a few mangy mutts and hold his composure whilst under fire for it, he'd certainly be able to eliminate a good chunk of the human population with dignified elegance.

As the untried, experimental mRNA vaccine pushed its way onto the world stage, public scrutiny kicked into high gear. Global lords had to be ready to neutralise public backlash, especially if this unproven antidote was to be injected into young children. By selecting an ambassador who made a career out of partaking in such controversial undertakings whilst maintaining the public's trust, global planners chose a delegate with an

533.) Yasmeen Abutaleb and Beth Reinhard. "Fauci Swamped by angry calls over beagle experiments after campaign that included misleading image." The Washington Post.com. November 19, 2021. https://www.washingtonpost.com/investigations/2021/11/19/fauci-beagle-white-coat-waste/?nid=top_pb_sign-in&arcld=VX675B4PTFA5VNTXHUYYETCSAU&account_location=ON-SITE_HEADER_ARTICLE and Ifhem Chelbi, Khouloud Maghraoui, Sami Zhioua, Saifedine Cherni, Imen Labidi, Abhay Satoskar, James G.C. Hamilton, and Elyes Zhioula. "Enhanced attraction of sand fly vectors of Leishmania infantum to dogs infected with zoonotic visceral leishmaniasis."PLOS.org. July 27, 2021. https://journals.plos.org/plosntds/article?id=10.1371/journal.pntd.0009647

indispensable skill set. Since this carefully groomed insider had the ability to coolly deliver calculated statements on a variety of controversial topics, Dr Fauci not only won the peasants' confidence, but received compliance with nearly all dictates and mandates as well.

The truth always remains hidden in plain sight. However, releasing small doses amongst a concoction of well-orchestrated lies, opinions and disinformation leaves most peasants in a state of bewilderment. As shown during the COVID-19 pandemic, easily confused peasants quickly handed over their decision-making duties to the establishment's health officials, virologists and genetic engineers funded by military biodefence/biowarfare programmes, leading pharmaceutical companies and the government.[534] Once the majority of peasants became frightened and confused well beyond their normal levels, it was easy to convince them that SARS-CoV-2 was so infectious and so dangerous that there were no existing medical drugs, treatment protocols, supplements, natural herbs, health practices or dietary or lifestyle changes that could strengthen their immune systems and protect them from serious illness, hospitalisation and death.[535]

Furthermore, by pummelling peasants with fear and withholding proactive solutions that could empower them on an individual level, most were keenly led to believe they had no choice but to follow orders, obey the rules of mask wearing and lockdowns, and wait for those in the pharmaceutical industry to offer, at warp speed, inadequately tested, genetically engineered vaccines.[536]

It's been a thing of pure beauty to witness, I might add.

> NOTE: Remember, this is global lord 101, i.e. to create a problem and then offer its solution. Gaining widespread cooperation will be nearly impossible unless the masses are coerced to desire your suggested course of action and are fear-motivated to cooperate.

The following hypothetical scenario provides a masterful blend of Kubark Interrogation Manual principles, coupled with COVID-19 narratives and mandates. The intent is to deepen your understanding of the techniques used during the actual pandemic by presenting real-world situations immediately after. Please pay special attention as to how closely the techniques and their ensuing outcomes (especially

---

534.) Mercola and Cummins, The Truth About COVID-19, 72-73.
535.) Mercola and Cummins, The Truth About COVID-19, 73.
536.) Mercola and Cummins, The Truth About COVID-19, 73.

early on in the crisis) parallel those listed in the Kubark Interrogation Manual.

Imagine yourself blindfolded and securely tied to a chair. After hours of isolation, you have the overwhelming feeling you're being studied and that someone wants something from you. You then hear a door open and the sound of footsteps as an unknown number of people enter the room where you're being held, followed by…silence. In this brief scenario, it's easy to imagine the fear that could surface and, in turn, be further enhanced, depending on the skill level of your tormentors. As I'm sure you'll agree, the greatest fear of all stems from the unknown.

You're then untied and your blindfold removed. Your captors exit and announce through a speaker from a safe area that a deadly pathogen has been released in the room and that one symptom of the resulting deadly disease is that there are no symptoms. Next, you're told it's unknown how it spreads. You're left in the room alone for many days, separated from your friends, family and loved ones. But you're left with disinfectant and a scouring pad, and you scrub everything vehemently to protect yourself.

NOTE: It's been observed that guinea pigs, whose symptoms and immune responses to various infections are eerily similar to humans, when raised in sterile environments with no bacteria, end up malnourished and dead at a young age.[537] By disturbing the symbiotic relationship developed between cells and germs that have evolved over billions of years, you can actually weaken the peasants' condition by having them over sterilise everything. After all, an immune system only strengthens when it's actively engaged and, of course, challenged.

For now, let's jump back into our interrogation scenario. Eventually, personnel come and go from your room and, although you don't feel sick, you don't know if you're infected or if those entering the isolated area are contagious. You avoid them and become suspicious of the food and drink they serve. The staff members have been wearing face shields and protective clothing due to the severity of the situation. You don't feel sick, but you haven't gotten any sunlight, fresh air, exercise or

537.) Danielle J. Padilla-Carlin, David N. McMurray, and Anthony J. Hickey. "The Guinea Pig as a Model of Infectious Diseases." NIH: National Library of Medicine. August, 2008. https://www.ncbi.nlm.nih.gov/pmc/articles/PMC2706043/ and Molika Ashford. "Could Humans Live Without Bacteria?" Live Science.com. August 12, 2010. https://www.livescience.com/32761-good-bacteria-boost-immune-system.html

a kiss or hug from a loved one in quite some time, and you find yourself spiralling into a growing state of despair. This, in turn, causes feelings of desperation and guilt should you pass on the disease to your captors. One is a Chinese man who enters your room multiple times per day flashing horrifying images of gruesome bats from his home country where this dreaded microorganism came from.

All along, mixed information is fed to you by the growing number of helpers entering your room. Some tell you, if you religiously wear a protective covering on your face, you cannot catch or spread the virus. You then decide that you don't want to eat or drink because that means you'd have to remove your face covering, but then you're told as long as you're eating or drinking, the pathogen cannot harm you. Others tell you it can only be passed by touching it directly and breathing fresh air will strengthen your immune system against it. You grow more and more confused by the day, which weakens your resolve.

Finally, a man in a white lab coat enters the room, grabs your head and jams a swab up your nose. Until this point, you've had no signs of illness but, suddenly, your eyes are watering profusely and you belt out an uncontrollable sneeze. The man exits the room with the swab. The next day, they slip a note under your door along with your daily meal (always served at different times of the day), stating that you have tested positive for the deadly agent. A couple of days later, at the completion of your meal (this time served ten minutes after your last previous meal was eaten), a large screen drops down from the ceiling and the man in the white coat appears. He explains the dire situation you're faced with. You panic. He then offers three possible scenarios to choose from.

The first is that you take an experimental treatment that has been proven effective against the pathogen. However, to receive it, you must remain in your room for pretty much the rest of your life. Occasionally, you'll be granted privileges and allowed to venture into other parts of the facility, but you're to wear a muzzle and will be forbidden to explain to anybody what you experienced. You must also be willing to take all further suggested treatments, and if full cooperation is received, you may be selected to promote the antidote to other captives and will be appropriately rewarded.

The second is that you're free to go. You may simply grab the few things you have and walk out the door. However, you've heard soldiers firing their weapons and performing drills outside your room. You've also been warned several times that if you try to escape, the soldiers will shoot to kill.

The third scenario ties into the second. You can refuse the experimental remedy and remain where you are, but you'll most likely die without the highly recommended treatment that, not so coincidentally, is offered to captives who no longer serve a useful purpose. If you choose the third option, you must also be muzzled and isolated, so you don't bring harm to other captives or staff members. Eventually, you won't be given care because you've failed to cooperate by not accepting the suggested course of action to reverse your condition.

In the real world, many of these same principles have been at play. When the virus was first released...dear me...I mean, when it first jumped species from bats to pangolins to Homo sapiens, one of the symptoms touted was that there were no symptoms. There were mixed messages and confusion as to how the virus could be spread and measures like removing basketball rims from parks were enacted, so people couldn't spread the disease (nor exercise, socialise or get necessary sunlight). Families were warned not to have gatherings and non-symptomatic *carriers* were told to self-quarantine. This was a most miraculous achievement, as it's the first time in human history that healthy people around the world were made to quarantine. Surprisingly, most people eagerly went along with it. Once again, much credit can be given to the RT-PCR test previously discussed that would prove to be a make-or-break factor in this false flag pandemic.

> NOTE: With the leeway to control test results through careful selection of the CT (cycle threshold), for example, fear can easily be heightened by way of increased testing. The more people who test and the more times they do so, the more likely they are to test positive, even when asymptomatic (a.k.a. noncontagious) or infected by one of thousands of less virulent strains of corona virus. With the help of charts, graphs and constant reporting of statistics, like inflated numbers of infections and deaths, mass hysteria can be conveniently reached.

As with any manufactured crisis, you'll need to repeatedly evaluate the herd's limits to see just how much prodding they'll accept. Remember, tightly governed societies aren't achieved by mass resistance, they're obtained through widespread compliance. By applying the techniques in this handbook, it's your job to see that this transition occurs as smoothly as possible. I know it may seem like I'm harping on you, but the biggest changes must be made early on in a crisis to convincingly sell the populace on their new reality.

By releasing the right biological agent in a proven location, you're laying the groundwork for a shock campaign of epic proportions. As the first test run of SARS-CoV-1 shows, the Chinese governmental system proved it was perfectly suited for the unimpeded and secretive spread of a proper contagion. Additionally, and especially since the onset of SARS-Cov-1, the entire world had grown accustomed to seeing Asians covering their faces with masks to protect themselves from germs, pollution, cold air and the like. Indeed, the seed was already planted. By flashing images of freshly slain animals that a westerner would never pet, let alone eat, on every news outlet across the globe every hour on the hour, along with nonsensical stories about the virus originating from these *wet markets*, there was hardly a peasant alive that was not captivated by the headlines and willing to trade in whatever freedom they had left in return for protection.

> NOTE: On the other hand, please be aware it's equally important to suppress and ridicule logical explanations for any fabricated calamity you impose.[538] As wonderfully executed by the Chinese government along with their silent affiliate, the World Health Organization, not only were they able to keep a tight lid on the viruses' initial release and rapid spread, but they were able to destroy all forensic evidence that could produce culpability for the orchestrators. All it took was some governmental directives and a little military prowess to seize and erase all existing proof that could lead to the virus's true origin.[539]

To add to the horrifying news coming out of China were reports of extreme lockdown measures, the collapse of a new hotel housing quarantine victims and another Asian dictator, Kim Jung Un, who had at least two people executed by way of firing squad for violating COVID protocols.[540] Certainly any Asian, or foreigner for that matter, stepping foot onto western shores would add to the already escalating panic. When the world economy began to shut down, fear of the unknown dominated the consciousness of the entire planet.

538.) Mercola and Cummins, The Truth About COVID-19, 16.

539.) Mercola and Cummins, The Truth About COVID-19, 17, 20.

540.) Yong Xiong, Theresa Waldrop, and Steven Jiang. "10 dead after coronavirus quarantine hotel collapses in China." CNN.com. March 8, 2020. https://www.cnn.com/2020/03/07/china/china-coronavirus-hotel-collapse/index.html and The Associated Press. "North Korea executed people, shut capital, South Korean spy agency says: Kim Jong Un has also banned fishing and salt production at sea to prevent seawater from being infected with the virus, lawmakers were told." NBC News.com. November 27, 2020. https://www.nbcnews.com/news/world/north-korea-executed-people-shut-capital-south-korean-spy-agency-n1249123

To the fast food, processed sugar, caffeine, alcohol, legal and illegal drug addicted land of the free, the United States of America, surely their state-of-the-art super society could not fall prey to a microscopic killer. If all that was required of their citizens was to wear masks and socially distance to *flatten the curve* for a couple of weeks, it was the least they could do. Once they did, it was a clear sign to the wise and stealthy behind-the-scenes players that the bait had been taken and integration of this new normal was well underway.

As we discussed earlier in this handbook, being the first to build the peasants' belief systems, according to how you want them to perceive the world, will give you greater control over every decision they make and each action they take throughout their lifetimes. Early training as outlined in Chapter 11, if done right, will give your anointed authority figures established credibility and, as long as you deliver your narrative first, you'll embed a nearly irreplaceable conviction about any given crisis in their easily mouldable brains.

In lockstep with the techniques outlined in the Kubark Interrogation Manual, early objectives during the COVID-19 pandemic such as isolation, the stripping of identity, shaming, provoking and exploiting guilt, inducing fear and helplessness, threats of force, achieving compliance through regression and establishing a father figure/authoritative dynamic over the subjects were obtained with a few non-enforceable directives. Amusing to note is that these random edicts contained no scientific or medical merit, but were parroted by pandemic stewards like Bill Gates and Dr Fauci, all the way down to the local dogcatcher. Remember, it's not what is said, but who says it and how. Your top pitchmen will require a certain degree of omnipotence to be accepted as credible. Once supremacy is established, new orders and updates will be more eagerly embraced and will quickly be accepted by the herd.

When looking at the psychological aspects of mandates like mask wearing, social distancing and quarantining, it's not hard to see the Kubark-esque principles assuring greater compliance. For instance, mask wearing not only stripped peasants of their identities but also bred fear, especially when first introduced to their **FARMS**. Those who refused to cooperate were shamed and even threatened by the obedient. This resulted in feelings of anxiety or guilt that led to regression and hence compliance. Widespread mask wearing not only served as a constant reminder of the invisible threat lurking everywhere, but it forced sceptics to contend with a mass submission of wills. This, in turn, provoked feelings of helplessness in even some of the strongest peasants, thus prodding them into conformity.

The masks also provided a few other subtle benefits for those looking to usurp the world's peasant farms. By removing personal expression and subtle, non-verbal communication from peasants' daily interactions, they were left detached from their own humanity and that of others. Measures such as social distancing, the prevention of gatherings and the quarantining of healthy people, etc. all had the same effect. These isolation techniques also aided in preventing a lord's worst nightmare, which is peasants figuring out their plight and uniting to prevent it. Furthermore, by muzzling them, their ability to exchange information was greatly reduced. At the same time, their intake of fresh oxygen, which is vital to their immune strength and well-being, was hampered, thus making them ripe for future infections. Historically, those made to cover their faces have always been considered the equivalent of mere chattel within their respective societies.

Now the same can be said of the entire human race.

What a rush!!!!

The Kubark Interrogation Manual discusses three Ds: debility, dependency and dread, considered necessary to obtain a response to coercion.[541] It's not hard to see how the closing of shops, restaurants, gyms, churches and the economy as a whole has stimulated one or all of these elements. By disrupting behavioural patterns, removing social stimuli and creating barren environments, orchestrators were able to cut peasants off from their familiar routines and plunge them into an ambiguous existence. The resulting trauma softened them into putty in their leader's hands.

Similar to the scene when Dorothy first meets the Wizard in the classic film *The Wizard of Oz*, you should blast fear through your media networks 24/7. You can use the old, reliable, colour-coded threat levels along with graphs and statistics to paralyse most peasants in their tracks. This had been accomplished to such a high level during the COVID-19 pandemic that anytime a peasant sniffled, they thought they were dying of the dreaded disease. This led them right into the trap as hordes of hapless peasants flocked to hospitals for care and right into the arms of unknowing health care professionals who were trained in medical schools owned and operated by the network's pharmaceutical companies. These same pharmaceutical companies also infiltrated

---

541.) CIA, Kubark, 84.

leading health institutions like the WHO, CDC and FDA where carefully placed insiders recommended treatments like Remdesivir and ventilators, exclusively, that lowered survival rates. As a result, these same approved treatments were sternly administered by the entire medical practice.[542] As deaths rates climbed, so did the fear. In the meantime, the bottom line expanded for the astute Malthusian industrialists who were able to acquire wealth and power well beyond their previous levels.

> NOTE: If you can find a drug such as Remdesivir that creates the symptoms of the very disease it's supposedly treating, you're well on your way to establishing plausible deniability. In this case, by shutting down the kidneys in roughly one third of the patients using it, fluids back up into areas like the lungs rather than being released from the body, thus simulating the effects of pneumonia which, conveniently, is an end-of-life symptom of COVID-19.[543]

There are also quite a few unintended beneficial consequences that the fear driven policies of mask wearing, social distancing and isolation lead to. I'll take time to bring a couple of them to your highly focused attention. For one, peasants were so jittery about catching the contagion from another person, the birthrate in countries like the United States, Italy, Spain and Portugal declined during the pandemic.[544] Whether it was happening to couples right under the same rooftops or was due to meeting places like nightclubs, shops and fitness centres curtailing

542.) Paul Frysh. "Complications of Ventilator Use." + WebMD.com. December 26, 2022. https://www.webmd.com/covid/ventilator-complications and Silvia Aloisi, Deena Beasley, Gabriella Borter, Thomas Escritt, and Kate Kelland. "Special Report: As virus advances, doctors rethink rush to ventilate." Reuters.com. April 23, 2020. https://www.reuters.com/article/us-health-coronavirus-ventila-tors-specia-idUSKCN2251PE and Dr. Cameron Kyle-Sidell, "Doctor warns of risk in using ventilators to treat COVID-19," YouTube video, WXYZ-TV Detroit | Channel 7, July 17, 2020, https://youtube.com/watch?v=Z5B2-7EpRvw and Dr. Bryan Ardis, "Most Important Video You'll See/Watch/Listen/Share With Loved Ones," BitChute video, 14:18, SwampNugget, September 5, 2021, https://www.bitchute.com/video/Pz0SBTvKrDrV/ and Mercola and Cummins, The Truth About COVID-19, 58, 117-118.

543.) Emily Mangiaracina. "26% of those prescribed Remdesevir for COVID died, according to Medicare database." LifeSite.com. September 29, 2021. https://www.lifesitenews.com/news/26-of-those-prescribed-remdesevir-for-covid-died-ac-cording-to-medicare-database/ and Ardis, "Most Important Video You'll See," 2:00-10:20.

544.) Cornell University. "COVID-19 slows birth rate in US, Europe." Science-Daily.com. September 15, 2021. https://www/sciencedaily.com/releas-es/2021/09/210915135129.htm

hours and enforcing unappealing masking policies, the statistics don't lie. Fewer babies were being made on affluent FARMS.

Second, with constant talk of overcrowding in hospitals, many peasants made the choice not to undergo treatments for non-COVID related chronic issues in order to avoid pandemic hot spots like doctor's offices, clinics and emergency rooms.[545] This not only allowed treatable conditions to worsen, but it made these medical care dodgers more fatally susceptible to the pathogen, since SARS-CoV-2 had a much higher kill rate on those suffering from underlying conditions that could have been corrected.[546]

Similarly, living with the fear of catching the virus also undermined the peasants' overall health as did experiencing psychological, financial and emotional stress caused by the pandemic. The further the misfortune spread, the weaker the masses became.

On the opposite side of the fear spectrum is flattery, another human compulsion technique that's incredibly useful when selling a narrative. For example, feel good stories of frontline workers battling the pandemic, heroic images of doctors saving the lives of the afflicted and uplifting slogans like *United We Stand* and *We Are All In This Together* gave the impression that everyone was pulling together for the sake of humanity. However, underhandedly these mantras and images were strategically placed before the masses to create breezy feelings in people to purposefully cut them off from their intuition. The reason being, should the commoners ever find out exactly who was orchestrating and cooperating in this large scale, soft kill depopulation agenda, where they were in the crosshairs, they may not react kindly. Let this be a warning to the wise.

There's no greater burden for a well-mannered and conscientious peasant to carry than being responsible for another peasant's life. However, if the planet needs a purging to sustain a STATE where resources are used to meet human needs without undermining the stability of the natural system,[547] it stands to reason that perhaps peasants

545.) Mark E. Czeisler; Kristy Marynak, MPP; Kristie E.N. Clarke, MD; Zainab Salah, MPH; Iju Shakya, MPH; JoAnn M. Thierry, PhD; Nida Ali, PhD; Hannah Mc-Millan, MPH; Joshua F. Wiley, PhD; Matthew D. Weaver, PhD; Charles A. Czeisler, PhD, MD; Shanta M.W. Rajaratnam, PhD; Mark E. Howard, MBBS, PhD. "Delay or Avoidance of Medical Care Because of COVID-19- Related Concerns – United States, June 2020." CDC.gov. September 11, 2020. https://www.cdc.gov/mmwr/volumes/69/wr/mm6936a4.htm

546.) Mercola and Cummins, The Truth About COVID-19, 3, 10-12, 53, 61, 76, 85.

547.) Wikipedia. 2002. "Sustainable development." Last modified January 29, 2023.

should be given faulty information on how to protect themselves from falling ill. Fortunately, much of that work had already been completed long before the launch of the COVID-19 pandemic.

We've discussed Béchamp vs Pasteur in Chapter 14 and, by golly, what an appropriate chapter. The war chapter!

If you doubt we're at war, a quote from our cherished pandemic general, Dr Anthony Fauci, will set you straight. Stated in his own authoritative words: 'We're dealing with the uncomfortable but real element of political divisiveness at a time when we are in the middle of a *war* against a virus.'[548]

Indeed good sir, indeed! There is little doubt we're in the midst of battle, but to achieve victory with a viral weapon exclusively, the enemy must be covertly and strategically undermined.

This has been largely accomplished by selling the masses on Pasteur's outside invader theory as opposed to Béchamp's internal conditions' philosophy. Sure, if you are symptomatic and truly love an elderly relative or friend, it's not a good idea to pay them a visit in a nursing home whilst you're shedding. However, as another closely guarded secret between us, the greatest protection you can provide yourself, and others, is building your natural immunity and thus keeping your body under optimal internal conditions. This is hardly an approach taken in the fast food, nutritionally depleted, environmentally toxic, modern societies of today.

Obviously, methods on how to best protect oneself and others should be kept from the masses if you wish them to succumb to illness. Instead, guilting peasants into complying with mandates whilst badgering them about how they don't care about others will not only dampen their spirits, but will help earn their cooperation as well. This will come in handy when experimental treatments are introduced.

In the recent past, when the world's incorporated peasant farms were operating at near full capacity, there were so many shiny objects in the marketplace that most subjects not only showed undying devotion to their careers, but were willing to give life and limb to have the finer things in life. Similarly, and as witnessed during this most recent grand experiment, as the world economic engine slowed to a crawl, many were just as eager, if not more so, to again step over and on their fellow man to pad their bottom line.

---

https://en.wikipedia.org/wiki_Sustainable_development

548.) Dr. Anthony Fauci interviewed by Ted Koppel. "Dr. Anthony Fauci: "I didn't create political divisiveness."" CBS News.com. November 14, 2021. https://www.cbsnews.com/news/dr-anthony-fauci-the-war-on-covid/

Throughout human history, bribery has been an effective way to bypass morality, ethics and good old fashion common sense in the pursuit of personal gain. The COVID-19 pandemic was certainly no exception. Furthermore, if targets can be terrorised into regression, they'll accept nearly any proposal offered in exchange for shallow and temporary promises like peer approval and a return to normalcy. It's during this heightened panic that critical thinking is lost, and the masses' willingness to cave in is at its highest. The clever world ruler understands this and will capitalise when the opportunity presents itself.

A few real-world examples will illustrate this technique in action.

During the onset of the pandemic, US citizens were told to wear masks, close their businesses and practice social distancing measures for a couple of weeks to *flatten the curve*. Although not immediately obvious, this two-week plea for cooperation was a form of bribery with a return to the new normal as the kickback. Dangling the return of societal perks like travelling, reopening schools, dining out and the reinstatement of public functions over an eager and complicit society's collective heads became an effective way of twisting arms whilst reshaping the entire world.

Hospitals and both local and state governments were perhaps the biggest benefactors of pandemic palm greasing, although peasants themselves were also slipped some hush money in the form of stimulus payments and rent forgiveness, etc. to keep them from destroying infrastructure and allowing, in general, a smoother transition into their own demise. As always, peasants were left to foot the bill through rising prices hidden in the secret lord, wealth-enhancing scheme known as inflation.

Hospitals gained easy financial perks in the tens of thousands of dollars per case based on the number of COVID patients they treated, the number of victims they placed on ventilators and for each SARS-CoV-2 death they oversaw.[549] It's easy to see why this was a worthwhile strategy. Hospitals were more inclined to exaggerate their numbers and offer a

---

549.) Michelle Rogers. ""Fact Check: Hospitals get paid more if patients listed as COVID-19, on ventilators." USA Today.com. April 24, 2020. https://www.usatoday.com/story/news/factcheck/2020/04/24/fact-check-medicare-hospitals-paid-more-covid-19-patients-coronavirus/3000638001/ and Dr. Scott Jensen interviewed by Laura Ingraham, "Dr. Scott Jensen With Laura Ingraham | The Ridiculous CDC Guidlines," YouTube video, 4:55, TheFelsyFamily, April 9, 2020, https://youtu.be/_qWmiWf81zI and Sage Edwards. "CDC Admits Financial Hospital Incentives Drove Up COVID-19 Death Rates." Organic Lifestyle Magazine.com. August 25, 2020. https://www.organiclifestylemagazine.com/cdc-admits-financial-hospital-incentives-drove-up-covid-19-death-rates and Mercola and Cummins, The Truth About COVID-19, 57.

treatment that might not otherwise be given without a promising stipend. If a **STATE** approved treatment were to result in more deaths, wouldn't it make more dollars and cents to administer it? If you're still reluctant, what if there were no repercussions because of the chaos and confusion taking place during a global health crisis in which death and destruction were expected?

If more fatalities could be falsely accredited to COVID-19, even though victims only had an assumed or non-lethal presence of the virus when they died, couldn't a few fudged results be used to fatten a hospital's bottom line? In return for these payouts, couldn't the higher death tolls be used to instil more fear into the masses? I'm not saying any of the fine men and women on the frontlines would consciously use a counterintuitive treatment like a ventilator to push up the death toll, but a savvy insider in the upper echelons of hospital management would certainly have enough plausible deniability to impose a policy that could boost his company's profits. After all, it's just business.

Local and state government payouts are the reason the national government must receive and distribute the largest percentage of the **FARM'S** spoils. Controlling the capital at the federal level will keep the subsidiaries in line with the **FARM'S** top-down policies through the release of funding. These *bribes* will incentivise local and state governments to comply with the national government's mandates to receive their kickbacks. Since these more localised offshoots will also need to turn around and bribe peasants, they should be awarded some additional federal play money to work with.

For our final reference to the Kubark Interrogation Manual, I must point out that the manual's position is that the *threat* of force is far superior to the actual *use* of force.[550] Although there's a time and place for physical coercion, much more can be accomplished by maintaining a looming presence rather than hastily breaking out the Billy club. However, this latter option should always be ominously present. Implied fear, along with a heaping dose of hysteria, mixed with a healthy pinch of bribery, using the perks peasants hold dear as leverage, can be combined to provide strong motivation for them to comply with all your demands. To achieve this most effortlessly, you must have a firm grasp on your **FARM'S** centres of power.

Since it should now be clear that the RT-PCR test was instrumental in selling the COVID-19 false flag pandemic, it's obvious that as a

---

550.) CIA, Kubark, 90-92.

condition of employment, attendance in schools and entry into certain buildings, institutions and events, it was necessary for the panic-stricken herd to acquiesce to mass swabbings. This allowed the continuation of the conditioning process that would eventually grant orchestrators the results they were striving for. This training phase began grooming the herd to submit to more invasive actions as they were introduced. Of course, along with less physically intrusive measures like mandatory temperature taking, questionnaires and contract tracing, making RT-PCR tests routine also helped sell the new, fear-based society being sold as the new normal. Fines backed with force, physical removal of the noncompliant from the premises and, in general, stirring peasants into a frenzy diverted their energy away from the true conspirators and their creation of the pathogen and pitted them against a more accessible enemy…each other.

China again served as a shining example during SARS-CoV-1 on how to incite mass hysteria, as in the Salem Witch Trials or the Inquisition, toward anyone who believed and behaved differently than what was approved by the ruling authority. This was all achieved with the mention of a simple buzzword…*science*. China's decisive military response during SARS-CoV-1 and SARS-CoV-2 set the standard for how the entire world, under the leadership of a select group of superior minds, should ideally operate. With the gains made on even the freest of **FARMS** during the COVID-19 pandemic, a more highly obedient and conformed global society has been poked, prodded and terrorised into existence. It's the job of every global lord to stand on the shoulders of those before them and fully capitalise on the concessions made by the peasants.

Are you ready for the challenge?

The more units, devices and consoles you can deliver official messages through, the more sway you'll hold over the masses. In today's brave new world (i.e. a chemically controlled society), drug companies can take a portion of the proceeds extracted from the comatose population and put it right back into a blitz of ads that constantly remind them of your credibility not to mention your lifesaving, vitality boosting cures, potions and pills.

It sure beats hauling your snake oils from town to town in a covered wagon and hopping up on a soapbox to deliver your spiel, wouldn't you say?

High production value and nicely wrapped messages assure mesmerised audiences of a drug's life-enhancing qualities despite the ominous warnings subtly layered under the commercial's feel-good visuals. To promote the legitimacy of these chemical manipulations of the human body, the pharmaceutical industry's most trusted insiders must be seated in positions of authority at the most respected health agencies. A few modern-day examples include the FDA, CDC, WHO, NIH, NIAID and all their spin-offs, now located on nearly every peasant farm on the planet. You'll be in an advantageous position when your subjects have complete confidence in these institutions and are willing to trust them with their lives, quite literally.

It's important for a budding global lord to understand that official health messages are really nothing more than paid advertising. For example, using loyal associates in recurring roles, we find ourselves once again admiring the services of Hill and Knowlton Strategies as we did in Chapter 14. As the genius behind the Kuwaiti babies in the incubators narrative, ole H & K, as I like to kindly refer to them, was hired by the WHO to seek out three tiers of influencers to help build trust in the pandemic planner's corona virus response.[551] These three tiers of influencers included celebrities with large social media followings, individuals with smaller but more engaged followings and *hidden heroes,* those users with slight followings but who, 'nevertheless shape and guide conversations'.[552]

One of the most highly persuasive illustrations of this three-tier strategy featured a public health Zoom interview with the man of the century, Dr Anthony Fauci. This video call was organised by the always alluring, commoner favourite, Kim Kardashian with appearances from widely recognised celebrities like Katy Perry, Ashton Kutcher, Mila Kunis, Gwyneth Paltrow and Orlando Bloom. Not only did these well-behaved socialites ask proper questions but they also posted important messages from Dr Faucheuse (French for grim reaper, as I like to politely refer to him) on their social media pages, thus reaching millions of people.[553] It's the least these over-compensated, glamourised freeloaders can do for serving little societal purpose other than distracting the masses with such irrelevant attributes as physical beauty, artistic abilities, lifestyle extravagances and personal drama.

Switching gears slightly, here's some friendly advice that should be taken seriously when buying influence and public opinion to facilitate a murderous, high-stakes agenda. Never donate directly to a company that's doing your dirty work. Always use a surrogate, for instance, a

551.) Mercola and Cummins, The Truth About COVID-19, 40.

552.) Mercola and Cummins, The Truth About COVID-19, 40.

553.) Rachel Yang. "Gwyneth Paltrow, Katy Perry, Kim Kardashian, and more starts spoke with Dr. Fauci about COVID-19 in group call." Entertainment Weekly. com. https://ew.com/celebrity/kim-kardashian-celebs-spoke-dr-fauci-covid-19-group-call/

charitable foundation. That has such a sweet ring to it, doesn't it…a charitable foundation? This holds true whether you're pumping money into public agencies like the NIH or WHO, media outlets that promote your public image or private companies where your charitable foundation holds a vested interest and will benefit greatly when your Tavistock Shock Doctrine event takes place.[554]

In regard to the COVID-19 pandemic, the master of this technique, Bill Gates, not only gave generous grants to organisations like the WHO through his philanthropic front, the Gates Foundation, but he also shared the wealth of his charity with many media companies such as the BBC, NBC, Al Jazeera, PBS News Hour, the Guardian and Washington Monthly that championed his public image and promoted his suggestions for a return to *normal* that were favourable to his financial and societal aims.[555] These non-negotiable ultimatums included vaccinations, tracking and tracing technologies and vaccine passports that peasants are still being conditioned to accept as mandatory.[556] By combining the benefits of tax-exempt charitable income that's, in turn, donated to companies helping to create pandemic profits for Mr Gates, this highly skilled mass manipulator discovered the perfect balance between advancing the global agenda and making a killing on COVID-19.[557] Such daring actions allowed his power and prestige to soar to new heights. Remember, everyone admires the bold; no one honours the timid.

Mr Gates, although gangly and nerdy in appearance, is no slouch, I tell you!

In addition, the former CEO of the Micro *Soft-kill* corporation had the presence of mind to sink his foundation funds into two research teams responsible for the US and UK lockdowns, the Imperial College COVID-19 Research Team and the Institute for Health Metrics and Evaluation.[558] This is a fine example of how it's done my darling pupil. If for some reason part of your audacious plan fails, follow it up with more bold actions. This will earn the respect and submission of the masses.

Not only were three tiers of influencers actively pursued by insider organisations, but Internet operatives were recruited as well. The sole purpose of these extremely valuable Internet operatives was to discredit and neutralise viewpoints that deviated from the official narrative.

554.) Mercola and Cummins, The Truth About COVID-19, 36-38.
555.) Mercola and Cummins, The Truth About COVID-19, 36-38.
556.) Mercola and Cummins, The Truth About COVID-19, 37.
557.) Mercola and Cummins, The Truth About COVID-19, 36-38.
558.) Mercola and Cummins, The Truth About COVID-19, 36.

Friend to the International Association of Lords, the United Nations, enlisted ten thousand digital volunteers in a campaign called the Verified Initiative, which was unleashed to rid the Internet of *false information* and dissenting medical opinions instead of UN verified science.[559]

Newsguard is a company predominantly funded by the multinational advertising and public relations company, Publicis. It's worth noting that Publicis serves many wonderful clients, but more importantly, it caters to the World Economic Forum and some of the world's top pharmaceutical companies. With self-appointed Internet watchdog Newsguard's stamp of approval or disapproval, denoted as reliable or fake, on just about every Internet search and posted article, pandemic organisers could be certain peasants saw things their way.[560] This brings me to my next point.

Adored and cherished by peasants, famous athletes and celebrities are provided an influential platform primarily for their endorsement and leadership positions on new undertakings introduced to a **FARM**. Their urgent and gleeful participation in important **FARM** policies quickly earns the trust of the well-conditioned peasants, who immediately begin sharing their viewpoints. Whilst brief fits of opposition add to the illusion of open debate, persistent, well-thought-out arguments should not be tolerated. Disruptive public authority figures should, quite rapidly, fall from grace. Without their art or sport, they'll dwell amongst the swine, unable to maintain their affluent lifestyles when their generous revenue streams are abruptly truncated. Of course, to do this, you must control the centres of power. On an advanced **FARM**, like the US, this includes having a hidden hand in the sports and entertainment industrial complexes, the media empire and the political structure. When you have a firm grasp on all three, you can use them interchangeably to guide the mesmerised masses in any direction you choose.

To help prevent peasant unification, your **FARM'S** political structure should play an integral role in splitting the **FARM** into two opposing political factions. You must also diligently strive to deepen any carefully arranged or naturally occurring divides that pit peasants against each other. This is especially true during a Tavistock Shock Doctrine event. Moreover, just like your medical establishment lackeys, your political cronies will benefit from their elevation to superstar status for their leading roles in an unfurling public health emergency.

559.) Mercola and Cummins, The Truth About COVID-19, 40.
560.) Mercola and Cummins, The Truth About COVID-19, 40-41.

This is particularly true when they're constantly broadcast on laptops, mobile phones and televisions across the globe.

Of course, by taking a firm political stance in line with their party's position on an issue, politicians not only feed the narrative (even if appearing to be opposed), but they energise their supporters to take on their point of view. One side's perspective should obviously be in stark contrast with the other. As the rift widens, tensions increase. This not only stirs up animosity between those with dissenting opinions, but it arouses feelings of helplessness when these public figures appear incapable of negotiating a commonsense strategy that works for everyone.

By politicising every aspect of a manufactured crisis, simple truths, along with the best practical solutions to resolve the matter, are so distorted they're unrecognisable to the average schlep. There's nothing more obnoxious than a group of squabbling baby-kissers arguing over insignificant hot-button issues meant to fire up their bases. The upside is that their repulsive public quarrels will cause even greater apathy amongst the herd, passing responsibility for the resolution to the same people creating the issue.

A wonderful example during the COVID-19 pandemic had Governor Andrew Cuomo and Mayor Bill de Blasio bickering with President Donald Trump over a stockpile of unused ventilators. In the process, peasants nearly bludgeoned each other to death over accusations of the other side's incompetence whilst creating a false demand for the machines that put an unhealthy amount of pressure on a victim's already compromised set of lungs.

Sheer brilliance, I must say!

Whether it was authority figures clamouring for adherence to masking mandates whilst they appeared at ballgames, hair salons and major public events bare faced or well-known figureheads critical of the mask's effectiveness attending group gatherings unclothed then contracting the virus, the results were the same. It all made for wonderful political theatre whilst, in the same breath, further selling the narrative and advancing the agenda. This type of whimsical, in-your-face behaviour helped stir the embers of fiery debate, adding to the widening divide between peasants. Many peasants found the process quite baffling.

Would you care to dream up a more ideal outcome?

But perhaps the most helpful tool at the politician's disposal is the use of emergency powers. Certainly, in dire times, even an alleged defender of the people must be willing to implement a miracle cure into widespread circulation at *Warp Speed* without animal trials and long-term effects' studies whilst removing liability for its profit driven manufacturers. To keep citizens *safe*, of course. Naturally, this slyly touted, devout, liberty loving leader was forgiven by his base for taking a few freedoms away to protect his **FARM**. Of course, to the devoted party member, it was the rascally opposition pressuring him to do so. If the political divide has been properly embedded into the psyche of your peasants, they'll blame their political rivals for transgressions carried out by their party's members to save face and protect their prepackaged belief systems.

Whilst this was happening in America in real time, liberties like freedom of assembly were taken away as well as the right to jury trials (in cases of vaccine injuries caused by corporate negligence). The right to dissent and free speech were curtailed with Orwellian type censorship whilst privacy and protection from illegal searches were breached through tracking and tracing programmes.[561] All the whilst, the peasants could not have been more unsuspecting.

Hail, Caesar!

Much of your success in a similar manufactured crisis will revert to your peasant training centres and their ability to properly prepare the masses to blindly follow nonsensical instructions and repeat meaningless tasks. It's not hard to see the wonderful results achieved by such efforts during the COVID-19 pandemic. Peasants didn't question the silly emergency orders, the legitimacy of the legal processes or the intent of the authority sources who commanded them.

An ideal situation, for sure.

Since this was an undertaking never achieved on a worldwide scale, trial and error was required. Would peasants follow arbitrary dictates that lacked peer reviewed science based on the scare of the day?

Well, they certainly remained masked and socially distanced, even though the curve reached unprecedented heights after nearly two years. But it sure was great fun to watch peasants comply with sidesplitting de-crees like having to wear a mask into a restaurant but being able to take them off whilst eating, only being allowed into bars to drink if they ordered food, permitting marching band members to play their instruments if they kept their masks on whilst puffing air through their blowholes and following one-way arrows marked on the floors of every corporate chain

561.) Mercola and Cummins, The Truth About COVID-19, viii.

store receiving special permission to remain open during lockdowns.

A greater social experiment has never been seen! As a pleasant afterthought, many who built their own businesses from the ground up were willing to lose everything to comply with random and unfounded orders of the day.

If the populace stood on their convictions, some paradoxes would have been intolerable and could have resulted in severe backlash for our beloved orchestrators. For instance, the closing of churches whilst liquor stores remained open as essential services is one hypocrisy that could have incited the herd. Surely, funnelling large numbers of people into enormous box stores is a much riskier proposition than spreading out the populace through small businesses across the land, yet not even a whimper. Finally, with a reasonable understanding of the past, one would think questions would arise over globally quarantining healthy people for the first time in human history. Thankfully, no serious inquiries ever came about, and many great technocratic systems were installed and activated during the shutdown.

However, the herd's adherence to lockdown orders, despite their health status, worked toward fulfilling the objective outlined in Chapter 11; to groom the survivors of the Great Reset to live in a prison-like society.

You haven't lived until you've visited a private, for-profit penitentiary from which you have received lucrative returns on your investment. The thrill involved in achieving this type of control over a society far exceeds any street drug that incarcerates the majority of these highly lucrative jail populations. Furthermore, like caged inmates, the hapless peasants, under strict COVID-19 pandemic isolation orders, relinquished their privacy, individual liberties and personal decision-making abilities whilst also being separated from their support systems.

The parallels are remarkably striking, are they not?

As we saw post 9/11, the use of emergency powers allowed the implementation of rash laws that required many concessions from peasants, just as the COVID-19 pandemic excused the push for new policies and experimental treatments in exchange for the false promise of safety and a return to *normal*, everyday life. Keep in mind, once a new precedent is set, peasants are inclined to adapt to the new way of doing things rather than revert to the past. Along these lines, once peasants buy into the response measures, it's important to continually test their limits to fully maximise the gains possible during any calamity.

As previously discussed, the initial phase of a manufactured crisis is the most opportune time to make the most significant changes on a **FARM**. Nonetheless, one shouldn't underestimate the advantages of gradual encroachments. A true master will skilfully apply both techniques. For instance, before the grand spectacle that launched the world into the Great Reset, a.k.a. the COVID-19 pandemic, there was the bird flu scare of 2005. This wonderfully played hoax generated billions of US$ in pharmaceutical sales as governments around the world stockpiled anointed drugs like Tamiflu, deemed the only medicine effective against the deadly H5N1 strain of the disease.[562] With many still traumatised from the horrifying memories of 9/11, citizens around the world became all too willing to place blind faith in their leaders for protection against the bugaboo of the day. Although the predicted death toll never materialised, this well-run fear campaign allowed the WHO to explore ways to expedite licensing and approval times for emergency pandemic vaccines.[563] A step that would prove quite valuable during today's viral scarefest.

Whilst the bird flu hysteria of 2005 provided a useful first step toward fast-tracking any new, state of emergency *pandemic cures*, the WHO also took some creative licence one month before the declared swine flu pandemic of 2009 to legitimise all future power grabs cleverly disguised as *public health emergencies*. This was done by redefining a key term that would justify the later and more intrusive actions witnessed during the COVID-19 live exercise.

By taking the term *pandemic* and making a few slight alterations to its meaning, a large snare was placed over nearly the entire world whenever anyone as much as sneezed. Just one month prior to the officially declared 2009 Swine Flu Global pandemic (that would claim a whopping 144 deaths worldwide), the original WHO definition of pandemic read: '[…] when a new influenza virus appears against which the human population has no immunity, resulting in several, simultaneous epidemics worldwide with enormous numbers of deaths and illnesses.'[564] However, by casually removing strong language like, for instance, 'enormous numbers of deaths and illnesses' and replacing it with a more generic phrase like 'a worldwide epidemic of disease',

---

562.) Geoffrey Lean and Jonathan Owen. "Donald Rumsfeld makes $5m killing on bird flu drug." Independent.co.uk. March 12, 2006. https://www.independent.co.uk/news/world/americas/donald-rumsfeld-makes-5m-killing-on-bird-flu-drug-6106843.html and Jeffrey A. Tucker. "A Retrospective on the Avian Flu Scare of 2005." American Institute for Economic Research.org. March 22, 2020. https://www.aier.org/article/a-retrospective-on-the-avian-flu-scare-of-2005/
563.) Mercola and Cummins, The Truth About COVID-19, 29.
564.) Mercola and Cummins, The Truth About COVID-19, 112.

they set a legal justification for any extreme actions taken for even the most frivolous of outbreaks.

> NOTE: When the *enormous numbers of deaths and illnesses* that are required to implement permanent changes on a **FARM** are not present, you must either find a way to exaggerate the numbers or use other creative techniques such as changing the meanings of key legal terms to justify your protective actions. Of course, as always, the option to gracefully implement a combination of methods can be applied. It'll be the skill level of the global lord and their associates, the size and scope of the agenda, the credibility and influence of their media outlets, the effectiveness of peasant training centres and a host of other factors that'll determine how much propaganda versus real-world calamity is needed to shock the herd into compliance. These factors will also play a hand in how often and when laws, policies and standard operating procedures need to be revamped to stack the deck in your favour.

Let's investigate a master class example from our friends at the World Health Organization on how to properly move the goalpost during a manufactured crisis. Let me start by saying it has been an utter joy to watch their website's explanation of *herd immunity* change right before the peasants' eyes. Until 9 June 2020, the definition on their forum read: 'the indirect protection from an infectious disease that happens when a population is immune either through *vaccination* or immunity developed through *previous infection.*' When their website was updated in mid-November 2020, the new meaning of *herd immunity* accidentally-on-purpose left out the overblown fact that human beings can actually develop their own natural resistance to a pathogen after being exposed or infected by it. When *herd immunity* was more eloquently established as 'a concept used for vaccination, in which a population can be protected from a certain virus if a threshold of vaccination is reached', it gave the impression that the only way to defeat any plague on humanity was to provide an approved inoculation given to a proper amount of people. In a real world vs. fictional world comparison, the WHO unquestionably gives George Orwell's *Ministry of Truth* strong competition.

> NOTE: In addition, if you wish to replace a tried and true treatment like a traditional vaccine with a new type of injectable prophylaxis, perhaps some sort of new, cutting edge mRNA technology that's unproven and would take up to a decade of flawless trials to find its way to the marketplace, an excitable

event is the perfect Trojan horse for you and your associates
to wheel your agenda serving elixir into the public forum. As
always, to remove culpability from the brilliant minds behind
such a bold undertaking, planners must publicly announce their
intentions to the herd before they act. If the peasants remain
silent regarding their subjugation to an experimental treatment,
the old legal maxim *qui tacet consentire videtur* or 'silence gives
consent,' applies.

In regard to the controversial mRNA technology introduced during
the COVID-19 pandemic, such a disclosure took place on Tuesday,
29 October 2019, at the Milken Institute Future of Health Summit. The
always dependable, Dr Anthony Fauci, and the former head of the US
Biomedical Advanced Research and Development Authority (BARDA),
Dr Rick Bright, led the conference. Their prediction of an *excitable
event* originating in China was a testament to their knowledge of the
field, not to mention a tribute to their insider connections. Nothing
will make you prouder than to help engineer such a world-changing
event without once hearing your name mentioned. If the entire planet
was not glued to this important C-SPAN 2 telecast on that particular
day, or the global population failed to perform their due diligence and
revisit this important panel discussion available for playback on one of
many social media platforms, one can hardly fault a global lord for this
blatant lack of interest.

Simply stated, the peasants were warned.

By convincing the masses that herd immunity can only be
achieved by protecting people from a virus as opposed to exposing
them to it, it's not hard to imagine the profits that can be generated
for those offering their *protective services*. Hence the reason for the
heightened desire to inundate the peasants with confidence-building
slogans such as 'Love, Trust, Protect #GetVax', 'Get vaccinated', 'Do
your part. Protect yourself. Protect each other' and 'Roll up your
sleeve'. In addition, badges of honour were pinned to the compliant,
boasting such self-congratulating declarations as 'Vaccinated Against
COVID-19'. With every peasant forced to foot the bill for the panacea
provided by the political institutions of the world as a *free* service to
their people, any upfront costs to fund this marketing bonanza of the
millennium were surely well worth the initial, risk-free investment
that forced government mandates provide. Remember, if you're also
funding the *science* behind the narrative and in control of the media

outlets and the political institutions, your bank account will flourish.

At first glance, you could surely suggest that a global pandemic can be primarily used to gain compliance from the peasants and unfreeze, change and then refreeze their behavioural patterns. However, an even stronger argument can be made that it's the opportune time to expand a global lord's wealth, power and influence. If you think about it, the world ruler lacking any of these necessary attributes will not retain their throne for long. Therefore, for as much time as you invest in planning and scheming the details of a false flag event, an even greater number of preparations must be made to enhance you and your associates' net worth and overall dominance over others.

Having the insight to predict a calamity in advance will allow global planners to focus their business investments on goods and services that will be used to usher in a new normal. Needless to say, you won't find a more opportune time to introduce new product lines unique to your vision for the upgraded reality you bring to pass. Remember, as a global lord, any changes implemented should give you more leverage over the herd's mental, physical, spiritual and financial well-being to rule over them more effectively. Total domination over every single human being, down to the cellular level, is a genuine possibility for the first time in mankind's existence.

An entire handbook could be written on how to prosper whilst creating desired changes on a **FARM** when either a manufactured or naturally occurring crisis arises. However, in the interest of time, the following tactics used during the COVID-19 pandemic should provide plenty of insight into the thought process required to shape the reality you and your associates aim to create whilst bilking the peasants to do so. Like the lucrative airport scanners The Chertoff Group cashed in on after the 9/11 *tragedy* that also allowed the US's evolving government to grossly violate its once *free* citizens,[565] the most obvious economic gains come from the industries equipping, supplying and servicing the **STATE**-sanctioned response to a crisis. This is why dominance of both the public and private sector is an absolute necessity when executing this type of large-scale operation.

As discussed in Chapter 14, the most beneficial reaction to

565.) Marcus Baram. "Fear Pays: Chertoff, Ex-Security Officials Slammed For Cashing In On Government Experience." HuffPost.com. November 23, 2010. https://www.huffpost.com/entry/fear/_n_787711 and Raven Clabough. "Getting Rich from the TSA Naked-Body Scanners." The New American.com. November 18, 2010. https://thenewamerican.com/getting-rich-from-the-tsa-naked-body-scanners/

a false flag event, according to a consortium of global lords, is war. This unanimously reached conclusion holds true whether that war is against a sworn enemy or a microscopic pathogen. Knowing an event is coming will provide the savvy and seemingly clairvoyant investor with a distinct advantage over the hapless peasants who must guess where to wager their hard-earned money. Of course, the old adage of 'follow the money' could certainly lead an astute peasant to any prospering conspirator but, if done properly, most will be too stunned or too caught up in the crisis to raise any serious concerns.

Paving the way to big dollars during the COVID scarefest were practical items like household cleaners, latex gloves, toilet paper (to placate the spoiled ingrates during lockdowns) and medical devices like face masks, RT-PCR tests and ventilators. What an absolute joy it has been to watch peasants scrubbing the skin from their knuckles in an attempt to sterilise a microbe out of existence.

Quite comically, one of the surface areas erected during the frenzy was the see-through divider. Common in prisons to serve as a protective barrier, these intrusive safety features disrupted natural air flow that could whisk the infectious agent away. Instead, these partitions allowed pathogens to collect in high traffic areas such as supermarket checkout counters and bank teller stations. You have to admit that it does add to the effect whilst, at the same time, increasing the spread of infection. In addition, obstructing peasants' breathing with protective barriers reduced the amount of precious air you had to share with them.

A win-win for any lord.

There's no greater time to implement technological advances on a **FARM** than during a war, especially one funded and waged through collusion between high tech megacorporations and the leading pharmaceutical companies. It gives special meaning to Charles Lieber's statement about blurring lines between digital and living systems (see page 369) and makes Aldous Huxley's prediction of a dystopian society under technological and pharmaceutical control all the more prophetic, does it not? Technological advancements such as track and trace systems, digital passports, biometric identity cards, along with computer applications that read and record private information from medical devices, all give you direct access to the peasants' whereabouts as well as their biological attributes. Furthermore, virus size transistors and mRNA technology can activate certain cell functions like the creation of proteins in the peasants' bodies. As I'm sure you can imagine, all these innovations could prove quite valuable should you ever need to track down or disable a peasant.

Of course, worldwide installation of the 5G network supports this ambition and strengthens a global lord's ability to monitor his subjects and regulate every aspect of their lives. This can be done through the manipulation of interactive devices such as Smart Appliances and medical contrivances that can be controlled from anywhere on the planet. Is there no better time to install such an invasive network of towers and satellites than when peasants are locked down in their cells...excuse me...I mean homes, praying the deadly agent does not seep through their walls?

If you were to release a snickering scowl, I certainly could not find fault with it. In fact, I would most likely declare you incompetent if you were unable to revel in some form of delight when discussing the peasants' demise.

Besides profiting financially from technological innovations, the collection of information obtained under the guise of both convenience and safety will prove invaluable. Not only will the herd allow you to breach their privacy if they feel it's for their own good, they'll cheerfully embrace the censorship, thus allowing you to more carefully maintain your narrative whilst controlling their speech. By establishing online platforms as a necessary part of the peasants' daily existence, these platforms have become trusted vehicles for peasants to share their innermost thoughts as well as to engage in revenue generating activities like shopping and commercial services and to attend school and training seminars, all from the privacy of their own homes. Peasants have become increasingly dependent on gadgets and gizmos, bringing them one step closer to their voluntary participation in a virtual peasant farm. Once fully realised, the living metaverse, micromanaged by artificial intelligence, will allow you to exploit, control and even terminate a peasant without lifting a finger, giving you even more time to enjoy your most decadent desires.

We've explored the importance of data collection as part of the Phoenix Program (see page 125) and the huge advantage it gave US forces in predicting, interrupting and eliminating those suspected of resisting US objectives. The same applies today with bands of *citizens* whose similar thought and behavioural patterns could result in armed insurrection. Identifying those with dissenting views in advance is an absolute must.

NOTE: The Phoenix Program provided the foundation for today's global enslavement blueprint, but it was not the first time authoritative governments collected information on citizens for agenda-driven purposes. Originally created for the 1890 US census, IBM's Hollerith punch card machines (a precursor to today's computer, named after its inventor, Herman Hollerith)[566] were used during the Holocaust to target prisoners for internment camp assignments. They recorded, tabulated and stored personalised details such as prisoners' registration (tattoo) numbers, ancestral and biological traits, and train schedules for the purpose of detaining, transporting and exterminating designated persons. The punch card details also contained a citizen's profession, labour skills, age group and language abilities. Individuals were selected via a mechanical sorter.[567] If deemed worthy and in possession of a useful and necessary talent, a prisoner was assigned to a work battalion and spared, at least temporarily.[568] Work assignments were doled out at Office D II of the SS Economics Office that received labour requirements from all the work camps under the watchful eye of General Oswald Pohl. The requirements were then matched with the results obtained from the Hollerith printouts.

General Pohl is credited with the *Extermination by Labour* programme that forced extra production out of prisoners who would've otherwise been terminated before serving the German cause.[569]

This is quintessential lord decision making and may be the type of dilemma you're faced with when enforcing your own, unique worldview.

Other useful specifics included discerning those of Jewish heritage and whether that ancestry derived from the mother, the father or both, the country of origin, i.e. whether one was a German or Polish Jew as well as many other useful personal traits and characteristics such as gender, religious affiliations, marital status, number of children, date of birth, occupation and assets. The tabulations did not end upon arrival to the concentration camps, however. Statistical tabulations followed the prisoners throughout their journey. Column 34, labelled 'Reason for Departure', included Code 2 designating transfer to another camp for continuing labour, Code 3 for natural death, Code 4 for execution, Code 5 for suicide and the infamous Code 6 that designated 'special handling', secretly meaning extermination either in a gas chamber, by hanging or by gunshot.[570]

566.) Edwin Black, IBM and the Holocaust: The Strategic Alliance Between Nazi Germany and America's Most Powerful Corporation (Washington DC: Dialog Press, 2012), 25-27.
567.) Black, IBM and the Holocaust, 21.
568.) Black, IBM and the Holocaust, 21.
569.) Black, IBM and the Holocaust, 21.
570.) Black, IBM and the Holocaust, 21.

Oddly enough, the first punch card designed by Herman Hollerith was the size of a dollar bill.[571] Not only did this reflect Mr Hollerith's understanding of his monopoly over the data processing industry, since his exclusive machines could only tabulate, sort and analyse his specifically designed punch cards but, in hindsight, and on a larger scale, it symbolised the increased wealth societies could attain after eliminating their dead weight (i.e. those unable to contribute). Once IBM took ownership of the Hollerith machine, it quickly realised that information equalled dollars and that doing business with governments that tightly regulated their societies meant a big boost to IBMs bottom line, regardless of the leader's overall intent.

There are a few startling similarities in regard to today's COVID affair. By the end of 1934, nursing homes, sanatoriums and German healthcare practitioners used punch cards to collect detailed information on their patients, launching a nationwide registry of anti-social citizens.[572] Does this sound eerily similar to the vaccine passport where those who are declared outcasts (unvaccinated) aren't only denied access to things like restaurants and sporting events but face the possibility of being forcefully relocated to an isolated area for quarantine?

In addition, Work Books,[573] completed by employers, further identified and regimented every worker in the Third Reich. By asking whether the worker fit the modified definition of 'foreigner or stateless', the system paved the way for further population scrutiny.[574] Jews were forbidden to work and, in the event they did and were discovered, they were terminated. Not only would lack of employment lead to starvation, but without a Work Book, Jews couldn't obtain ration cards to purchase food.[575]

In today's modern world, with peasants completely dependent on Big Agriculture, cutting off access to the local supermarket can achieve the same results. Anyone objecting to the technocratic pharmaceutical agenda can be denied access to society and basic living essentials.

Lastly, the Nazi's *final solution* was all justified and done in the wonderful, beloved name of, you guessed it, *science*. Medical doctors,

---

571.) Black, IBM and the Holocaust, 97.
572.) Black, IBM and the Holocaust, 103.
573.) Workbooks were documents that were required for employment in Nazi Germany. They were handed in at an employee's workplace and listed the worker's skills and previous occupations. They were used to manage and coordinate labor deployment.
574.) Black, IBM and the Holocaust, 103.
575.) Black, IBM and the Holocaust, 103.

corrupted professionals, profit-minded industrialists and a clique of scientists fed into the hysteria, and despite their prestigious academic credentials, found it more beneficial to support the authorised narrative than oppose the rising fervour in the name of such overrated characteristics as moral decency and professional ethics.[576] After all, it's much simpler to lead one thousand men by their prejudices than it is to lead one man by reason, is it not?

The Nazi/IBM data collection operation continues to serve lords. Never before have so many people been identified so precisely, so silently, so quickly and with such far-reaching consequences.[577] I think it's fair to say that the information age was inspired by one's need to completely enslave his fellow man, and by acquiring technological control over their subjects, the modern-day lord will finally be able to obtain the type of absolute power that's been craved for centuries.

Inspired by noteworthy results like those achieved in Nazi Germany, fear, new laws and improved coordination between a multitude of enforcement authorities were cleverly utilised to allow orchestrators of the COVID-19 pandemic to effectively clamp down on the entire planet. For instance, businesses, with only slight pressure from government regulators, fell in line not only to satisfy authoritative directives handed down by pandemic orchestrators, but to appease peasants clamouring for compliance. Frightened subjects were easily swayed away from professionals, businesses and institutions that **STATE** leaders categorised as a threat. Meanwhile, behind closed doors, **STATE** leaders secretly worked in collusion with their generous corporate financiers to reshape humanity.

When fear-based suggestions failed to stick, emergency power mandates accompanied by fines, backed with the threat of force, ensured mass cooperation. Of course, besides fear and force, the other four human compulsion techniques of flattery, bribery, guilt and shame were also employed. The result was a massive upward shift of wealth to those with a personal stake in the technocratic business model being thrust into place.

On the international level, non-compliant countries like Tanzania, (whose leader attempted to make a mockery of the entire affair by swabbing a goat and a pawpaw for RT-PCR testing) were depicted as rogue and backwards to the rest of the world.[578] For effect, an inflated

---

576.) Black, IBM and the Holocaust, 47.
577.) Black, IBM and the Holocaust, 104.
578.) Judd Devermont and Marielle Harris. "Implications of Tanzania's Bungled Response to Covid-19." Center for Strategic International Studies.org. May 26, 2020.

number of COVID cases and deaths were reported to give the narrative a boost and to make an example of Tanzania by exaggerating the dangers of non-compliance.[579] During a pandemic, such reports will stop an industry like tourism dead in its tracks and will provide the perfect guise for many other forms of economic terrorism such as the rerouting of trucks, ships and planes carrying essential supplies to and from these *highly infected* areas.

CEOs of large superstores and dominant online retailers, conspiring with a conglomeration of global technocrats, had their businesses deemed essential and remained open, whilst smaller and more local competitors faced stringent repercussions for defying health and safety protocols if they refused to close. This created a go-along-to-get-along mentality amongst the herd that rapidly spread across the globe. Non-essential businesses were put at a severe disadvantage during lockdowns when bewildered customers were redirected into big box stores that reaped the benefits, as if this was a safer proposition. Don't worry, one-way directional arrows, cattle lines, social distancing and mask mandates accomplished what millions of years of evolution could not…complete immunity from a contagious pathogen. Of course, this was only possible inside of superstores and as long as peasants obeyed their orders.

For those too panic-stricken to leave their homes, online shopping and delivery services began the immobilisation of the public. Eventually peasants will be confined to limited areas as their freedom to move about is greatly reduced. Naturally, delivery personnel, as essential workers, and the products they carried could not transmit SARS-CoV-2 whilst peasants were led to believe everything else, including themselves, could.

What good fortune for governments that people do not think.

As a *quid pro quo* for the unfair marketplace advantages these large retailers received, their adherence to the strictest of protocols and total commitment to the narrative was the least these trusted associates could do to express their gratitude. As they say, the best way to lead is by example. Online giants such as Facebook, Google and Amazon are shining examples of businesses that flourished during the lockdowns whilst remaining faithful to the official story. In fact, so much so, that anyone

https://www.csis.org/analysis/implications-tanzanias-bungled-response-covid-19 and Reuters. "Goat and pawpaw 'test positive' for COVID-19 in Tanzania." Reuters.com. May 4, 2020. https://www.reuters.com/video/watch/idOVCCIUZCJ

579.) Joe Parkinson. "Tanzania Denied Covid-19 As Thousands Likely Died." Wall Street Journal.com. November 15, 2021. https://www.wsj.com/story/tanzania-denied-covid-19-as-thousands-likely-died-71ab47d3 .

opposing the pandemic narrative faced an interruption of services, public shaming through false information claims and a severe reduction in free speech.[580] Surely, who could forget the breaches of privacy intelligence agencies were afforded to conduct their data mining operations?[581] Whilst appearing to serve peasants, these wonderful electronic advancements made keeping tabs on them, from surveillance of their shopping habits to constant updates on their state of mind, movements, affiliations and whereabouts, easier than ever before.

With constant technological evolution since the early punch card days, artificial intelligence can now collect, store, analyse and manage information on a much faster and more expansive scale than previously possible. Owning and controlling these types of leading technologies is an absolute *must* for any modern-day lord.

A word to the wise, the emperor who ceases to find new and innovative ways to subjugate their herd will find themselves unseated from the throne of their world empire.

Of course, the companies at the forefront of the COVID-19 live exercise manufactured things like masks, digital and nanotechnologies, plastic shields, biohazard suits, ventilators, FDA approved medicines, thermometers, RT-PCR tests and the biggest revenue generator of them all…the mRNA vaccine.

In true lord fashion, one must create a problem to offer an even worse solution that creates an even bigger problem for the peasants. Their worsening condition will force them into a greater state of dependence on their ruler and the ruler's trusted institutions.

I'll use a fictitious local business, Joe's Sporting Goods, to represent the duress caused to unconnected players spread across the land of the consumer (the USA), by way of a meticulous strategy implemented before, during and after the COVID-19 pandemic.

Even though exercise, exposure to sunlight and social interaction, all facilitated by the products sold at Joe's Sporting Goods, could be justified as essential, Joe disqualified his business as essential because it wasn't specifically mentioned as such by the **STATE**. He decided

---

580.) Michelle Crouch. "12 Things You Can't Post About the Coronavirus on Facebook." AARP.org. February 24, 2021. https://www.aarp.org./health/conditions-treatments/info-2021/facebook-blocks-coronavirus-misinformation. html and Carmen Ferri. "Social media's response to COVID-19 misinformation." APC.org. April 21, 2020. https://www.apc.org/en/news/social-medias-response-covid-19-misinformation and Mercola and Cummins, The Truth About COVID-19, 10.

581.) Mercola and Cummins, The Truth About COVID-19, 44-47.

to close his doors and obey the directives piped into every home and business with a television or computer and onto the palm of every peasant with a mobile phone.

Joe's employees, all living paycheque to paycheque, were awarded unemployment benefits. With an additional emergency allotment tacked onto the bi-weekly unemployment cheque, Joe's staff members now had more discretionary spending money than they had when they were working full time. In addition, they no longer had to endure Joe's poor hygiene habits or his intrusive micromanagement style. After seeing the perks acquired by Joe's Sporting Goods' employees, others left their jobs in both *essential* and *non-essential* businesses, overburdening workers who continued working and prided themselves on being self-reliant.

> NOTE: When a drastic reduction in numbers is necessary on a **FARM**, the self-reliant are an excellent choice for those you can work to death. They'll eagerly take on more and more responsibility in pursuit of their narrow self-interests. Besides, what good is it to have peasants who wish to be independent of your authoritative rule still alive at the end of your population reduction programme?

Joe soon developed a shrewd outlook on the situation and promptly realised that if he didn't open his doors for business, he would never win back his regular customers who were developing new shopping habits and might never visit his shop again. Joe, already fully aware of the unfair advantages superstores had over his mom-and-pop operation, bucked lockdown orders and offered to pay his employees under the table.[582] This incentivised some of them to return to work, since they could still collect unemployment whilst double-dipping at Joe's shop and make more money than they ever had. Joe also sensed his small business was a dying breed as customers were embracing the money saving convenience of online shopping. Joe was

---

582.) Ned Resnikoff. "Walmart benefits from billions in government subsidies: Study." MSNBC.com. April 14, 2014. https://www.msnbc.com/msnbc/walmart-government-subsidies-study-msna307306 and Horiko Tabuchi. "Walmart's Imports From China Displaced 400,000 Jobs, a Study Says." The New York Times.com. December 9, 2015. https://www.nytimes.com/2015/12/09/business/economy/walmart-china-imports-job-losses.html and Nathan Layne. "Wal-Mart puts the squeeze on suppliers to share its pain as earnings sag." Reuters.com. October 18, 2015. https://www.reuters.com/article/us-wal-mart-suppliers-insight-iduskcn0s-d0cz20151019 and Good Jobs First. "How Wal-Mart Uses Taxpayer Money to Finance Its Never-Ending Growth." Wal-Mart Subsidy Watch.org. www.walmart-subsidywatch.org

in a desperate position and began thinking of unconventional ways to protect his wealth.

Although Joe didn't mind bending a few rules to secure his financial future, including obtaining a COVID-19 Paycheck Protection Program loan (PPP) to invest in pharmaceutical stocks, he deeply cared for the welfare of his customers. To prove it, Joe used a small portion of the loan money to purchase latex gloves, masks, hand sanitiser and disinfectants. He also installed a plexiglass checkout barrier and refused to accept cash since it could harbour the deadly virus.

In spite of these measures, nothing could stop disruptions in the supply chain caused by labour shortages and business closures. There were plenty of reasons for customers to be upset with Joe. Many of his most popular products were on backorder, his prices kept rising due to limited supply and inflation, and he strictly enforced masking and social distancing protocols.

Whilst some in the community appreciated proprietors keeping them *safe*, disenfranchised customers refused to enter Joe's shop due to what these agitators believed were nonsensical, tyrannical orders.

> NOTE: I'd be lying if I didn't admit it brought me sheer joy to watch the ruckus. Never before in modern history have so many families, friends, co-workers and neighbours been so successfully pitted against each other because of differing positions on an issue. You'll know you have mastered the divide-and-conquer technique if you achieve similar results.

Joe's valiant effort in *stopping the spread* is worthy of applause, even if it did little to strengthen his business into the foreseeable future. However, imagine adding up the profits earned on not just the small businesses complying with these *necessary* mandates, but the large businesses, hospitals, jails, airports, police stations and any other open to the public institutions and private sector participants now required to purchase RT-PCR tests, cleaning supplies, plastic shields, masks, gloves and AI helmets. The results are almost unprecedented, and we haven't even arrived at the most lucrative seller of them all, the miracle antidote. However, before we do, I'll make a few more suggestions for maximising wealth whilst expanding your power.

For one, whilst you and your team of associates are working tirelessly to subdue humanity, part of the profits generated from the unfair advantages you create for yourself and your partners must be invested back into the control grid you're installing. I know this may seem like common sense, but it must be mentioned to keep everyone on the level. You can provide additional perks to those willing to contribute to your realm's upgraded framework by using your **FARM'S** political and economic systems. Allowing associates to benefit from the use of an advanced **FARM'S** military can incentivise them to kickback a portion of their proceeds into that **FARM'S** surveillance system. This is in their best interest, since the herd may not react too kindly if their abuse of power is discovered. Additionally, a **FARM'S** military can help ensure compliance from those who reaped the benefits of the distinct privileges they were afforded yet suddenly become reluctant to pay their fair share.

Ultimately, however, isn't it always the commoners who pay the greatest price for their own enslavement?

As seen during the COVID-19 pandemic, political institutions were used as buffers to shield orchestrators from the harm caused by their Malthusian remedies. By creating laws that indemnified pharmaceutical companies for the damages incurred by their emergency, hurried to market *vaccines*, profits were maximised due to the removal of liability for any wrongful injuries and deaths these antidotes caused. Since governments are able to provide emergency panaceas *free of charge* by billing and then, in turn, more heavily taxing peasants, why shouldn't peasants foot the bill for the hardships incurred from these emergency treatments? This is done simply by redirecting peasants back to the government for any injurious claims brought on by the *vaccines*. It'll then be the government that absorbs the lawsuits which, not so coincidentally, are reimbursed by peasants through even more taxation.

This is a win-win scenario for any canny lord.

As previously discussed, a good crisis should never go to waste.

When a herd is devoutly loyal to an apparition in the sky as opposed to their true overlord here on Earth, you can wisely use the political structure. During the COVID-19 global pandemic, the **STATE** dismantled families and support systems by minimising the number of peasants allowed to gather in one setting, resulting in the favourable Kubark Interrogation manual technique of isolation (see page 249). A god-fearing society directs peasants' attention away from the **STATE**, which in the new, high tech pharmaceutical society is the exact opposite of what should occur, as the **STATE** should replace the **FARM'S** divine entity of choice. The transition can easily occur through science worship and its many breakthroughs, like those that make lords appear all-seeing and all-knowing. You can enhance this effect by dumbing down the masses, which makes every advanced technology introduced to society seem like a mysterious, unexplainable miracle performed by the **STATE**. One day, in the name of safety, and in the not-too-distant future, the **STATE** will truly become godlike by knowing every single thought entering a peasant's mind.

Those in positions to seize the opportunity gained greater control over the world's industries during the false flag pandemic. When you control the planet's political bodies, laws can be rewritten, emergency state powers enacted and arbitrary, non-binding mandates randomly muttered by various authority figures. The net effect is the absolute economic power to decrease production at will, which you can use to create controlled shortages that yield higher profits.

To be in an ideal position to conquer the planet, a world economy that revolves around a single, major supplier-nation, preferably under a totalitarian regime that all other **FARMS** are dependent on, *must* be established. Then, when the time is ripe, simply shut down the supplier-nation. Political and social upheavals of epic proportions will ensue on even the strongest of **FARMS**. As clearly explained in this handbook and through unbiased observations by anyone with a modicum of sense, the current workshop of the world fitting this description is China.

It's easy to imagine the calamity that could arise should this type of scenario unfurl in today's modern world. However, for the live exercise currently taking place, I would like to point out a couple of major achievements that the current modern-day lords might attain should they continue to offer a bold vision for humanity.

For one, by dismantling the current system whilst also maintaining firm control of **STATE** institutions and essential industries, today's exciting team of rising technocrats has been able to strong arm societies around the civilised world to adopt their new business model. With a workforce too afraid to enter proximity to one another, the moment has finally arrived to confine most of humanity to their quarters. From there, they can conduct their daily activities without squandering the Earth's precious resources that are in dire need of more sustainable management. The ideal result of this fourth industrial revolution features a much smaller herd size but one still capable of producing, maintaining and servicing the control grid, all essential supplies and, most importantly, all the earthly pleasures that an exquisite group of technocratic lords so rightly deserve.

In this prisonlike setting, peasants can experience the illusion of freedom through the interactive, computer-generated reality created to limit the need for their actual presence in physical locations. This can already be seen in many occupations, like teaching, where virtual class-rooms are transitioning peasants of today into the metaverse of tomor-row. Occupations in sales and service have also begun the transforma-tion process whilst institutions like hospitals and prisons are replacing actual, in-person visits with live streaming, further reducing human contact. It's easy to see that this is an inconspicuous way to sequester peasants. The biggest upside to these types of interactions is that they can be recorded and then monitored by artificial intelligence, making secret plots and rebellions a thing of the past.

The political body can also inconspicuously impose all six human compulsion techniques, especially that of bribery, to gain cooperation from peasants whilst simultaneously lining the pockets of its master. For instance, dangling a peasant's ability to clothe and feed their family over their head is a sure way to encourage cooperation with testing requirements, mask wearing directives and even injections of an ex-perimental DNA altering substance into a healthy human body. Peas-ants will hit even greater levels of desperation and hence willingness to conform as the world economy starts to unhinge. In addition, the advantage of transitioning from a relatively free society where peasants can readily move about, to one with much tighter controls and limited mobility, is that peasants can be offered a return to *normal* in exchange for compliance.

Would you like to return to school kiddies? If so, you must wear spirit crushing masks that, with prolonged use, raises the carbon dioxide levels in your bloodstreams.[583] Are you interested in attending a large event or taking a trip to France? Well, most certainly, but you'll be required to submit to an RT-PCR test, and when available, you must receive a shot manufactured NOT by those who profit from your sickness but by those who deeply care for you and all of humanity.

Shall I continue?

Coming up a little short on your mortgage payment this month? Sorry to hear that, but since your co-worker's wife bowls with a woman whose husband tested positive for COVID-19, you're going to have to

---

583.) Harold Walach, Helmut Traindl, Juliane Prentice, Ronald Weikl, Andreas Di-emer, Anna Kappes, Stefan Hockertz. "Carbon dioxide rises beyond acceptable safety levels in children under nose and mouth covering: Results of an experi-mental measurement study in healthy children," ScienceDirect.com. https://www.sciencedirect.com/science/article/pii/S001393512200891X

stay home from work and take an RT-PCR test even though you show no symptoms of the disease. Whilst waiting for the results, you'll have to burn some annual leave to cover your absence. Were you notified of your responsibility to pay the cost of the rapid test so you can return to work sooner, thereby preserving your annual leave for your already pre-paid yearly trip to the Canary Islands?

Are the underlying motives of this form of coercion becoming glaringly obvious?

On a large scale, mass punishment can be equally effective. For example, do you want to return to the beach this summer or eat out at your favourite restaurant? Then most of the population *must* receive the one and only **STATE** recommended treatment that can return society back to its most cherished activities. By the way, as suggested by Kurt Lewin in his *Force Field Analysis* and as put into effect by complicit members of society, withholding an activity that everyone enjoys until they meet a certain demand is a great way to put additional pressure on those refusing to cooperate with their orders.

Have I made myself clear? Please remember, if you need to prolong the crisis for an indefinite period of time, grant privileges but then randomly revoke them as quickly as you issue them. This will condition peasants to adapt to their new normal. Your mastery over the herd will hit its apex when they immediately adhere to whatever directives you issue.

The new normal ambitiously strives to grant lords the luxury of reigning over the last bastion of freedom an isolated individual has left, their thoughts. It's the human spirit that's the great intangible separating mankind from all other species. It's this unbridled X factor that has lifted humans through the darkest of times and elevated them above the fiercest of oppressors. If there's a way to change what it is to be human and dampen this unique quality, shouldn't it be pursued with the utmost urgency?

It's imperative that the peasants' overall condition continuously deteriorates. This will afford an aspiring world ruler the greatest degree of leverage. This has been performed with subtle mastery during the COVID-19 pandemic. Whether strict enforcement crackdowns like those in New York or Los Angeles were naturally occurring or induced through well-coordinated efforts of a sleek, underground network, the results are the same. Peasants were either scurrying to areas that offered safety from the lethal virus or, conversely, were moving away from localities with heavy-handed restrictions intended to *protect* citizens from the microbe. Little did either camp know they were unknowingly depleting themselves financially whilst uprooting themselves from their established support systems.

The opportunistic lord is in an ideal position to exploit such a situation, by setting a trap. In our current example, this can be done by creating a haven for resistors to flock to in order to escape STATE coercion. Once a majority of peasants take the bait, the trap can be sprung, and even more invasive measures put into effect at this once desirable place of refuge. You can accomplish this with the insertion of a key political figure, a new governor perhaps, who is friendly to the network and its overall plan. With little to no personal wealth remaining due to things like inflation, moving costs and underemployment, transplanted peasants will find themselves in a more precarious position. The cornered and vulnerable peasants will have little choice but to comply with the new demands. Both the novice and well-seasoned lord must understand this sort of strategy requires time and patience.

Any level of peasant ownership, let alone taking over the entire world, can be actualised only by taking chances. However, if you are to completely conquer the planet, the risks must be minimised and eliminated whenever possible, as the room for error is incredibly slim. To flesh out a couple of important lessons for creating a world empire, let's look at a peasant favourite, the sports industry.

First, when grown adults are paid astronomical sums to play a kids' game like American football, you'll know your FARM has hit a high level of economic success. These overpaid, modern-day gladiators can serve many useful purposes. The games distract peasants from their mundane lives, relieve stress, and keep them occupied, preventing them from focusing on bigger issues. Ancillary markets created by the sports industrial complex add a healthy boost to the economy and offer an aggressive outlet for those who might disrupt established order, whether they're players at the highest level or spectators rooting for their favourite team.

Since society turns the most talented athletes into idols by trumpeting their salaries, lifestyles, and accolades, whilst also providing wonderful workplace banter when one of them falls from grace, it's easy to see why these publicly adored sports heroes heavily influence the chattels' perception of the world. It's this power of persuasion over the masses that can be a lord's most valuable asset when attempting to motivate the citizenry into a desired course of action. During the

COVID-19 pandemic, the sports crazed American public was led by its favourite athletes who were glistening examples of the proper way to handle the crisis. If this meant masking up in public, avoiding large stadium crowds or routinely testing for the virus as directed by health officials, every peasant had a public figure they adored that helped influence their decision.

Pro athletes had a lot to lose if they refused to go along with the agenda. This was an advantageous position for lords. With the entire world watching, professional athletes were held to the highest of standards whilst being ordered to comply with whimsical directives. American professional sports leagues including the National Basketball Association (NBA), the National Football League (NFL) and Major League Baseball (MLB) coined the term *COVID-19 Health and Safety Protocols*. With the amount of money made on professional sports, in particular gambling, and with trusted associates in control of testing, it was the ideal setting to rig a game by sidelining a few key players, creating an advantage for connected, sports betting profiteers. After all, money is power, and the successful lord must always be on the lookout for ways to enhance their riches at the expense of the unenlightened masses.

> NOTE: If it's time to shrink a farm's economy, an event like a pandemic or similar false flag attack is the perfect time to cut back on bread and circus industries serving no useful purpose other than diverting the peasants' attention. Surely, no commoner will complain when these overpaid professionals receive wages comparable to their own. Once a wealthy farm begins its decline into fiscal calamity, those chosen to flaunt the excesses of that society can be wrangled back in, as there will no longer be a need for a golden calf for the peasants to chase, as most will struggle to survive.

The second major discussion point regarding celebrity athletes and entertainers has to do with the miracle vaccine. When a new gene therapy, never shown to be effective, is suddenly pushed onto the entire populace, naturally a few commoners will be sceptical. Unless, of course, their favourite poster boy for good health and athletic prowess not only willingly succumbs to the jab himself, but strongly encourages others to do so.

I mean, who could possibly refuse?

In a similar situation, depending on what you put into your remedy, you may want to inject those in visible positions with a saline solution in case there are adverse effects. The last thing you need is for a highly regarded public figure who is endorsing your money-making treatment to suddenly keel over whilst forcing the befuddled masses to watch.

On that note, I believe it's time to discuss the most important part of a well-orchestrated outbreak, the antidote.

Chapter 18

THE MIRACLE ANTIDOTE AND THE WORLD OF TOMORROW

By 2100, our destiny is to become like the gods we once worshipped and feared. But our tools will not be magic wands and potions but the science of computers, nanotechnology, artificial intelligence, biotechnology and most of all, the quantum theory.
—Michio Kaku

Compromising the peasants' well-being has been a repetitive theme throughout this handbook, but it must once again move to the forefront of your consciousness if you're to receive the most benefit from our next discussion. My goal is not to guide you through every possible scenario but to stimulate your thinking in a direction that allows you to plan a strategy for any situation so that it brings you greater abundance and dominance.

Klaus Schwab, Founder and Executive Chairman of the World Economic Forum, candidly states in his prophetic book, *COVID-19: The Great Reset*: 'History shows that epidemics have been the great resetter of countries' economy and social fabric.'[584] I'll use the COVID-19 mRNA vaccine rollout to illustrate how to reboot society and thrust mankind into its most magnificent evolution to date.

For starters, can you tell me what the foundation of life is? You may suggest water or salt or some other external element like fire, but the answer is more basic and even more obvious. It's carbon. Carbon is the primary component of all life on Earth mainly because of its ability to readily bond with other elements and its capacity to form essential compounds.[585]

I would be amiss if I were to hold back the fact that some

584.) Klaus Schwab and Thierry Malleret, COVID-19: The Great Reset (Cologny/Geneva, Switzerland: Forum, 2020), 38.

585.) CK-12 Foundation. "Significance of Carbon." LibreTexts Biology.org. March 5, 2021. https://bio.libretexts.org/Bookshelves/Introductory_and_General_Biology/Book%3A_Introductory_Biology_(CK-12)/01%3A_Introduction_to_Biology/1.09%3A_Significance_of_Carbon

very clever technocratic aspirants have toyed with the notion of manipulating carbon to possess certain qualities that would allow living organisms to coexist in both the physical world and a virtual world as part of a living Internet, commonly known as the metaverse.

In fact, one such discovery that offers a ton of potential is a pure carbon material called graphene. Possessing ideal properties such as flexibility, off the chart tensile strength, and thermal and electrical conductivity, it's oxidised derivative, graphene oxide, also proves to have intelligence in the form of black goo.[586] The British MI6 weaponised this murky substance and referred to it as 'sentient fluid' due to its response to electrical stimulation.[587] On a more top-secret level, graphene oxide is quite capable of connecting the human brain to a computer and, in turn, the Internet, serving as a bridge between man and machine.[588]

NOTE: If you truly desire to rule over men, I believe you may already intuitively understand the importance of choosing a dark spiritual path for summoning your supernatural strength. One glaring detail to point out is that carbon is number six on the periodic table of the elements and contains six protons, six neutrons and six electrons. That's 6-6-6.[589] I'm afraid that

586.) Dave Roos. "Graphene: 200 Times Stronger Than Steel, 1,000 Times Lighter Than Paper.howstuffworks.com. August 18, 2020. https://science.howstuffworks.com/innovation/new-inventions/graphene.htm and Tarun Radadiya. "A Properties of Graphene." ResearchGate.net. September 2015. https://www.researchgate.net/publication/321036338_A_PROPERTIES_OF_GRAPHENE and DeepStateDamage. "The Substance Ruling the World: Black Goo/Graphene Oxide." Forensichealing.com. https://forensichealing.com/the-substance-ruling-the-world-black-goo-graphene-oxide/ and Jason Kehe. "The Biggest Threat to Humanity? Black Goo. Wired.com. August 24, 2022. https://www.wired.com/story/biggest-threat-to-humanity-black-goo/

587.) "Black Goo Coming Out of Bathroom in England/Sentient Fluid," BitChute video, 2:36, Jeff_P, October 14, 2021, https://www.bitchute.com/video/9erIJaGtl0sO/

588.) Sarah Westall. "Can Graphene Oxide Turn the Human Body into a Networked Biological Computer?" Sarah Westall.com. July 22, 2021. https://sarahwestall.com/can-graphene-oxide-turn-the-human-body-into-a-networked-biological-computer/ and "Graphene shown to safely interact with neurons in the brain." University of Cambridge.ac.uk. January 29, 2016. https://www.cam.ac.uk/research/news/graphene-shown-to-safely-interact-with-neurons-in-the-brain and "Nanotechnology: Hacking Humans, Its Potentials, and Real Risks," YouTube video, 4:36, CISO Global, June 29, 2019, https://youtu.be/nsGvcejqzb4 and "America's Book Of Secrets: DARPA's Secret Mind Control Technology (Season 4) | History," YouTube video, 5:57, HISTORY, July 10, 2021, https://youtu.be/wZRkfBsTTt8

589.) "Protons Neutrons & Electrons of All Elements (List and Images)." Periodic Table Guide.com. July 9, 2022. https://periodictableguide.com/protons-neu-

nothing is by accident, and to rule in this principality you must
serve the true lord of this world, the great bearer of light, Lucifer.
As you can clearly see, it's written into the code of every material
substance on the planet. You'd be playing with eternal fire to
believe otherwise.

Cancer researchers found that by attaching a specific drug to a
nanoparticle of graphene oxide then targeting the tumour location
with a magnetic field, the nanoparticle would take the desired drug
to the afflicted area.[590] When the magnetic field was discontinued, the
graphene oxide would disperse back into the body but would leave
the drug with the distressed tissue requiring it. Quite miraculous,
one might say. Unfortunately, or should I say fortunately, for the
global planner looking to spark a worldwide pandemic, the side
effects of nanoparticle graphene oxide bear a striking resemblance
to the symptoms of COVID-19. First, there is a platelet reduction
because of blood clotting. Then, as toxicity increases, oxidative stress
occurs, leading to an immune system collapse (known as a cytokine
storm).[591] Does the term *cytokine storm* sound familiar? It should as
this final stage of human response attributed to SARS-CoV-2 was
popularised on every news programme across the globe. Not only
are the lethal progressions of graphene oxide toxicity and COVID-19
indistinguishable, inhalation of nanoparticle graphene oxide initiates
inflammation of the mucous membranes, resulting in the loss of taste
and smell.[592]

As a bonus, nanoparticle graphene oxide has the rare ability
to penetrate the impermeable blood-air, blood-brain and placental
barriers, allowing access to these previously forbidden yet highly
critical biological safe zones.[593] Imagine, if you will, the amazing

trons-and-electrons-of-elements/
590.) Ya-Shu Huang, Yu-Jen Lu, Jyh-Ping Chen. "Magnetic graphene oxide as a carrier for targeted delivery of chemotherapy drugs in cancer therapy." ScienceDirect.
com. October 10, 2016. https://www.sciencedirect.com/science/article/abs/pii/
S030488531632515X#:~:text=A%20magnetic%20targeted%20functionalized%20
graphene%20oxide%20%28GO%29%20complex,FE3%20O%204%20magnet-
ic%20nanoparticles%20on%20GO%20nano-platelets.
591.) Dr. Ricardo Delgado interviewed by Michel Chossudovsky, "Graphene Oxide: A
Toxic Substance in the Vial of MRNA Vaccine – Interview With Ricardo Delgado," BitChute video, 24:45, Centre for Research on Globalization, July 17, 2021,
https://www.bitchute.com/video/17S4PiXkfU6t/
592.) Delgado interviewed by Chossudovsky," Graphene Oxide," 3:58-4:07.
593.) Monique Culturato Padiha Mendonca, Edilene Siqueira Soares, Marcelo Bispo

capabilities of graphene oxide coupled with Dr Charles Lieber's transistors and both working in conjunction at the nanoparticle level within the human body. Instructions and information could theoretically be sent and received via an electronic device using the properties of graphene oxide. Once the graphene oxide receives a message, it could activate or seek out a nano transistor and deliver instructions to a strategic part of the body ready to carry out the task requested by the external source. Can you see the wide range of possible applications? Of course, as always, these technologies are developed as dual-purpose where the potential benefits are sold to peasants to gain their consent for internal use, whilst their detrimental applications (for peasants anyway) are kept in the strictest of confidence. This will allow plausible deniability in situations where a deadly disease is triggered, or a kill switch is activated.

I'm not implying any of this was done as part of the COVID-19 mRNA drive but suppose it had been. Are we not in a war? As stated in Chapter 14, is there no better time to experiment on living human beings? Are typical laws not suspended as part of a state of emergency?

For fun, let's explore what would happen if these *world of tomorrow* technologies were slipped into the COVID-19 mRNA vaccine already approved for emergency use. Even though the methods used to deliver such transformational advancements into peasants are only limited by the creative boundaries of their architects, for this discussion, assume peasants will be compromised by injection. In reality, at the time of this writing, not only is this the most effective way to infiltrate a target, but it's also the most widely accepted. Even more importantly, peasants grant their legally required consent by voluntarily submitting to these experimental

de Jesus, Helder Jose Ceragioli, Monica Siqueira Ferreira, Rodrigo Ramos Catharino, Maria Alice da Cruz-Hofling. "Reduced graphene oxide induces transient blood-brain barrier opening : an in vivo study." NIH: National Library of Medicine.gov. October 30, 2015. https://pubmed.ncbi.nlm.nih.gov/26518450/ and Anju S. Mohanan P.V.. "Can nanographene cross the placental barrier? Atlas of Science.org. February 11, 2020. https://atlasofscience.org/can-nanog-raphene-cross-placental-barrier/ and Rogue Male. "Graphene Oxide: a Vial Concoction for Mass Murder." RogueMale.org. July 7, 2021. https://roguemale.org/2021/07/07/graphene-oxide-a-vial-concoction-for-mass-murder/#:~:text=G-FNs%20can%20induce%20acute%20and%20chronic%20injuries%in,accumu-lating%20in%20the%20lung%2C%20liver%2C%20and%20spleen%20etc. and Lingling Ou, Bin Song, Huimin Liang, Jia Liu, Xiaoli Feng, Bin Deng, Ting Sun, and Longquan Shao. "Toxicity of graphene-family nanoparticles: a general review of the origins and mechanisms." BioMedCentral.com. October 13, 2016. https://particleandfibretoxicology.biomedcentral.com/articles/10.1186/s12989-016-0168-y#citeas

treatments. Is it so wrong to swap out one lesser-known technology for another when their overall objectives are exactly the same?

For instance, in the COVID-19 mRNA vaccine, a strand of RNA (made of nucleotides and reverse transcriptase (a biological catalyst)) instructs the cell to manufacture spike proteins, triggering an immune response that produces antibodies that will more readily respond to the virus spike protein.[594] It looks good on paper anyway. However, it's important to realise that when the presence of nanoparticles (a technological catalyst) is detected inside the host, a natural, internal response triggers the body to innately form biomolecular coronas on the nanoparticles.[595] The type of corona protein formed depends on factors such as the physiochemical properties of the nanoparticle as well as the health of the carrier.[596]

If the right nanoparticle is found, say one whose side effects, when in the body, match those of SARS-CoV-2, is it unreasonable for you to assume that these nanoparticles produce the same corona proteins as the virus that causes COVID-19?[597] In a 'Which came first, the chicken or the egg?' scenario, did the right nanoparticles under the right conditions create the corona spike proteins that lead to COVID-19? Or, did the SARS-CoV-2 virus already exist and the right nanoparticles just so happened to create the same symptoms as SARS-CoV-2? Regardless of which one predated the other, could the injection of specific nanoparticles incite the body to create corona proteins that the body then learns to form immunity against? If so, can you think of

---

594.) National Center for Immunization and Respiratory Diseases (NCIRD), Division of Viral Diseases. "Understanding How COVID-19 Vaccines Work." CDC.gov. February 3, 2023. https://www.cdc.gov/coronavirus/2019-ncov/vaccines/different-vaccines/how-they-work.html

595.) Jie Gao, Li Zeng, Linlin Yao, Ziniu Wang, Xiaoxi Yang, Jianbo Shi, Ligang Hu, Qian Liu, Chunying Chen, Tian Xia, Guangbo Qu, Xian-En Zhang, and Guibin Jiang. "Inherited and acquired corona of coronavirus in the host: Inspiration from the biomolecular corona of nanoparticles." PubMed Central. NIH: National Library of Medicine. April 17, 2021. https://ncbi.nlm.nih.gov/pmc/articles/PMC8052473/

596.) Daniel Nierenberg, Annette R. Khaled, and Orielyz Flores. "Formation of a protein corona influences the biological identity of nanomaterials." College of Medicine. University of Central Florida.edu. May 28, 2018. https://med.ucf.edu./akhaled/files/2020/09/Niemberg-RPOR-2018.pdf

597.) Ricardo Delgado and Prof Michele Chossudovsky. "Video: Graphene Oxide : A Toxic Substance in the Vial of the COVID-19 mRNA Vaccine." Truthcomestolight.com. July 17, 2021. https://truthcomestolight.com/an-interview-w-richard-delgado-impacts-of-graphene-oxide-nano-particles-contained-in-the-vial-of-the-mrna-vaccine/

any additional benefits that injecting nanoparticles of graphene oxide into peasants may bring?

Let's discuss the replacement of mRNA strands in the COVID-19 vaccines with nanotransistors (a technological catalyst). These nanotransistors may or may not be made of graphene or a derived substance. Additionally, they may or may not be accompanied by nanoparticles of graphene oxide to assist in their function. Recall the words of Dr Charles Lieber: 'Digital electronics are so powerful that they dominate our daily lives. When scaled down, the difference between digital and living systems blurs....'[598] Therefore, whether cells are receiving instructions to manufacture spike proteins from strands of RNA, messages are delivered to nanotransistors that, in turn, relay them to penetrated cells to produce the spike proteins or biomolecular coronas innately form on graphene nanoparticles inside the human, the net result is the same. The spike protein is manufactured within a host due to a lab created catalyst that triggers the immune system to respond.

To encourage progressive thinking, it would be incredibly beneficial from a financial and authoritative standpoint if nanotechnology could be used to create new and evolving strains of viruses within the human body. The costs involved in running and maintaining large facilities could be reduced if peasants became walking bioweapon laboratories. Simply click on your favourite biological agent, activate it within a targeted group of individuals and boom, your next wave of disease emerges, sending them running to their lord for a cure.

If they're the defiant type, I see no reason you should grant remedies for unruly subjects. For peasants worth keeping, an unlimited number of boosters for an evolving number of variants can be administered. The cost for each **STATE** regulated cure should, of course, be docked from the peasants' pay.

If the technology has not been delivered into human systems during this most recent opportune time, I suggest that a rising lord seize the next opportunity to launch humanity into this bold, new frontier. Rulers possessing the most sophisticated combination of both human and artificial intelligence will manage this technocratic super state. This quantum leap into the future will be so abrupt and so spectacular, peasants will barely notice, nor care, how and when it all came about!

Playing devil's advocate, if an ideal scenario such as the

598.) Shaw, "Virus-Sized Transistors."

COVID-19 pandemic is not presented, you must consider other delivery systems. As always, it's important that peasants volunteer their consent to receive these exploratory scientific advancements. However, with naked-to-the-human-eye technology, the temptation exists to secretly inundate the masses through common environmental and commercial means.

Does the late, great Dr Shiro Ishii come to mind?

With these nanotechnologies nearly impossible to detect or trace back to their source, ideas include atmospheric aerosol droplets, water supplies, medical masks, RT-PCR test swabs and even supermarket-bought food wrapped in *scientifically advanced* packaging material. In days of old, an emerging virus could have been delivered via a common seasonal flu vaccine.

Are you surprised by this concept? Well, if you think about it, unless regulatory agencies like the CDC have a crystal ball, how would they predict which flu strain would be prevalent that year?

Psst. Could it be that some vaccines contained an active strain, bringing that year's outbreak to fruition?

Nah. Never. It would be unethical to sicken people for the mere sake of profit and power. That's exactly why lords must always present themselves in the most humanitarian light possible whilst using their institutions to hammer the importance of high ethical standards into the herd's thick skulls. This will create the illusion that lords play by the same rules as their subjects. However, it'll be those willing to step outside of a **FARM'S** ethical boundaries who will truly separate themselves from the pack. At the same time, the astute ruler is cleverly building an additional layer of defence, since many of his **FARM'S** devout subjects would never suspect that *credible* positions were attained by violating their **FARMS**' sacred moral standards.

As the great pharmaceutical leader Baxter Corporation learned, a conscientious and untrusting peasant could potentially discover a live virus or any other mysterious ingredient secretly implanted in the vials. Unfortunately in 2009, a research facility in the Czech Republic discovered the live avian flu virus in the seasonal flu vaccine that was distributed by Baxter to eighteen different countries including Austria, Slovenia and Germany.[599] This, as a result, sidelined years of planning,

---

599.) The Canadian Press. "Baxter admits flu product contained live bird flu virus." CTVNews.ca. February 27, 2009. https://www.ctvnews.ca/baxter-admits-flu-product-contained-live-bird-flu-virus-1.374503 and The Canadian Press. "How were bird flu viruses sent to unsuspecting labs?" CTV News.ca. February 26,

research and billions of dollars spent on inoculations containing the live bird flu virus, never injected into the arms of properly conditioned test subjects...good heavens...I mean citizens.[600] If not for this setback, the new and much more subversive methods of implementation may never have been realised. The moral of the story is, stay committed to the task at hand and use each difficulty as a learning experience. The advancements made to date are proof that when one door closes another portal leading to a more obsequious world opens.

Let us raise a toast to human conquest!

If your knees buckle at the thought of peasants becoming wise to such calculated plots, here's a quote by Gustav LeBon: 'The masses have never thirsted after truth. They turn aside from evidence that is not to their taste, preferring to deify error, if error seduced them. Whoever can supply them with illusions is easily their master; whoever attempts to destroy their illusions is always their victim.' I thought it might encourage you to hear a grouping of such eerily prophetic words from someone other than me.

Let's continue our quest to transcend humanity, whether through the manipulation of their DNA, nanotechnology or a splendid combination of both.

In the land of Hollywood, if a mysterious new plague haunted mankind, those using science for the noblest of causes would quickly discover and produce a cure, and widely distribute it to every man, woman, and child, saving humanity from a disastrous fate. Then the film credits would roll and peasants, whose endorphins were raised to overdrive by the film, would have trouble discerning fact from fiction should a similar, real-life scenario present itself.

Since the comfortable and highly entertained peasants rarely face this type of life-or-death crisis in their pampered reality, the information

2009. https://www.ctvnews.ca/how-were-bird-flu-viruses-sent-to-unsuspecting-labs-1.374153 and Jason Bermas, "Baxter Puts Live Avian Flu In Vaccines And Sends It Out to 18 Countries," YouTube video, 8:41, harrythomasinfo, March 9, 2009, https://youtu.be/RqBWr5xY6N0 and Mike Adams. "Vaccines as Biological Weapons? Live Avian Flu Virus Placed in Baxter Vaccine Materials Sent to 18 Countries." Natural News.com. March 3, 2009. https://www.naturalnews.com/025760.html

600.) Robert Roos. "YEAR-END REVIEW: Avian flu emerged as high-profile issue in 2005."CIDRAP University of Minnesota.edu. January 5, 2006. https://www.cidrap.umn.edu/avian-influenza-bird-flu/year-end-review-avian-flu-emerged-high-profile-issue-2005 and Jeffrey A. Tucker. "A Retrospective on the Avian Flu Scare of 2005." American Institute for Economic Research.org. March 22, 2020. https://www.aier.org/article/a-retrospective-on-the-avian-flu-scare-of-2005/

they're fed through the various media outlets provides the foundation for their belief systems. Therefore, this trusted source of news (or 'Ministry of Truth' if comparing it to George Orwell's *1984)* must win the battle for the monopoly on *credible* information. To do this, it must inundate peasants with official narratives whilst relentlessly censoring the opposition.

In reality, whether a COVID-19 type scenario arises by chance, or through a concerted effort to weaken, shrink down, profit on, or in some other way alter the herd, the goal should be the same. That is, to inject as many test subjects as possible with an agenda-serving *treatment* that accomplishes one or all the objectives just mentioned.

For those who aren't of the Malthusian ilk, conquering the planet and enslaving humanity is simply a delusion of grandeur. I'd be surprised if such a person could put a worm on a fishing hook.

Should an up-and-coming lord decide to experiment with a miraculous new ingredient capable of elevating the human race by uniting it into one living, breathing virtual world (of course, I'm referring to nanoparticles of graphene oxide), he must expect setbacks, physical complications, illnesses and even death. But hasn't that been the case throughout human history, where a few sacrificial lambs were offered for the sake of progress? To avoid negative repercussions, however, a grand risk-taker should apply a common lord tactic, cloaking his ambitious and sometimes dark undertakings by obscuring details with confusing nomenclature.

The food industry has accomplished this with remarkable success.

When the ill effects of trans fats raised a bellowing cry from the herd due to their negative impact on human circulatory systems, trans fats were simply relabelled hydrogenated oils.[601] For any aspiring lord wondering why a harmful, artery clogging food preservative would be renamed instead of removed from the market, they may need to be reminded of their Malthusian ideals. Not only were gazillions made on heart surgeries, heart medicines, type 2 diabetes, strokes and continued trans fat sales, but the peasants' overall condition was weakened, and FARM populations were kept in check.

One of the *blood thinners*, Warfarin, originally patented as a rat poison, also sold for decades under the brand names of Coumadin and Jantoven.[602] Slight tweaks in their formulas justified the new names that

601.) Andrea Donsky., RHN. "Label Loophole: Why Trans Fat-Free Foods Are Often Far From It." naturallysavvy.com. https://naturallysavvy.com/eat/label-loophole-why-trans-fat-free-foods-are-often-far-from-it/

602.) Gregory B. Lim. "Warfarin: from rat poison to clinical use." Nature.com.

subsequently provided just enough shade to help disguise their lethal roots.[603] Furthermore, Warfarin has another close cousin operating under the brand name of Heparin, again providing another degree of separation from its rodent-killing past.

> NOTE: Warfarin was named after the Wisconsin Alumni Research Foundation (WARF) that funded the research of biochemist, Karl Link, Warfarin's inventor. WARF was awarded the patent for the original discovery of dicoumarol in 1941 from which many subsequent anti-blood clotting derivatives were born.[604]

Both Warfarin and Heparin interrupt the body's natural clotting process, although in different ways. Warfarin stops the liver from processing vitamin K into substances that trigger the clotting function whereas Heparin drugs interfere with certain factors that activate thrombin, an enzyme that helps clot blood.[605] Misleadingly sold as *blood thinners*, it should be carefully noted that none of the variations do anything to thin blood or reduce the buildup of plaque on the walls of veins and arteries caused by things like trans fats. Instead, these *blood thinners* stop blood from producing clots that would otherwise get stuck in the narrowing passageways, thus preventing even more blood flow from travelling through these hardened, collagen corridors. The beauty of this approach is that, should a peasant need his blood to clot due to an internal or external injury, that function is deactivated, thus leading to another monumental problem, which generates even more revenue for those overseeing the *practice* of medicine.

Unlike Hydroxychloroquine, whose lethal effects outside of its small, specific permissible range were widely broadcasted during the COVID-19 pandemic and, as a result, its use discouraged, Warfarin and Coumadin were nonchalantly switched out with similar compounds listed under new brand names such as Xarelto, Pradaxa and Eliquis to

December 14, 2017. https://www.nature.com/articles/nrcardio.2017.172 and "Warfarin (Oral Route)." Mayo Clinic. March 1, 2023. https://www.mayoclinic.org/drugs-supplements/warfarin-oral-route/description/drg-20070945

603.) "Warfarin (Coumadin/Jantoven)." Sarasota Memorial Health Care System.com. https://home.smh.com/sections/services-procedures/medlib/patient_health_education/Warfarin/compiled%20coumadin%20education.pdf

604.) Lim, "Warfarin: from rat poison to clinical use."

605.) Paul Frysh. "A Comparison of Blood Thinners Warfarin and Heparin." WebMD.com. August 9, 2022. https://www.webmd.com/dvt/warfarin-heparin-comparison

further extend the public's trust in their heavily marketed *benefits*.[606]

From earlier discussions, the reason should be so obvious not one in a million can figure it out. Can you? Are you reaching a point in your comprehension skills where you take something you read and put it to practical use when needed? If so, then you remember that an emergency vaccine can only be approved for use in most developed *countries* if no other treatments are available. Granted there are some risks with Hydroxychloroquine when used to treat COVID-19 and the patient must be closely monitored when it's administered, but such is the case with anticoagulants like Coumadin (or should I say Warfarin?) and any other rat poison derivative.

The lesson to be learned is that, as a modern-day lord, you promote the treatments and products that suit your needs, and not the needs of your peasants. I cannot emphasise this point enough.

In summation, even though Hydroxychloroquine helps carry zinc into the cells preventing SARS-CoV-2 replication, it had to be downplayed as an effective medical treatment for COVID-19 so that no other licenced pharmaceuticals existed in the marketplace to cure COVID-19. This provided the special justification needed for an emergency use vaccine.[607] Although severe and, at times, lethal effects arise from irresponsible administration of Hydroxychloroquine, it is purposefully shunned, whilst a long list of coumarins that have more unpredictable and equally devastating effects on a wider array of patients is enthusiastically promoted.[608] I will not insult your intelligence by reiterating the reasons why, since it's quite clear the coumarin business is thriving and accomplishing its Malthusian aims with little to gain from an emergency use vaccine.

As a final thought on this matter, even though the likes of Xarelto, Pradaxa and Eliquis require less clinical observation than their predecessors due to their slightly better track record, when it comes to life threatening complications, Warfarin is still the top selling *blood*

606.) Sandee LaMotte, CNN. "Popular blood thinner warfarin no longer recommended for most atrial fibrillation cases." CNN health.com. January 28, 2019. https://www.cnn.com/2019/01/28/health/blood-thinner-warfarin-atrial-fibrillation-afib/index.html

607.) "Emergency Use Authorization for Vaccines Explained." FDA.gov. November 20, 2020. https://www.fda.gov/vaccines-blood-biologics/vaccines/emergency-use-authorization-vaccines-explained

608.) Kathy Moncivais, Ph.D. "Most Dangerous Drugs: Xarelto, Pradaxa and Other Blood Thinners." ConsumerSafety.org. July 16, 2020. https://www.consumersafety.org/news/most-dangerous-drugs-xarelto-pradaxa-and-other-blood-thinners/

thinner on the market.[609] This is due to its drastically reduced cost after many years on the market, putting it in the generic/expired patent category as opposed to the slightly altered old drug, posing as a new drug, hiding behind a new brand name category.[610] Hopefully, it's quite clear that the more control a modern-day lord has over his peasants purchasing power, the easier it is to steer them into less expensive yet more detrimental food and medicines that will inconspicuously degrade their health.

Graphene oxide was once known as graphitic oxide, graphite oxide and graphitic acid.[611] However, perhaps even greater protection can be achieved by assigning it an alphanumeric code, tucked into an undisclosed patent, protected by the courts and governmental structure.[612] When applying this tactic, experience has clearly shown that peasants are none the wiser.

NOTE: For those with a tight grip on their **FARM**'s power centres, a campaign of deception like the one beautifully conducted by the pharmaceutical behemoth Pfizer during the COVID-19 pandemic can serve as a shining example. From it, we can learn how to conceal suspicious ingredients during a genetic experiment on the populace, whilst at the same time, burying their harmful effects. The bold choice made by the FDA, on behalf of Pfizer, was to simply tuck away over 451,000 pages of documents that only required 108 days of review to

609.) Nazneen Memon, BHMS, PGDCR. "What Are the Top 5 Blood Thinners?" MedicineNet.com. October 27, 2022. https://www.medicinenet.com/what_are_the_top_5_blood_thinners/article.htm

610.) Heart Health. "How Do I Know What Blood Thinner Is Right for Me?" Cleveland Clinic.org. November 30, 2018. https://health.clevelandclinic.org/how-do-i-know-what-blood-thinner-is-right-for-me/

611.) Kaylan Raidongia, Alvin T.L. Tan, and Jiaxing Huang. "Chapter 14 – Graphene Oxide: Some New Insights into an Old Material." ScienceDirect.com. July 25, 2014. https://www.sciencedirect.com/science/article/pii/B9780080982328000140 and H. Vidya, B.E. Kumara Swamy, S.C. Sharma, G.K. Jayaprakash and S.A. Hariprasad. "Effect of graphite oxide and exfoliated graphite oxide as a modifier for the voltametric determination of dopamine in presence of uric acid and folic acid." Nature.com. December 15, 2021. https://www.nature.com/articles/s41598-021-01328-w and Wikipedia. 2008. "Graphite oxide." February 20, 2023. https://en.wikipedia.org/wiki/Graphite_oxide

612.) Rogue Male. "Graphene Oxide: a 'Trade Secret.'" Roguemale.org. July 30, 2021. https://roguemale.org/2021/07/30/graphene-oxide-a-trade-secret-hidden-in-plain-sight/ and Shanghai National Engineering Research Center for Nanotechnology Co Ltd. "Nano coronavirus recombinant vaccine taking graphene oxide as carrier." Google Patents.com. January 15, 2021. https://patents.google.com/patent/CN112220919A/en

perform the intricate task of licensing Pfizer's COVID vaccine.[613] As witnessed during its brilliant execution, once pressed by the peasants for the dossier's general release, Pfizer simply dictated...oops-a-daisy...I mean, negotiated a deal with the tightly controlled courts to only trickle out five hundred pages per month for public scrutiny.

Hilariously, at this rate, it would take seventy-five years to release the complete set of documents, meaning many of the interested peasants would surely be deceased by the time all the information was released.[614]

You have to give the little buggers credit for their effort. Legal counsel for the group of thirty scientists and professors who stepped up to the challenge of launching a Freedom of Information Act request to gain access to the tightly guarded data, gave the awkwardly positioned drug giant 108 days to answer their complaint. They demanded the release of all related files within this short 108-day time frame.[615] The plaintiff's somewhat admirable logic was that if the FDA could licence an unproven product containing 451,000 pages of clinical trial results in 108 days, they could surely complete the much simpler task of redacting confidential trade secrets and personal privacy information from the files in that same amount of time.[616] I tip my hat to their ambitious argument. However, the triumphant and long-lasting ruler *must* always be right even when he is—well—he's always right.

Of course, for an agency that employs over 18,000 people and has a budget of over six billion dollars, making these files available to the public should have been a pretty straightforward task.[617]

Now this, my prudent understudy, is where your utmost attention is required. The following is why a modern-day lord *must* stringently control the authoritative institutions on a **FARM**. The FDA, under normal conditions, would and should have been ready to hand over the data upon approval of the vaccine's licence due to its own code's

---

613.) Russia Today. "Disclosing Pfizer vaccine data "may take until 2096."" RT.com. December 9, 2021. https://www.rt.com/usa/542616-fda-years-declassify-pfizer/

614.) Russia Today. "Disclosing Pfizer vaccine data."

615.) Jenna Greene. "Wait what? FDA wants 55 years to process FOIA request over vaccine data." Reuters.com. November 18, 2021. https://www.reuters.com/legal/government/wait-what-fda-wants-55-years-process-foia-request-over-vaccine-data-2021-11-18/

616.) Greene. "Wait what?"

617.) Greene. "Wait what?"

provision found in CFR Title 21 subchapter F.[618] This section stipulates that it make *immediately available* all documents underlying licensure of a vaccine.[619] However, this type of legal obstacle can easily be bypassed if your network controls the world's most dominant drug companies that in turn, have their trusted insiders appointed to agencies like the WHO, CDC and FDA. Equally important is assuring fellow secret society members oversee your **FARMS**' most influential court proceedings. Once a true boss's most loyal assets are in place, peasants can hum and haw all they want, but they *must never* be privy to these types of confidential matters.

Please excuse my coarseness but, quite frankly, it's none of their damn business how their lords conduct their affairs!

Whether injuries occur due to random coincidences, unknown effects of experimental ingredients, or preplanned calculations, an orchestrator can do much damage control by assigning investigations to the manufacturer of the accused treatment. In regard to COVID-19, this meant that each pharmaceutical company inspected the harm done by its *own* mRNA *vaccine*. If a network is in total control, those working inside the governmental agencies will be deeply aligned with the major industries and, in this case, the leading drug companies. Naturally, these well-paid government insiders can ignore any foul play related to a well-connected vaccine manufacturer's assessment of its own test trials, any claims filed against it, and any dazzling yet manipulated statistics boasting their treatment's efficacy. These calculated oversights, guided by carefully placed regulators, created a leakproof plan designed to win the public's trust.

For those not so easily sold, along with those who just needed a little nudge in the right direction, the old standbys were always there. For instance, bribery came in many forms as payouts were awarded to ensure compliance with vaccine mandates. Just like masking, lockdowns, and RT-PCR tests, societal negotiations with the general public were again in full force. As a quick reminder, permission to dine out, travel, attend a concert or sporting event, and even keep one's job were held over the majority's collective heads. Even those not directly required to comply felt the pressure to do so, to retain *normalcy* and peace of mind. On an individual level, not only were the shots put on the peasants' tab

---

618.) Greene. "Wait what?"

619.) Code of Federal Regulations. "Title 21 Chapter 1 Subchapter F Part 601 Subpart F Section 601.51." National Archives. March 10, 2023. https://www.ecfr.gov/current/title-21/chapter-I/subchapter-F/part-601/subpart-F/section-601.51

and then offered *free of charge,* but bonuses of several hundred dollars were offered to healthcare workers who *willingly* cooperated with the vaccine initiative.

Similarly, commissary funds were credited to state inmates who played along in an orderly fashion, and many corporations including Wal-Mart (that offered store and warehouse employees $150 to get vaxed) began jumping on the vaccination rewards bandwagon.[620] **STATE** corporations weren't opposed to the idea either. The 'Shot and a Beer' programme offered New Jerseyans who received a shot a free beer at one of thirteen participating breweries if they rolled up their sleeve. Furthermore, 'Vax and Scratch' gave participating New Yorkers a $20 lottery ticket that dangled a five-million-dollar jackpot above their blood clotted heads.[621]

Feeding into the inoculation frenzy were peasants themselves, who even initiated their own programmes, like 'Pot for Shots,' where a marijuana dispensary in Michigan gave out free joints for those succumbing to the mighty jab. On the opposite side of the world in the Indian city of Rakjot, Gujarat, goldsmiths banded together to give women free gold nose pins if they agreed to the inoculation whilst men were offered free hand blenders.[622] More obscure yet simplistic door prizes included donuts, Girl Scout cookies and fishing or hunting licences.[623] I think you would agree that it's been very inspiring to see peasants sacrificing so much of themselves, including the commodities from their very own depleted businesses, in order to achieve their owner's overall goal of eliminating the majority of them.

There were those of us who knew it was possible, but I don't think

620.) Joseph Darius Jaafari and Jamie Martines. "Two Pa. Prisons have vaccinated more than 70% of inmates; incentive program may be making a difference." The Daily Item.com. March 17, 2021. https://www.dailyitem.com/coronavirus/two-pa-prisons-have-vaccinated-more-than-70-of-inmates-incentive-program-may-be-making/article_a819432a-8707-11eb-82cf-5bf70b5800a2.html and Kenneth Terrell. "These Companies Are Paying Employees to Get Vaccinated: Paid time off, one-time payments give hourly and gig workers incentive to get shots." Aarp.org. September 10, 2021. https://www.aarp.org/work/companies-paying-employees-covid-vaccine/

621.) Jack Hunter. "From beer to Tinder boosts: The bribes for people to get jabbed." BBC.com. May 21, 2021. https://www.bbc.com/news/world-57201111

622.) Hunter. "From beer to Tinder boosts."

623.) Sophie Dodd and Janine Henni. "How to Get Promotions, Prizes and Freebies with your COVID-19 Vaccine: From free beer to college scholarships and a $5 million lottery, here's a list of some of the coolest COVID-19 vaccine incentives." People.com. June 8, 2021. https://people.com/health/covid-19-vaccine-freebies-incentives-rewards/

anyone could've imagined it would be this easy. It proves that, if you educate/train them early, achieve chemical dependence with medicines, foods, beverages, and recreational drugs, and offer a wide array of time-consuming diversions like mind-numbing, sexually explicit entertainment and 24/7 impulse shopping venues right in the privacy of their own homes, your task of completely enslaving them becomes much more palpable.

It's important for modern-day lords to recognise that the one redeeming quality peasants have is their outdated, pie-in-the-sky religions. Although an effective religion will pull the peasants' attention into a false reality where they are told their good deeds earn them gold stars in the afterlife, contrary to a lord's aims, a congregation's focus also shifts away from worldly possessions and their faith is placed outside of the **STATE**. This provides just enough of a buffer to evade a ruler's complete dominance.

Now can you see why **STATE** endorsed science must replace monotheistic religions? Man has now discovered the keys to becoming godlike and through this knowledge, people like you, who possess these secrets, will be the focus of human adulation.

Any aspiring lord should understand the following two truths.

To assemble devotees, *evangelists*, *pastors* and *clerics* must convince their followers to believe in a divine being's existence. Second, in science, with its theories and formulas too complex for the average human mind to comprehend, **STATE** approved *experts* must persuade the public to unwittingly trust the conclusions and recommendations *experts* put forth. Therefore, it only makes sense that with the right type of conditioning, someone blindly believing in one could foolishly be led to put full faith in the other.

New York Governor Kathy Hochul wonderfully exhibited this when she stood before a Christian congregation in her jab jewellery, stressing that God wants them to be vaccinated.[624]

Hallelujah sister Hochul. God's spirit has anointed you to lead the flock into the final stage of their new God's plan, their transhuman ascension into the metaverse.

Praise be to Gates!

Thank you, Fauci!

624.) Kathy Hochul, "NY Governor Hochul: God Wants You To Get Vaccinated," YouTube video, 3:07, TheDC Shorts, September 28, 2021, https://youtu.be/Q8T-Di3v6uS8 and Shannon Thaler. "Viral style! How 'jab jewelry' is being worn by vaccine advocates like NY Gov Kathy Hochul to tell the world to get jabbed." Daily Mail.com. September 28, 2021. https://www.dailymail.co.uk/news/article-10037689/How-jab-jewelry-sold-Amazon-worn-vaccine-advocates-like-NY-Gov-Kathy-Hochul.html

For those who remain defiant, once the majority's new behavioural patterns are locked in place, they will either comply or fade out of existence. As it stands now, once the herd buys into vaccine passports and other digital technologies, they can more readily be convinced to accept physically embedded devices that will allow easy access to their biological systems.[625] At this point, total ownership will be complete. Therefore, getting as many on board with the vaccination agenda as possible conditions the herd for these long-term goals, where passive cooperation is attained.

When bribing them doesn't work, perhaps shaming the unvaxed with demeaning terms like *plague rats* may appeal to their better judgment. Buzz words like *refuse* can effectively exert a burdensome moral pressure on a resisting peasant. Can you see the negative stigma that comes with refusing to do something?

Good! Use it to your advantage.

In the rapidly approaching, futuristic world, as part of the Great Reset, worldwide digital passports will allow peasants to function within this new invisible prison whilst being constantly monitored. To get to this final stage, one more Tavistock Shock Doctrine event may be necessary. The Earth's habitat has, regrettably, been heavily compromised to build and support the current control grid developed, predominantly, by today's technocratic overlords. This degradation of the planet has been partly on purpose and partly natural consequence.

'Why would it be done on purpose?' you ponder.

A compromised environment impairs the peasants' robustness and jeopardises their well-being. In addition, should the need arise to downsize your **FARM** or force the herd into complete dependency on your industries, a depleted ecosystem will be to your advantage. Perhaps one day, you can harness the herd's energy and create profitable industries of your own that begin the clean-up process and unite the **FARMS** of the world against a *common adversary* that threatens their very existence, unless collective action is taken.

By the way, that common adversary can be anything from a ravaged landscape to contaminated waterways to the littering and wasteful human beings themselves.

With some *experts* suggesting that greenhouse pollution was

625.) Holly Evarts. "Tiny, Wireless, Injectable Chips Use Ultrasound to Monitor Body Processes." Columbia|Engineering.edu. May 12, 2021. https://www.engineering. columbia.edu/news/shepard-injectable-chips-monitor-body-processes

reduced by 17% in April 2020 when human activity stopped, further lockdowns and other restrictions can easily be justified.[626] Because many peasants have already adapted to working from home whilst having many of their necessities delivered to their doorsteps, and young, budding plantation toilers have been receiving at least a portion of their *education* at home, limiting the peasants' movements and activities has become an established trend.

Is there a more beautiful way to unite the world under one government and one financial system than another invisible, common enemy the herd must sacrifice their privileges and even themselves to defeat? After all, an elusive and vast enemy distracts the commoners' attention and prevents them from uniting against the actual network implementing the drastic, life-altering changes imposed upon them.

One sure way to reduce the peasants' carbon footprints is to eliminate the unnecessary peasants themselves. If a wave of remorse sweeps over you as a result of this statement, it's with purposeful intent that I direct you to a manuscript, similar to this one, written as far back as 1954 (although the exact date is unknown), mistakenly left inside a photocopier, then discovered at a government clearance sale in 1986.[627]

Please, you must use great care if you're in possession of such a confidential exposé. On page seven of the accidentally discovered, top-secret document *Silent Weapons for Quiet Wars* was the painfully accurate quote: 'A nation or world of people who will not use their intelligence are no better than animals who do not have intelligence. Such a people are beasts of burden and steaks on the table by choice and consent.'[628] I have yet to find a more accurate expression to validate the tactics described in this handbook.

All lords must possess this mentality to prevent the disintegration of their **FARMS**' social hierarchies and the platforms from which they rule.

The latest disruption in global production was the beginning of a cascade of events to slow down the world economic engine. This was done to save the planet for those enlightened enough to maintain it and

---

626.) Mercola and Cummins, *The Truth About COVID-19*, 3.

627.) Science Guided By Faith. *Silent Weapons for Quiet Wars*. What Is Really Going On.com. November 20, 2022. https://whatisreallygoingon.substack.com/p/silent-weapons-for-quiet-wars

628.) "Silent Weapons for Quiet Wars", 7.

those deemed important enough to remain. Is there a better reason to reign over mankind than the preservation of yourself and your genetic line?

It's my hope that you will perform as instructed when the opportunity arises. It's time for you to demonstrate to your colleagues, and all of humanity, what you're made of.

Conclusion

Bravo! You've made it to the end of the manual, written to intrigue the mere novice or enthral the seasoned master. The principles and intricacies detailed lay an unshakeable foundation for those beginning their quest for global domination, and will also assist those already at the top of their game in need of a refresher course. As any successful world ruler can attest, to assert your supremacy and achieve your aims, it's imperative you attain compliance from the peasants.

We live in an exciting time where advanced control tools, once only dreamed about, are now game changers in human conquest. By adhering to the proven techniques passed down by our daring predecessors whilst also warmly embracing a plethora of ever-evolving scientific advancements, total control over every aspect of human life is genuinely possible.

An authoritative system of surveillance will give you a distinct advantage over your broadening herd. To sustain your meteoric rise as ruler of humanity, your political structure must retain all its secrets whilst peasants maintain none.

This handbook has focused almost entirely on the philosophical framework needed to enslave humanity. The advances made and the courageous actions taken over the past two hundred years have set the stage for an up-and-coming lord like yourself to thrive, whilst utilising undesirable humans or eliminating them from the face of the planet.

To ensure a successful global takeover, a strong worldview coupled with a detailed plan are essential. It's also imperative that you and your associates carry out your ruling actions absent of both fear and guilt. Since the techniques provided in this volume have been expertly applied, to save time, you may simply want to join the current ruling class rather than build from the ground up, as even peasants who recognise their predicament don't have the inner fortitude to undo this elaborate web of control.

To continue the trend toward a *prison planet*, you must apply the proven techniques herein to keep peasants in a false reality that disconnects them from their inner selves and each other. You must also keep them ignorant of their true history. If the herd is constantly divided, distracted and ill-informed, not to mention mentally, physically and spiritually repressed, it will be much easier for you to rule over them and less likely they will *unite* against you.

Hopefully, this handbook serves as a blueprint that inspires you to not only take action, but to develop even more satisfying ways to rule over your inferiors.

For those with less serious ambitions, I believe your PlayStation is calling.

Acknowledgements

I would like to extend a sincere thank you to Christopher Snyder for trawling through this document and for providing his impeccable proofreading services. I am forever indebted. A warm expression of gratitude is also owed to Marcia Breece for her keen eye and encouragement throughout the editing process. I especially appreciate her resolve when challenging me to write the best book possible. It is a working relationship I am blessed to have. Finally, I would like to thank my friends, loved ones and acquaintances (too many to mention) who have offered their optimism and support for this endeavor that, as a result, have inspired this book to fruition. Lastly, this acknowledgement would not be complete without paying homage to a love affair that dates back hundreds of years. Mary, Queen of Scots, your beauty, strength and charm have provided the perfect muse to bring this task to completion and your light has guided my every step. Be it known, my love for you is as steadfast as the Highlands.